AF575488

The Story of God Bible Commentary Series Endorsements

"Getting a story is about more than merely enjoying it. It means hearing it, understanding it, and above all, being impacted by it. This commentary series hopes that its readers not only hear and understand the story but are impacted by it to live in as Christian a way as possible. The editors and contributors set that table very well and open up the biblical story in ways that move us to act with sensitivity and understanding. That makes hearing the story as these authors tell it well worth the time. Well done."

Darrell L. Bock
Dallas Theological Seminary

"The Story of God Bible Commentary series invites readers to probe how the message of the text relates to our situations today. Engagingly readable, it not only explores the biblical text but offers a range of applications and interesting illustrations."

Craig S. Keener
Asbury Theological Seminary

"I love The Story of God Bible Commentary series. It makes the text sing and helps us hear the story afresh."

John Ortberg
Senior Pastor of Menlo Park Presbyterian Church

"In this promising new series of commentaries, believing biblical scholars bring not only their expertise but their own commitment to Jesus and insights into today's culture to the Scriptures. The result is a commentary series that is anchored in the text but lives and breathes in the world of today's church with its variegated pattern of socioeconomic, ethnic, and national diversity. Pastors, Bible study leaders, and Christians of all types who are looking for a substantive and practical guide through the Scriptures will find these volumes helpful."

Frank Thielman
Beeson Divinity School

"I'm a storyteller. Through writing and speaking I talk and teach about understanding the Story of God throughout Scripture and about letting God reveal more of his story as I live it out. Thus I am thrilled to have a commentary series based on the story of God—a commentary that helps me to Listen to the Story, that Explains the Story, and then encourages me to probe how to Live the Story. A perfect tool for helping every follower of Jesus to walk in the story that God is writing for them."

Judy Douglass
Director of Women's Resources, Cru

"The Bible is the story of God and his dealings with humanity from creation to new creation. The Bible is made up more of stories than of any other literary genre. Even the psalms, proverbs, prophecies, letters, and the Apocalypse make complete sense only when set in the context of the grand narrative of the entire Bible. This commentary series breaks new ground by taking all these observations seriously. It asks commentators to listen to the text, to explain the text, and to live the text. Some of the material in these sections overlaps with introduction, detailed textual analysis and application, respectively, but only some. The most riveting and valuable parts of the commentaries are the stories that can appear in any of these sections, from any part of the globe and any part of church history, illustrating the text in any of these areas. Ideal for preaching and teaching."

Craig L. Blomberg
Denver Seminary

"Pastors and lay people will welcome this new series, which seeks to make the message of the Scriptures clear and to guide readers in appropriating biblical texts for life today."

Daniel I. Block
Wheaton College and Graduate School

"An extremely valuable and long overdue series that includes comment on the cultural context of the text, careful exegesis, and guidance on reading the whole Bible as a unity that testifies to Christ as our Savior and Lord."

Graeme Goldsworthy
author of *According to Plan*

LEVITICUS

Editorial Board
of
The Story of God Bible Commentary

Old Testament general editor
Tremper Longman III

Old Testament associate editors
George Athas
Mark J. Boda
Myrto Theocharous

New Testament general editor
Scot McKnight

New Testament associate editors
Lynn H. Cohick
Michael F. Bird
Dennis R. Edwards

Zondervan editors

Senior acquisitions editor
Katya Covrett

Senior production editor, Old Testament
Nancy L. Erickson

Senior production editor, New Testament
Christopher A. Beetham

The Story of God Bible Commentary

LEVITICUS

Jerry E. Shepherd

Tremper Longman III & Scot McKnight
General Editors

ZONDERVAN ACADEMIC

Leviticus
Copyright © 2021 by Jerry E. Shepherd

Requests for information should be addressed to:
Zondervan, *3900 Sparks Dr. SE, Grand Rapids, Michigan 49546*

Zondervan titles may be purchased in bulk for educational, business, fundraising, or sales promotional use. For information, please email SpecialMarkets@ Zondervan.com.

Library of Congress Cataloging-in-Publication Data

Names: Shepherd, Jerry E., author.
Title: Leviticus / Jerry E. Shepherd.
Description: Grand Rapids : Zondervan, 2021. | Series: The Story of God Bible commentary. | Includes bibliographical references and index.
Identifiers: LCCN 2021003612 (print) | LCCN 2021003613 (ebook) | ISBN 9780310490739 (hardcover) | ISBN 9780310490746 (ebook)
Subjects: LCSH: Bible. Leviticus--Commentaries.
Classification: LCC BS1255.53 .S54 2021 (print) | LCC BS1255.53 (ebook) | DDC 222/.13077--dc23
LC record available at https://lccn.loc.gov/2021003612
LC ebook record available at https://lccn.loc.gov/2021003613

All Scripture quotations, unless otherwise indicated, are taken from The Holy Bible, New International Version®, NIV®. Copyright © 1973, 1978, 1984, 2011 by Biblica, Inc.® Used by permission of Zondervan. All rights reserved worldwide. www.Zondervan.com. The "NIV" and "New International Version" are trademarks registered in the United States Patent and Trademark Office by Biblica, Inc.®

Scripture quotations marked ESV are taken from the ESV® Bible (The Holy Bible, English Standard Version®). Copyright © 2001 by Crossway, a publishing ministry of Good News Publishers. Used by permission. All rights reserved.

Scripture quotations marked MSG [or The Message] are taken from *THE MESSAGE*. Copyright © 1993, 1994, 1995, 1996, 2000, 2001, 2002 by Eugene H. Peterson. Used by permission of NavPress. All rights reserved. Represented by Tyndale House Publishers, Inc.

The Scripture quotations marked NRSV are taken from the New Revised Standard Version Bible. Copyright © 1989, Division of Christian Education of the National Council of the Churches of Christ in the United States of America. Used by permission. All rights reserved.

Any internet addresses (websites, blogs, etc.) and telephone numbers in this book are offered as a resource. They are not intended in any way to be or imply an endorsement by Zondervan, nor does Zondervan vouch for the content of these sites and numbers for the life of this book.

All rights reserved. No part of this publication may be reproduced, stored in a retrieval system, or transmitted in any form or by any means—electronic, mechanical, photocopy, recording, or any other—except for brief quotations in printed reviews, without the prior permission of the publisher.

Cover design: Ron Huizinga
Cover photo: iStockphoto.com

Printed in the United States of America

---

21 22 23 24 25 26 27 28 29 30 31 /TRM/ 15 14 13 12 11 10 9 8 7 6 5 4 3 2 1

Dedicated to my instructors in
the study of the Old Testament:

Ronald L. Reinert†
J. Alan Groves†
Raymond B. Dillard†
Tremper Longman III
Bruce K. Waltke

What the Lord said about the faithful Levitical
priests could also be said about you:

"He revered me and stood in awe of my name.
True instruction was in his mouth and nothing false
was found on his lips. He walked with me in peace
and uprightness, and turned many from sin."
(Mal 2:5b–6)

Old Testament series

1 ▪ Genesis—*Tremper Longman III*
2 ▪ Exodus—*Christopher J. H. Wright*
3 ▪ Leviticus—*Jerry E. Shepherd*
4 ▪ Numbers—*Jay A. Sklar*
5 ▪ Deuteronomy—*Myrto Theocharous*
6 ▪ Joshua—*Lissa M. Wray Beal*
7 ▪ Judges—*Athena E. Gorospe*
8 ▪ Ruth/Esther—*Marion Ann Taylor*
9 ▪ 1–2 Samuel—*Paul S. Evans*
10 ▪ 1–2 Kings—*David T. Lamb*
11 ▪ 1–2 Chronicles—*Carol M. Kaminski*
12 ▪ Ezra/Nehemiah—*Douglas J. Green*
13 ▪ Job—*Martin A. Shields*
14 ▪ Psalms—*Elizabeth R. Hayes*
15 ▪ Proverbs—*Ryan P. O'Dowd*
16 ▪ Ecclesiastes/Song of Songs—*George Athas*
17 ▪ Isaiah—*Mark J. Boda*
18 ▪ Jeremiah/Lamentations—*Andrew G. Shead*
19 ▪ Ezekiel—*Havilah Dharamraj*
20 ▪ Daniel—*Wendy L. Widder*
21 ▪ Minor Prophets I—*Beth M. Stovell*
22 ▪ Minor Prophets II—*Beth M. Stovell*

New Testament series

1 ▪ Matthew—*Rodney Reeves*
2 ▪ Mark—*Timothy G. Gombis*
3 ▪ Luke—*Kindalee Pfremmer DeLong*
4 ▪ John—*Nicholas Perrin*
5 ▪ Acts—*Dean Pinter*
6 ▪ Romans—*Michael F. Bird*
7 ▪ 1 Corinthians—*Justin K. Hardin*
8 ▪ 2 Corinthians—*Judith A. Diehl*
9 ▪ Galatians—*Nijay K. Gupta*
10 ▪ Ephesians—*Mark D. Roberts*
11 ▪ Philippians—*Lynn H. Cohick*
12 ▪ Colossians/Philemon—*Todd Wilson*
13 ▪ 1, 2 Thessalonians—*John Byron*
14 ▪ 1, 2 Timothy, Titus—*Marius Nel*
15 ▪ Hebrews—*Radu Gheorghita*
16 ▪ James—*Mariam J. Kamell*
17 ▪ 1 Peter—*Dennis R. Edwards*
18 ▪ 2 Peter, Jude—*C. Rosalee Velloso Ewell*
19 ▪ 1, 2, & 3 John—*Constantine R. Campbell*
20 ▪ Revelation—*Jonathan A. Moo*
21 ▪ Sermon on the Mount—*Scot McKnight*

Contents

Acknowledgments

There are so many people to thank for the ways in which they have contributed to this commentary.

I have dedicated this volume to my former Old Testament professors, both those that are still living and those who have passed away. I am thankful not only for their instruction but also for their inspiration, modeling, and personal investment in my life and teaching career.

My thanks go to Tremper Longman III, general editor for The Story of God Bible Commentary series on the Old Testament (and my Doktorvater) for the invitation to make this contribution to the series. And I am very thankful to both Tremper and associate editor George Athas, who was assigned to the editing of my volume, for their encouragement, careful interaction, and valuable suggestions. This is a far better commentary than it would have been without their engagement (even if I did not always follow their suggestions).

I also express my appreciation to Mark J. Boda and Myrto Theocharous, the other two associate editors of this series, for their encouraging comments and suggestions upon reading my initial commentary on the earliest passages in Leviticus.

The careful work of the editors at Zondervan is much appreciated. Though I did not know him well, comments on my early work by the late Verlyn D. Verbrugge were extremely helpful. I appreciate the input and assistance that Katya Covrett, senior acquisitions editor, provided during the initial stages of my research and writing. And I am very grateful to Nancy Erickson, senior production editor, for her careful work, not only in the clerical editing of the volume, but also with regard to substantial suggestions she made for the book's content.

I am thankful to Jay A. Sklar and Roy E. Gane, who have written excellent monographs and commentaries on Leviticus, for conversations we had about the book, and for their gracious attempts to answer my numerous queries.

It has been delightful to become acquainted with Hans M. Moscicke and to engage the work he has done on the scapegoat narrative in Leviticus 16. My thanks to him for passing along to me relevant articles he has written, as well as his recently published dissertation.

Of course, I am grateful for all those who have written commentaries on

Leviticus over the centuries. As has been said in many book acknowledgements, we stand on the shoulders of the giants who have come before us.

I thank the administration and board of Taylor Seminary for granting me a sabbatical, during which I was able to do a major portion of the research for this commentary. I appreciate my supportive colleagues on the Taylor Seminary faculty for their prayers and encouragement. And my appreciation goes also to the students of a course I taught on Leviticus, though, unfortunately, I was not able to incorporate their questions and comments into my already submitted manuscript.

Of course, I express, not just thankfulness, but my love for my beautiful wife of forty-six years, Cheryl. She has known what it is to be a doctoral student's spouse, a seminary professor's spouse, and a commentator's spouse, with all the patience those roles require. My thanks to her for her love, her encouragement, and her support.

I also express my love for, and appreciation for the support of, my grown children, their spouses, and their children: for Jennifer and her husband Jason, for Joel, and for Tim and his wife Holly, and their children. Of course, the delight of one's older years is one's grandchildren. Brody Allan Shepherd, Chase Levi(!) Shepherd, and Annabelle Elizabeth Grace Shepherd, I pray that you may grow up in the fear of the Lord, and that perhaps, one day, you might crack open a commentary on Leviticus written by your adoring grandfather.

Of course, my deepest appreciation, and worship, go to the Triune God: Father, Son, and Holy Spirit. It has been my conviction during the writing of this commentary that Leviticus is the word of God—and to put that more pointedly, that the words of Leviticus are just as much the words of Christ as are those that are found in the Gospels. I pray that the God of the covenant, our Rock and our Redeemer, will be pleased with the words from my pen, and the meditations of my heart.

JERRY SHEPHERD

The Story of God Bible Commentary Series

Why another commentary series?

In the first place, no single commentary can exhaust the meaning of a biblical book. The Bible is unfathomably rich and no single commentator can explore every aspect of its message.

In addition, good commentary not only explores what the text meant in the past but also its continuing significance. In other words, the Word of God may not change, but culture does. Think of what we have seen in the last twenty years: we now communicate predominantly through the internet and email; we read our news on iPads and computers. We carry smartphones in our pockets through which we can call our friends, check the weather forecast, make dinner reservations, and get an answer to virtually any question we might have.

Today we have more readable and accurate Bible versions in English than any generation in the past. Bible distribution in the present generation has been very successful; more people own more Bibles than previous generations. However, studies have shown that while people have better access to the Bible than ever before, people aren't reading the Bibles they own, and they struggle to understand what they do read.

The Story of God Bible Commentary hopes to help people, particularly clergy but also laypeople, read the Bible with understanding not only of its ancient meaning but also of its continuing significance for us today in the twenty-first century. After all, readers of the Bible change too. These cultural shifts, our own personal developments, and the progress in intellectual questions, as well as growth in biblical studies and theology and discoveries of new texts and new paradigms for understanding the contexts of the Bible—each of these elements work on an interpreter so that the person who reads the Bible today asks different questions from different angles.

Culture shifts, but the Word of God remains. That is why we as editors of The Story of God Bible Commentary, a commentary based on the New International Version 2011 (NIV 2011), are excited to participate in this new series of commentaries on the Bible. This series is designed to speak to this generation with the same Word of God. We are asking the authors to explain what the Bible says to the sorts of readers who pick up commentaries so they can understand not only what Scripture says but what it means for today. The Bible does not change, but relating it to our culture changes constantly and in differing ways in different contexts.

As editors of the Old Testament series, we recognize that Christians have a hard time knowing exactly how to relate to the Scriptures that were written before the coming of Christ. The world of the Old Testament is a strange one to those of us who live in the West in the twenty-first century. We read about strange customs, warfare in the name of God, sacrifices, laws of ritual purity, and more and wonder whether it is worth our while or even spiritually healthy to spend time reading this portion of Scripture that is chronologically, culturally, and—seemingly—theologically distant from us.

But it is precisely here that The Story of God Bible Commentary series on the Old Testament makes its most important contribution. The New Testament does not replace the Old Testament; the New Testament fulfills the Old Testament. We hear God's voice today in the Old Testament. In its pages he reveals himself to us and also his will for how we should live in a way that is pleasing to him.

Jesus himself often reminds us that the Old Testament maintains its importance to the lives of his disciples. Luke 24 describes Jesus's actions and teaching in the period between his resurrection and ascension. Strikingly, the focus of his teaching is on how his followers should read the Old Testament (here called "Moses and all the Prophets," "Scriptures," and "the law of Moses, the Prophets and Psalms"). To the two disciples on the road to Emmaus, he says:

> "How foolish you are, and how slow to believe all that the prophets have spoken! Did not the Messiah have to suffer these things and then enter his glory?" And beginning with Moses and all the Prophets, he explained to them what was said in all the Scriptures concerning himself. (Luke 24:25–27)

Then to a larger group of disciples he announces:

> "This is what I told you while I was still with you: Everything must be fulfilled that is written about me in the law of Moses, the Prophets and the Psalms." Then he opened their minds so they could understand the Scriptures. (Luke 24:44–45)

The Story of God Bible Commentary series takes Jesus's words on this matter seriously. Indeed, it is the first series that has as one of its deliberate goals the identification of the trajectories (historical, typological, and theological) that land in Christ in the New Testament. Every commentary in the series will, in the first place, exposit the text in the context of its original reception. We will interpret it as we believe the original author intended his contemporary audience to read it. But then we will also read the text in the light of the death and resurrection of Jesus. No other commentary series does this important work consistently in every volume.

To achieve our purpose of expositing the Old Testament in its original setting and also from a New Testament perspective, each passage is examined from three angles.

Listen to the Story. We begin by listening to the text in order to hear the voice of God. We first read the passage under study. We then go on to consider the background to the passage by looking at any earlier Scripture passage that informs our understanding of the text. At this point too we will cite and discuss possible ancient Near Eastern literary connections. After all, the Bible was not written in a cultural vacuum, and an understanding of its broader ancient Near Eastern context will often enrich our reading.

Explain the Story. The authors are asked to explain each passage in light of the Bible's grand story. It is here that we will exposit the text in its original Old Testament context. This is not an academic series, so the footnotes will be limited to the kinds of books and articles to which typical Bible readers and preachers will have access. Authors are given the freedom to explain the text as they read it, though you will not be surprised to find occasional listings of other options for reading the text. The emphasis will be on providing an accessible explanation of the passage, particularly on those aspects of the text that are difficult for a modern reader to understand, with an emphasis on theological interpretation.

Live the Story. Reading the Bible is not just about discovering what it meant back then; the intent of The Story of God Bible Commentary is to probe how this text might be lived out today as that story continues to march on in the life of the church.

Here, in the spirit of Christ's words in Luke 24, we will suggest ways in which the Old Testament text anticipates the gospel. After all, as Augustine famously put it, "the New Testament is in the Old Testament concealed, the Old Testament is in the New Testament revealed." We believe that this section will be particularly important for our readers who are clergy who want to present Christ even when they are preaching from the Old Testament.

The Old Testament also provides teaching concerning how we should live today. However, the authors of this series are sensitive to the tremendous impact that Christ's coming has on how Christians appropriate the Old Testament into their lives today.

It is the hope and prayer of the editors and all the contributors that our work will encourage clergy to preach from the Old Testament and laypeople to study this wonderful, yet often strange, portion of God's Word to us today.

Tremper Longman III, general editor Old Testament
George Athas, Mark Boda, and Myrto Theocharous, editors

Abbreviations

AB	Anchor Bible
ABD	*Anchor Bible Dictonary*. Edited by David Noel Freedman. 6 vols. New York: Doubleday 1992
ACCS	Ancient Christian Commentary on Scripture
ACW	Ancient Christian Writers
ANET	*Ancient Near Eastern Texts Relating to the Old Testament*. Edited by James B. Pritchard. 3rd ed. Princeton: Princeton University Press, 1969
ANF	*Ante-Nicene Fathers*
ApOTC	Apollos Old Testament Commentary
BBR	*Bulletin for Biblical Research*
BBRSup	*Bulletin for Biblical Research, Supplements*
BSC	Bible Student's Commentary
CBQ	*Catholic Biblical Quarterly*
ConcC	Concordia Commentary
COS	*The Context of Scripture*. Edited by William W. Hallo. 3 vols. Leiden: Brill, 1997–2002
CurBR	*Currents in Biblical Research*
ECC	Eerdmans Critical Commentary
ESV	English Standard Version
FC	Fathers of the Church
HCOT	Historical Commentary on the Old Testament
HSM	Harvard Semitic Monographs
HTR	*Harvard Theological Review*
IBC	Interpretation: A Bible Commentary for Teaching and Preaching
ICC	International Critical Commentary
Int	*Interpretation*
ITC	International Theological Commentary
JBL	*Journal of Biblical Literature*
JETS	*Journal of the Evangelical Theological Society*
JHebS	*Journal of Hebrew Scriptures*
JSNT	*Journal for the Study of the New Testament*

JSOTSup	Journal for the Study of the Old Testament Supplement Series
NAC	New American Commentary
NET	New English Translation
NIB	*The New Interpreter's Bible*. Edited by Leander E. Keck. 12 vols. Nashville, Abingdon, 1994–2004
NIBCNT	New International Biblical Commentary on the New Testament
NIBCOT	New International Biblical Commentary on the Old Testament
NICNT	New International Commentary on the New Testament
NICOT	New International Commentary on the Old Testament
NIDOTTE	*New International Dictionary of Old Testament Theology and Exegesis*. Edited by Willem A. VanGemeren. 5 vols. Grand Rapids: Zondervan, 1997
NIGTC	New International Greek Testament Commentary
NIV	New International Version
NIVAC	New International Version Application Commentary
NJPS	*Tanakh: The Holy Scriptures: The New JPS Translation according to the Traditional Hebrew Text*
NovT	*Novum Testamentum*
NRSV	New Revised Standard Version
NSBT	New Studies in Biblical Theology
OBT	Overtures to Biblical Theology
OTL	Old Testament Library
ProEccl	*Pro Ecclesia*
RB	*Revue biblique*
SGBC	The Story of God Bible Commentary
SNTSMS	Society for New Testament Studies Monograph Series
StBoT	Studien zu den Boğazköy Texten
TOTC	Tyndale Old Testament Commentaries
WAW	Writings from the Ancient World
WAWSup	Writings from the Ancient World Supplement Series
WBC	Word Biblical Commentary
WUNT	Wissenschaftliche Untersuchungen zum Neuen Testament

Introduction to Leviticus

In 1878 a theology professor at a German university wrote an introduction to Old Testament history. In the book's introduction he told of his own days as a student of Old Testament at university:

> In my early student days I was attracted by the stories of Saul and David, Ahab and Elijah; the discourses of Amos and Isaiah laid strong hold on me, and I read myself well into the prophetic and historical books of the Old Testament. Thanks to such aids as were accessible to me, I even considered that I understood them tolerably, but at the same time was troubled with a bad conscience, as if I were beginning with the roof instead of the foundation; for I had no thorough acquaintance with the Law, of which I was accustomed to be told that it was the basis and postulate of the whole literature. At last I took courage [!] and made my way through Exodus, Leviticus, Numbers. . . . But it was in vain that I looked for the light which was to be shed from this source on the historical and prophetical books. On the contrary, my enjoyment of the latter was marred by the Law; it did not bring them any nearer me, but intruded itself uneasily, like a ghost that makes a noise indeed, but is not visible and really effects nothing.[1]

This individual was Julius Wellhausen, Professor of Theology at the University of Greifswald. The book was his subsequently famous *Prolegomena to the History of Ancient Israel.* One of his primary theses was that the legal and ritual material in the Pentateuch did not come at the beginning of Israel's history but nearly a thousand years later, after the end of the Babylonian exile, and that these books were essentially a perversion of the pure religion of Israel found in the rest of the Old Testament. In the words of Jon Levenson, Wellhausen's view was that the legal and ritual material of the Pentateuch is representative of a Judaism that is, in essence, "Israelite religion after it has died."[2] Levenson goes on to say that Wellhausen regarded this Judaism as

1. Julius Wellhausen, *Prolegomena to the History of Ancient Israel,* repr. and trans. of German second edition, 1883 (New York: Meridian, 1957), 3.

2. Jon D. Levenson, *The Hebrew Bible, the Old Testament, and Historical Criticism: Jews and Christians in Biblical Studies* (Louisville: Westminster John Knox, 1993), 11.

merely "the ghost of ancient Israel."[3] Additionally, Wellhausen believed that it was left for Christianity and the New Testament, especially the apostle Paul, "the great pathologist of Judaism," to restore pure Israelite religion and to declare the "freedom of the children of God."[4]

Wellhausen's estimation of the value, or rather lack of value, of the legal, sacrificial, and ritual material in the book of Leviticus has been shared by many. Christianity has been regarded as containing a totally different spirit than what may be found in Leviticus, indeed, a breath of fresh air. And various Christian theologians would agree with this assessment, in accord with the old cliché that the Old Testament is law and the New Testament is gospel; that the Old Testament, and especially Leviticus, is just dead works and darkness, but the New Testament is life and light.

Yet, there are many Christians who would disagree strongly with this assessment. They would argue that Christianity and the New Testament cannot be understood without the book of Leviticus. And they would say this, not to argue that the New Testament provides a contrast with Leviticus, but because the two are in essential continuity with each other. Popular Christian author David Platt, based on his conviction that the Bible is the very word of God, declares:

> I believe it is more important for you and me to read Leviticus than it is for us to read the best Christian book ever published, because Leviticus has a quality and produces an effect that no book in the Christian marketplace can compete with. If we want to know the glory of God, if we want to experience the beauty of God, and if we want to be used by the hand of God, then we must live in the Word of God.[5]

Or consider this anecdote from one recent commentator on Leviticus, Jay Sklar, after having been asked by an interviewer what the modern Christian can get from studying Leviticus. He responds by referring to the time when he was doing doctoral studies in England:

> Maybe I can answer that with this just really brief story. When I was in England, I'm studying sin, impurity, atonement, sacrifice, and about a

3. Ibid., 11.

4. Wellhausen, *Prolegomena*, 425 and 315 respectively; cited in Levenson, *Hebrew Bible*, 12.

5. David Platt, *Radical: Taking Back Your Faith from the American Dream* (Colorado Springs: Multnomah, 2010), 192.

> year into that I had this new experience in church that started happening. We would be singing a song about atonement or about sacrifice or about ransom, and it was really hard for me not to cry. Because I had studied these things so deeply in Leviticus, what ended up happening is the work and ministry of Jesus became that much more beautiful to me.[6]

Many similar statements have been articulated in both academic and more popular Christian writings. But in addition to this, it is important to note that the New Testament itself seems to agree with them. A little-known fact is that the commandment that Jesus says is the second greatest comes from the book of Leviticus (Lev 19:18, "Love your neighbor as yourself"). This verse is actually the most quoted Old Testament verse in the New Testament. Additionally, the favorite New Testament book of the author of this commentary is the book of Hebrews, a book that perhaps pays more attention to the significance of the sacrificial death of Christ than any other New Testament book. One simply cannot understand the book of Hebrews without understanding the book of Leviticus. And the book of Hebrews does not by any means declare that the work of Christ has invalidated Leviticus; rather, the work of Christ fulfills Leviticus.

In some ways, my own story bears some resemblance to that of Wellhausen. For the most part, my studies in Old Testament have been primarily in the Psalms, the wisdom literature, and the prophets. The Pentateuch has not been one of my major research interests. When the opportunity came to contribute a commentary to this series, I was excited on account of the series' focus on each book's Christological and New Testament connections. But I must admit that when the invitation came to do the commentary on Leviticus, I was not especially thrilled. Nevertheless, this has proved to be one of the most valuable studies in which I have been engaged. It has, to use the old cliché, truly been a labor of love.

There is a sad epitaph to the Wellhausen narrative. Several years after he published his *Prolegomena* he resigned from his position as professor of theology. Part of his resignation letter reads as follows:

---

6. The video of this interview may be accessed at Faithlife, "Dr. Mike Heiser on Every Day Bible | Dr. Jay Sklar on Leviticus," *Faithlife Today*, Episode 8, 12 March 2015, https://www.youtube.com/watch?v=WpF3os52YNI&ab_channel=Faithlife. In another interview, Sklar relates how a tribe in Papua New Guinea was converted to Christianity as a result of connecting the dots between Leviticus and the sacrifice of Jesus, Faithlife Today, "Should Christians Study Leviticus?" *Faithlife Blog*, 9 July 2020, https://blog.faithlife.com/blog/2020/07/should-christians-study-leviticus-7/.

> I became a theologian because the scientific treatment of the Bible interested me; only gradually did I come to understand that a professor of theology also has the practical task of preparing the students for service in the Protestant Church, and that I am not adequate to this practical task, but that instead despite all caution on my own part I make my hearers unfit for their office. Since then my theological professorship has been weighing heavily on my conscience.[7]

Wellhausen had complained that the book of Leviticus was no more than a ghostly sign that the pure religion of the Old Testament had come to a demise. But the more accurate testimony with regard to the book's contents and value comes from the Lord whose words are preserved in the book:

> Keep my decrees and laws, for the person who obeys them will live by them. I am the LORD. (Lev 18:5)

This promise includes those who would study, and meditate on, these laws as well.

Composition, Transmission, and Canonicity

Authorship and Date

On a surface reading of the book of Leviticus, it would appear to be one of the five books of Moses, recording the words of the LORD to Moses at some point in the second half of the second millennium BC. Traditionally, then, based on when one considers the exodus from Egypt to have occurred, the Pentateuch has been understood to have been written by Moses sometime around 1450–1200 BC.

However, the work of Julius Wellhausen mentioned above, based on the previous writings of Karl Heinrich Graf, resulted in the position known as the Graf-Wellhausen or Documentary Hypothesis. This hypothesis is that the Pentateuch should be understood as comprised of four independent source documents that an editor or redactor (or a group or series of editors or redactors) combined into the form that we now have as the Pentateuch.

The four sources are referred to as the Yahwist, Elohist, Deuteronomist, and Priestly documents, thus resulting in the acronym JEDP (the J comes

7. Cited in Rudolf Smend, "Julius Wellhausen and His Prolegomena to the History of Israel," *Semeia* 25 (1982): 6.

from the German Jahwist). The dates that Wellhausen assigned to these sources were: J (tenth or ninth century BC); E (eighth century); D (seventh century); and P (fifth or fourth century). Of special importance for us is that Leviticus is considered in this hypothesis to be the work of the Priestly writer or school and does not come into existence until perhaps a century after the return of the Judahites from the exile in Babylon. It was also theorized that the Priestly writer incorporated into his work another source comprised of Leviticus 17–26. These chapters were regarded as having been written by a Holiness writer or school, and are thus referred to as H.

In the nearly century-and-a-half since this hypothesis was articulated by Wellhausen, there have been several alternative theories as to how the Pentateuch came together. However, the Documentary Hypothesis may still be considered the most prominent critically held theory, though with a number of proposed alterations. For example, the existence of a separate E document has been questioned, the presence of many additional hands in the editorial process has been proposed, and a number of scholars have argued, against Wellhausen's theory, that the order of the documents should be JEPD, rather than JEDP, with the Priestly material being considerably older than Wellhausen had theorized. Even for many of those who retain the JEDP order, they may argue that the traditions recorded in P regarding sacrifice and ritual, though perhaps not written down until after the exile, are nevertheless reflective of Israelite worship, perhaps as early as the foundation of the nation.[8]

How should we respond to this theory? First, it is important to note that while the narrative in the Pentateuch certainly highlights Moses's role in receiving laws from God and communicating them to the people, there are actually very few references to Moses's writing activity. Nothing necessarily prevents the possibility of figures after Moses being the actual individuals who committed part, or even the bulk, of these laws to writing.

Second, there are a number of valid reasons to believe that there were different sources used in the composition of the Pentateuch. There do seem to be strands running through the five books that are characterized by different stylistic features and emphases. I am convinced that these different sources actually existed and that an editor or editors took these different sources and skillfully wove them together into a narrative whole.

---

8. For a survey of the different views, see Gordon J. Wenham, "Pondering the Pentateuch: The Search for a New Paradigm," in *The Face of Old Testament Studies*, ed. David W. Baker and Bruce K. Waltke (Grand Rapids: Baker Books, 1999), 116–44.

Third, the New Testament informs us that the Scriptures are breathed out by God (2 Tim 3:16). While, traditionally, the Christian church has thought of this inspiration process as the act of God on a single individual writer, I believe we should expand our understanding of this. Leslie Allen approvingly cites the words of H. L. Ellison, "No doctrine of inspiration is worth its salt that does not take the work of editors into account."[9] While we have tended to think only of an inspired writer (and that is certainly true), the passage in Timothy emphasizes the inspiration of the words themselves. The final form of the book, consisting of the work of the author and editor(s), is to be regarded as the inspired word of God.

Finally, I refer to the work of Brevard Childs in his *Introduction to the Old Testament as Scripture*. Childs was a critical scholar who nevertheless argued that our faith and theologizing must be based on the final form of the text. It is only this final form that is canonical and theologically authoritative, not our theorizings or reconstructions as to what really took place and how the canonical book came together. This is how Childs relates his emphasis on the final form of the text to the book of Leviticus:

> The canonical effect of structuring the book in such a way as to connect all the material of Leviticus directly to the revelation at Sinai is of crucial importance in understanding how the book was shaped in its role as authoritative scripture for Israel. All the laws of Leviticus which stemmed originally from very different periods, and which reflected strikingly different sociological contexts, were subordinated to the one overarching theological construct, namely, the divine will made known to Moses at Sinai for every subsequent generation.[10]

To rephrase what Childs says here, as I understand it, we may have plausible, and perhaps even very likely, reconstructions as to when the materials in the book of Leviticus were variously written and how the book came together. But our reconstructions are not canonical, and they are not theologically authoritative. Only the received final form of the text is canonical and authoritative for faith and practice. Those who are responsible for the final form of the text have taken pains to faithfully present the text as the words that God gave to Moses at Mount Sinai.

---

9. Leslie C. Allen, *Ezekiel 20–48*, WBC 29 (Dallas: Word, 1990), xxv.

10. Brevard S. Childs, *Introduction to the Old Testament as Scripture* (Philadelphia: Fortress, 1979), 185–86.

When I preach from a text in the Pentateuch, I do not get up in the pulpit and ask the congregation to turn to J, or P, or H. No, I ask them to turn to Genesis or Exodus or Leviticus, the final form of the text that the church has received as canonical Christian Scripture. I place my trust in the Lord of the canon that this accurately reflects how he wants the church to receive these Scriptures and that, after having read them, I can truly and faithfully say, "This is the word of the Lord," to which the congregation can respond, "Thanks be to God."

Textual Witnesses

The Hebrew text of Leviticus, on which practically all modern scholarly commentaries on the book are based, is known as the Masoretic Text, named after the Masoretes, scribal scholars who were active in approximately the fifth to tenth centuries AD. All available evidence points to the faithfulness of this guild of scholars in transmitting the text that they received from previous generations of scribes. While they did add vowel markings to what had before been a text that only had consonantal characters, they were preservers and not innovators. The discoveries in the twentieth century of older manuscripts, as early as the third century BC, have confirmed the faithfulness and accuracy of the Masoretes in their transmission of the text. Any variations between these older texts and the Masoretic Text are fairly insignificant and are usually orthographic (pertaining to spelling) in character.

These older manuscripts are often referred to as Proto-Masoretic—that is, they form the base from which the Masoretes produced their manuscripts. Approximately sixteen such manuscripts of Leviticus have been found among the Qumran or Dead Sea Scrolls (DSS). Due to erosion and decay these manuscripts are fragmentary, and none of them contain the complete text of Leviticus. However, except for chapter 12, all the chapters of Leviticus are represented among them. Additionally, every chapter of Leviticus is referred to somewhere among the nonbiblical scrolls among the DSS—that is, scrolls that are not copies of biblical texts. This indicates the importance of the book of Leviticus for the Qumran community.[11]

There are also ancient translations (versions) of the text of Leviticus in Greek, Aramaic (Syriac), and Latin. None of these versions have proven to contain demonstrably superior readings to that of the Masoretic Text.

11. Martin Abegg, Jr., Peter Flint, and Eugene Ulrich, *The Dead Sea Scrolls Bible* (New York: HarperCollins, 1999), 77. See also their larger discussion of the Leviticus scrolls. Also, see most recently, Baesick Choi, *Leviticus and Its Reception in the Dead Sea Scrolls from Qumran* (Eugene, OR: Wipf & Stock, 2020).

Title and Canonicity

The ancient Hebrew and modern Jewish title for Leviticus is *wayyiqra'*, taken from the book's first word, meaning "and he called." Our current English title, Leviticus, comes to us by way of the Greek Septuagint (*Leuitikon*) and Latin Vulgate (*Leviticus*), and means "concerning the Levites." In essence, then, our English title is simply a transliteration of the Latin title. On the one hand, this designation is somewhat misleading, since the term Levite in the book of Leviticus only occurs in 25:32–33. Evidence suggests, however, that when the translators of these ancient versions used the term *Leuitikon* or *Leviticus* to refer to the book, they actually had in mind the idea of "Levitical priesthood." So, this name is not too far removed from another ancient rabbinic designation, "book of the priests."

There has never been any controversy over the book's canonical status. Regarded as a book of Moses, it has always been accorded canonical status in both the Jewish and Christian communities. In ancient times, Leviticus was the first biblical book with which Jewish children began their education, recognized in this way as foundational for Judaism. According to the rabbis, there are 613 laws in the Torah, and nearly half of them are contained in Leviticus.

Literary Analysis

Genre

The various types (genres) of writing or literature to be found within the book are not especially diverse. The book could fairly be characterized as containing laws, rules, regulations, and instructions for carrying out the rituals described in the book. A number of laws have motive clauses attached to them; for example, the Israelites are to be holy because the Lord is holy (Lev 19:2). Some of the laws have purpose clauses attached to them, indicating what was supposed to be the result of keeping the laws. Commentators often wish there were more motive and purpose clauses attached to the laws; it would have been nice, for example, to have pronounced rationales for the dietary laws!

Along with the giving of the laws and regulations, there are statements that can sound almost prophetic in their tone, with regard to the threat attached to violations. In chapter 26 these warnings sound like the kind of pronouncements one would find in ancient Near Eastern international treaties or covenants.

The book of Leviticus exists within a narrative already in place within the Pentateuch. When the book begins, it picks up the narrative with which the book of Exodus comes to a close. More will be said about this below.

Within this overall narrative, the book also contains a few of its own imbedded narratives. Even though chapters 8–10 contain a good deal of instruction, the chapters actually constitute a narrative about the ordination of Aaron and his sons, as well as the death of two of Aaron's sons, Nadab and Abihu, when they violate ritual proscriptions. The Day of Atonement ritual prescribed in chapter 16 is also related to this last incident, and the chapter concludes by noting that the instructions for celebrating the Day of Atonement were actually carried out. Finally, a narrative in chapter 24 deals with an individual who blasphemed the name of LORD and what was to be done with him.

One genre designation for the book as a whole, which is somewhat correct but can be misleading, is that of "priestly manual." However, if the book was meant to be a priestly manual, then it falls somewhat short. Some of the instructions are ambiguous as to exactly what the priest was to do or how a particular ritual act was to be carried out. Not enough information is given. Also, even though the instructions are, in many cases, aimed at how the priests were to perform their assigned responsibilities, they were also meant for the people's awareness. The "lay" Israelites were also to be familiar with these priestly instructions. They had the responsibility, not only of knowing what was happening in the various rituals, but also that of holding the priests accountable for performing these actions in accord with the directives of a holy God. They had a vested interest in the priests doing their work responsibly and carefully. Their lives depended on it.

All in all, with regard to the overall genre for the book, I agree with Longman and Dillard that perhaps the best generic label would be that of "instructional history."[12] This genre designation indicates that the book's purpose is to provide instructional material within a narrative framework and that the instruction cannot be separated or understood apart from its narrative setting.

Style

The book's instructional character results in a presentation that is fairly straightforward with little stylistic variety, which can be somewhat repetitive. The individual sentences and legal instructions were not intended to have any ornate aesthetic properties. So there really is not much by way of literary artistry at the individual sentence level.

---

12. Tremper Longman III and Raymond B. Dillard, *An Introduction to the Old Testament*, 2nd ed. (Grand Rapids: Zondervan, 2006), 83.

However, commentators and scholars have called attention to what they understand to be the use of structural literary artistry or symbolism on a macro-level. Some of these suggestions include:

1. The use of terms that occur exactly seven times within a passage, symbolic of divine origin, wholeness, completeness, and therefore holiness.
2. Certain rituals are demonstrated to be made of up seven ritual acts, or seven ritual instructions, also communicating a sense divine origin, completeness, and holiness.
3. The use of *inclusio*—an instruction or narrative beginning and ending with mirroring terms and clauses.
4. Chiasms: certain sections or chapters are said to be arranged in an inverted pattern shaped like an X.

In a commentary of this type, space precludes referring to all these postulated literary devices, but I will do so in particular instances. There is at least some indication that the authors/editors of the final form of Leviticus intentionally incorporated these literary devices to reinforce the teaching of the book.

Structure

The book of Leviticus may be outlined at various levels of detail. I have chosen to provide a more broadly simplified outline here, and one that does not separately list brief introductory or summary statements.

- I. Sacrificial Offerings (1:1–7:38)
  - A. From the Offerer's Perspective (1:1–6:7)
    1. Burnt Offering (1:1–17)
    2. Grain Offering (2:1–16)
    3. Fellowship Offering (3:1–17)
    4. Sin Offering (4:1–5:13)
    5. Guilt Offering (5:14–6:7)
  - B. From the Priest's Perspective (6:8–7:38)
    1. Burnt Offering (6:8–13)
    2. Grain Offering (6:14–18)
    3. Ordination Grain Offering (6:19–23)
    4. Sin Offering (6:24–30)
    5. Guilt Offering (7:1–10)

6. Fellowship Offering (7:11–21)
7. Prohibition against Consumption of Blood and Fat (7:22–27)
8. The Priests' Portions (7:28–38)

II. Narrative of Priestly Ordination, Service, and Violation (8:1–10:20)
A. Ordination of Aaron and His Sons (8:1–36)
B. Initial Priestly Service (9:1–24)
C. First Priestly Violation (10:1–20)

III. Purity Legislation (11:1–15:33)
A. Dietary Laws (11:1–47)
B. Childbirth (12:1–8)
C. Unclean Skin Diseases (13:1–46)
D. Unclean Fabric (13:47–59)
E. Purification from Skin Diseases (14:1–32)
F. Unclean Houses (14:33–57)
G. Unclean Discharges (15:1–33)

IV. The Day of Atonement (16:1–34)

V. Holiness Legislation (17:1–22:33)
A. Regulations Regarding Blood (17:1–16)
B. Laws Regarding Incest and Other Sexual Violations (18:1–30)
C. A Miscellany of Laws (19:1–37)
D. Punishments for Capital, Sexual, and Other Serious Violations (20:1–27)
E. Rules for Priest and Their Families (21:1–24)
F. Rules for Consumption of Sacrifices and for Unacceptable Sacrifices (22:1–33)

VI. Festival Calendar (23:1–44)
A. Sabbaths (23:1–3)
B. Passover and Unleavened Bread (23:4–8)
C. Firstfruits (23:9–14)
D. Weeks (23:15–22)
E. Trumpets (23:23–25)
F. Day of Atonement (23:26–32)
G. Tabernacles (23:33–44)

VII. Regulations Regarding the Holy Place (24:1–9)

VIII. Narrative Regarding a Blasphemer (24:10–23)

IX. The Sabbath Year and the Jubilee (25:1–55)
A. Sabbath Year (25:1–7)
B. Jubilee (25:8–55)

X. Blessings and Curses (26:1–46)

A. Blessings (26:1–13)
B. Curses (26:14–46)
XI. Vows and Gifts to the Lord (27:1–34)

Historical Background

Historical Setting of the Contents of the Book

The book of Exodus narrates God's deliverance of the Israelites from Egypt. Within three months of their departure from Egypt they arrive at Mount Sinai (Exod 19:1). All the events that follow, from Exodus 19:1 to Numbers 10:11, take place within the next ten months. Exodus 25–31 details the instructions the Lord gave Moses for the construction of the tabernacle. Exodus 32–34, the golden calf narrative, is an interruption that even threatens to bring the entire Israelite nation to an end. But after this interruption chapters 35–40 narrate how the instructions for the construction of the tabernacle are carried out.

Nine months into this period, just two weeks shy of the first anniversary of the Israelites' departure from Egypt, the tabernacle is finally erected and dedicated. At this dedication the glory of the Lord fills the tabernacle, signaling his move from the top of Mount Sinai to take up residence in the tabernacle. At this point the book of Leviticus continues the narrative: "The Lord called to Moses and spoke to him from the tent of meeting" (1:1). Now Yahweh no longer speaks to Moses from the top of Mount Sinai, but from within the tabernacle. The significance of this dramatic development will be explored in the commentary on chapter 1. This timeline suggests that the entire book of Leviticus, all the Lord's instructions and the narratives in the book, takes place within a month-and-a-half time period, though there are some chronological issues with this understanding. Nevertheless, within the narrative flow of the Pentateuch, the book of Leviticus is seen as occupying approximately a month and a half of the forty-year journey of the Israelites in the wilderness of Sinai. The narrative has almost come to a standstill. The significance of this will also be discussed in the commentary on chapter 1.

Ancient Near Eastern Background

Israel's worship of its God did not take place in a vacuum, and it only stands to reason that, in many respects, Israel's worship would look like the worship of the surrounding nations. To be sure, there are many disconnects, and God declares certain practices, especially among the Egyptians and Canaanites, prohibited for the Israelites in their worship of him. Nevertheless, there are many commonalities: priests, sacrifice, blood manipulation, incense, sanctuary complexes with different grades of holiness, special festivals at appointed times, food offerings, anointings, purity regulations, etc. At many places in this commentary we will call attention to these similarities as well as the contrasts.

The salvation history that the Scriptures present to us is a culturally imbedded history. Israel, despite being the LORD's special possession and despite benefitting from the LORD's special protection, did not live in a divine glass bubble. The LORD dealt with his special people as the ancient Near Eastern people that they were and in the cultural milieu in which they existed. It only makes sense, then, that the LORD spoke to his people utilizing the cultural forms, concepts, and idioms with which they were familiar. As John Calvin so famously emphasized, God, in his revelation of himself, has accommodated himself to our understanding. He has stooped down to our level, "lisping" to us as a parent would to their small child.[13] Inspired Scripture is a fully divine and a fully human product. So we certainly confess with the psalmist, "Your word, LORD, is eternal; it stands firm in the heavens" (Ps 119:89). But we also believe that this culturally embedded word reflects its cultural context.

In our investigation of how the book of Leviticus was used in the New Testament and how it is to be used by Christians today in the twenty-first century, we have to attempt to discern how this culturally embedded text speaks to readers in very different contexts. We will, of course, do this imperfectly, but we have to make the attempt, which we will do throughout this commentary.

Theological Message

Theology of the Book

The Divine Presence

From prior accounts in Scripture—the garden of Eden narrative, the establishment of the Abrahamic covenant, as well as the Mosaic covenant—it is clear that God wished to dwell among his people, that he would be their God, and the Israelites would be his people (Gen 17:8; Exod 25:8; 29:45–46). Now, in a very special development, God takes up residence among his people in a way that he had not before. He no longer merely dwells above them from atop Mount Sinai, but he dwells among them in the tabernacle, in a tent that is squarely in the middle of the camp, surrounded by all the tents of the

13. John Calvin, *Institutes of the Christian Religion*, ed. John McNeill, trans. Ford Lewis Battles, Library of Christian Classics (Louisville: Westminster John Knox, 1960), 1.xiii.1:121. See also the very fine discussion of this concept in Ford Lewis Battles, "God Was Accommodating Himself to Human Capacity," *Int* 31.1 (1977): 19–38.

Israelites. The King is in residence.[14] God, as their covenant King who has taken up residence among them, is to be given all the respect, honor, glory, and obedience that would be given to any earthly monarch. Failure in this area is not simply an act of disrespect. Intentional failures can only be regarded as acts of treason.

Worship

Seven times in the early chapters of Exodus, God articulates the reason why Pharaoh should release the Israelites and allow them to leave:

> "Let my son go, so he may worship me." (Exod 4:23)
>
> "Let my people go, so that they may worship me in the wilderness." (Exod 7:16)
>
> "Let my people go, so that they may worship me." (Exod 8:1, 20; 9:1, 13; 10:3)

In the course of the dialogue between Moses and Pharaoh, it becomes clear that Pharaoh recognizes that this worship will involve offering sacrifices (8:8; see also 3:18 and 5:3). Moses reinforces this understanding in 8:26. Moses also says, in 10:9, that they must go out to worship the Lord, "with our flocks and herds, because we are to celebrate a festival to the LORD" (see also 5:1). At one point, even though Pharaoh knows this worship is to involve sacrifice, he tells Moses that they can go out and worship in the wilderness, but they have to leave their flocks and herds behind (10:24). But Moses responds that they must take their flocks and herds because they must offer some of them as sacrifices, and they will not know exactly which ones to offer until they get there (10:25–26).

So all the elements are there. The Israelites must be allowed to go because they are to worship the LORD. They must go out into the wilderness to do this. They must take their animals with them to make sacrifices in the wilderness. They will not know which animals to use until they get there. And they will indeed celebrate a festival to the LORD. All these elements are fulfilled in the book of Leviticus. They arrive at Mount Sinai in the wilderness. They receive instructions as to which animals to use for which sacrifices. They worship and

---

14. Jay Sklar has a very fine discussion of this royal imagery in his commentary. See Jay Sklar, *Leviticus: An Introduction and Commentary*, TOTC 3 (Downers Grove, IL: InterVarsity Press, 2014), 37–44.

celebrate a festival to the LORD. We can very appropriately say that Leviticus is the goal of the Exodus! Exodus happens so that Leviticus will happen. The purpose for the Exodus—and this is not simply a deceptive ploy or subterfuge to get Pharaoh to let the people go—is that Israel might worship God in the wilderness. The heart, the middle point, the focus, the purpose, the goal of the Pentateuch is—Leviticus!

Ritual

Ceremonies and rituals of worship were by no means regarded by the ancients, as they often are today, as meaningless repeated acts devoid of real value and devotion on account of their lack of spontaneity. Rather, the rituals were an important part of the faithful response of the Israelites toward God. More will be said about this in the commentary on chapter 1, but here I note briefly five important reasons why this was the case:

1. God was the one who commanded and authorized these rituals. When the Israelites observed these rites, they were simply obeying God's commands.
2. Even today there are protocols that must be observed when coming into the presence of royalty, holders of government offices, and courtroom judges. Ancient Israelite rituals can be seen as royal protocols in which the people showed proper respect, not only for the one who was King of Israel, but King of the universe. These rites were intended to assure proper behavior and decorum in the presence of the King.
3. Ritual is an exercise in world formation. As Mark Boda says, "The priestly legislation constructs a ritual world, designed to foster the covenant relationship between Yahweh and his people."[15] When the Israelites went through their rites of worship, they were led to acknowledge that the outside world, the world of Egyptian oppressors, pagan Canaanites, empires, business, commerce, a world in which injustice may have often seemed to prevail, was something less than full reality. Indeed, ritual presented them with an alternate reality, a world in which God was King—not Pharaoh, nor the Hittite, Assyrian, or Babylonian emperor, nor any of the oppressive rulers of the neighboring countries. Ritual provided a vision, a worldview, a guide for faithful living for those who were the special possession of this great King.

15. Mark J. Boda, *A Severe Mercy: Sin and Its Remedy in the Old Testament*, Siphrut 1 (Winona Lake, IN: Eisenbrauns, 2009), 50.

4. There is an important corporate dimension to worship that is enhanced by ritual. "Ritual enables corporate participation in a single act, which thereby creates community around the act of worship."[16]
5. Along with this last-mentioned point, it is also important to note that ritual ties together the worship of generations across time. "Ritual enables continuity with the past—the same thing being done through the ages creates a commonality across history."[17]

Holiness

The topic of holiness is a huge one. For our purposes here, we may categorize the discussion with regard to God, things and animals, and human beings:

1. God is holy. Perhaps most Christians regard this as a statement about God's moral or ethical holiness. I do not believe this understanding is wrong, but it is incomplete. Rudolf Otto has argued that the idea of moral or ethical holiness is actually secondary to the original understanding of holiness, that God is transcendent, "wholly other"; the term indicates God's separateness from his creation.[18] I believe Otto is correct to call attention to this dimension; and yet, an ethical and moral understanding of God's holiness must also be present in order for the statement in Leviticus 19:1, "Be holy because I, the Lord your God, am holy," to actually provide behavioral motivation. So, I think it is best to understand that from the very beginning a variety of concepts are included in the idea of God's holiness: wholly otherness, separateness, and ethical purity. On the last element, it is also important to note that God's ethical and moral purity does not conform to some external standard outside himself. He himself is his own standard.
2. Things and animals can be holy. The concern here has to do with ritual status. Various schemes have been used by commentators to provide a grid for understanding this. Two pairs of contrasting concepts must be laid out.

   First, there is the opposition between holy and profane or common. If something is holy, it is understood as being separated for use by God or by his cultic personnel. If something is common or profane, it is not so set apart. There is nothing necessarily bad about an object being common or profane; it simply is not reserved solely for God's use.

16. George Athas (personal communication, 2018).
17. George Athas (personal communication, 2018).
18. Rudolf Otto, *The Idea of the Holy* (London: Oxford University Press, 1923); see also John G. Gammie, *Holiness in Israel*, OBT (Minneapolis: Augsburg Fortress, 1989).

Second, there is the opposition between clean and unclean, or pure and impure. If something is clean, it is not ritually defiling. If something is unclean, it is ritually defiling.

Now one might think that, based on this description, there are four states: holy, common, clean, and unclean. Actually, there are only three possible combinations:

- Holy and clean
- Common and clean
- Common and unclean

Again, it is important to note that common and profane are not derogatory terms. That which is common or profane is bad only if it is also unclean, and, as mentioned earlier, these are all categories of ritual status. That which is holy is reserved for Yahweh's use and for use by the priests, Levites, and their families. That which is common may still be brought into the tabernacle complex if it is ritually clean, but that which is unclean may not.

3. People can be holy. The same oppositions exist for humans as with things and animals. Again, these are ritual categories. For the most part, only the priests are regarded as holy in Leviticus. Clean Israelites may enter the tabernacle courtyard and take part in the rituals. Unclean Israelites may not.

   There can be degrees with the polar oppositions, so some things and persons can be holier than others. The high priest is in a holier ritual state than the regular priests. Some uncleannesses are more unclean than others, and the purification process to move someone or something from unclean to clean may be more involved and longer for some than for others.

Finally, within Leviticus there are only a handful of references to people other than priests as holy. In Leviticus 11:43–45 those who do not defile themselves by coming into contact with unclean animals or carcasses sanctify themselves and are referred to as holy. Then, in addition to that which is purely ritual, in the so-called Holiness Code people other than priests are referred to as holy on account of their ethical behavior (19:2; 20:7–8, 26; 22:32).

We will call attention to these various distinctions within the course of the commentary.

Sacrifice and Offerings

There are five major sacrifices described within the first seven chapters of Leviticus. There are several observations to make about these sacrifices. First, most modern commentators and some translations use different designations to refer to these sacrifices than have been traditionally used. The NIV, the base text for this commentary, employs the traditional designations.

- The burnt offering is often referred to by modern commentators as the ascending offering.
- The grain offering has, by some commentators, been referred to as the tribute or gift offering.
- The fellowship offering (also traditionally referred to as the peace offering) has now been designated by some commentators as the offering of well-being.
- The sin offering is referred to by most commentators as the purification offering.
- The guilt offering is referred to by most commentators as the reparation offering.

There are good and cogent reasons for the alternate designations. However, I am going to retain the more traditional way of referring to these sacrifices, for three reasons: (a) so that the person who is using this commentary along with the NIV text will not be unnecessarily confused; (b) the traditional designations are not so much wrong as they are perhaps imprecise or incomplete; and (c) even some modern academic commentaries have decided to retain or revert to the traditional names.[19] We will discuss these alternate designations in the course of the commentary.

Second, I agree with a number of commentators that, broadly speaking, all the sacrifices are to some extent propitiatory in their function. Traditionally, it is the sin and guilt offerings that are thought of as being propitiatory. But to some degree all the sacrifices are propitiatory—that is, they are intended to appease and please the deity and to avert his displeasure and wrath. This propitiatory function is indicated in the biblical text by the effect they produce, "a pleasing aroma" to the Lord (some translations have "a soothing aroma"). Some might think of bargaining with God as a jaded view of sacrifice, but this does not have to be case; all sacrifices to deities in the ancient Near East were

19. For example, James W. Watts, *Leviticus 1–10*, HCOT (Leeuven: Peeters, 2013), 306–10, 332–33.

for the purpose of bringing pleasure to the deity and seeking his favor. This is no less the case with Israel and with Israel's God.

Finally, commentaries will often make a distinction between voluntary and mandatory sacrifices, with the burnt, grain, and fellowship offerings being examples of the voluntary, and the sin and guilt offerings being examples of the mandatory (since sin must be atoned for). However, while the first three offerings are, indeed, strictly voluntary in essence, the better way to refer to them is "voluntary but expected." When one goes to visit a great person, it is customary to bring a gift. To not bring a gift would be regarded as a sign of disrespect. To be sure, this was the case in ancient Israel as well. God was Israel's great King. One should not visit that King empty-handed.

Atonement

> *Sacrifice, primal and universal, is nothing more than the visible representation that evil can be removed, sin can be erased, defilement can be cleansed, harmony can be restored. Leviticus outlines the foundations of the world.*

In this way Myrto Theocharous, one of the editors of this commentary series, eloquently captures the vision of the book of Leviticus.[20] There seems to be something innate in human beings that understands that when a person does something wrong they must "make up" for it. Whenever we think we may have offended someone, a common reaction is to say to the person, "How can I make it up to you?" In the movie *The Mission*, the slaver Rodrigo Mendoza has to atone for kidnapping members of a native Paraguayan tribe and selling them into slavery; he does so by climbing a high waterfall while carrying a large sack containing all his heavy armor and weapons. In Charles Dickens's *A Tale of Two Cities*, Sydney Carton makes up for a promising but wasted life by sacrificing himself to save the life of Charles Darnay, a rival suitor for the woman he loves. In Ian McEwan's novel *Atonement* (subsequently made into a movie of the same name), Briony Tallis, as a young teenager, makes a false rape accusation. Several years later she has the opportunity to set things right but does not have courage to do so, ruining several lives by her failure. Fifty years later, dying and suffering from dementia, she writes a novel about the incident, attempting by means of the novel to perform—yet rather lamely and dubiously—the act of atonement she failed to perform sixty years earlier. These examples illustrate that the concept of atonement is by no means missing from contemporary culture.

20. Personal communication, 2017.

As for the biblical narrative, this need for sacrifice and atonement is indeed primal. It goes back to Abel's offering in Genesis 4:4, and perhaps even to a sacrifice performed by God himself in Genesis 3:21.[21] It is universal: the nations in the ancient Near East also perform atoning sacrifices. It is significant that when God relocates from the top of Mount Sinai to the newly dedicated tabernacle, his first speeches from this new location have to do with sacrifice and atonement. Even though the primary atonement offerings, the sin and guilt offerings, are described last in the series, the burnt offering is one that "will be accepted on your behalf to make atonement for you" (Lev 1:4). So Leviticus emphasizes the necessity of sacrifice in order that God may indeed dwell among his people, as was the original intention at the creation of the world and as was the purpose of the tabernacle: "Have them make me a sanctuary, so that I may dwell among them" (Exod 25:8; NRSV). The sacrifices ensure this continued presence. Leviticus, indeed, "outlines the foundations of the world."

Much more will be said about this in the commentary, but I will be defending the position that the sacrifices of atonement are indeed substitutionary. The sacrificial animal dies in place of the offerer. In this way, God's wrath, either actual or potential, is averted; the offerers are ransomed and purified; and their sins are atoned for and forgiven. The atoning sacrifices both expiate sin (remove it) and propitiate God (avert his wrath). Communion between God and the offerers is established or re-established. God continues to walk among them and be their God, and they continue to be his people, his treasured possession.

Ethics

For God to dwell among his people, they must not only be in right relation to him, they must also be in right relationship with each other. Especially, then, in the latter chapters of the book, the so-called Holiness Code (chs. 17–26), emphasis is laid on how the people may imitate, and share in, the ethical and moral holiness of God by dealing with one another in love and justice. They must be holy as he is holy (19:2). Therefore, every area of their lives must conform to his expectations. They must be pure in their sexual, financial, family, and interpersonal relationships.

The Israelites, both in their relationship with God and in their relationships with each other, are to be regulated in their conduct according to the covenant. Obedience to the LORD's commandments in all their relationships is a matter

21. It is debated whether God's clothing the first human pair with animal skins also involves sacrifice. For a cogent defense of this position, as well as exploration of connections to Leviticus, see Kenneth A. Mathews, *Genesis 1–11:26*, NAC 1A (Nashville: Broadman & Holman, 1996), 254–55.

of covenantal obligation. If they are obedient, they will enjoy the blessings of the covenant. If they disobey, they risk being subjected to the curses of the covenant, which may eventually result in being cut off from the presence of the LORD and being exiled from the land of promise. All this highlights the necessity of the people's right conduct in both their ritual and ethical behavior.[22]

Reading in the Context of the Old Testament

We have already discussed Leviticus's role in the context of both the narrative flow and theology of the Pentateuch. In this section I wish to focus on only two areas.

First, in some Old Testament scholarship in the earlier part of the twentieth century there was an emphasis placed on the supposed antithesis between the Pentateuchal laws, especially those contained in Leviticus, and the prophetic books of the Old Testament. The understanding was that the prophets were highly critical of the cult, the sacrificial system, and ritual. Passages like those found in Isaiah 1:10–20; Jeremiah 7:21–25; and Micah 6:6–8 were taken as being wholesale condemnations of sacrifice and ritual. However, this older understanding has receded as scholars have more correctly understood that the prophets were not against sacrifice and ritual per se; rather, their concern was a sinful lifestyle that did not accord with participation in the ritual observances of the cult, thus rendering their participation in those rituals to be hypocritical. What they were against is the same as that depicted in the movie *The Godfather*, when Michael Corleone, standing as godfather at the baptism of his nephew, confesses his belief in the doctrines of the Catholic Church, renouncing Satan and all his works, while at the very same moment his goons are carrying out contract hits against Corleone's enemies.

While we should not swing the pendulum too far and suggest that the prophets were all avidly pro-cult, it should be pointed out that a number of the prophets seem to have cultic associations. For some prophets, like Ezekiel, Haggai, and Zechariah (and, I would even argue, Isaiah and Jeremiah), their relationship to sacrifice and ritual is quite significant. For Ezekiel the priest, who is also critical of hypocritical ritual observance, his connection to the book of Leviticus is especially significant. We will call attention to those connections in the course of the commentary.

Second, it is important to recognize the significance of this material for passages like Psalm 119 and the interesting slant this provides for us to understand

---

22. For an excellent treatment of this topic, see Christopher J. H. Wright, *Old Testament Ethics for the People of God* (Downers Grove, IL: InterVarsity Press, 2004).

how psalmists and prophets regarded the Pentateuchal laws and the book of Leviticus. In Psalm 119, not only does the psalmist regularly proclaim his admiration and love for, and intense devotion to, the law of God, but he even goes so far as to say the following:

> I run in the path of your commands, for you have set my heart free. (v. 32; NIV 1984)
>
> I will walk about in freedom, for I have sought out your precepts. (v. 45)

About such statements of intense devotion, and the psalmist's maintaining that the law of God actually provides him freedom, Robert Davidson declares:

> What is remarkable . . . are the words used to describe the psalmist's attitude to and response to Torah: "liberty," "freedom," "delight," or joy, and the repeated "love." These are not the words you find in the context of a harsh legalism. They are the words which the New Testament uses again and again to describe the Christian's relationship to Christ (e.g., John 8:36; Phil. 4:4; 1 John 4:7–12).[23]

Picking up on Leviticus 26:13, Childs argues that in the book of Leviticus

> [a] witness is given that the institutions and rites which determine how Israel is properly to worship God derived from divine revelation. Israel's cult is not her own invention. There is no tension between spirit and form of the covenant. Rather in the service of the tabernacle the sons of the covenant realize their new life of freedom to "walk erect."[24]

The book of Leviticus and the book of Psalms both affirm that in the commands of the Lord are found life and joy and delight—and freedom.

Reading from the Perspective of the New Testament

One particular focus of this commentary series is how the Old Testament text is utilized by, and points forward to, the New Testament. We will be doing this in every chapter of the commentary, so I will keep my remarks here more brief and general.

---

23. Robert Davidson, *The Vitality of Worship: A Commentary on the Book of Psalms* (Grand Rapids: Eerdmans, 1998), 394.

24. Childs, *Introduction to the Old Testament as Scripture*, 187.

Fleming Rutledge, in her justly praised volume on the crucifixion, remarks:

> A preacher on the radio observed that the New Testament tells us almost nothing about what went on in Jesus' mind; then he said "If you want to know what went on in Jesus' mind, read the Old Testament." That is a dazzlingly simple way of stating what every biblical scholar knows but seldom says. We tend to forget that what we call the Old Testament was the only Bible that Jesus, Paul, and the earliest Christians had. Not only so, but the Torah, the Prophets, and the Psalms were known to them by heart in a fashion that we today can scarcely imagine. There are many things that we do not know about Jesus, but of this we can be sure: his mind and heart were shaped by intimate, continuous interaction with the Scriptures. If we are to have the mind of Christ (1 Cor. 2:16), we need to know the Old Testament.[25]

There have been efforts, both ancient and modern, to relativize and marginalize the Old Testament and to squeeze the teaching of the Old and New Testaments into formulations such as law versus gospel, letter versus spirit, bondage versus freedom, relevant versus irrelevant, and abrogated versus valid. But, as Rutledge and her radio preacher point out, the truth of the matter is quite the opposite. Jesus and the apostles lived in the world of the Old Testament. It was their joy and delight. Jesus declared that these words from God are the very words by which we live, demonstrating that to be the case as he quoted from the book of Deuteronomy in his contest with Satan in the wilderness (Matt 4:1–11). In the last week of Jesus's life on earth before his crucifixion, he made constant references to various books of the Old Testament, citing at least a dozen different Old Testament books. In particular, he cited at least seven different psalms. Among the "seven sayings" Jesus uttered as he hung from the cross, at least three of them (possibly four) were quotations from the Psalms. Yes, if you want to know the mind of Jesus, read the Old Testament.

The book of Leviticus may not be as front and center in the New Testament as other Old Testament books. However, as I have already noted above, the most cited Old Testament verse in the New Testament comes from Leviticus, and it could be argued that, in many ways, the teaching of the book of Leviticus "undergirds the logic of the New Testament."[26] Leviticus plays a

25. Fleming Rutledge, *The Crucifixion: Understanding the Death of Jesus Christ* (Grand Rapids: Eerdmans, 2015), 107.

26. George Athas (personal communication, 2018).

major role in the book of Hebrews. As many have argued, Leviticus seems to play a significant role in the letter in Acts 15 that the apostles send to gentile believers, instructing them with regard to the law. It has been maintained that James demonstrates a significant acquaintance with Leviticus in his epistle.

All this presents us with a bit of a quandary. On the one hand, Paul does seem to set up oppositions similar to the ones I mentioned earlier: law versus faith, letter versus spirit, bondage versus freedom. So it would appear that we do not need Old Testament law. Yet, it is Paul himself who uses Old Testament law to encourage believers in their training in righteousness (for example, the well-known 2 Tim 3:16; see also 1 Cor 9:7–10; 14:34; Eph 6:1–3), and he does declare that the law is good for those who use it properly (1 Tim 1:8). Jesus himself says he came to fulfill the law. This does not mean simply that he came to fulfill it in his own person, though that is certainly part of what he meant; he also places a high value for his followers on obeying the law, issuing a dire warning for those who would do and teach otherwise (Matt 5:17–20).

I called attention in the last section to Robert Davidson's observation that the psalmist of Psalm 119 speaks of God's laws with an intensity of devotion and language that resembles statements in the New Testament made about devotion to Christ. Ultimately, I conclude that, for believers in Christ, there is no actual contradiction. We declare our devotion to Christ. But Christ himself was one who delighted in the law of God. Jesus is the blessed man of Psalm 1 who "delights in the law of the Lord." Jesus is the psalmist of Psalm 119 who regards the words of God to be his joy and his delight. Jesus is the psalmist of Psalm 40, who, according to the author of Hebrews, said as he entered this world, "Here I am—it is written about me in the scroll—I have come to do your will, my God" (Heb 10:7; see Ps 40:7). Yes, we delight in Jesus. But precisely because we delight in Jesus, we also delight in the law of God (see Rom 7:12, 22), which means we also delight in Leviticus.

Reading from the Perspective of the Twenty-First Century

In at least one important respect, there is no difference between reading Leviticus from the perspective of the twenty-first century and that of reading Leviticus in the second half of the first century AD. First-century believers and twenty-first century believers can both say that we are those "on whom the culmination of the ages has come" (1 Cor 10:11). Both first-century and twenty-first-century believers can say, "Christ has come, Christ has died, Christ has risen, Christ has sent his Holy Spirit, and we are now living in the last days." In essence, the situation has not changed from the first century to the twenty-first century. Yet it is also true that every generation must discern how best to live out the truth of Scripture and the gospel of Jesus Christ in the midst of their temporal, geographical, and cultural contexts.

Kevin Vanhoozer has presented a helpful "dramatic" metaphor for understanding the way we should seek to live out the truth of the biblical text.[27] The biblical text is our canonical script, and we are now called upon to act out the play that God has written before our audience, the world. Vanhoozer says,

> [t]hough the Bible is not, strictly speaking, a play script, there is much therein for disciples to learn and perform. The Bible is the primary text from which disciples learn how to act as disciples, because it is from the Bible that they learn about the divine protagonist and the nature of the triune action, the drama "behind" the doctrine, which doctrine helps us better to understand: "To learn how to interpret these scripts well by playing them out in one's life is to learn how to be a disciple."[28]

Additionally, Vanhoozer argues that we do not act out this play as individuals but as a community: The church is "an acting company that performs the drama at the heart of the Gospels and apostolic letters."[29]

To put a bit of my own twist on the way Vanhoozer has articulated his metaphor, I would put it this way: The Bible, the canon of Scripture, is the script for the play that we as Christians are being called upon to act out before the audience, the world. We must study the script, and we must study how the play has been performed by previous generations of actors. Indeed, we must study how Jesus himself, the main character in the very first "Passion Play," lived, died, and rose again, according to the Script(ures).

Also important for Vanhoozer's drama metaphor is that the actors are not expected to merely mimic the script or to repeat the lines verbatim. Rather, we are expected by the writer of the play to do a bit of improvisation in our performance. This improvisation is the way we communicate the gospel and the truth of the Script in all our varied temporal, geographical, and cultural contexts. These are not absolutely free improvisations. The canonical Script provides parameters and limits as to what we can do.

---

27. Kevin J. Vanhoozer, *The Drama of Doctrine: A Canonical-Linguistic Approach to Christian Theology* (Louisville: Westminster John Knox, 2005); Kevin J. Vanhoozer, *Faith Speaking Understanding: Performing the Drama of Doctrine* (Louisville: Westminster John Knox, 2014).

28. Vanhoozer, *Faith Speaking Understanding*, 143–44. The words in the quotation come from Terrence W. Tilley, *The Disciples' Jesus: Christology as Reconciling Practice* (Maryknoll, NY: Orbis, 2008), 73

29. Vanhoozer, *Faith Speaking Understanding*, 36.

Of course, this improvisation is a tricky business, which is why we need the canonical parameters and limitations; this is the reason we study how Christ and the apostles played out the Script, and it is also why we study how previous generations of Christians performed the play. We learn from them, and we are constrained by them.

To act out the book of Leviticus requires a carefully studied act of improvisation. Various models have been suggested. For example, there is the "moral, civil, ceremonial" model. What usually happens here is that it is suggested that we as Christians still need to follow the moral law, but we no longer need to follow the civil law, since we are not a theocracy; we do not need to follow the ceremonial or ritual law, because Christ has fulfilled that law in his death and crucifixion.

There is indeed a certain heuristic value in using these categories from our standpoint today. But there are three significant problems with the model. The first is that our modern division of moral, civil, and ceremonial is indeed our own modern overlay on the text. This construal would have made no sense to the ancient Israelites. The ceremonial law was civil and moral; the civil law was ceremonial and moral; the moral law was ceremonial and civil.[30]

The second problem is that, when we do this, we cut off ourselves off from the ways that even the New Testament used this material. For example, the commands to present ourselves as living sacrifices, to be a holy temple in the Lord, and so on are actually ways in which we improvise on the so-called ceremonial law. Many of the directions which Paul gives to the churches in his epistles, especially in the Corinthian letters, can validly be seen as the application of so-called civil law to the way in which churches should conduct their ecclesiastical affairs.

The third problem is that this kind of division into moral, ceremonial, and civil often betrays, at least in North America, a western moralist and anti-ceremonial perspective that also tends to regard itself, with its individualistic and democratic orientation, to be the only perspective. However, when the gospel is acted out in other parts of the world, the so-called ceremonial aspects of Leviticus may actually serve to be as, or even more, important than our focus on the so-called moral aspects.[31] And it may well be that so-called civil aspects of Leviticus may be quite relevant in those parts of the world where

30. For another critique of the moral, civil ceremonial distinction, see Wright, *Old Testament Ethics for the People of God*, 288–89, 292–93.

31. I am thinking here, for example, of those places where ritual sacrifice is still a very important part of the larger culture.

there is a much closer connection between state and religion than is the case in North America.[32]

In this commentary we will try to suggest ways in which the teaching of Leviticus as a whole, as refracted through the pages of the New Testament, may be improvised in our communication of the gospel and in our ways of behaving ethically and responsibly in our Christian communities, before a watching world. May God be pleased with, and add his blessings to, this effort.

---

32. There are several countries where there is at least a nominal understanding that the government of the country is Christian. More substantial is the example of Samoa, which has recently strengthened its already understood status—as a nation founded on Christian principles—to that of truly being a Christian state rather than a secular one, with a provision in its constitution that reads: "Samoa is a Christian nation founded of God the Father, the Son and the Holy Spirit." It also states that the government will operate "within the limits prescribed by God's commandments." In this context there is an increased potential for the biblical text to have substantial influence in legislative and courtroom situations. See Grant Wyeth, "Samoa Officially Becomes a Christian State," *The Diplomat*, 26 June 2017, https://thediplomat.com/2017/06/samoa-officially-becomes-a-christian-state/.

Resources for Those Teaching or Preaching the Book of Leviticus

Among the commentaries that I would most recommend are those by Milgrom and Hartley on the more academic and technical side; and Wenham, Gane, Sklar, Balentine, Hess, Levine, and Kleinig, as still academic, but perhaps more accessible by those not trained in Hebrew. Aside from commentaries, I would also recommend the following resources.

Balentine, Samuel E. *The Torah's Vision of Worship*. OBT. Minneapolis: Augsburg Fortress, 1999.

Gammie, John G. *Holiness in Israel*. OBT. Minneapolis: Augsburg Fortress, 1989.

Longman, Tremper III. *Immanuel in Our Place: Seeing Christ in Israel's Worship*. The Gospel According to the Old Testament. Phillipsburg, NJ: P&R, 2001.

Morales, L. Michael. *Who Shall Ascend the Mountain of the Lord?: A Biblical Theology of the Book of Leviticus*. NSBT 37. Downers Grove, IL: InterVarsity Press, 2015.

Wright, Christopher J. H. *Old Testament Ethics for the People of God*. Downers Grove, IL: InterVarsity Press, 2004.

CHAPTER 1

Leviticus 1:1–17

LISTEN to the Story

[1:1]The LORD called to Moses and spoke to him from the tent of meeting. He said, [2]"Speak to the Israelites and say to them: 'When anyone among you brings an offering to the LORD, bring as your offering an animal from either the herd or the flock.

[3]"'If the offering is a burnt offering from the herd, you are to offer a male without defect. You must present it at the entrance to the tent of meeting so that it will be acceptable to the LORD. [4]You are to lay your hand on the head of the burnt offering, and it will be accepted on your behalf to make atonement for you. [5]You are to slaughter the young bull before the LORD, and then Aaron's sons the priests shall bring the blood and splash it against the sides of the altar at the entrance to the tent of meeting. [6]You are to skin the burnt offering and cut it into pieces. [7]The sons of Aaron the priest are to put fire on the altar and arrange wood on the fire. [8]Then Aaron's sons the priests shall arrange the pieces, including the head and the fat, on the wood that is burning on the altar. [9]You are to wash the internal organs and the legs with water, and the priest is to burn all of it on the altar. It is a burnt offering, a food offering, an aroma pleasing to the LORD.

[10]"'If the offering is a burnt offering from the flock, from either the sheep or the goats, you are to offer a male without defect. [11]You are to slaughter it at the north side of the altar before the LORD, and Aaron's sons the priests shall splash its blood against the sides of the altar. [12]You are to cut it into pieces, and the priest shall arrange them, including the head and the fat, on the wood that is burning on the altar. [13]You are to wash the internal organs and the legs with water, and the priest is to bring all of them and burn them on the altar. It is a burnt offering, a food offering, an aroma pleasing to the LORD.

[14]"'If the offering to the LORD is a burnt offering of birds, you are to offer a dove or a young pigeon. [15]The priest shall bring it to the altar, wring

off the head and burn it on the altar; its blood shall be drained out on the side of the altar. [16]He is to remove the crop and the feathers and throw them down east of the altar where the ashes are. [17]He shall tear it open by the wings, not dividing it completely, and then the priest shall burn it on the wood that is burning on the altar. It is a burnt offering, a food offering, an aroma pleasing to the LORD.

Listening to the Text in the Story: Biblical Texts: Genesis 8:20; 22:1–18; Exodus 10:24–26; 19:1; 20:24; 24:5; 29:42; 40:33–38; Ancient Near Eastern Texts: A Punic Sacrificial Tariff; Establishing a New Temple for the Goddess of the Night; Epic of Gilgamesh

The book of Leviticus begins with seven chapters that give instructions concerning offerings and sacrifices. The first five chapters (through 6:7) are more oriented toward the offerers of the sacrifices; the last two chapters (beginning at 6:8) are more oriented toward the duties of the priests who oversee the sacrificial process.

The subject of this first chapter is the whole burnt offering, which, unlike the other offerings, is completely burned up on the altar. There are three contexts in which the instructions in this chapter should be examined: related ancient Near Eastern texts, other significant references to the burnt offering in the Old Testament, and the narrative context.

Ancient Near Eastern Texts

Sacrifice was a widespread phenomenon in the ancient Near East, but it seems that the whole burnt offering was unknown in Egypt and Mesopotamia. There are, however, a number of texts from Anatolia and Syria-Palestine that mention the offering. For example, in a Hittite text, Establishing a New Temple for the Goddess of the Night, there are several references to sacrifices of lambs. At one point the text says that the "fat is burned up. No one eats it."[1]

In a Phoenician document known as the Marseilles Tariff or Punic Sacrificial Tariff, there are several references to burnt offerings, either by themselves or in combination with other offerings, particularly fellowship or well-being offerings. One part of this text reads:

1. "Establishing a New Temple for the Goddess of the Night," trans. Billie Jean Collins (*COS* 1.70:176).

> In (the case of) a mature bovine: (whether it be) a whole offering, or a presentation-offering, or a whole well-being offering, the priests receive ten (shekels) of silver for each (animal offered); in (the case of) the whole offering they receive in addition to this fee [three-hundred (shekels)-weight of] meat.[2]

There is some ambiguity as to whether the text is, in fact, referring to a wholly burnt offering, but it is at least possible and most likely the case.

There are several observations to make with regard to the ancient Near Eastern context.

First, even though, apparently, the burnt offerings were completely burned up, this may not have been the case in all instances. Gerstenberger expresses some skepticism when he observes that "the sacrificial literature of the ancient orient . . . offers hardly any evidence for the whole burning of sacrificial animals," suggesting that the "completely burned sacrifice is probably an Israelite peculiarity."[3] I believe he may have overstated the case, but the evidence does suggest that the whole burnt offering had greater significance in Israel than among the surrounding peoples, deriving "from the theological and literary need to emphasize complete devotion to Yahweh."[4]

Second, the biblical text incorporates instructions about the performance of sacrifice into the narrative history of Israel and the law codes of the Pentateuch. However, none of Israel's neighbors did the same. Although they considered instructions about sacrifice to be the will of the gods, this was more explicitly the case with Israel herself. Over fifty times in Leviticus the clause "The Lord says," or its equivalent, stands behind the ritual instructions. The prescriptions in Leviticus are Yahweh-willed prescriptions.

Third, in Leviticus 1 and the following chapters we will see the importance of the manipulation and handling of the blood of the sacrificial animals. This aspect of the Israelite sacrificial system, while not absent in the literature of Israel's neighbors, is comparatively negligible. With Israel, on the other hand, it is of paramount importance.

Finally, while it is certainly appropriate to call attention to the differences between the sacrificial rites of Israel and those of her neighbors, it is also possible to overplay the differences. For example, the "Epic of Gilgamesh"[5] narrates a flood story similar to the flood narrative in Genesis 6–9. It has a

---

2. "A Punic Sacrificial Tariff," trans. Dennis Pardee (*COS* 1.98:306–7).

3. Erhard S. Gerstenberger, *Leviticus: A Commentary*, OTL (Louisville: Westminster John Knox, 1996), 33–34.

4. Ibid., 34.

5. "Gilgamesh," trans. Benjamin R. Foster (*COS* 1.132:458–60).

scene comparable to the one in Genesis 8, in which Noah, after leaving the ark, offers burnt offerings to the LORD. While Gilgamesh does not refer to the offerings as burnt offerings, as Genesis 8 does, it does refer to how the gods (plural) "smelled the sweet savor" of the offerings. It would be unfair to argue that the Gilgamesh Epic is describing the gods as literally smelling the aroma of the offering while at the same time suggesting that Genesis 8 or Leviticus 1 refer to Yahweh smelling the aroma of the sacrifices only anthropomorphically. The same may be said about the idea that Israel's neighbors were obsessed with the literal "care and feeding of the gods" in their sacrifices, while in Israel the presentation of food offerings to Yahweh was only symbolic[6] (see further comments in Explain the Story below).

Burnt Offering in the Old Testament

Leviticus 1 is not the first place in the Old Testament to mention burnt offerings, though it is the first place where detailed instructions are given for their performance. The biblical texts listed in Listening to the Text in the Story above narrate prior occurrences of this offering.

Additionally, in Exodus 29:15–40 the LORD gives instructions for the burnt offerings to be performed as part of the ordination procedures for Aaron and his sons. During the giving of these instructions the LORD specifies that burnt offerings are also to be performed every morning and evening, for the "generations to come" (v. 42). The bronze altar in the courtyard of the tabernacle is specifically named the "altar of burnt offering" (Exod 30:28), indicating that the burnt offering would undoubtedly be the most common of all the Israelite sacrifices.

Finally, Numbers 28–29 expands beyond Exodus 29:42 in detailing the procedures for the community burnt offerings, both for the regular daily offerings and those offered during special feast days. But in Leviticus 1 the focus is on the voluntary, individual presentations of burnt offerings rather than the prescribed daily and special occasion burnt offerings for the whole community.

The Narrative Context

There are three important things to emphasize here. The first is that Leviticus is embedded in a larger narrative. There are several ways in which this is evidenced:

---

6. On the caution that needs to be employed in this regard, see Gary A. Anderson, *Sacrifices in Ancient Israel: Studies in Their Social and Political Importance*, HSM 41 (Atlanta: Scholars Press, 1987), 14–19.

- The book begins, more literally than the NIV translates, with the words, "*And* the Lord called" (emphasis added; Heb. *wayyiqra'*). A number of biblical books begin with the conjunction "and," so it could be argued that this is simply stylistic. There is, nevertheless, a true narratival connection between the end of Exodus and the beginning of Leviticus.
- This opening, "*And* the LORD *called* to Moses" (emphasis added), continues a series of such statements, begun in Exodus 3:4 and continued in 19:20 and 24:16. The statement in Leviticus 1:1 keeps the narrative going.
- The instructions for the priestly ordination procedure for Aaron and his sons, given in Exodus 29, are then carried out in Leviticus 8–9. Rather than simply being a book that contains instructions for sacrificial performance, Leviticus is a vital part of the narrative flow of the Pentateuch.

Second, picking up on this point, an important distinction must be made between the *wayyiqra'* in Leviticus 1:1 and its three prior occurrences. On each of the prior occasions the LORD calls to Moses from Mount Sinai, a mountain where the glory of the LORD settled and that the Israelites were not allowed to ascend or even touch. But now, as we come to Leviticus 1:1, there has been a startling development. The glory of the LORD is no longer on the mountain. Rather, it is now in the tabernacle, the tent of meeting. This tent is not atop Mount Sinai. Rather, it is right in the middle of the camp. Samuel Balentine rightly captures the profound significance of this development:

> Leviticus presents what God now says to Moses, and what Moses must now speak to the community of Israel, as the most immediate and intimate revelation from God available in the cosmos. . . . This is surely an astonishing claim. The closest parallel in Christian Scripture is the assertion that God is fully present in Jesus (John 1:14–16).[7]

This is of tremendous significance as we approach the book of Leviticus. We are about to hear the word of the living God, not from the top of some lofty mountain but from within the middle of the camp, where God has taken up residence among his people.

7. Samuel E. Balentine, *Leviticus*, IBC (Louisville: John Knox, 2002), 20.

Third, we should note how the narrative has come to almost a screeching halt. Time has slowed down to a crawl. Things have become almost ethereal, a kind of "twilight zone." The Pentateuchal narrative covers thousands of years. At times, within the flow of the Pentateuchal narrative, hundreds of years are covered in just a few verses. But all of a sudden, starting with Exodus 19:1 when Israel arrives at the foot of Mount Sinai three months after they left Egypt, the narrative pace slows way down. It will not pick up again until Numbers 10:11–12, when the Israelites leave Sinai approximately nine or ten months later. Though the Pentateuchal narrative covers thousands of years, over forty percent of that narrative, from Exodus 19 to Numbers 10, is devoted to describing what happened in just one of those years. This fact leads Balentine to declare, "In this conceptualization, the Pentateuch presents worship as the goal of creation."[8]

In this regard, note Moses's requests to Pharaoh in Exodus 4:23; 5:1, 3: "Let my son go, so he may worship me"; "Let my people go, so that they may hold a festival to me in the wilderness"; "let us take a three-day journey into the wilderness to offer sacrifices to the Lord our God." Perhaps the Israelites thought the goal was only the promised land. To be sure, it was the ultimate goal. But from the narrator's (and Yahweh's) perspective, the more immediate goal was the worship that God would institute among the people that year at Sinai as he constituted them as his own treasured possession. How important, then, it is to listen to what the Lord said when he called to Moses from the tent of meeting.

EXPLAIN the Story

In this chapter the Lord gives Moses instructions for the Israelites regarding the performance of burnt offerings. It is customary in commentaries to note that the three offerings described in chapters 1–3 are voluntary offerings, as opposed to the ones in chapters 4–5, which are required for dealing with sin. While this distinction is helpful on one level, it is potentially misleading on another. The offerings may be voluntary, but they are also expected. All three offerings have to do with devotion to, paying honor to, and maintaining a good relationship with Yahweh. The Israelite who never brought these

8. Samuel E. Balentine, *The Torah's Vision of Worship*, OBT (Minneapolis: Fortress, 1999), 66, and the larger discussion in pp. 65–70; see also his *Leviticus*, 17–18.

sacrifices would not truly be a loyal devotee of Yahweh. So the situation is really not if but when one will bring one of these offerings to the LORD. For the burnt offering, the initial choice in the chapter is whether one's offering will be from the herd or the flock. For those whose economic situation precludes either one of these choices, the option is given later in the chapter to bring a dove or pigeon instead.

The Hebrew word translated "burnt offering" is *'olah*. It comes from a verb that means "to ascend," suggesting that this offering ascends to God via the smoke. So, it could be referred to as the "ascending offering." However, the smoke from all the offerings placed on the altar ascended to God. Instead, traditionally, it has been referred to as the "burnt offering." Even this designation does not make for a precise distinction since portions of all the offerings were burned on the altar. More accurately, it could be referred to as the "whole burnt offering," though I will refer to it as the burnt offering for the sake of convenience. In contrast to the other offerings, in which edible portions of the sacrifice go to the priest, the offerer, or both, in the whole burnt offering all edible portions are completely burned up on the altar.

There has been much discussion as to what the purpose of the burnt offering was. One might surmise that the purpose is spelled out in verse 4: "it will be accepted on your behalf to make atonement for you." However, it could also be argued that this is only a secondary goal along the way and that another one of the offering's effects—indicated in verses 9, 13, and 17—is the ultimate goal of the offering: to present a food gift to the LORD, which will be a pleasing aroma to him. If this is correct, then the atonement in verse 4 could be understood as a penultimate goal and effect, by no means unimportant but nevertheless serving the ultimate goal of presenting Yahweh with something that pleases him.

Beyond this, a survey of all the places in the Old Testament where burnt offerings are made demonstrates that there were a number of purposes for the burnt offering: dedication of people or things to the LORD (Exod 29 and 40); celebration of special occasions (Num 10:10); to accompany vows and other offerings (Num 15:3; Ps 66:13); to dedicate plunder to the LORD (Deut 13:16); to accompany prayer and petition (1 Sam 7:9); to accompany acts and songs of praise (2 Chr 29:27–28); to invoke the LORD's presence or affirmation and validation (2 Chr 7:1); and to request the LORD's assistance in battle (Ps 20:3).[9]

9. For an excellent discussion see Richard E. Averbeck, "*'ōlâ*," *NIDOTTE* 3:405–15.

The procedure for the burnt offering seems fairly straightforward, though there are some interpretive issues. One of the questions has to do with who does what. It is not entirely clear which actions are performed by the offerer and which actions are performed by the priests. The NIV 2011 provides its own answer to this question by using the second person to refer to these actions (e.g., "you are to slaughter," v. 5; "you are to skin," v. 6; "you are to wash," v. 9). However, in the Hebrew these verbs are all third person (as can be seen in NIV 1984). Also, there is the possibility that on some occasions the third-person verbs ought to be understood as impersonal verbs, such that the Hebrew text really is ambiguous as to who performs the action. So, for example, for verse 5 NIV has "You are to slaughter"; NIV 1984 has "He is to slaughter" (referring to the offerer); and NRSV has "The bull shall be slaughtered," rendering the verb impersonally and leaving open the question as to whether the slaughtering is done by the offerer or the priest. I tend to agree with the NIV (both 1984 and 2011) that the offerer does the slaughtering, since the act of slaughtering in verse 5 is mentioned before any priest has been referred to. But it is not as clear who performs the flaying and washing.

A second question has to do with the significance of the offerer placing their hand on the head of the sacrificial animal (*samak*, more literally, "pressing" or "leaning" their hand; v. 4). Perhaps the traditional and still most popular understanding, based on Leviticus 16:21, is that this action transfers the sin of the offerer to the sacrificial animal. However, there are a number of objections to this understanding. One is that in Leviticus 16:21 Aaron places two hands on the head of the "scapegoat," whereas in Leviticus 1 the offerer places only one hand on the sacrifice. Another objection is that in Leviticus 16 Aaron places his hands not on the animal that is slaughtered but on the animal sent into the wilderness, which is not a sacrifice per se. While these objections are not unanswerable, they do suggest that the purpose of the hand placement in the burnt offering sacrifice might not be identical to the purpose of the hand placement on the Day of Atonement.

An alternative understanding of the hand placement is that it simply indicates that the animal belongs to the offerer and that when the offerer presents the animal to the LORD, it is in the offerer's power to do so. However, the majority of scholars see this answer as being too restrictive or banal. Perhaps it is best to understand that the offerer is not simply declaring the animal one's own but also making identification with the animal. The animal is offered to the LORD, both representatively and substitutionally. The sacrificed animal represents the offerer and dies in place of the offerer. So while the hand-leaning rite does not technically transfer the offerer's sins, as such, onto the sacrificial animal, it does, in some respect, transfer the offerer's own person as one who is a sinner. The hand-leaning rite thus also ensures that the benefits to be accrued from the death of the animal go to the offerer. A number of scholars believe that it is during the hand-leaning rite that the offerer may have vocalized a prayer or confession, comparable to that found in Leviticus 16:21 and Deuteronomy 21:6–9.[10]

A third issue is the meaning of the word translated as "make atonement" (v. 4), the Hebrew word *kipper*. There is considerable controversy as to the meaning of this word, and I am going to postpone a fuller discussion of this issue until we come to the commentary on the sin offering in chapter 4. For the present, I will simply say that the verb refers both to the idea of removing sin and, consequently, appeasing Yahweh's wrath, whether actual or potential.[11] The sacrifice is both a food offering to Yahweh as well as, somewhat paradoxically, a means of atonement to render the offerer qualified to enter the LORD's courts to make the offering. Perhaps, in distinction from the purification and reparation offerings, which deal with particular sins, the burnt offering deals with the offerer's sin in general.[12]

A fourth interpretive issue concerns the symbolism of the blood "splashing" in verses 5 and 11 (*zaraq*, alternatively "splattering," "dashing," "throwing"; but not "sprinkling" as in NIV 1984). Again, I will postpone this discussion until we look at the sin and guilt offerings in chapters 4–6.

A fifth issue to address here is the concept of presenting a food offering to the LORD, who smells its pleasing aroma. First, it should be observed that, as opposed to NIV 1984's phrasing in verses 9, 13, and 17 ("offering made by fire"), NIV 2011 has what is perhaps the more accurate rendering, "food offering." The Hebrew word in question is *'isheh*, which translators and commentators took to be derived from the similar sounding Hebrew word for "fire," *'esh*. However, more recently commentators have noticed that *'isheh* sometimes occurs in texts where no fire is involved (e.g., Lev 24:8–9). Most translations and commentaries now take *'isheh* to mean "food offering," though "offering by fire" still has its scholarly defenders.[13]

10. Gordon J. Wenham, *The Book of Leviticus*, NICOT (Grand Rapids: Eerdmans, 1979), 61–62; John E. Hartley, *Leviticus*, WBC 4 (Nashville: Nelson, 1992), 21.

11. Frank H. Gorman Jr., *Divine Presence and Community: A Commentary on the Book of Leviticus*, ITC (Grand Rapids: Eerdmans, 1997), 23; Wenham, *Leviticus*, 58.

12. Sklar, *Leviticus*, lxix.

13. See Watts, *Leviticus 1–10*, 210–11; Christian A. Eberhart, "A Neglected Feature of Sacrifice in the Hebrew Bible: Remarks on the Burning Rite on the Altar," *HTR* 97.4 (2004): 489–90. For a fuller discussion, see Richard E. Averbeck, "*'iššeh*," *NIDOTTE* 1:540–49.

Second, as mentioned earlier, it is by no means clear that we should understand the idea of Yahweh being presented with food offerings and smelling the aroma simply as instances of anthropomorphism. Commentators often refer to passages like Psalm 50:13 (where the LORD queries, "Do I eat the flesh of bulls or drink the blood of goats?") as proof that there never was any idea in the sacrificial system itself that Yahweh consumed the food offerings that were brought to him and that such ideas were perversions of God's revelation of himself. However, I believe it is more in line with the data to say that, at this early stage of Israel's history, the LORD *accommodated* his revelation to the people. In Genesis 8:21 the narrator says that "the LORD smelled the pleasing aroma" of Noah's burnt offerings. And in stark language in Numbers 28:2 the Lord says to Moses,

> Command the Israelites and say to them, "My offering, my food for my food offerings, my pleasing aroma—be careful to present to me at their appointed time." (author's translation)

I believe that a more nuanced view would be that when God gave these commands to the Israelites, he was indeed accommodating his revelation to the cultural milieu of the ancient Near East. Perhaps the Israelites understood from the very beginning that this was an accommodation. Nevertheless, by the command of the LORD himself, he wanted his people to envision what they were doing as presenting food offerings to their God and King. Hess notes that the "cutting of the offering into pieces prepares it as a meal . . . as though it were being offered to a king or someone else who would be served a meal of meat."[14] George Athas has also pointed out that, especially in regard to the fellowship offering, this was understood as a "shared meal" between God and his worshipers in his house, in which God "invites Israel to participate in his own household. Eating, being a basic activity, is therefore part of the normal household activity."[15] The Israelites surely knew that God did not literally eat the food of these offerings. Nevertheless, God still gave the people a visualization as if this was what was really happening. The later perversion of this picture, which Psalm 50:13 addresses, was that God was in some way dependent on these offerings, that the people were actually keeping God fed, and that if they did not bring these offerings, God would go hungry. But as

---

14. Richard S. Hess, "Leviticus," in *Expositor's Bible Commentary*, ed. Tremper Longman III and David E. Garland, rev. ed., 13 vols. (Grand Rapids: Zondervan, 2008), 1:590.

15. Personal communication, 2018.

originally communicated, the revelation encouraged the people to understand that their offerings pleased and brought delight to the heart of their covenant Lord and King.

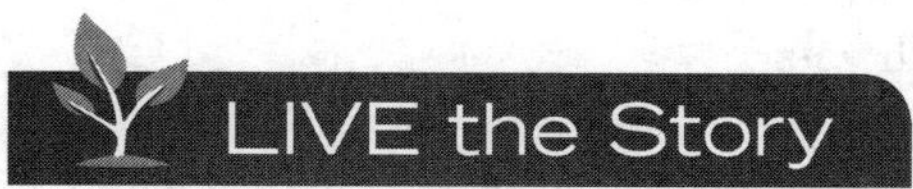

Christians no longer bring bulls or lambs to a tabernacle or temple, slaughter the animal in front of a priest, and offer the animal to the Lord. Nor do they believe that, if they did so, the sacrifice would atone for their sins. What, then, is the relevance of a passage like Leviticus 1 for the twenty-first-century Christian and the twenty-first-century church? Below I make five suggestions for understanding the importance of this chapter.

Complete and Utter Devotion

I suggested above that even though commentators refer to the offerings of these first three chapters as voluntary offerings, we should qualify this somewhat and think of them rather as "voluntary but expected." Though there may have been no specified set times for the presentation of individual burnt offerings (as opposed to community burnt offerings), they were not, however, optional. There is, indeed, a certain *must*-ness to these offerings.[16] Noordtzij rightly says that the offering "signifies the complete self-surrender and total subjection to the Lord of the person who brings it."[17]

Analogously, Christians should also give expression of this self-surrender to the Lord who bought them (1 Cor 6:19–20). Christians do not consider themselves to be their own persons; rather, they belong to Jesus Christ. They do not present bulls and rams and lambs and goats as offerings to the Lord but their own persons as "a living sacrifice, holy and pleasing to God," which is their "true and proper worship" (Rom 12:1). Paul "urges" his readers to do this, "in view of God's mercy." This is, indeed, an expectation. Christians can emulate the faith of the Old Testament saints and learn from those who expressed their faith in God and their devotion to him in the bringing of their offerings.

Pleasing the Lord

It is not uncommon to hear something like this from church pulpits:

16. Gerstenberger, (*Leviticus*, 23), also recognizes the mandatory character of the offering.
17. A. Noordtzij, *Leviticus*, BSC (Grand Rapids: Zondervan, 1982), 31.

> Since Christ has come, we no longer live under law but under grace. We don't operate on the performance model any more. So you need to stop trying to please God. God will not be any less or any more pleased with you than he already is. There is really nothing you can do to please God anyway. God is already pleased with you.

The problem with this way of expressing things is that it is almost completely unbiblical. Rather than providing a contrast with the New Testament on this point, Leviticus actually prepares the way for New Testament teaching about the necessity of living a life that pleases the Lord. Indeed, as we see in Romans 12:1–2, "true worship" results in a life that is "pleasing" to God. If the offerer of the burnt offering had presented a defective animal; if things had not been done according to the protocol laid out in the instructions; if the offerer had harbored sin or presented the offering grudgingly, the offering would not have been an "aroma pleasing to the LORD" (Lev 1:9). The offerers simply could not have done things any way they wanted to, disregarding the LORD's instructions, and still have expected the LORD to bless their efforts.

In the same way, there is no understanding in the New Testament that simply because Christians have been saved by God's grace and are indwelt by the Holy Spirit they can now live their lives on autopilot and that there is nothing they can do that could possibly displease God. Rather, there are many injunctions in the New Testament to give diligent attention to living a life that pleases God (e.g., Rom 12:1–2; 2 Cor 5:9–10; Eph 5:8–10; Col 1:10; 1 Thess 4:1). Aside from Romans 12:1–2, another couple of passages seem to be alluding to Leviticus 1. Paul refers to the gifts of financial aid that the Philippians sent him as "a fragrant offering, an acceptable sacrifice, pleasing to God" (Phil 4:18). The author of Hebrews tells his readers to not forget to do good and to share with others, "for with such sacrifices God is pleased" (Heb 13:16). So Leviticus and the New Testament speak with one mind on this issue.

A Royal Waste of Time and Goods

Marva Dawn, in her book *A Royal "Waste" of Time*, has written eloquently about the seeming impracticality of the act of worshiping God:

> To worship the Lord is—in the world's eyes—a waste of time. It is, indeed, a royal waste of time, but a waste nonetheless. By engaging in it, we don't accomplish anything useful in our society's terms. . . . Worship ought not to be construed in a utilitarian way. Its purpose is not to gain numbers

for our churches to be seen as successful. Rather, the entire reason for our worship is that God deserves it.[18]

To bring Leviticus 1 into this discussion, evidently worship is not simply a royal waste of time but also a royal waste of goods. What could possibly be the purpose of taking one's prize bull, offering it to God, and burning it up completely so that it becomes nothing more than smoke in the atmosphere? Richard Boyce uses an analogy to demonstrate the apparent senselessness of this:

> One of the fun questions this offering has provoked for me goes like this. An elder walks into the pastor's study and announces, "Preacher, I want you to come out to the church parking lot with me. This morning I'm overwhelmed by God's goodness, and I'm under compulsion to do something extravagant. See this stack of $100s? Let's go outside and burn 'em." What would you do?
>
> Be clear. If you simply say, "No, no. Let's take that money and give it to Church World Service," you may unintentionally demonstrate that you are more enamored by the power of money than the power of worship! A prize cow was as close to a stack of bills as the Israelites got. It could fill the stomachs and provide security for many people. But if this cow was selected by its owner for a Burnt Offering, all this life-giving potential "went up in smoke."[19]

Doctors who have spent tens of thousands of dollars to earn their medical degrees and who then go to work with Ebola patients, subjecting themselves to catching the disease, possibly dying, and causing all those thousands of dollars to be a royal waste. . . . Christians who, when given the option of recanting their faith or being martyred, choose martyrdom—what a royal waste; they should have gone ahead and lied, recanted, and gone on to some friendlier environment where they could perhaps win many people to Christ. . . . Brilliant musicians and artists, successful entrepreneurs and corporation executives, highly recruited athletes, popular movie stars and rock idols who, at the height of their success, abandon these pursuits and pursue instead a life of service in missions, church work, and cross-cultural ministries—what

18. Marva J. Dawn, *A Royal "Waste" of Time: The Splendor of Worshiping God and Being Church for the World* (Grand Rapids: Eerdmans, 1999), 1.

19. Richard Nelson Boyce, *Leviticus and Numbers*, Westminster Bible Companion (Louisville: Westminster John Knox, 2008), 17.

a royal waste; they could have been so much more effective in their fields of expertise, making it possible for Christianity to be seen as a cool, hip, popular religion. But the burnt offerings in Leviticus 1 don't work that way. Nor did Jesus Christ. Nor did the woman who wasted a year's wages worth of perfume to pour it on Jesus's head and feet. Nor did the apostles who poured out their lives like drink offerings (Phil 2:17; 2 Tim 4:6). Nor should we.

Suspension in Time

As mentioned earlier, over 40 percent of the Pentateuch, which narrates thousands of years of history, is taken up with just one year, from Exodus 19–Numbers 10. Balentine argues that the purpose for this intense slowdown in the narrative is to show us that, indeed, the goal of creation and the theme of the Pentateuch is the worship of God. A large part of that one year at the foot of Mount Sinai is taken up in teaching the Israelites the rhythms of ritual.

Ritual is, for many people, a pejorative term. Ritual is bad; spontaneity is good. For them, to talk about "empty ritual" is a redundancy. Ritual is inherently empty, a symptom that the religion employing the ritual has died.

However, ritual can be a powerful tool in the Christian's and the church's arsenal of tools for the work of spiritual formation and transformation. Ritual affords the participant an opportunity to play a role in a spiritual drama. It is a dramatic, embodied, visible way of portraying spiritual realities.[20] Perhaps more to the point, ritual is a way to portray an alternative reality, to portray the "real" reality, in opposition to the potentially false picture of reality painted by the world. Ritual is, as Frank Gorman articulates it, a "means for world construction."[21]

Six days a week we live in the world of commerce, highways, politics, the Internet, business, fashion, entertainment, mortgages, interest rates, stocks and bonds, sports, air travel, and conflict on any number of local, national, and international stages. By the end of that sixth day we might be tempted to think that this world is all there is. But then, on the seventh day, we go to a worship service, we hear Scripture, sing hymns, participate in responsive readings, listen to testimonies, and hear sermons. If those involved in leading this worship have done their jobs well, we begin to realize that there is an alternative reality, a "real" reality, one that relativizes the world's reality. A new world is constructed for us, a new Jerusalem, what Augustine referred to as the City of God. Of late, however, the push in many churches has been to

20. Gorman, *Divine Presence*, 5.

21. Frank H. Gorman, Jr., *The Ideology of Ritual: Space, Time and Status in the Priestly Theology* (Sheffield: JSOT Press, 1990), 59.

construct a service that looks pretty much just like the world we came out of when we entered the sanctuary. The justification for this is that the church must be relevant. However, a well-constructed ritual helps us to realize that, in at least some respects, the church should be dearly and gloriously irrelevant.

When the Israelite worshipers entered the courtyard of the tabernacle or temple, they were entering into an alternate reality. The sacrifices, the psalms, the hymns, the rituals, the liturgical movements—they all served to demonstrate that there in that courtyard something was happening that was more important and more true than anything that was happening on the outside. There was a suspension of time that, paradoxically, provided a window through which to view eternity.

Our church services need to do the same today. They need to provide us with a suspension of time, in which we see an alternative world, a glorious eternity, a glimpse of the kingdom of God that allows us to "see with new eyes."[22] A well-constructed ritual and liturgy can help to achieve that goal.

Christ, the Glory of the Lord, and the Burnt Offering

There are several ways in which Leviticus 1 points us toward Jesus Christ. As mentioned above, Exodus 40 narrates how God took up residence in the tabernacle. This takes place just five verses before Leviticus 1. Indeed, the first report of divine speech after the glory of the Lord fills the tabernacle comes in Leviticus 1:1–2. Balentine avers that this is, for the Old Testament, as astonishing a narration as when the Gospel of John tells us that "The Word became flesh and made his dwelling among us" (John 1:14).[23]

This same narrative also foreshadows the exchange that takes place between Jesus and the Samaritan woman in John 4. In Exodus 40–Leviticus 1 God takes up residence in the tabernacle after having previously revealed himself from atop Mount Sinai. But now he has changed locations. In John 4, Jesus tells the Samaritan woman that there is coming a time when the Lord will not be worshiped on Mount Gerizim, or Mount Zion, or (let us supply here) Mount Sinai (v. 21). Rather, he will be worshiped in spirit and in truth (v. 24). Does "spirit" here refer to the Holy Spirit, the human spirit, or both? I would argue that it is, indeed, a double entendre and that part of the message here is that the location of true worship has moved from a fixed geographical point to the human spirit, or into the midst of like-minded believers. Interestingly, the Samaritan woman focuses on the role of the Messiah as one who will be a

---

22. From the song by John Michael Talbot and Terry Talbot, "Behold Now the Kingdom," 1 February 2017, https://www.youtube.com/watch?v=fb5sndufa7Y.

23. Balentine, *Leviticus*, 20.

prophet and teacher. So, even as God in Exodus 40 took up residence in the tabernacle, and this is then followed by the speech of the Lord in the book of Leviticus, in the same way in John 4, after Jesus tells of how God will take up residence in the human heart, this is then followed by a narrative emphasis on Jesus as prophet and teacher (see vv. 29, 39, and 41–42).

Analogous to the movement in Exodus 40 and Leviticus 1, in the account of Jesus's transfiguration in Matthew 17:1–8, we come across the same pattern of a glorious transformation followed by an emphasis on speech. Jesus is transfigured (Peter refers to him receiving "glory from the Father;" 2 Pet 1:17), and then a voice from heaven instructs the three disciples whom Jesus took with him to "Listen to him!" (Matt 17:5). Even as God took up residence in the tabernacle and then "spoke" the book of Leviticus, so Jesus is transfigured with his heavenly glory and then his disciples are commanded to pay heed to his words.

In Ephesians 5:2 Paul tells us that Christ "loved us and gave himself up for us as a fragrant offering and sacrifice to God." While we understand that Jesus did this to rescue us from our sins, it is equally important to recognize here that this is also something Jesus did for God his Father. His sacrifice, just like the burnt offering in Leviticus 1, is a "fragrant offering"—that is, in the words of Leviticus, "an aroma pleasing to God" (Lev 1:9).

Finally, in Hebrews 10:5–10 the author of Hebrews puts the words of Psalm 40:6–8 on Christ's lips:

> Therefore, when Christ came into the world, he said:
>
> "Sacrifice and offering you did not desire,
> but a body you prepared for me;
> with burnt offerings and sin offerings
> you were not pleased.
> Then I said, 'Here I am—it is written about me in the scroll—
> I have come to do your will, my God.'"

It is important to note here, against faulty understandings of this passage, that, in the overall context and theology of the book of Hebrews, the author is not quoting Psalm 40 in order to argue that God didn't really want burnt offerings and sacrifices. Rather, his point is that the burnt offerings and sacrifices that God commanded in the Old Testament sacrificial system could not ultimately provide a real atonement for sin because, as he says in Hebrews 10:4, "It is impossible for the blood of bulls and goats to take away sin." The problem was not with sacrifice per se; the problem was with what was sacrificed. So, in order to accomplish what the sacrifice of bulls and goats could not, Christ offered himself as the truly perfect sacrifice, so that "we have been made holy through the sacrifice of the body of Jesus Christ once for all" (v. 10). It was Christ's determination to accomplish the will of the Father. God called to the Israelites and gave them instructions about sacrifices. Jesus is the one who ultimately heard that call and determined to offer himself as the full and final sacrifice.[24] And it is by that determination, by his sacrifice on the cross, and by the will of the Father that we have been saved, made holy, and have been granted life in God's presence—forever.

24. See Ephraim Radner, *Leviticus*, Brazos Theological Commentary on the Bible (Grand Rapids: Brazos, 2008), 35.

CHAPTER 2

Leviticus 2:1–16

LISTEN to the Story

2:1“‘When anyone brings a grain offering to the LORD, their offering is to be of the finest flour. They are to pour olive oil on it, put incense on it 2and take it to Aaron's sons the priests. The priest shall take a handful of the flour and oil, together with all the incense, and burn this as a memorial portion on the altar, a food offering, an aroma pleasing to the LORD. 3The rest of the grain offering belongs to Aaron and his sons; it is a most holy part of the food offerings presented to the LORD.

4“‘If you bring a grain offering baked in an oven, it is to consist of the finest flour: either thick loaves made without yeast and with olive oil mixed in or thin loaves made without yeast and brushed with olive oil. 5If your grain offering is prepared on a griddle, it is to be made of the finest flour mixed with oil, and without yeast. 6Crumble it and pour oil on it; it is a grain offering. 7If your grain offering is cooked in a pan, it is to be made of the finest flour and some olive oil. 8Bring the grain offering made of these things to the LORD; present it to the priest, who shall take it to the altar. 9He shall take out the memorial portion from the grain offering and burn it on the altar as a food offering, an aroma pleasing to the LORD. 10The rest of the grain offering belongs to Aaron and his sons; it is a most holy part of the food offerings presented to the LORD.

11“‘Every grain offering you bring to the LORD must be made without yeast, for you are not to burn any yeast or honey in a food offering presented to the LORD. 12You may bring them to the LORD as an offering of the firstfruits, but they are not to be offered on the altar as a pleasing aroma. 13Season all your grain offerings with salt. Do not leave the salt of the covenant of your God out of your grain offerings; add salt to all your offerings.

14“‘If you bring a grain offering of firstfruits to the LORD, offer crushed heads of new grain roasted in the fire. 15Put oil and incense on it; it is a grain offering. [16]The priest shall burn the memorial portion of the crushed grain and the oil, together with all the incense, as a food offering presented to the Lord.

Listening to the Text in the Story: Biblical Texts: Genesis 3:17; 4:1–3; 18:1–15; Ancient Near Eastern Texts: Instructions to Priests and Temple Officials; Purifying A House: A Ritual for the Infernal Deities; The *Zukru* Festival; Six Months of Ritual Supervision by the Diviner

The second of the three voluntary (but expected) offerings detailed in the book of Leviticus is the grain offering. The offering of grain products to deities was common among Israel's neighbors, and the ancient Near Eastern texts listed above are only a representative few of the many documents that contain references to such offerings. Purifying A House: A Ritual for the Infernal Deities (Hittite) lists a number of grain and other agricultural products to be placed before the deity.[1] Instructions to Priests and Temple Officials (Hittite) makes reference to "thick bread" and "thin bread," which one should "not omit" to offer to a god.[2]

A text from Emar, Six Months of Ritual Supervision by the Diviner, emphasizes, with reference to their ritual calendar, the need to give special attention to the planting and cultivation of different grain products to be presented to the god Dagan, designated as "the Lord of the Seed."[3]

Also from Emar, The *Zukru* Festival text may shed light on our understanding of what is meant by the term "memorial" (*'azkarah*) in Leviticus 2:2, 9, 16, which seems to be related to the Akkadian term *zukru*.[4] On the one hand, it may be understood that the *zukru* festival was an opportunity for the celebrants to "remember" the deity. However, it may be argued that the festival was for the purpose of invoking the deity to remember the offerers.[5]

The story of Abraham's hospitality to "three men" in Genesis 18 may have

1. "Purifying a House: A Ritual for the Infernal Deities," trans. Billie Jean Collins (*COS* 1.68:168–71).

2. "Instructions to Priests and Temple Officials," trans. Gregory McMahon (*COS* 1.83:218).

3. "Six Months of Ritual Supervision by the Diviner," trans. Daniel Fleming (*COS* 1.124:436–39); see also the discussion in Richard S. Hess, *Ancient Israelite Religions* (Grand Rapids: Baker Books, 1997), 120.

4. "The *Zukru* Festival," trans. Daniel Fleming (*COS* 1.123:431–36). See also discussion in Hess, *Ancient Israelite Religions*, 114.

5. See the discussion in Daniel E. Fleming, *Time at Emar: The Cultic Calendar and the Rituals from the Diviner's Archive* (Winona Lake, IN: Eisenbrauns, 2000), 121–26.

special relevance for the grain offering. When Abraham sees the three men, one of whom the reader knows to be the Lord, he immediately goes to meet them and offers them "something to eat" (v. 5). NIV's "something to eat" is more literally a "morsel of bread" or "piece of bread." The Hebrew word translated "morsel" or "piece" (*pat*) does not occur again in the Old Testament until Leviticus 2:6, with its instructions regarding one possible form that the grain offering could take. NIV's "crumble" (*patat*) could be more literally translated as "break it into pieces," with the word for "pieces" being the same as that in Genesis 18:5. Richard Hess argues that "[t]he Israelites, who understood the history of their patriarch Abraham," . . . would have seen "in each grain offering the continued 'entertaining and fellowship' between themselves and the God of Abraham."[6] Hess's suggestion seems likely, especially in light of how a number of incidents in the Abraham narratives seem to foreshadow events in the history of Israel.[7] It certainly seems plausible that the authors/editors of the Pentateuch wanted the reader to catch this connection. When the Israelites brought their grain offerings to the tabernacle, they joined with their ancestor Abraham and replicated his actions in providing hospitality and respect to the honored deity who resided in the tabernacle. The grain offering was no inferior offering, but one very important way in which the Israelites were to pay tribute to their covenant Lord.

EXPLAIN the Story

The chapter lays out five different options for the form which the grain offering could take. It could be:

1. uncooked wheat flour;[8]
2. baked in an oven, made into larger thick or thin loaves;
3. prepared on a griddle, made into smaller cakes, possibly ring-shaped or perforated;
4. cooked in a pan (perhaps with a lid), made into smaller cakes; or
5. roasted grain (in this case probably barley rather than wheat).

---

6. Hess, "Leviticus," 601.

7. For example, Abraham's time in Egypt in Gen 12:10–13:1 seems to foreshadow Israel's slavery and exodus from Egypt four hundred years later.

8. What the NIV translates as "fine flour" is actually more coarse than the translation suggests. The Hebrew word indicates something like semolina, more grits-like in texture. See Jacob Milgrom, *Leviticus 1–16: A New Translation with Introduction and Commentary*, AB 3 (New York: Doubleday, 1991), 179.

Several elements of this offering call for interpretive attention.

Grain offering. Even though NIV and most translations render the Hebrew word *minhah* as "grain offering," the word does not mean "grain" per se but simply "offering" or "gift." Indeed, outside the more narrowly legal and ritual texts of the Old Testament, the word is translated more regularly as "gift," "offering," or "tribute." However, within the legal and ritual texts, the word seems to almost always refer to the grain offering specifically, but the underlying idea of gift or tribute should not be overlooked. When the Israelites brought their grain offerings, they were bringing gifts to their covenant Lord, tribute to their great king. We could rightly refer to the offering as a tribute or a declaration of loyalty.

The grain offering should also be seen as possibly having an expiatory or atoning purpose. There are at least three reasons that make this a possibility. First, in ancient rabbinical writings there was often the suggestion that the grain offering was the poor man's burnt offering, which was an expiatory offering. While this is not stated in the text itself, interestingly, when we come to Leviticus 4–5 and the discussion of the sin offering we will see that, in addition to the animal sacrifices, there is also provision for a grain sacrifice (5:11–13).[9] Second, in some places where the word *minhah* occurs, there is a clear reference to the idea of appeasing anger (Gen 32:20; 1 Sam 26:19). Third, there are passages where grain offerings are mentioned alongside the other offerings as being for the purpose of atonement (e.g., Ezek 45:15, 17). Additionally, the burnt, grain, and fellowship offerings were regularly offered together. Perhaps the safest conclusion is that the grain offering, while not primarily intended as expiatory per se, nevertheless could have an expiatory function, especially in conjunction with the other offerings.[10]

The five options. Some have speculated that, to some extent, the differences between the five options reflect the economic circumstances of the offerer. Though this is a possibility, the instructions do not so specify, and it is by no means certain. They may all be equally valid options.

Incense. For the two loose grain options, the text specifies that incense (more precisely, frankincense) is to be put on the offering. Some have suggested that this was for the purpose of covering up the odor of the blood and entrails of the animal sacrifices. While this utilitarian purpose may have been

9. This argument is mitigated somewhat by the statement in 5:11 that oil and incense are not to be added to the grain offering for sin, because it is a sin offering, unlike the case with the regular grain offering here in ch. 2. This does not necessarily mean, however, that the regular grain offering had no expiatory function at all.

10. See the discussion in Milgrom, *Leviticus 1–16*, 196–98.

part of the motivation, it is more likely that the frankincense is added to the uncooked offerings for the purpose of giving them a bit of aroma, as opposed to the cooked grain offerings which would have their own aroma.

Memorial portion. For all five options, the priests are instructed to take a small part of the offering and burn it on the altar as a "memorial portion" (Hebrew *'azkarah*). But does the token symbolize the offerer remembering the LORD? Or is the token for the purpose of causing the LORD to remember the offerer? While the choices are not necessarily mutually exclusive, it seems likely that the latter idea is the more dominant one. The offering is for the purpose of reminding the LORD that the offerer is a loyal covenant partner and asks that the LORD keep that in mind and respond to the offerer faithfully and graciously. Some commentators have suggested that the superscriptions of Psalms 38 and 70, which contain the related word *zakar* (NIV "petition"), reinforce this idea and that these psalms may have even been recited in accompaniment to the grain offering.[11]

Most holy. This phrase, in verses 3 and 10 (*qodesh qodashim*, literally, "holy of holies"), refers to food that is to be eaten only by the priests and only within the confines of the tabernacle courtyard. In the commentary on chapters 4 and 10 we will look more closely at the significance and symbolism involved in the act of a priest eating food that is offered to God.

Without yeast or honey. This is perhaps because yeast had come to represent the idea of corruption and lack of purity. Honey, which most likely refers to the pulp of a fruit such as dates rather than that produced by bees, evidently also came to represent the idea of corruption.

Salt. Not only does the text indicate that salt must be added to the grain offering, but, in particular, "the salt of the covenant of your God" (Lev 2:13). The salt property most likely alluded to here is that of lastingness, perhaps even eternality. Numbers 18:19 seems to draw this out specifically with the phrase "an everlasting covenant of salt" (see also 2 Chr 13:5; Ezra 4:14 [note that in the Ezra passage, NIV's "under obligation" is literally "the salt of the palace is our salt"]). God had entered into a covenant with Abraham and his descendants (Gen 12:1–3; 15:7–19; 17:1–14). It was on account of his faithfulness to that covenant that God had come to the rescue of the Israelites in Egypt (Exod 2:24; 6:4–5; Deut 7:8). God renewed that covenant with the Israelites when they arrived at Mount Sinai (Exod 19:1–7; 24:1–8). Several commentators have noted that there is a saying among some Arab peoples, "there is salt between us," referring to the concept of a lasting commitment.

11. See, for example, A. Noordtzij, *Leviticus*, 44; Erhard S. Gerstenberger, *Leviticus*, 42.

It has also been noted that in ancient Near Eastern treaties, when one party violated the treaty, one of the possible penalties was to have their fields salted to destroy their fruitfulness (see Deut 29:23; Judg 9:45; Ps 107:34; Jer 17:6; 48:9; Zeph 2:9). So, it is possible that the salt imagery cuts two ways: on the one hand, it was symbolic of the covenant's everlastingness,[12] but it also served to symbolize the ramifications of breaking the covenant.

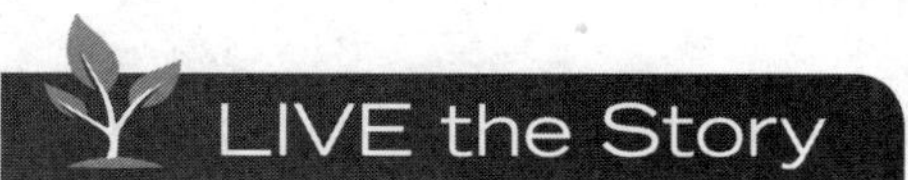

Paying Tribute to the Lord

The Lord is the great king. He is Israel's covenant Lord, and he has condescended to dwell no longer on a lofty mountain but in the midst of his people. His dwelling place is now situated right in the middle of all the tents of the Israelite tribes. It was only to be expected that his subjects would display their loyalty by bringing him gifts of tribute. Even so today, God dwells in his people, both individually and corporately. It is only fitting that his people should demonstrate their loyalty to this King by their acts of worship, giving, and service. To fail to do these things is to insult the great King who lives among us. The apostle Paul tells his readers that acts of worship, even the presentation of our very own lives as living sacrifices, are both "true and proper" (Rom 12:1). To do so, indeed, brings pleasure to the one we worship (Rom 12:2).

"O Lord, Do Remember Me"

We noticed above that there is some ambiguity regarding the exact meaning and purpose of the "memorial portion," but two ideas do seem to emerge. The first is that this memorial portion is a token that represents the entire offering. Even though only a token portion is actually burnt on the altar and produces the "aroma pleasing to the Lord" (Lev 2:9) and the rest goes to the priests, still the token portion is indicative that the whole offering belongs to God. Indeed, the offering itself is actually a token portion, indicating that the offerer's entire being and all his or her possessions belong to God.

The second concept, which is probably the more dominant one, is that the offerer, by presenting this offering to the Lord, is invoking the Lord's favor and asking to be remembered by him. As mentioned earlier (Explain the Story,

12. It may be that since salt does not melt or turn into smoke, thus surviving the sacrificial fire, this may have enhanced salt's association with everlastingness (Tremper Longman, personal communication, 2018).

p. 50), it is possible that Psalms 38 and 70, which in their superscriptions contain a word (translated "petition" in NIV) formed off the same root as the word "memorial," may have been sung in accompaniment to the grain offering. If so, note the petitions in these psalms:

> LORD, do not forsake me;
> do not be far from me, my God.
> Come quickly to help me,
> my Lord and my Savior. (Ps 38:21–22)

> But as for me, I am poor and needy;
> come quickly to me, O God.
> You are my help and my deliverer;
> LORD, do not delay. (Ps 70:5)

It might be objected that since the LORD is omniscient and obviously cannot forget anything, it makes no sense to ask him to remember us, especially since the coming of Christ in the New Testament. But, of course, such an objection would actually put an end to all prayer. It is still right and proper for us to ask the Lord to be with us, to look on us with favor, and to ask him to remember our deeds and labors of love in God's service, to remember us by coming to our aid (Heb 6:10; 13:16).

Taking Care of God's Servants

Not only do our offerings honor God, they also honor God's servants. The offerings the Israelites brought to the LORD also served to provide the priests who worked at the tabernacle with an income and means of support. This practice and principle are no less operative today. The apostle Paul states,

> Don't you know that those who serve in the temple get their food from the temple, and that those who serve at the altar share in what is offered on the altar? In the same way, the Lord has commanded that those who preach the gospel should receive their living from the gospel. (1 Cor 9:13–14)

Those who benefit from the ministry and work of the church but fail to contribute to the work of the Lord are robbing both God and God's servants. A friend of mine related to me how the church he pastored full time, which could easily have paid him a more sustaining and reasonable salary, chose not to do so. He was forced, then, to obtain a second, part-time job just to make ends meet and take care of his family. He told me that, interestingly, the people in the church had greater respect and praise for his getting this part-time job than they ever gave him for carrying out his pastoral duties! Unfortunately, stories like this are numerous. A church should make sure that its ministers, in the fulfillment of their pastoral responsibilities, do not have to worry about how they are going to barely eke out a living. Those who have the heavy responsibility of caring for congregations should be well cared for by those congregations.

Participatory, Prescribed, and Focused Worship

In the services of the tabernacle, the ritual was prescribed *by* God, even down to fine details, and the worship was focused *on* God. Additionally, the Israelites who brought their sacrifices to the tabernacle were not relegated to spectator status. They had their part to play in the preparation of the sacrifices and were expected to do so according to the prescriptions. At the same time, neither they nor the priests were the stars of the show. The worship was for God. Derek Tidball catches these interrelated aspects eloquently and applies them appropriately to Christian worship today:

> In the worship of Israel the worshippers were the players, not the audience, and they were assigned an active role. It was God who was the audience for whose benefit the drama was presented, and God who was to be satisfied. For that reason, the rituals were carefully prescribed and observed. How different from much present-day worship that turns the congregation into an audience of passive onlookers.[13]

Of course, these factors are all on a spectrum. Some churches are more formal and set in their ritual. Others seem to be more free and extemporaneous. Even with the grain offering, there was considerable freedom—there were five different options for what could be presented! But within those options, there were prescriptions as to how each one should be prepared and offered. In any case, we learn that within the freedom of worship, care should also be given to what is prescribed. Some kind of balance should be aimed for. When this is done well and "in a fitting and orderly way" (1 Cor 14:40), the result should be a worship that is focused away from ourselves and fastened squarely on God.

---

13. Derek Tidball, *The Message of Leviticus: Free to Be Holy*, The Bible Speaks Today (Downers Grove, IL: IVP Academic, 2005), 47.

Ritual Begins at Home

At least half of the directions in this chapter have to do with things that are to be done *before* the grain offering is brought to the tabernacle. They have to do with baking, cooking, frying, putting in or withholding of particular ingredients, and so on. The rituals for the tabernacle begin in the offerer's home. Gorman remarks:

> The fact that the preparation is completed away from the tent does not disqualify it as ritualized activity. It is incorrect to argue that the ritual begins only at the time of the presentation. Such a view removes ritual from the dynamics of life. The instructions for the grain offerings provide a framework for the enactment of the ritual that intersects with the rhythms of daily life.[14]

Similarly, today, we should not consider the act of worship to be one that only starts the moment the worshiper sets foot in the house of worship. Worship should start at home as the worshiper, Sunday morning, or perhaps even Saturday night, or earlier in the week, begins to get his or her heart in a state of readiness for the worship. There are a number of different elements that may take place in the worship service: reading of Scripture, singing of hymns, confession of sins, affirmation of faith, giving of gifts, etc. Perhaps the worshiper could prepare for these things by doing them or contemplating them prior to the actual worship service: read the assigned Scriptures, search one's heart, engage in prayer, go ahead and write the check. Perhaps those words we often associate with death, "Prepare to meet thy God," are ones that should be more appropriately thought of as describing what we should do in getting ourselves ready to attend a worship service.

Covenant Commitment

The word "covenant" (2:13, *berit*) only occurs nine more times in Leviticus: once in chapter 24 and eight times in chapter 26. Nevertheless, covenant really provides the context for the book. The heart of God's covenant with Israel was that he would be their God, they would be his people, and he would dwell among them. Leviticus could rightly be considered a book that is focused on the maintenance of that covenant agreement. The salt that the Lord commands the offerer not to leave out of the grain offering is symbolic of the covenant. As is often the case with a sign or symbol, it has a double-edgedness

---

14. Gorman, *Divine Presence*, 28.

to it. On the one hand, it symbolizes enduringness and everlastingness. On the other hand, it also represents what might happen to the covenant violator—their fields covered with salt to destroy the fertile soil.

We who are members of the new covenant should remember that our two covenant signs have this double-edged character as well. The initiatory covenant sign, baptism, positively symbolizes the removal of sin, being washed from sin, being united with Christ, being reborn to new life. But, more negatively, we should note that in two different places in the New Testament baptism is analogized to the great flood in Genesis 6–9 (1 Cor 10:1–2) and the Red Sea crossing in Exodus 14 (1 Pet 3:18–22). While Noah and his family are saved from the waters of the flood, the rest of humanity is destroyed. And while the Israelites cross the Red Sea on dry ground, Pharaoh and his army are drowned in the waters that come crashing back over them. Baptism is a death sign. The covenant renewal sign, the Lord's Supper, is positively a communion with the Lord and our brothers and sisters in Christ. But more negatively, it is possible for a person to take part in the Lord's Supper in an unworthy manner and thus "eat and drink judgment on themselves," even to the point of death (1 Cor 11:27–30). The Lord's Supper, like baptism, is a death sign.

There are those who would argue that there are both conditional and unconditional covenants and that the new covenant is an unconditional one. I would argue, however, that all covenants have conditional elements to them, and the new covenant, as is evidenced particularly by the 1 Corinthians passage, should be considered as having conditional elements as well. In baptism and the Lord's Supper we pledge, to the death, to be Christ's loyal covenant partners and to follow him all of our days.

What this means is that as Christians, to use an old phrase that still shows up in the instructions that some officiants incorporate in their prefatory remarks before the Lord's Supper, we should "neither presume, nor despair." We have been saved by grace, by the death of Christ, by God entering into covenant with us through our Lord Jesus Christ; we should never despair of that grace. However, as loyal covenant partners, neither should we presume on this grace and live in such a way that would bring displeasure to our covenant Lord. We should not leave the salt of the covenant out of the offering of ourselves as living sacrifices. We should be fully committed to our Lord and seek to please him with our whole lives.

Jesus Christ as Bread of Life and Redeemer

Christ has chosen bread, the fruit of the earth, to serve as one of the symbols for himself as life-giver and redeemer. Jesus is the "bread of God . . . that comes down from heaven and gives life to the world" (John 6:33). He is the "bread of life" (John 6:48). Jesus says that "[t]his bread is my flesh, which I will give for the life of the world" (John 6:51). Jesus speaks of himself as the "kernel of wheat" that "falls to the ground and dies" and "produces many seeds" (John 12:24). And then, perhaps most surprisingly, at the institution of the Lord's Supper he chooses bread, rather than the meat of the lamb, to be the symbol of his broken body. Leviticus, at least on an initial, surface reading, seems to regard the animal sacrifices as the ones that are expiatory and propitiatory, doing away with sin and appeasing God. Yet Jesus, by choosing the kernel of grain and the broken bread as symbols for his sacrificial death, seems to have actually gone back, not only to the animal sacrifices, but also to the grain offering for his symbolism. If indeed, as was argued earlier, the grain offering did in some measure contribute to the expiation of sin in the priestly system of offerings, we may appropriately understand even the grain offering as anticipating the great sacrifice of our Lord, his body broken for us.

LISTEN to the Story

3:1"'If your offering is a fellowship offering, and you offer an animal
from the herd, whether male or female, you are to present before the
LORD an animal without defect. 2You are to lay your hand on the head of
your offering and slaughter it at the entrance to the tent of meeting. Then
Aaron's sons the priests shall splash the blood against the sides of the altar.
3From the fellowship offering you are to bring a food offering to the LORD:
the internal organs and all the fat that is connected to them, 4both kidneys
with the fat on them near the loins, and the long lobe of the liver, which
you will remove with the kidneys. 5Then Aaron's sons are to burn it on
the altar on top of the burnt offering that is lying on the burning wood;
it is a food offering, an aroma pleasing to the LORD.

6"'If you offer an animal from the flock as a fellowship offering to
the LORD, you are to offer a male or female without defect. 7If you offer
a lamb, you are to present it before the LORD, 8lay your hand on its head
and slaughter it in front of the tent of meeting. Then Aaron's sons shall
splash its blood against the sides of the altar. 9From the fellowship offering
you are to bring a food offering to the LORD: its fat, the entire fat tail
cut off close to the backbone, the internal organs and all the fat that is
connected to them, 10both kidneys with the fat on them near the loins,
and the long lobe of the liver, which you will remove with the kidneys.
11The priest shall burn them on the altar as a food offering presented to
the LORD.

12"'If your offering is a goat, you are to present it before the LORD, 13lay
your hand on its head and slaughter it in front of the tent of meeting. Then
Aaron's sons shall splash its blood against the sides of the altar. 14From what
you offer you are to present this food offering to the LORD: the internal
organs and all the fat that is connected to them, 15both kidneys with the
fat on them near the loins, and the long lobe of the liver, which you will

remove with the kidneys. [16]The priest shall burn them on the altar as a food offering, a pleasing aroma. All the fat is the LORD's.

[17]"'This is a lasting ordinance for the generations to come, wherever you live: You must not eat any fat or any blood.'"

Listening to the Text in the Story: Biblical Texts: Exodus 12–13; 18:12; 24:5; 32:1–34:15; Ancient Near Eastern Texts: Establishing a New Temple for the Goddess of the Night; Ugaritic Rites for the Vintage; Kirta Epic

A third type of offering is introduced in this chapter: the fellowship offering, sometimes translated as a "well-being" or "peace" offering. The "fellowship" aspect of this offering is that it is the only one in which the offerer, in addition to the deity and the priestly personnel, is given the privilege of eating part of the sacrifice (7:15–21).

Israel's ancient Near Eastern neighbors also had sacrifices which they designated as *shelamim* offerings. A Hittite text, Establishing a New Temple for the Goddess of the Night, refers to a well-being offering (consisting of flour, soups, fruit, beer, wine, and a sheep) that is placed before a deity. At one point the text tells of a female deity whose image is brought into a newly dedicated temple for her and has a well-being offering placed before her. There is reference made to the officiant "rewarding" the deity, priest, and attendant women, perhaps referring to the apportionment of food from the offering.[1]

Another text, Ugaritic Rites for the Vintage, refers multiple times to a well-being offering to be presented to Baal in conjunction with burnt offerings.[2] In another Ugaritic text, the Kirta Epic, there is an instance of this offering being made not to a deity but as an offer of appeasement from one king to another.[3]

Though this chapter supplies the procedure for the fellowship offering within the context of the Levitical and tabernacle ritual system, such offerings had already been narrated in prior texts. For example, Jacob, in Genesis 31:54, offers a sacrifice and invites his relatives to the meal. We should probably understand the Passover sacrifice in Exodus 12–13 to be essentially a fellowship offering as well (see especially 12:27, which uses the term *zebah*, which is the word translated as "offering" in Lev 3; see also Exod 34:25). Moses, Jethro,

1. "Establishing a New Temple for the Goddess of the Night," *COS* 1.70:173–77.

2. "Ugaritic Rites for the Vintage," trans. Baruch A. Levine, Jean-Michel de Tarragon, and Anne Robertson (*COS* 1.95:299–301).

3. "The Kirta Epic," trans. Dennis Pardee (*COS* 1.102:335).

and the Israelite elders, in Exodus 18:12, participate together in a fellowship offering before God. In Exodus 24:5 fellowship offerings are employed in the ratification of the covenant.

Interestingly, one fellowship offering in the book of Exodus that actually constitutes a parody of a legitimate fellowship offering is the one that occurs in Exodus 32, where the people, after having presented fellowship offerings to the golden calf, "sat down to eat and drink and got up to indulge in revelry" (v. 6). This is especially important because of how the very existence of the nation was imperiled on account of this fellowship offering. Due to Moses's prayers on their behalf and the action of the Levites in playing an executioner role, the nation as a whole is spared. Still, at the conclusion of the golden calf narrative, the LORD issues a strong warning: "Be careful not to make a treaty with those who live in the land; for when they prostitute themselves to their gods and sacrifice [*zabah*] to them, they will invite you and you will eat their sacrifices [*zebah*]" (34:15). So behind the procedural prescriptions in Leviticus 3 for the fellowship offering lies the memory of a deliverance accomplished by a Passover fellowship offering (Exodus 12), a covenant ratified over fellowship offerings (Exodus 24), and a covenant that was also violated by means of a fellowship offering (Exodus 32). The privilege of dining in the presence of God is not one that is to be taken lightly.

EXPLAIN the Story

Terminology, Meaning, and Purpose.

"Fellowship offering" translates the Hebrew *zebah shelamim*. Not only the entire phrase, but either word occurring separately, can be used to denote this particular sacrifice in the Old Testament. The noun *zebah*, "slaughter" or "sacrifice," is derived from the verb *zabah*, "to slaughter or sacrifice." Literally, the Hebrew would be translated as "slaughter of *shelamim*," that is, "a sacrifice of the *shelamim* variety."[4] The real issue in understanding the phrase, then, is the meaning of *shelamim*. While it is often taken for granted that this word is derived from *shalom*, popularly understood as meaning "peace," the word *shalom* actually has a broad range of meanings. Other suggestions have been given by the various translations and commentators to denominate the offering, including "fellowship," "shared," "communion," "peace," "well-being," "prosperity," "wholeness," "recompense," "restoration," "gift," "greeting," and "tribute." It is perhaps unnecessary to land on just one of these meanings

4. Milgrom, *Leviticus 1–16*, 218.

since the concepts overlap to a considerable extent. However, "fellowship," "shared," and "communion" perhaps more directly relate to the fact that this is the only offering in which the offerer is allowed to participate in the eating of the offering. So whenever the phrase *zebah shelamim* occurs, or its individual components separately, a sacrifice in which the offerer shares the meal with the deity is designated. We will see below, however, that perhaps the better way to put it is that the deity shares the meal with the offerer.

Peace/Fellowship Celebrated? or Peace/Fellowship Established?

Does this offering celebrate a peaceful relationship that is already in place, or is it for the purpose of establishing such a relationship? It is probably not a matter of either/or but both/and. On the one hand, the offerer would not even be able to enter the courtyard of the tabernacle to present the offering if there were not a prior relationship between God and the offerer. Additionally, it appears to have been a fairly common practice to offer the fellowship offering along with, or after, the burnt offering. This is pointed out specifically in 3:5, where it is stated that the parts of the sacrificial offering to be burned on the altar are to be placed on top of the burnt offering that is already there. It is unclear whether this burnt offering is the daily community burnt offering or one brought by the individual offerer. In either case, the parts of the fellowship offering to be burned on the altar are placed atop (or alongside) the burnt offering, which we already know from 1:4 has an atoning function. The fellowship offering, then, is understood to be an offering brought by someone whose sins have been atoned for; thus, it properly celebrates a relationship already established.

On the other hand, even though it seems that the burnt offering bears the brunt of this atoning function when the two are offered together, there are, nevertheless, indications that the fellowship offering had its own expiatory and propitiatory aspects (expiation having to do with the removal of sin, and propitiation with appeasing or averting the deity's wrath). First, the hand-leaning in verses 2, 8, and 13, as discussed earlier in the comments on chapter 1 (pp. 36–37), seems to indicate an identification between the offerer and the sacrificial animal, an identification that includes the offerer's identity as sinner. Second, Leviticus 17:11, though perhaps more specifically applying to the burnt, sin, and guilt offerings, is not without meaning for the fellowship offering: "the life of a creature is in the blood, and I have given it to you to make atonement for yourselves on the altar; it is the blood that makes atonement for one's life." Finally, there are other passages that seem to indicate that the fellowship offering had an atoning function (1 Sam 3:14 [the Hebrew there for "sacrifice" is *zebah*]; Ezek 45:15, 17). Note especially that in Exodus 29:27–34 part of the procedure for the priestly ordination rite is the presentation and eating of a fellowship offering, of which it is said in verse 33 that priests are to "are to eat these offerings by which atonement was made for their ordination and consecration." So it is best to understand that the fellowship offering both celebrates a reconciliation already achieved and functions, to at least some extent, as an expiatory offering in establishing and maintaining that relationship.

Occasions

Aside from the main signification of the fellowship offering, it should be noted that there are certain designated occasions and purposes for the fellowship offering. It was noted above that the offering played a role in the priestly ordination rite (Exod 29:27–34). Additionally, Leviticus 7:11–21 provides information regarding different types of fellowship offerings. There, it is indicated that the offerings could be classified as thank offerings, freewill offerings, or votive (vow) offerings. We should probably not understand this to be an exhaustive list. In some respects, one might say that the fellowship offering was a kind of all-purpose offering, an offering whose overtones were more celebratory and joyful (with some exceptions) and could be offered on any occasion deemed appropriate for the offerer and his family, relatives, and guests (including even the larger public and the poor) to participate in the eating of the sacrifice.

God as Host

In opposition to the other types of offering, because of the communal nature of the fellowship offering, the portrait that emerges is that of God as the one who is hosting a meal for the offerers, his guests. If the burnt and grain offerings portray God as the one who receives tribute from his loyal subjects, the fellowship offering portrays God as one who receives tribute but then takes part of that tribute and hosts a dinner for his loyal covenant partners. It is important to note the elements of both immanence and transcendence that are demonstrated in this hosted dinner. On the one hand, there is tremendous condescension and accommodation in this act. The tabernacle is not just the royal residence of Israel's king but also the place where this royal king entertains his loyal subjects. Employing a striking metaphor, Calvin says that God deigns "to make Himself, as it were, the messmate of His worshippers."[5] At the same time, however, the text also makes it clear that God and his worshipers are not equal opportunity diners. God is the King, and there are parts of the

5. John Calvin, *Commentaries on the Last Four Books of Moses Arranged in the Form of a Harmony* (trans. Charles William Bingham; 1852–1855; repr., Grand Rapids: Eerdmans, 1950), 2:334.

sacrificial animal that only the deity consumes. This is particularly true of the fat, considered in the ancient Near East to be a choice portion of the animal; in this offering it is reserved for God alone. This contrast leads Hartley to remark rightly, "Thus the ritual procedure of this offering communicated both the bond and the distance between Yahweh and humans."[6]

Sacrificial Animals

As with all offerings, the animals were to be without defect; it would not be right to offer Israel's King an inferior sacrifice. The animal could come from either the flock or herd. The animal could be either male or female. Since the greater portion of the offering was returned to the offerer, there was no need to specify the gender as was the case with the other offerings.[7] In addition to the fat, mentioned above, other parts reserved for Yahweh and burnt on the altar were the internal organs, the kidneys, and the long lobe of the liver. Possibly the internal organs are symbolic of the offerer's devotion to the LORD. The lobe of the liver may have been burnt on the altar on account of the role that examination of the liver played in ancient divinatory techniques (cf. Ezek 21:21), to discourage such actions among the Israelites.

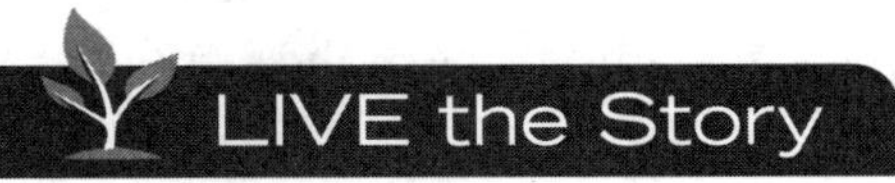

LIVE the Story

At the seminary where I teach, I regularly offer a course entitled "Motifs in Biblical Theology." In this course I take a number of images, type-scenes, motifs, and the themes they symbolize and trace them through the entire Bible. One of these studies is the "Dining" motif, in which the class looks at what theological lessons may be learned in looking at the large number of passages that deal with food and the various dining scenes in the Scriptures. For example, the creation narrative in Genesis 1 specifies different kinds of food for both animals and humans. It is instructive that the first human pair is told they may eat from any of the trees in the garden, including the tree of life, but must not eat the fruit of the tree of the knowledge of good and evil. This then introduces both their first temptation and their first sin. Interestingly, the first punishments are on the order of "the punishment fits the crime." The serpent now has to "eat" dust. Adam now will only be able to eat after having exerted strenuous labor. And humans are now barred from access to the tree of life.

6. Hartley, *Leviticus*, 42.
7. Milgrom, *Leviticus 1–16*, 204.

When we come to the book of Revelation, the same motifs show up again. A major temptation described there has to do with whether people will take the mark of the beast on their persons, a mark that, if they take it, will enable them to buy and sell, which of course would include food (13:16–17). Those who are faithful to God and refuse the mark are banned from buying and therefore are not allowed to sustain themselves. As Revelation draws to a close, the great economic prostitute, Babylon, is defeated; the saints of God rejoice at the wedding banquet of the Lamb (Rev 19:7–9); the animals, in particular the birds, are given a special food provision (the flesh of the fallen mighty; Rev 19:17–18, 21); and access is again granted to the tree of life (Rev 22:2). This is just one small snippet of what this motif looks like, but it provides a sample of some of the themes the dining motif symbolizes when traced all the way through the Scriptures: allowances, prohibitions, temptation, sin, punishments, reward, and so on. This is only as it should be; after all, everyone has to eat.

Leviticus 11, with its lists of clean and unclean animals, contributes significantly to this motif, and we will see how that plays out when we come to that chapter. But the present chapter dealing with the fellowship offering, a shared meal, is quite significant as well. In what follows I hope to show how this chapter fits into the dining motif and how it contributes to our understanding of the themes the motif symbolizes.

God as Host

Not only is the fellowship offering the only one in which the offerer gets to partake of the offering that he or she brings, but it is also important to recognize that the imagery and symbolism of the offering highlights that God is the one who hosts the offerer and provides the meal. When the offerer brings the animal to the deity's home, the tabernacle, the entire offering becomes the Lord's. God, then, in his graciousness and kindness, returns most of the meat back to the offerer to be eaten and shared with the offerer's family and friends. The fellowship offering, then, looks both backward and forward to other occasions when God is the divine host. As already mentioned, when God creates the first human pair, he places them in his garden and provides every tree in the garden for their sustenance. Indeed, many Old Testament scholars have argued that the garden of Eden should be seen as a tabernacle/temple in which God places his first human servants.[8] If so, in this particular respect the

8. For just two such examples, see G. K. Beale, *The Temple and the Church's Mission: A Biblical Theology of the Dwelling Place of God*, NSBT 17 (Downers Grove, IL: InterVarsity Press, 2004), 66–80; Tremper Longman III, *Immanuel in Our Place: Seeing Christ in Israel's Worship*, The Gospel According to the Old Testament (Phillipsburg, NJ: P&R, 2001), 7, 12, 26, 35, 47, 57, 69, 72–73.

fellowship offering should be seen as replicating the garden of Eden situation, with God providing for the needs of his servants.

This offering also mirrors what is happening in the very context of the Israelite wanderings in the wilderness. God is sustaining his people with water out of the rock, manna from heaven, quail from the sky. Indeed, God is "spreading a table" for them in the wilderness (see Ps 78:18–20).

This offering anticipates other texts in the Old Testament. The author of Psalm 23 is the guest of Yahweh, who prepares (*'araq*, "spreads" [v. 5]; same Hebrew verb as in Ps 78:19) a table for him in full view of his enemies, anoints his head with oil (as ancient Near Eastern royal hosts would do), and makes sure his cup is always overflowing. And, in a more eschatological text, Yahweh himself is the one who will, on Mount Zion, "prepare a feast of rich food for all peoples, a banquet of aged wine—the best of meats and the finest of wines" (Isa 25:6).

When we come to the New Testament, again God, in the person of Jesus Christ, is the divine host. Jesus feeds the five thousand (Matt 14:13–21) and then the four thousand (Matt 15:29–39). Jesus makes all the arrangements for and then hosts the Passover meal (which was one form of the fellowship offering) with his disciples, the "Lord's Supper" (Matt 26:17–30). And, of course, God and his Christ are the hosts for the great messianic banquet at the end of the ages (Matt 22:1–14; Rev 19:7–9).

A popular saying among many Christians is that God is the "unseen guest at every meal." As wonderful as that thought is, we may go beyond this conception and recognize, perhaps more perceptively, that God is the royal host and we are his guests. Every meal, then, becomes an opportunity to reflect on the graciousness and kindness of our divine host and to anticipate the great banquet yet to come.

Possibility of Perversion

Unfortunately, there are two ways in which this imagery of being hosted by and sharing a meal with the divine host can be perverted.

The first of these ways is by accepting another deity's invitation rather than the one from Yahweh. As mentioned earlier, the offerings that the Israelites made to the golden calf in Exodus 32 should most likely be understood as fellowship offerings. So, the Israelites rejected their unseen host and worshiped instead the golden calf that they could see; they regarded the calf as their host and fellowshipped with it instead. There was, throughout Israel's history, the temptation to regard other deities as their hosts and benefactors. One example is recorded in Hosea 2, where the Israelites regarded Baal (and not Yahweh) as the one who "gave her the grain, the new wine and oil" and worshiped him instead (Hos 2:8). The apostle Paul probably utilizes this imagery in 1 Corinthians 10:21 when he says that we "cannot drink the cup of the Lord and the cup of demons too," that we "cannot have a part in both the Lord's table and the table of demons." We who have been invited to sit at the table to which the Lord has so graciously offered us must refuse the devil's invitation to dine with him.

Second, it is also possible to dine at the Lord's table in a perverse manner. The ancient Israelites could bring their fellowship offerings to the Lord in a very insincere manner, harboring sin in their hearts such that the Lord pronounced he would have no regard for and would not accept such offerings (Isa 1:11; Amos 5:22). The adulteress/prostitute in Proverbs 7 could declare to her customer/client that she needed the money from the transaction in order to pay for her fellowship offerings (v. 14).[9] The Lord's table can also be despised by bringing impure or inferior offerings (Mal 1:12–13). And, of course, there are recorded in the Bible acts of treachery in conjunction with meals. The psalmist, foreshadowing what would happen at the Lord's Supper, declares, "Even my close friend, someone I trusted, one who shared my bread, has turned against me" [more lit., "has lifted his heel against me"] (Ps 41:9). Indeed, at the Lord's Supper, which should be seen as a fellowship meal, Judas lifts his heel against the Lord (John 13:18, 26–28). The other disciples, too, engage in actions at the table that are less than praiseworthy (Luke 22:20–30). As the apostle Paul says, those who would eat at the Lord's table should examine their hearts before doing so (1 Cor 11:28).

Benevolence

Those who are invited to dine at the Lord's table, unworthy as they are in themselves, should in turn be gracious hosts. The fellowship offering, accordingly, was an occasion for offerers to become benefactors, and there are several passages in the Old Testament that seem to indicate that a benevolent meal sharing with those less fortunate was a regular part of these offerings. One such example is found in Psalm 22 where the psalmist, having received from the Lord the deliverance for which he prayed, declares in verse 25 that he will fulfill his vows, most likely by bringing to the Lord a fellowship offering (see Lev 7:16). It is then noted in verse 26 that the "poor will eat and be satisfied." So, an example is set for us: we who have received mercy should also extend mercy. Almost certainly this understanding lies behind Paul's complaint against

9. Note also how the dining motif plays a role in the contest between Woman Folly and Woman Wisdom in Prov 9.

the Corinthian Christians that at their love feasts/Lord's Supper celebrations, the poorer persons in the congregation were being humiliated by the richer persons' refusal to share with them. The practice of many churches, therefore, of taking up a benevolence offering in connection with the Lord's Supper is entirely appropriate and profoundly scriptural (see also Heb 13:15–16).

Atonement

Finally, as noted before, the ideas of atonement, expiation, and forgiveness of sins are not by any means absent, though they should probably not be seen as the primary purpose of the fellowship offering. The Passover meal, which was one form of the fellowship offering and which the Lord celebrated with his disciples the night before his crucifixion, was transformed by him into the Lord's Supper, a special fellowship offering that symbolized both the establishment of the new covenant in his blood (just as the fellowship offering established the Mosaic covenant in Exodus 24:4–8) as well as the forgiveness of sins by the shedding of that blood. Every time we take part in the Lord's Supper, we are being hosted by our gracious Lord, the one who, at the cost of his blood, has entered into covenant with us and has provided redemption for us, the forgiveness of our sins.

CHAPTER 4

Leviticus 4:1–5:13

LISTEN to the Story

4:1The LORD said to Moses, 2"Say to the Israelites: 'When anyone
sins unintentionally and does what is forbidden in any of the LORD's
commands—

3"'If the anointed priest sins, bringing guilt on the people, he must
bring to the LORD a young bull without defect as a sin offering for the sin
he has committed. 4He is to present the bull at the entrance to the tent of
meeting before the LORD. He is to lay his hand on its head and slaughter
it there before the LORD. 5Then the anointed priest shall take some of the
bull's blood and carry it into the tent of meeting. 6He is to dip his finger
into the blood and sprinkle some of it seven times before the LORD, in
front of the curtain of the sanctuary. 7The priest shall then put some of the
blood on the horns of the altar of fragrant incense that is before the LORD
in the tent of meeting. The rest of the bull's blood he shall pour out at the
base of the altar of burnt offering at the entrance to the tent of meeting.
8He shall remove all the fat from the bull of the sin offering—all the fat
that is connected to the internal organs, 9both kidneys with the fat on them
near the loins, and the long lobe of the liver, which he will remove with the
kidneys—10just as the fat is removed from the ox sacrificed as a fellowship
offering. Then the priest shall burn them on the altar of burnt offering.
11But the hide of the bull and all its flesh, as well as the head and legs, the
internal organs and the intestines—12that is, all the rest of the bull—he
must take outside the camp to a place ceremonially clean, where the ashes
are thrown, and burn it there in a wood fire on the ash heap.

13"'If the whole Israelite community sins unintentionally and does
what is forbidden in any of the LORD's commands, even though the community is unaware of the matter, when they realize their guilt 14and the sin
they committed becomes known, the assembly must bring a young bull as
a sin offering and present it before the tent of meeting. 15The elders of the

community are to lay their hands on the bull's head before the Lord, and the bull shall be slaughtered before the Lord. 16Then the anointed priest is to take some of the bull's blood into the tent of meeting. 17He shall dip his finger into the blood and sprinkle it before the Lord seven times in front of the curtain. 18He is to put some of the blood on the horns of the altar that is before the Lord in the tent of meeting. The rest of the blood he shall pour out at the base of the altar of burnt offering at the entrance to the tent of meeting. 19He shall remove all the fat from it and burn it on the altar, 20and do with this bull just as he did with the bull for the sin offering. In this way the priest will make atonement for the community, and they will be forgiven. 21Then he shall take the bull outside the camp and burn it as he burned the first bull. This is the sin offering for the community.

22" 'When a leader sins unintentionally and does what is forbidden in any of the commands of the Lord his God, when he realizes his guilt 23and the sin he has committed becomes known, he must bring as his offering a male goat without defect. 24He is to lay his hand on the goat's head and slaughter it at the place where the burnt offering is slaughtered before the Lord. It is a sin offering. 25Then the priest shall take some of the blood of the sin offering with his finger and put it on the horns of the altar of burnt offering and pour out the rest of the blood at the base of the altar. 26He shall burn all the fat on the altar as he burned the fat of the fellowship offering. In this way the priest will make atonement for the leader's sin, and he will be forgiven.

27" 'If any member of the community sins unintentionally and does what is forbidden in any of the Lord's commands, when they realize their guilt 28and the sin they have committed becomes known, they must bring as their offering for the sin they committed a female goat without defect. 29They are to lay their hand on the head of the sin offering and slaughter it at the place of the burnt offering. 30Then the priest is to take some of the blood with his finger and put it on the horns of the altar of burnt offering and pour out the rest of the blood at the base of the altar. 31They shall remove all the fat, just as the fat is removed from the fellowship offering, and the priest shall burn it on the altar as an aroma pleasing to the Lord. In this way the priest will make atonement for them, and they will be forgiven.

32" 'If someone brings a lamb as their sin offering, they are to bring a female without defect. 33They are to lay their hand on its head and

slaughter it for a sin offering at the place where the burnt offering is slaughtered. [34]Then the priest shall take some of the blood of the sin offering with
his finger and put it on the horns of the altar of burnt offering and pour
out the rest of the blood at the base of the altar. [35]They shall remove all the
fat, just as the fat is removed from the lamb of the fellowship offering, and
the priest shall burn it on the altar on top of the food offerings presented
to the LORD. In this way the priest will make atonement for them for the
sin they have committed, and they will be forgiven.

[5:1]" 'If anyone sins because they do not speak up when they hear a
public charge to testify regarding something they have seen or learned
about, they will be held responsible.

[2]" 'If anyone becomes aware that they are guilty—if they unwittingly
touch anything ceremonially unclean (whether the carcass of an unclean
animal, wild or domestic, or of any unclean creature that moves along
the ground) and they are unaware that they have become unclean, but
then they come to realize their guilt; [3]or if they touch human uncleanness
(anything that would make them unclean) even though they are unaware
of it, but then they learn of it and realize their guilt; [4]or if anyone thought-
lessly takes an oath to do anything, whether good or evil (in any matter
one might carelessly swear about) even though they are unaware of it, but
then they learn of it and realize their guilt—[5]when anyone becomes aware
that they are guilty in any of these matters, they must confess in what way
they have sinned. [6]As a penalty for the sin they have committed, they must
bring to the LORD a female lamb or goat from the flock as a sin offering;
and the priest shall make atonement for them for their sin.

[7]" 'Anyone who cannot afford a lamb is to bring two doves or two
young pigeons to the LORD as a penalty for their sin—one for a sin offering
and the other for a burnt offering. [8]They are to bring them to the priest,
who shall first offer the one for the sin offering. He is to wring its head
from its neck, not dividing it completely, [9]and is to splash some of the
blood of the sin offering against the side of the altar; the rest of the blood
must be drained out at the base of the altar. It is a sin offering. [10]The priest
shall then offer the other as a burnt offering in the prescribed way and
make atonement for them for the sin they have committed, and they will
be forgiven.

[11]" 'If, however, they cannot afford two doves or two young pigeons,
they are to bring as an offering for their sin a tenth of an ephah of the

finest flour for a sin offering. They must not put olive oil or incense on it, because it is a sin offering. [12]They are to bring it to the priest, who shall take a handful of it as a memorial portion and burn it on the altar on top of the food offerings presented to the LORD. It is a sin offering. [13]In this way the priest will make atonement for them for any of these sins they have committed, and they will be forgiven. The rest of the offering will belong to the priest, as in the case of the grain offering.'"

Listening to the Text in the Story: Biblical Texts: Exodus 29:14, 36; 30:10; Ancient Near Eastern Texts: Various Hittite Ritual Texts

The passages listed above are the only previous mentions of the sin offering in the biblical narrative leading up to the book of Leviticus, all of which are prescriptive anticipations of the ordination of Aaron and his sons as priests in Leviticus 8–9 and of the Day of Atonement in Leviticus 16. There are no previous accounts of an actual occurrence of a sin offering.

While Israel's neighbors were certainly conscious of the need to deal with sin and impurity, their remedies, for the most part, were not close analogues of the biblical sin offering and did not involve the same extensive employment of blood manipulation. Indeed, for a considerable part of the twentieth century, scholars and commentators believed that Israel's sin offering was unique in its blood rite. However, over the last few decades a corrective to this understanding has been provided by several scholars. Yitzhaq Feder, for example, in a comparison between a number of mid-second millennium Hittite texts dealing with the sin offering, has noticed, among others, the following correspondences:

Smearing of the blood on cultic furniture
Fat reserved for the deity
Sacrifice of birds
Emphasis on one or more of the following:
    expiating sin
    appeasing divine wrath
    removing impurity[1]

1. Yitzhaq Feder, *Blood Expiation in Hittite and Biblical Ritual: Origins, Context, and Meaning*, WAWSup 2 (Atlanta: SBL Press, 2011), 125–43.

Correspondences with other of Israel's neighbors also exist, though not to the same degree. So, it is important to note that the sacrificial laws that God gave to Israel were not imparted in a vacuum, and the Israelites would already be acquainted with the conceptual categories.

It is important, however, to draw attention to some general differences as well. Quite often, Israel's neighbors offered their sacrifices and performed their blood manipulations to ward off demonic activity and to appease the more malevolent gods of the underworld—gods who could be quite capricious in their demands and perceived threats. They could offer their sacrifices to more benevolent deities, as well, and on account of actions that were truly sinful and ethically immoral. Nevertheless, the concern with demons and malevolent gods was dominant.

By contrast, Israel's sacrifices for sin were not to be offered to underworld deities but only to their one covenant God, the one who ruled over and was superior to all other gods, the one who forbade Israel to sacrifice to any other god, much less underworld deities (e.g., Lev 17:1–8; unfortunately, Israel often failed in these prohibitions). Israel's sacrifices for sin were to be offered to a holy God, one whose only complaint against his people was for ethical violations that fell short of the ideal he had for them: that they might be a holy people, fully devoted to the Lord their God.

EXPLAIN the Story

The basic flow of the instructions for the sin offering is as follows:

- 4:1—The introductory verse indicates that the directions that follow are for sins committed by Israelites unintentionally.
- 4:2–12—If the priest is the one who brings a sin offering, he must offer a young bull. Some of the bull's blood is to be sprinkled either on or in front of the veil that separates the holy place from the most holy place, and he also puts some of the blood on the horns of the incense altar.
- 4:13–21—If it is the entire community that has sinned, the offering is, again, to be a young bull, and the blood is manipulated in the same way as for the priest.
- 4:22–26—If it is a leader of the community who has sinned, he is to bring a male goat. The goat's blood is to be put on the horns of the altar of burnt offering in the courtyard of the tabernacle.

4:27–35—If it is a regular community member who has sinned, the offering to be brought is either a female goat or lamb. Again, the blood is to be placed on the horns of the altar of burnt offering.

5:1–6—There is a representative list of sins for which the sin offering is to be presented. In verse 6 the sin offering of the regular Israelite is again indicated, either a female goat or lamb.

5:7–10—A concession is made for someone who is too poor to offer a goat or lamb. They may offer instead two doves or two young pigeons, one of which will be a sin offering and the other a burnt offering.

5:11–13—A further concession is made for someone who is too poor to even offer birds. They may bring a grain offering instead.

The instructions for the sin offering raise several questions.

What Should This Offering Be Called?

Traditionally, this offering has been referred to as the sin offering, and with good reason. The passage under consideration here does indeed deal with sins, offenses against God, and a check of most modern translations reveals that this is still the preferred designation. However, it has become almost commonplace in modern commentaries to argue that the offering is better referred to as a purification offering. One of the main arguments for this is that the offering is also to be presented when there is no real question of any sin having been committed by the offerer. When a woman gives birth to a child, she has not sinned in giving birth, yet she must present a sin offering at the sanctuary for her purification (Lev 12:6). A sin offering is to be presented for a house that has had some kind of mold within its walls (Lev 14:48–53), yet inanimate houses cannot sin. A sin offering is to be offered to purify the sanctuary (Lev 16:15–16), yet the sanctuary has not sinned. So the suggestion has been made, and largely adopted, that the better name would be the purification offering. However, more recently, and for various reasons, several scholars have made the case for the more traditional "sin offering" designation.[2] At the very least, it must be recognized that, in the priestly conception of the world, there is no such thing as an impurity that is not, at least indirectly, the result of or associated in some way with sin. So, when we examine the various impurities in chapters 12–15 for which sin offerings have to be presented, we will see there that, while the impurities may not directly be the result of some sin on

2. Watts, *Leviticus 1–10*, 306–10, 332–33; Feder, *Blood Expiation*, 99–108; Yitzhaq Feder, "A Sin Offering for Birth Anxiety," *The Torah*, n.d., http://thetorah.com/a-sin-offering-for-birth-anxiety/.

the part of the offerer, nevertheless the impurity is the result of sin that exists in the world. The sin offering atones not only for actual sinful acts the offerer has committed; it also atones for impurities that are symbolically understood to have resulted from the sin in the world that lies behind all impurities, even though the impure person has not necessarily acted sinfully in contracting the impurity. The sin offering is the appropriate offering in both cases, in that both sinful acts and impurities are caused by sin and both sinners and impure persons need to have their sin and impurities removed and their lives ransomed.[3] Consequently, both for the sake of the typical NIV reader of this commentary as well as by conviction, I will retain the traditional "sin offering" designation.

What Does This Offering Do?

Certainly, as far as the present passage is concerned, the offering has to do with sin—that is, violations of the LORD's commandments. The Hebrew word for both "sin" and "sin offering" is *hatta't*. The verb from the same root, in one stem (*qal hata'*) means "to sin," and in another stem (*piel hitte'*) means to "offer a sin offering" and thus to "de-sin," or to "purify" from sin. The interesting thing about this last verb is that it is used later in Leviticus to refer to "de-sinning" or cleansing inanimate objects, such as the altar of incense (8:15) or houses (14:49, 52). This is part of the reason many scholars suggest that the offering is better labeled as a purification offering. However, for the reasons given above, I believe "sin offering" still captures the essence of what this offering does, especially in the present passage.

Related to this discussion is the meaning of the Hebrew word *kipper*, translated "make atonement" in this passage (4:20, 26, 31, 35; 5:6, 10, 13). Previously in Leviticus this term only occurred in 1:4. I noted briefly in the commentary for that passage that I would postpone a fuller discussion until we came to this chapter. The issue is a complicated one, involving the history of the word, its relationship to apparent cognate words in other ancient Near Eastern languages, and even whether there might be two different roots from which the verb is derived. However, the basic questions have to do with (1) whether the verb means "to ransom" or "to purify," and (2) what are the effects of this atonement. I basically agree with Jay Sklar that to a large extent the questions pose a false dichotomy, and that *kipper* refers to both ransoming

3. For an informative discussion on the relationship between sin and impurity, see Jay Sklar, *Sin, Impurity, Sacrifice, Atonement: The Priestly Conceptions*, Hebrew Bible Monographs 2 (Sheffield: Sheffield Phoenix, 2005), 109, n. 16, 130, 135–36, 139–59, 183–87.

and purifying, though in any one passage one idea might be more prominent than in another.[4] The verb means "to ransom" (related to the noun *kopher*, "ransom"), and it also means to purify from the uncleanness or impurity of sin. In short, then, for the present passage, the sin offering atones (ransoms) the life of the offerer, as well as atoning for, or purifying, the offerer from their sin. In later passages, especially chapters 12–15, we will see that the notion of purifying may well be more prominent, but even in those passages, though the purification may be for inanimate objects, the idea of providing a ransom for the life of the offerer is still in the background.

Also related to the use of the verb *kipper* is the question as to whether the sin offering provides expiation or propitiation. Does the sin offering expiate—that is, remove sin—or does it also propitiate—that is, appease or placate God's anger/wrath against sin? Again, I believe that this question introduces a false dichotomy. Almost all scholars are agreed that the sin offering expiates sin. But as soon as this stipulation is made, it must be asked, "Why does sin need to be expiated?" The answer must certainly be that the expiation of sin also propitiates God's wrath. The expressions of God's anger against sin are multiple in the Torah. One scholar, while admitting that God's anger "is an important aspect of God's attitude to humanity in the Bible," goes on to say that "there is hardly any book in which it is less prominent than Leviticus."[5] But it is hard to understand this as fairly representing the book of Leviticus, a book that uses all kinds of phrases and formulations to describe God's wrath against both sin and sinner. And it is hardly fair to the book of Leviticus in its narrative context within the Pentateuch. To be sure, in the chapters that deal with sacrifice in particular, explicit references to God's anger are few. But with regard to what is implied in these chapters, one must ask what would have happened if those who sinned had not presented their offerings, their sin had not been atoned, and they had not been forgiven.[6] Certainly the language of being "cut off," which occurs multiple times in the book, even with regard to ritual infractions, is operative here (see 7:20–27; 17:4–14; 18:29; 19:8;

4. Sklar, *Sin, Impurity, Sacrifice, Atonement*; Jay Sklar, "Sin and Impurity: Atoned or Purified? Yes!" in *Perspectives on Purity and Purification in the Bible*, ed. Baruch J. Schwartz et al., Library of Hebrew Bible/Old Testament Studies 474 (New York: T&T Clark, 2008), 18–31.

5. John Goldingay, "Your Iniquities Have Made a Separation between You and Your God," in *Atonement Today: A Symposium at St. John's College, Nottingham*, ed. John Goldingay (London: SPCK, 1995), 51.

6. See Baruch A. Levine, *Leviticus; Va-Yikra: The Traditional Hebrew Text with the New JPS Translation*, JPS Torah Commentary (Philadelphia: Jewish Publication Society, 1989), 20. He correctly notes that "in Leviticus the sense of the reality of divine wrath should not be underestimated. Mitigating and preventing that wrath is a major objective of the religious life."

20:3–6, 18; 22:3).[7] Additionally, non-ritual use of the verb *kipper* also suggests an appeasing element. For example, the very first occurrence of the word in the Old Testament, in Genesis 32:20, refers to Jacob's attempt to *pacify* Esau's anger with a gift of animals from his flocks and herds.

For Whom/What Is This Offering Made?

Jacob Milgrom, in his magisterial commentary on Leviticus, as well as in a highly influential article, has argued that the sin offering does not actually atone for the offerer; rather, it purifies the *sancta*—that is, the tabernacle and its altars and furniture. The offerer's sin is forgiven, not because of the sacrifice of the sin offering but because of the offerer's repentance. All that is required for forgiveness in the Old Testament is the sinner's genuine repentance and confession. The sin offering is not necessary for the sinner's purification but for the tabernacle's purification. Whenever an Israelite sins, the impurity produced by that sin becomes a miasma that airborne, as it were, contaminates the tabernacle aerially. The blood of the sin offering, which is variously applied to the horns of the altar in the courtyard or to the altar of incense in the holy place, serves to cleanse the *sancta* from this airborne impurity.[8] And then, once a year, on the Day of Atonement, a major house cleaning takes place, in addition to the regular sin offerings made during the prior months of the year.

While Milgrom's proposal has won a sizable number of followers, it has also justly drawn considerable criticism. In the present passage, in particular, there is nothing said about atonement or purification for the tabernacle. Rather, atonement is made "for the community" (4:20); "for the leader's sin" (4:26); and "for him" (NIV "for them," 4:31, 35; 5:6, 10, 13). Nevertheless, it is also important to note that, while Milgrom is definitely correct to note the role of repentance in the obtaining of forgiveness, the text certainly seems to make the forgiveness contingent, chronologically, on the sacrifice of the sin offering.

Additionally, the entire premise of an airborne miasma that contaminates the tabernacle must be called into question. The handful of texts Milgrom uses to support his thesis, while capable of being interpreted along the lines Milgrom suggests, are in my opinion more satisfactorily interpreted with reference to direct physical contact rather than airborne contact. For example,

---

7. For a discussion of the various theories as to what this "cutting off" is, as well as an emphasis on the fact that God is the one who executes the penalty, see Milgrom, *Leviticus 1–16*, 457–60.

8. Milgrom, *Leviticus 1–16*, 254–61; Jacob Milgrom, "Israel's Sanctuary: The Priestly 'Picture of Dorian Gray,'" *RB* 83 (1976): 390–99.

one passage to which Milgrom points is Leviticus 20:3, in which the Lord declares that the person who sacrifices his children to Molek "has defiled my sanctuary."[9] Milgrom claims that this defilement takes place aerially, from afar. However, in a similar passage, Ezekiel 23:39, the Lord's complaint is, "On the very day they sacrificed their children to their idols, they entered my sanctuary and defiled it." Here the sanctuary defilement is the result of direct physical contact rather than airborne contact. In my opinion, the defilement in Leviticus 20:3 is also direct physical contact, and there is simply an ellipsis or gap in the text that the reader should take into account. That the defilement to the sanctuary would have come about by way of direct contact is to be understood.[10]

All in all, it seems that the sin offering is better understood as atoning for the offerer, or at least primarily so, rather than the *sancta*. As well, the forgiveness mentioned in the text, though certainly tied to repentance, is still contingent on the presentation of the sin offering.[11]

What Is the Role of Blood in This Offering?

It would be difficult to say for sure what the consensus is as to what the blood of the sacrificial animal actually does in the sin offering. Somewhat vaguely, many commentators state that the blood atones for sin and provides purification. But exactly how does it do this? Jacob Milgrom, for example, in conjunction with his miasma theory, argues that the blood sprinkled, splattered, or daubed on the altar of burnt offering, the altar of incense, the veil, and the ark of the covenant[12] acts as a detergent to purify them from the sins of the Israelites, both serially during the year as well as on a much larger scale on the Day of Atonement.

A number of scholars, however, have argued that the blood, rather than acting as a detergent with regard to the sanctuary, acts as a contaminant. In the initial act of the sin offering, there is a ritual symbolic transfer of sin from the sinner to the sacrificial animal, and especially to its blood. Then, subsequently, when the blood of the animal is applied to the horns of the altar

9. See also Num 19:13, 20.

10. For only a few of the critiques of Milgrom's theory, in part or in whole, see Roy E. Gane, *Cult and Character: Purification Offerings, Day of Atonement, and Theodicy* (Winona Lake, IN: Eisenbrauns, 2005), 106–62; Angel M. Rodríguez, "Transfer of Sin in Leviticus," in *The Seventy Weeks, Leviticus, and the Nature of Prophecy*, ed. Frank B. Holbrook (Washington, DC: Biblical Research Institute, 1986), 169–97; Gammie, *Holiness in Israel*, 37–41.

11. See also Boda, *Severe Mercy*, 75.

12. Sprinkling on the veil or toward the veil would have been symbolic of sprinkling the ark of the covenant; see the discussion in Hartley, *Leviticus*, 60.

of burnt offering in the courtyard or to the altar of incense, the veil, or the ark inside the sanctuary, the sins that were originally transferred to the animal are now transferred to the tabernacle and its altars and furniture. The sin of the sinner, via the blood of the sacrificial animals, has now been transferred to the tabernacle. Symbolically, the tabernacle has absorbed the sins of the Israelites. The Israelites' sins are atoned for by being transferred to the very dwelling place of God.[13] Symbolically this would mean, as Roy Gane argues, that "God has freed offerers from 'debt' toward him by accepting/absorbing the cost."[14] And again, "Forgiveness by YHWH carries with it a cost that he must bear."[15]

Despite the objections that could be raised against this understanding, I find myself in substantial agreement with it. If the hand-leaning rite, as was argued in the commentary on Leviticus 1:4 essentially established an identification between the offerer and the sacrificial animal, then it would seem that, in a ritually symbolic sense, not just the offerer's sins but the offerer's entire person are transferred to the animal. The animal dies in place of the offerer,[16] and the blood of the animal carries the defilement from the offerer's sins. The animal "bears" the offerer's sins.

How Can an Offering of Grain Count as a Sin Offering?

It has been traditionally understood in the history of the Christian church that a blood sacrifice was necessary for the forgiveness of sins. This understanding seems to be supported by passages like Leviticus 17:11,

> For the life of a creature is in the blood, and I have given it to you to make atonement for yourselves on the altar; it is the blood that makes atonement for one's life.

---

13. This thesis has been argued most strongly by Gane, *Cult and Character*, 167–97, 274–84, 334–37; Roy Gane, *Leviticus, Numbers*, NIVAC (Grand Rapids: Zondervan, 2004), 104–10, 148–50, 277–83; Angel M Rodríguez, *Substitution in the Hebrew Cultus*, Andrews University Seminary Doctoral Dissertation Series 3 (Berrien Springs, MI: Andrews University Press, 1979), 117, 133–49, 193–224, 238–44, 255–260; Rodríguez, "Transfer of Sin in Leviticus"; Noam Zohar, "Repentance and Purification: The Significance and Semantics of *Hatta't* in the Pentateuch," *JBL* 107.4 (1988): 609–18.

14. Gane, *Leviticus, Numbers*, 106.

15. Gane, *Cult and Character*, 335.

16. Hartley, *Leviticus*, 65: "It needs to be underscored that the sacrificial system loudly proclaims that the penalty of sin is death. Thus the giving of a life (*nephesh*) on the altar for the life of the offerer upholds justice." See also Levine, *Leviticus*, 20–22; Christopher J. H. Wright, "Leviticus," in *New Bible Commentary: 21st Century Edition*, ed. D. A. Carson et al., 4th ed. (Downers Grove, IL: InterVarsity Press, 1994), 127.

as well as by its New Testament equivalent,

> In fact, the law requires that nearly everything be cleansed with blood, and without the shedding of blood there is no forgiveness. (Heb 9:22)

Of late, those who have been opposed to the idea of penal substitutionary atonement—that Christ's death and the shedding of his blood is a sacrifice for and pays the penalty for our sins—have used the concession made in 5:11–13 to argue against this understanding. If the offering of a bit of grain could qualify as a sin offering, then obviously the death of an animal was not actually necessary; this should put the whole concept of sacrificial atonement into question. After all, as J. S. Whale so famously phrased it, "You cannot punish a cupful of barley."[17]

At least two responses can be offered to this objection. First, note that the text takes care to indicate that the memorial portion of the grain offering is to be burned on the altar "on top of the food [or fire] offerings presented to the LORD" (5:12). As several commentators have noted, this may well indicate that even though the use of grain as a sin offering is a concession, it is nevertheless a concession made with stipulations. The instruction that this offering is to be placed on top of the other food/fire offerings suggests that this concession offering, in large measure, derives its efficacy from the other offerings on which it is placed.[18]

Second, it is important to keep things in perspective and to realize that this is indeed a concession, an exception that serves to prove the rule. God's special gracious concession in this instance is just that, a gracious concession; to suggest otherwise is, as Henri Blocher has argued, hardly different from a "mere cavil."[19] The principle as stated in Leviticus 17:11 and Hebrews 9:22 stands.[20]

---

17. J. S. Whale, *Victor and Victim: The Christian Doctrine of Redemption* (Cambridge: Cambridge University Press, 1960), 53.

18. For this argument, see R. K. Harrison, *Leviticus: An Introduction and Commentary*, TOTC (Downers Grove, IL: InterVarsity Press, 1980), 73; F. Duane Lindsey, "Leviticus," in *The Bible Knowledge Commentary*, ed. John F. Walvoord and Roy B. Zuck, 12 vols. (Wheaton: Victor, 1983), 1:182; Oswald T. Allis, "Leviticus," in *The New Bible Commentary*, ed. Donald J. Guthrie and J. Alec Motyer, 3rd ed. (London: Inter-Varsity Press, 1970), 146; Michael L. Brown, *Answering Jewish Objections to Jesus*, 3 vols. (Grand Rapids: Baker Books, 2000), 2:113, 289 n. 186.

19. Henri Blocher, "Biblical Metaphors and the Doctrine of the Atonement," *JETS* 47.4 (2004): 642.

20. For a much more extensive academic response, see my forthcoming article, "You Cannot Punish a Cupful of Barley."

What Does It Mean That This Offering Is for Unintentional Sins?

For both the sin offering and the guilt offering, it is specified in the instructions that they are for "unintentional" sins (sin offering: 4:1, 13, 22, 27; guilt offering: 5:15, 18). Yet, in some of the examples of the kinds of sins for which these two offerings are to atone (5:2–6; 6:1–7), it would appear that there is at least some level of intentionality to them. Since the issue is actually more pronounced with the guilt offering than for the sin offering, I will reserve the discussion of this issue for the commentary on Leviticus 5:14—6:7

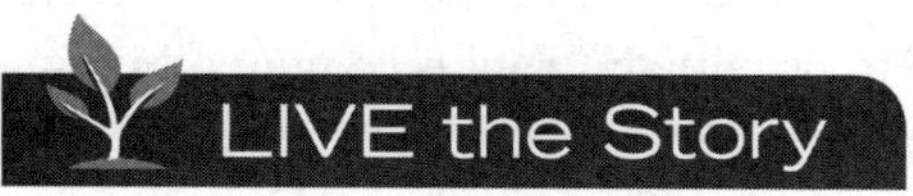

Jesus, the Ransoming and Purifying Sin Offering

In Mark 10:45 Jesus refers to himself as a "ransom for many." In addition to the verse's allusion to the "many" of Isaiah 53:11, the Greek term *lytron* ("ransom") is almost certainly a reference to the *kopher* ("ransom") of the Old Testament and the verb *kipper* ("atone"), which play such an important function in the sin offering. Jesus refers to his own death as an atonement for sin. More explicitly, Jesus refers to his blood being poured out for "many for the forgiveness of sins" (Matt 26:28). This is indeed the function of the sin offering: the animal is slaughtered, the blood is shed, atonement is made, and sins are forgiven.

Near the end of Luke's travel narrative (approximately Luke 9:51–19:47), which recounts Jesus's determination to go to Jerusalem to die on the cross, Jesus tells the story of the Pharisee and the tax collector who entered into the temple to pray (18:9–14). The Pharisee was thankful that he was not like "robbers, evildoers, adulterers—or even like this tax collector" (v. 11). But the tax collector prays for God to have mercy on him. The NIV's "have mercy" is the Greek *hilaskomai*, which only occurs twice in the New Testament: here and in Hebrews 2:17, where it is translated with reference to Jesus that he would "make atonement for the sins of the people." It particularly relates to the idea of atonement and propitiation; it is this same verb, with an attached preposition, that the Septuagint uses to translate the Hebrew word *kipper*. So, the tax collector's prayer in Luke 18:13 could appropriately be translated as "be propitiated toward me, a sinner." It is entirely possible that Luke has narrated this account with this word in particular, rather than the usual word for having mercy (*eleeō*), precisely to highlight that it is for this very reason that Jesus is making this determined journey to Jerusalem, to die on the cross as an atonement for sin, which will provide the propitiation for which the tax collector prayed.[21]

John the Baptist, in John 1:29, points to Jesus and declares, "Look, the Lamb of God, who takes away the sin of the world!" While John may be alluding here to the Passover lamb, it is likely that he is also referring to the lamb of the sin offering (see also Heb 10:11; 1 John 3:5), whose death removed sins from the offerer.

Paul in Romans 3:21–26 refers to how "God presented Christ as a sacrifice of atonement, through the shedding of his blood." The term "sacrifice of atonement" is the Greek *hilastērion*, which is from the same root as the previously mentioned verb *hilaskomai*, "to propitiate." Paul is certainly thinking here of the sin offering when he states that God presented Christ as a sacrifice of atonement (see also, with reference to the blood of Christ in the Pauline literature, though not with the same explicit sacrificial language, Rom 5:9; Eph 1:7; 2:13; Col 1:20).[22]

Even more graphically, Paul in Romans 8:3 says that God sent "his own Son in the likeness of sinful flesh to be a sin offering. And so he condemned sin in the flesh." The NIV's translation, "sin offering," is perhaps a bit overinterpretive here (the Greek simply says "for sin") but nevertheless captures Paul's thought. Indeed, the essential correctness of the reasoning behind this translation is validated by the phrase, "condemned sin in the flesh." The majority of Romans commentators believe that the flesh referred to here is the flesh of Jesus Christ. That is, God condemned sin in the flesh of Jesus Christ, or, to put that another way, God executed the penalty against sin in the flesh of Jesus Christ. This is what I have argued takes place in the sin offering. The sacrificed animal receives the penalty against sin in its flesh. Jesus received the penalty against sin in his flesh.

In 2 Corinthians 5:20–21 Paul states that "God made him who had no sin to be sin for us." An important interpretive issue in this verse is whether the second occurrence of the word "sin" should be translated rather as "sin offering." We have already seen how the Hebrew word *hatta't* can mean either sin or sin offering. The Septuagint, mimicking the Hebrew in this regard, also often (not always) translates *hatta't*, when it definitely means sin offering,

---

21. John W. Kleinig, *Leviticus*, ConcC (St. Louis: Concordia, 2003), 121–22.

22. It may be that *hilastērion* in Rom 3:25, as has been argued more recently, is referring not to Christ as sacrifice but rather to Christ as the "place of atonement," i.e., the atonement cover or the "mercy seat" on the ark of the covenant. But even if this is the case, the verse still emphasizes the role of Christ's blood in the act of atonement. Atonement covers do not bleed. In this case, then, Christ is the atonement cover, the sacrifice whose blood is sprinkled on the cover, and the priest who does the sprinkling!

with the Greek word for sin, *hamartia*. The question then is whether Paul does the same thing in 2 Corinthians 5:21. It is at least possible that this is the case, though probably the majority of commentators think it should simply be translated as "sin." Regardless, Paul is describing Christ either as a sin offering or as having sin imputed (transferred) to him, even as happens with the sacrificial animal in the sin offering.

The book of Hebrews has much to say about Christ as a sacrifice for sin and has the sin offering of Leviticus 4–5 as its background. The Old Testament high priest first had to sacrifice for his own sins before he offered a sacrifice for the people (Heb 5:2–3). Christ, however, who is "blameless, pure, set apart from sinners," did not need to sacrifice for his own sins (7:26–27). Furthermore, whereas the Old Testament priest had to perform these sacrificial rituals over and over again, Christ, by virtue of the truly sinless nature of the sacrifice that he offered (that is, himself), made that sacrifice "once for all" (7:27; 9:25–28; 10:10–14; see also 1:3; 2:17). The Old Testament sacrifices, while certainly serving a purpose in their own time, could not ultimately pay for sin or "clear the conscience of the worshiper" (9:7–9). Christ, however, when he died as a ransom for sin, truly set those for whom he died free from their sins and cleared their consciences (9:11–15). However, even though the Old Testament sacrifices served a purpose, the blood of animals could not ultimately provide a sacrifice for sin. But Christ, by the sacrifice of himself, has truly provided forgiveness, satisfaction, redemption, purification, and perfection (Heb 10:1–18). Christ is, indeed, the sin offering who has made "the people holy through his own blood" (13:12).

In 1 John there are two specific references that use the Greek word *hilasmos*, related to the previously mentioned *hilaskomai* and *hilastērion*, to describe Christ's sacrifice. In 2:2 Christ is the "atoning sacrifice for our sins." And in 4:10 the author says that God "loved us and sent his Son as an atoning sacrifice for our sins."

This survey of the New Testament's use of sacrificial language is not exhaustive, and there are other passages where one may well find echoes of Old Testament sacrifices (e.g., 1 Pet 1:2, 19; 2:24; Rev 1:5). Nevertheless, what we have seen is instructive and has significant implications for how we live our lives as Christians. The title of this section is Live the Story. The idea is to identify ways we can take the passage and its exposition to help us live out the story. However, the important takeaway from this particular part of the biblical story is that, in some respect, we cannot live it out. We do not bring sacrifices to the temple. We certainly do not bring these sacrifices day after day. Rather, the takeaway from what we have looked at is that it is Jesus Christ himself who has lived the story, and he has done so precisely so that we do not have to. The required response from us is to fall on our knees in praise, wonder, love, worship, and adoration, echoing the language of the angels, living creatures, and elders in Revelation 5:12,

> "Worthy is the Lamb, who was slain,
> to receive power and wealth and wisdom and strength
> and honor and glory and praise!"

We still offer sacrifices (e.g., Rom 12:1), but we do not do so in order to secure atonement and forgiveness. Rather, we do so because we have already received the atonement and been forgiven. Indeed, the sacrifices we make have a role to play in the advance of the gospel (Col 1:24). Christ has died, and there is no more sacrifice for sin (Heb 10:18). Christ has died, Christ has risen, Christ will come again. And when he does, it will not be to bear sin but to bring to completion the salvation of "those who are waiting for him" (Heb 9:28).

CHAPTER 5

Leviticus 5:14–6:7[1]

LISTEN to the Story

[14]The Lord said to Moses: [15]"When anyone is unfaithful to the Lord by sinning unintentionally in regard to any of the Lord's holy things, they are to bring to the Lord as a penalty a ram from the flock, one without defect and of the proper value in silver, according to the sanctuary shekel. It is a guilt offering. [16]They must make restitution for what they have failed to do in regard to the holy things, pay an additional penalty of a fifth of its value and give it all to the priest. The priest will make atonement for them with the ram as a guilt offering, and they will be forgiven.

[17]"If anyone sins and does what is forbidden in any of the Lord's commands, even though they do not know it, they are guilty and will be held responsible. [18]They are to bring to the priest as a guilt offering a ram from the flock, one without defect and of the proper value. In this way the priest will make atonement for them for the wrong they have committed unintentionally, and they will be forgiven. [19]It is a guilt offering; they have been guilty of wrongdoing against the Lord."

[6:1]The Lord said to Moses: [2]"If anyone sins and is unfaithful to the Lord by deceiving a neighbor about something entrusted to them or left in their care or about something stolen, or if they cheat their neighbor, [3]or if they find lost property and lie about it, or if they swear falsely about any such sin that people may commit—[4]when they sin in any of these ways and realize their guilt, they must return what they have stolen or taken by extortion, or what was entrusted to them, or the lost property they found, [5]or whatever it was they swore falsely about. They must make restitution in full, add a fifth of the value to it and give it all to the owner on the day they present their guilt offering. [6]And as a penalty they must bring to the priest, that is, to the Lord, their guilt offering, a ram from the flock, one

1. Note that the English and Hebrew verse enumerations are slightly out of sync here. English 6:1–7 is in the Hebrew text 5:20–26.

without defect and of the proper value. [7]In this way the priest will make atonement for them before the LORD, and they will be forgiven for any of the things they did that made them guilty."

Listening to the Text in the Story: Ancient Near Eastern Texts: Instructions to Priests and Temple Officials; Prayer to Every God

This passage deals with the guilt offering. What distinguishes this offering from the previous atoning offerings (the burnt and sin offerings) is that it deals not simply with sin in general but with sin that is characterized as violating the *sancta*, the tangible holy things of God, which are understood, in some way, as having been damaged (perhaps rendered unholy or unclean) or misappropriated. Accordingly, not only does there have to be a sacrifice, but the sacrifice has to be accompanied by some kind of reparation or compensatory payment, plus a 20 percent penalty. It has to be a "value added" sacrifice. The sacrifice itself may be seen as providing ritual compensation, which atones for the offerer and results in forgiveness, but there must also be real financial compensation, with accompanying penalty. Additionally, this sacrifice may also be offered in cases where the offerer has defrauded a neighbor with regard to various property issues. For this reason, many commentators have argued that rather than "guilt offering," a better name would be "reparation offering." However, the Hebrew word *'asham* does in fact refer to "guilt" or "culpability"; "guilt offering" certainly constitutes a proper rendering as well (more about this in Explain the Story below, p. 85).

In various texts from the ancient Near East there are concerns expressed about the violation of the *sancta*. For example, the Hittite text Instructions to Priests and Temple Officials details the various ways these might violations might occur.[2] Roy Gane nicely summarizes some of these by noting that this text

> takes pains to specify and prohibit several categories of sacrilege, including temple personnel appropriating sacrificial portions that are not theirs or taking dedicated things from the temple for their families, and farmers cheating gods out of property or delaying presentation of dedicated offerings.[3]

---

2. "Instructions to Priests and Temple Officials," *COS* 1.83:217–21.

3. Roy E. Gane, "Leviticus," in *Zondervan Illustrated Bible Backgrounds Commentary of the Old Testament*, ed. John H. Walton, David W. Baker, and Daniel I. Block, 5 vols. (Grand Rapids: Zondervan, 2009), 1:296.

There was also great concern for having possibly committed a sacrilege without knowing it. Thus, in the Babylonian text Prayer to Every God, the complainant is distressed because

> In ignorance I have eaten that forbidden of my god;
> In ignorance I have set foot on that prohibited by my goddess. . . .
>
> The transgression which I have committed, indeed I do not know;
> The sin which I have done, indeed I do not know.
> The forbidden thing which I have eaten, indeed I do not know;
> The prohibited (place) on which I have set foot, indeed I do not know.[4]

EXPLAIN the Story

As noted above, this offering addresses the sin of sacrilege against the *sancta*, the holy things of God. The "holy things" would include the tabernacle complex itself, the furniture, all implements, and, of course, the sacrificial offerings. If an Israelite defiled or misappropriated any of these holy objects, they would have to present a ram as a guilt offering (*'asham*), so that their sin might be atoned for and be forgiven. In addition, they would have to bring a 20 percent monetary payment to make reparation and provide compensation for this violation.

Interestingly, this guilt offering was also necessary for certain violations committed against other Israelites (6:1–5). The relationship between this passage and the laws of restitution in Exodus 22:1–15, which prescribe a higher rate of compensation, is not entirely clear. What is clear is that the property crimes committed against fellow Israelites in Leviticus 6:1–5 are regarded as being specifically sins of "unfaithfulness" (*ma'al*) against the Lord, just as the earlier violations in 5:14–19 were also characterized as "unfaithfulness" (*ma'al*) against the Lord.

The major interpretive issue for this passage is one that I briefly raised in the previous chapter dealing with the sin offering in 4:1–5:13 (see Explain the Story, p. 79). There I noted that, for both the sin offering and the guilt offering, there is a problem with the fact that these offerings are denoted as being for sins that have been committed unintentionally.

---

4. "Prayer to Every God," trans. Ferris J. Stephens (*ANET*, 391–92).

The Sin Offering

4:1—"When anyone sins unintentionally"
4:13—"If the whole Israelite community sins unintentionally"
4:22—"When a leader sins unintentionally"
4:27—"If any member of the community sins unintentionally"

The Guilt Offering

5:15—"When anyone is unfaithful to the LORD by sinning unintentionally"
5:18—"The wrong they have committed unintentionally"

There is a problem, however, in that, for both offerings, but most prominently for the guilt offering, a number of the violations for which these offerings are said to atone for can hardly be regarded as unintentional:

failure to speak up when asked to testify
uttering a rash oath
deceiving a neighbor
cheating a neighbor
lying about lost property
swearing falsely

Commentators have dealt with this issue in various ways. Some have argued that the translation "unintentional" for the Hebrew *shegagah* is too restrictive and the term should be understood as simply indicating a straying or waywardness that could be either intentional or unintentional.[5] Others, whether they adopt this particular argument or not, suggest that the real concern of these chapters has not so much to do with strict intentionality or non-intentionality but that the term is being used to make a distinction between the sins that could be atoned for by these offerings versus sins that Numbers 15:30 refers to as "defiant" sins (literally, "with a high hand," *beyad ramah*), which could not be atoned for by offerings.[6] While I appreciate the potential explanatory force of both these arguments, I believe the answer may lie along a different track.

Jacob Milgrom engages in an extensive discussion on this issue in his commentary. I provide some extended quotations here in order to properly interact with them.

5. See, for example, Walter C. Kaiser, Jr., "Leviticus," in *NIB*, vol. 1 (Nashville: Abingdon, 1994), 1033–34, 1039.

6. See, for example, the very helpful discussion in Sklar, *Leviticus*, 42–44.

> Confession is the legal device fashioned by the Priestly legislators to convert deliberate sins into inadvertences, thereby qualifying them for sacrificial expiation.[7]

> Although he [the offender] has deliberately taken a false oath—lying to God's face as it were—his sin is absolved through sacrifice, an absolution that elsewhere is permitted only for involuntary sins. Thus conscience is the source of a legal force that can convert a deliberate sin against God, always punishable by death, into an involuntary sin, now expiable by sacrifice.[8]

> Thus the paradox raised at the outset confronts us again: how can deliberate crime be expiated by sacrifice? . . . One is forced to deduce that a death sentence has been commuted to sacrificial expiation![9]

> I submit that the repentance of the sinner, through his remorse and confession, reduces his intentional sin to an inadvertence, thereby rendering it eligible for sacrificial expiation.[10]

In essence, Milgrom argues that the Priestly legislators have created what could be referred to as a "legal fiction"[11] (though Milgrom himself is reticent to call it that), in which deliberate sins have been moved into the category of inadvertent sins. And what allows them to do this? It is the act of confession and repentance on the part of the offerer of the sacrifice. The priest makes a judgment as to the sorrow and sincerity with which the offerer comes and, having judged the confession to be truly sincere and heartfelt, allows the offerer to bring the guilt offering, atoning for the offerer's sin and pronouncing forgiveness. Milgrom even goes so far as to argue that the Priestly legislators did this, arrogating to themselves the right to "commute the death sentence imposed by the heavenly court," and in doing so, they have "overruled the will of God!"[12]

I find much to resonate with in Milgrom's thesis and argumentation. First, it leaves the traditional understanding of the Hebrew word *shegagah* intact. The offering does indeed have to do with unintentional sins. Second, it properly recognizes that "unfaithfulness" (*ma'al*) certainly goes beyond what is

7. Milgrom, *Leviticus 1–16*, 301–2.
8. Ibid., 372.
9. Ibid., 373.
10. Ibid.
11. Ibid., 374.
12. Ibid., 373.

normally thought of unintentional. Indeed, when one looks at the occurrences of the noun and the corresponding verb in the Old Testament, it is hard to escape the conclusion that *ma'al* could be seen as very much characterizing the sins that, as mentioned above, are regarded in Numbers 15:30 as sins committed with a "high hand." Representative translations for *ma'al* are terms like "unfaithful," "treacherous," "break faith," "treason," "treachery," and so on. Furthermore, it is paired up with words like "disobedience," "rebellion," and "hostility." Milgrom is certainly correct when he characterizes this as sin deserving of death.

I differ from Milgrom in two respects. First, although confession, repentance, sincerity, and heartfelt sorrow should certainly accompany the ritual sacrificial act, I do not think this alone can account for the reclassification from intentional to unintentional. Sincere repentance would be the normal accompaniment with the offerer's sacrifice in any case.

Second, this move is not to be chalked up to "Priestly legislators" who "encroached upon the divine sphere" and "arrogated to themselves the power to alter God's decree," thus overruling the "will of God."[13] Rather, this decree comes from God himself. What stands behind it? An act of sheer grace and mercy on the part of Yahweh, signaled from the very start by the harsh clash in 5:15 of the word "unfaithfulness" (*ma'al*) being used in the same sentence as the word "unintentional" (*shegagah*). Already, from the very beginning of the description, there is signaled the intention to atone for both unintentional and intentional sins, even sins that might be thought to be ones of defiance, with a "high hand." Not the priests, but God himself has issued this decree. The decree to treat intentional sins as unintentional ones comes from the same place as the decree to regard the blood of sacrificial animals to be atonement for sin. It is purely an act of grace on the part of the sovereign God.

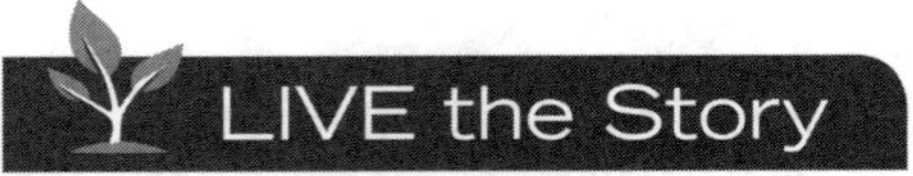

Jesus, the Guilt Offering for "Ignorant" Sinners

One of the most important passages in the Old Testament for understanding the death of Jesus Christ is Isaiah 53 (more precisely, 52:13–53:12). What is not so well recognized, and sometimes obscured by modern translations (including the NIV), is the likely reference to the guilt offering, the *'asham*,

13. Ibid., 374.

in 53:10. Altering the NIV translation to account for this would result in the following:

> Yet it was the LORD's will to crush him and cause him to suffer,
> and though the LORD makes his life a *guilt offering*,
> he will see his offspring and prolong his days,
> and the will of the LORD will prosper in his hand.
> (author's translation; emphasis added)

Not all scholars are convinced that the *'asham* in verse 10 is necessarily a reference to the guilt offering as described in Leviticus 5–6. For example, some have argued that the word was a secular term before it was a cultic/religious term, and the sense in 53:10 is more likely a reference to compensation in general rather than specifically a cultically sacrificial term.[14] This does not necessarily prevent them from seeing the servant's suffering and death as atoning in some respect. Indeed, some of them would argue that even if the *'asham* is seen as more of a general economic term, it can still be understood as the servant making restitution or reparation for the people. The servant still acts vicariously to take away the sin debt of the people, which they themselves were unable to pay, by bearing it in his own person in his suffering and death. This understanding is not implausible.

However, I think it is more likely, in light of what I consider to be other cultic/sacrificial language in the passage,[15] that the *'asham* in this verse is in fact the cultic/sacrificial *'asham*. But, if the author of this chapter wanted to portray the servant as an offering for sin, why not use the term "sin offering" rather than *'asham*, the "guilt offering"? My answer is that the *'asham* term is in fact the more appropriate one, because it actually relates more directly to the context in Isaiah 53.

The servant figure in this chapter has undergone tremendous suffering. Those sufferings are described in Isaiah 50:4–9. The servant was beaten, his beard was pulled out by his tormentors, he was mocked, and he was spat upon. Then, in 52:13–53:12, he is described as one whose "appearance was so disfigured beyond that of any human being" and whose "form [was] marred beyond human likeness" (52:14). He was a "man of suffering" and "familiar with pain" (53:4). He was despised and held in low esteem.

14. Bernd Janowski, "He Bore Our Sins: Isaiah 53 and the Drama of Taking Another's Place," in *The Suffering Servant: Isaiah 53 in Jewish and Christian Sources*, ed. Bernd Janowski and Peter Stuhlmacher (Grand Rapids: Eerdmans, 2004), 66–70.

15. See Boda, *Severe Mercy*, 208–10.

There is a "we" group in the chapter which speaks in the first-person plural. They confess that at one point they thought very ill of this servant figure. They were among those who despised him. They looked at his sufferings and concluded that he deserved them, that God was the one who was punishing him, and that he was being afflicted and stricken by God himself. Indeed, if there is a story line, a narrative plot line that connects the "Servant Songs" in the book of Isaiah (42:1–9; 49:1–13; 50:4–9; and 52:13–53:12)—and I believe there is—then it is likely that this "we" group was actively involved in afflicting suffering on the servant, thinking that they were doing God a great service in being his agents to carry out this punishment of the servant.

This "we" group was, in fact, correct in their assumption that the servant was afflicted by God. What they were mistaken about, however, was that they thought the sufferings that the LORD was inflicting on the servant were on account of the servant's own sins and transgressions—the servant was being punished for his own crimes. But then they come to the realization that the servant was not suffering for his own sins, but for their sins! They still acknowledge that the LORD "has laid on him . . . iniquity" (53:6) and that "it was the LORD's will to crush him cause him to suffer" (53:10), but now they understand that the LORD did this, not on account of the servant's wickedness but theirs.

> But he was pierced for our transgressions,
> he was crushed for our iniquities;
> the punishment that brought us peace was on him,
> and by his wounds we are healed.
> We all, like sheep, have gone astray,
> each of us has turned to our own way;
> and the LORD has laid on him
> the iniquity of us all. (53:5–6)

> For the transgression of my people he was punished. (v. 8)

And this is where the *'asham*, the guilt offering, seems to be especially appropriate. God had sent the servant to establish justice in the earth (42:1–4). The servant was especially chosen by God to "be a covenant for the people" (42:6). He was given the mission of bringing Jacob back to the LORD and gathering Israel to himself (49:5). And yet the people of Israel had despised this abhorred servant (49:7), mocked him, spat on him, and physically abused him, all the while thinking that he was cursed by God when in fact he was

God's chosen servant to restore Israel back to the God of their fathers. If ever there was an act of unfaithfulness with regard to the *sancta*, the holy things (and persons) of God, this was it. If there was ever a need for a guilt offering to atone for sinners who had acted so horribly to the LORD's own beloved servant, this was it. The author of Isaiah 53 could have chosen *hatta't*, "sin offering," to describe the sacrifice of the servant for the sins of the people. But the *'asham*, "guilt offering," seems especially appropriate in this chapter. It is appropriate because (1) it has to do with an act of unfaithfulness toward a chosen servant of the LORD, and (2) because the guilt offering, as was explained above, is especially focused (more expressly so than the sin offering) on taking a deliberate sin, which could not actually be atoned for and for which the prescribed penalty would have been death, and regarding it as an inadvertent sin. The sins of the people are reckoned to be unintentional sins that were committed in ignorance. Indeed, in some measure, this is the case, for they thought they were doing God a service by inflicting punishment on the one they considered already being punished by God.

This theme of sins committed in ignorance also continues as we come to the New Testament. I have highlighted relevant terms in the passages below.

Luke 23:34

> Jesus said, "Father, forgive them, for *they do not know* what they are doing."

Acts 3:17

> Now, fellow Israelites, I know that you acted in *ignorance*, as did your leaders.

1 Timothy 1:13–14

> Even though I was once a blasphemer and a persecutor and a violent man, I was shown mercy because I acted in *ignorance* and unbelief. The grace of our Lord was poured out on me abundantly, along with the faith and love that are in Christ Jesus.

Hebrews 5:1–3

> Every high priest is selected from among the people and is appointed to represent the people in matters related to God, to offer gifts and sacrifices for sins. He is able to deal gently with those who are *ignorant and are going astray*, since he himself is subject to *weakness*. This is why he has to offer sacrifices for his own sins, as well as for the sins of the people.

Hebrews 9:7

But only the high priest entered the inner room, and that only once a year, and never without blood, which he offered for himself and for the sins the people had committed in *ignorance*.

Hebrews 4:14–15

Therefore, since we have a great high priest who has ascended into heaven, Jesus the Son of God, let us hold firmly to the faith we profess. For we do not have a high priest who is unable to empathize with our *weaknesses*.

What is especially to be noted about these passages is that though the sins referred to are said to have been committed in ignorance, they were nevertheless committed intentionally. Forgiveness is offered to sinners who had been very intentional in committing their sinful acts, and yet they are reckoned as having committed them in ignorance, even unintentionally. This is the decree of God himself, the same God who designated his Son as a guilt offering for sin, whose precious blood renders intentional sins as unintentional ones, and who atones for them by the command and decree of God.

Additionally, I note here that even if Milgrom is correct (even partially) in his thesis that it is sinners' sincere repentance and sorrow for their sins that causes their sins to be moved from deliberate to inadvertent, in the New Testament even repentance is seen as effected by God in the sinner's heart (emphases added):

Acts 5:31

God exalted him to his own right hand as Prince and Savior *that he might bring Israel to repentance* and forgive their sins.

Acts 11:18b

So then, even to Gentiles *God has granted repentance* that leads to life.

Romans 2:4

Or do you show contempt for the riches of his kindness, forbearance and patience, not realizing that *God's kindness is intended to lead you to repentance*?

2 Timothy 2:25

Opponents must be gently instructed, *in the hope that God will grant them repentance* leading them to a knowledge of the truth.

In sum, regarding all the sins that people can commit, this verse from the book of Psalms sums up what God is doing in the sacrificial system, in the sin offering, and especially the guilt offering:

> Psalm 103:13–14 (emphasis added)
> As a father has compassion on his children,
> so the LORD has compassion on those who fear him;
> *for he knows how we are formed,*
> *he remembers that we are dust.*

In the Live the Story section in chapter 4, in noting that Christ is the fulfillment of the sin offering, I remarked that in some respect we cannot live out the story but can only worship the one who has become the sin offering and has already lived out the story in his own life and death as a sacrifice for sin (pp. 81–82). The same thing could be said for this chapter with relation to the guilt offering. However, I would like to go on to note that if God has shown such grace to us in sympathizing with us in our weakness, to forgive us in our ignorance, and to reckon our deliberate sins to be inadvertent ones, then that means it also imperative for us to show the same grace, mercy, compassion, and forgiveness to those who have sinned against us. To put the issue in a Shakespearian-like phrase, "To forgive or not to forgive—that is ***NOT*** the question!" Forgiveness for the Christian is not optional, it is imperative.

> Matthew 6:14–15
> For if you forgive other people when they sin against you, your heavenly Father will also forgive you. But if you do not forgive others their sins, your Father will not forgive your sins.

> Matthew 18:35
> This is how my heavenly Father will treat each of you unless you forgive your brother or sister from your heart.

> Mark 11:25
> And when you stand praying, if you hold anything against anyone, forgive them, so that your Father in heaven may forgive you your sins.

> Luke 17:3–4
> If your brother or sister sins against you, rebuke them; and if they repent, forgive them. Even if they sin against you seven times in a

day and seven times come back to you saying "I repent," you must forgive them.[16]

Ephesians 4:32

Be kind and compassionate to one another, forgiving each other, just as in Christ God forgave you.

Colossians 3:13

Bear with each other and forgive one another if any of you has a grievance against someone. Forgive as the Lord forgave you.

Dietrich Bonhoeffer has put it especially well:

There is another kind of suffering and shame which the Christian is not spared. While it is true that only the sufferings of Christ are a means of atonement, yet since he has suffered for and borne the sins of the whole world and shares with his disciples the fruits of his passion, the Christian also has to undergo temptation, he too has to bear the sins of others; he too must bear their shame and be driven like a scapegoat from the gate of the city. . . . "Bear ye one another's burdens, and so fulfill the law of Christ" (Gal. 6.2). As Christ bears our burdens, so ought we to bear the burdens of our fellow-men. The law of Christ, which it is our duty to fulfil, is the bearing of the cross. My brother's burden which I must bear is not only his outward lot, his natural characteristics and gifts, but quite literally his sin. And the only way to bear that sin is by forgiving it in the power of the cross of Christ in which I now share. Thus the call to follow Christ always means a call to share the work of forgiving men their sins. Forgiveness is the Christlike suffering which it is the Christian's duty to bear.[17]

In sum, if I as a Christian have been forgiven by God in my ignorance and even my intentional waywardness, then, if I do not forgive, I have not been forgiven. If I withhold forgiveness, then perhaps it is because I am not remembering that I am Christian who has been forgiven.[18]

16. I do believe that, though a Christian should have an attitude in which they are ready to forgive, the actual forgiveness is conditional on repentance (see, for example, Luke 17:3–4).

17. Dietrich Bonhoeffer, *The Cost of Discipleship*, rev. ed. (New York: MacMillan, 1963), 100.

18. I have put this paragraph in the first-person singular. This is how I judge myself. This means that I do not necessarily have the right to judge another for how they forgive, especially in particularly egregious situations—though I would still encourage them to forgive the truly remorseful and repentant offender.

For a recent example of what I am referring to here, consider the statement that Rachael Denhollander made in January, 2018, at the trial of Dr. Larry Nassar, in which Nassar was convicted for multiple instances of sexual abuse committed against members of the United States women's gymnastic team, as well other female athletes he had treated over a number of years. Denhollander, during her victim impact statement, addresses Nassar directly and says:

> Should you ever reach the point of truly facing what you have done, the guilt will be crushing. And that is what makes the gospel of Christ so sweet. Because it extends grace and hope and mercy where none should be found. And it will be there for you. I pray you experience the soul crushing weight of guilt so you may someday experience true repentance and true forgiveness from God, which you need far more than forgiveness from me—though I extend that to you as well.[19]

Such forgiveness is not easy. And it is costly. Christ tells us to take up our cross and follow him. Sometimes we employ the language of cross-bearing far too lightly and far too casually. The cross we bear is not some physical ailment—whether it be an ingrown toenail or a deadly cancer. It is not some financial setback or the loss of a job. It is not loneliness or the loss of loved ones.

Rather, it is those things we actively do to share in the sufferings of Christ. And since Christ, when he was crucified, asked his Father to forgive those who played their various roles in his crucifixion, it would seem that the act of taking up our cross and following Christ involves first and foremost forgiving those whom we consider to have done us wrong. Furthermore, it must be an action we are prepared to do every day for all our lives. We take up our cross daily and follow him. We ask God to forgive those who have trespassed against us. We cannot very well ask God to forgive them unless we are prepared to forgive them as well. The Christian's daily cross is to forgive sins.

An Interesting Postscript

I referred earlier to Jesus's prayer on the cross in Luke 23:34, "Father, forgive them, for they do not know what they are doing." It is interesting to think of those for whom Jesus prayed that day, and who were involved in his arrest, trial, and crucifixion. Among the participants that Luke lists were:

---

19. For the full statement, see CNN, "Read Rachael Denhollander's full victim impact statement about Larry Nassar," 30 January 2018," *CNN*, https://www.cnn.com/2018/01/24/us/rachael-denhollander-full-statement/index.html.

Roman soldiers (including a centurion and regular soldiers)
Pharisees
Priests and Sadducees (the primary members of the Sanhedrin)
A large crowd

When we then turn to the book of Acts, the second volume of Luke's two-volume work, it is instructive, then, to notice some of the converts to the faith to which Luke calls attention:

A Roman centurion (Acts 10)
A Roman jailer (Acts 16)
A Pharisee (Acts 9; see also 15:5)
A number of priests (Acts 6:7)
A large crowd (Acts 2:36–41)

It seems that for those whom Jesus prayed for forgiveness, there are representative figures in the book of Acts who came to faith, receiving the forgiveness that is to be found in Christ Jesus. Forgiveness is, indeed, the way of the kingdom. More pointedly, it is the way of evangelism, the way in which the good news, the gospel, is spread. The church is founded on, and propagated by, forgiveness—and not just the forgiveness which Jesus offers, but also that which is offered by his followers (Stephen, Acts 7:60—"Lord, do not hold this sin against them").

Again, forgiveness is not an option. It is, in fact, a *sine qua non* for the Christian faith, and for the very existence of the church of Jesus Christ.

CHAPTER 6

Leviticus 6:8–7:38[1]

LISTEN to the Story

[6:8]The LORD said to Moses: [9]"Give Aaron and his sons this command: 'These are the regulations for the burnt offering: The burnt offering is to remain on the altar hearth throughout the night, till morning, and the fire must be kept burning on the altar. [10]The priest shall then put on his linen clothes, with linen undergarments next to his body, and shall remove the ashes of the burnt offering that the fire has consumed on the altar and place them beside the altar. [11]Then he is to take off these clothes and put on others, and carry the ashes outside the camp to a place that is ceremonially clean. [12]The fire on the altar must be kept burning; it must not go out. Every morning the priest is to add firewood and arrange the burnt offering on the fire and burn the fat of the fellowship offerings on it. [13]The fire must be kept burning on the altar continuously; it must not go out.

[14]"'These are the regulations for the grain offering: Aaron's sons are to bring it before the LORD, in front of the altar. [15]The priest is to take a handful of the finest flour and some olive oil, together with all the incense on the grain offering, and burn the memorial portion on the altar as an aroma pleasing to the LORD. [16]Aaron and his sons shall eat the rest of it, but it is to be eaten without yeast in the sanctuary area; they are to eat it in the courtyard of the tent of meeting. [17]It must not be baked with yeast; I have given it as their share of the food offerings presented to me. Like the sin offering and the guilt offering, it is most holy. [18]Any male descendant of Aaron may eat it. For all generations to come it is his perpetual share of the food offerings presented to the LORD. Whatever touches them will become holy.'"

[19]The LORD also said to Moses, [20]"This is the offering Aaron and his sons are to bring to the LORD on the day he is anointed: a tenth of an

1. Note that the English and Hebrew verse enumerations are slightly out of sync here. English 6:8–30 is in the Hebrew text 6:1–23. Beginning at 7:1, the enumerations are the same again.

ephah of the finest flour as a regular grain offering, half of it in the morning and half in the evening. 21It must be prepared with oil on a griddle; bring it well-mixed and present the grain offering broken in pieces as an aroma pleasing to the Lord. 22The son who is to succeed him as anointed priest shall prepare it. It is the Lord's perpetual share and is to be burned completely. 23Every grain offering of a priest shall be burned completely; it must not be eaten."

24The Lord said to Moses, 25"Say to Aaron and his sons: 'These are the regulations for the sin offering: The sin offering is to be slaughtered before the Lord in the place the burnt offering is slaughtered; it is most holy. 26The priest who offers it shall eat it; it is to be eaten in the sanctuary area, in the courtyard of the tent of meeting. 27Whatever touches any of the flesh will become holy, and if any of the blood is spattered on a garment, you must wash it in the sanctuary area. 28The clay pot the meat is cooked in must be broken; but if it is cooked in a bronze pot, the pot is to be scoured and rinsed with water. 29Any male in a priest's family may eat it; it is most holy. 30But any sin offering whose blood is brought into the tent of meeting to make atonement in the Holy Place must not be eaten; it must be burned up.

7:1" 'These are the regulations for the guilt offering, which is most holy: 2The guilt offering is to be slaughtered in the place where the burnt offering is slaughtered, and its blood is to be splashed against the sides of the altar. 3All its fat shall be offered: the fat tail and the fat that covers the internal organs, 4both kidneys with the fat on them near the loins, and the long lobe of the liver, which is to be removed with the kidneys. 5The priest shall burn them on the altar as a food offering presented to the Lord. It is a guilt offering. 6Any male in a priest's family may eat it, but it must be eaten in the sanctuary area; it is most holy.

7" 'The same law applies to both the sin offering and the guilt offering: They belong to the priest who makes atonement with them. 8The priest who offers a burnt offering for anyone may keep its hide for himself. 9Every grain offering baked in an oven or cooked in a pan or on a griddle belongs to the priest who offers it, 10and every grain offering, whether mixed with olive oil or dry, belongs equally to all the sons of Aaron.

11" 'These are the regulations for the fellowship offering anyone may present to the Lord:

12" 'If they offer it as an expression of thankfulness, then along with this

thank offering they are to offer thick loaves made without yeast and with
olive oil mixed in, thin loaves made without yeast and brushed with oil,
and thick loaves of the finest flour well-kneaded and with oil mixed in.
[13]Along with their fellowship offering of thanksgiving they are to present
an offering with thick loaves of bread made with yeast. [14]They are to bring
one of each kind as an offering, a contribution to the LORD; it belongs
to the priest who splashes the blood of the fellowship offering against the
altar. [15]The meat of their fellowship offering of thanksgiving must be eaten
on the day it is offered; they must leave none of it till morning.

[16]" 'If, however, their offering is the result of a vow or is a freewill offering, the sacrifice shall be eaten on the day they offer it, but anything left
over may be eaten on the next day. [17]Any meat of the sacrifice left over till
the third day must be burned up. [18]If any meat of the fellowship offering
is eaten on the third day, the one who offered it will not be accepted. It
will not be reckoned to their credit, for it has become impure; the person
who eats any of it will be held responsible.

[19]" 'Meat that touches anything ceremonially unclean must not be
eaten; it must be burned up. As for other meat, anyone ceremonially
clean may eat it. [20]But if anyone who is unclean eats any meat of the
fellowship offering belonging to the LORD, they must be cut off from
their people. [21]Anyone who touches something unclean—whether human
uncleanness or an unclean animal or any unclean creature that moves along
the ground—and then eats any of the meat of the fellowship offering
belonging to the LORD must be cut off from their people.' "

[22]The LORD said to Moses, [23]"Say to the Israelites: 'Do not eat any of
the fat of cattle, sheep or goats. [24]The fat of an animal found dead or torn
by wild animals may be used for any other purpose, but you must not
eat it. [25]Anyone who eats the fat of an animal from which a food offering
may be presented to the LORD must be cut off from their people. [26]And
wherever you live, you must not eat the blood of any bird or animal.
[27]Anyone who eats blood must be cut off from their people.' "

[28]The LORD said to Moses, [29]"Say to the Israelites: 'Anyone who brings
a fellowship offering to the LORD is to bring part of it as their sacrifice to
the LORD. [30]With their own hands they are to present the food offering to
the LORD; they are to bring the fat, together with the breast, and wave the
breast before the LORD as a wave offering. [31]The priest shall burn the fat
on the altar, but the breast belongs to Aaron and his sons. [32]You are to give

the right thigh of your fellowship offerings to the priest as a contribution.
[33]The son of Aaron who offers the blood and the fat of the fellowship offering shall have the right thigh as his share. [34]From the fellowship offerings
of the Israelites, I have taken the breast that is waved and the thigh that
is presented and have given them to Aaron the priest and his sons as their
perpetual share from the Israelites.'"

[35]This is the portion of the food offerings presented to the LORD that
were allotted to Aaron and his sons on the day they were presented to
serve the LORD as priests. [36]On the day they were anointed, the LORD
commanded that the Israelites give this to them as their perpetual share
for the generations to come.

[37]These, then, are the regulations for the burnt offering, the grain
offering, the sin offering, the guilt offering, the ordination offering and
the fellowship offering, [38]which the LORD gave Moses at Mount Sinai in
the Desert of Sinai on the day he commanded the Israelites to bring their
offerings to the LORD.

Listening to the Text in the Story: Biblical Texts: Exodus 29:38–46; Leviticus 1:1–6:7; Ancient Near Eastern Texts: Instructions to Priests and Temple Officials (Hittite)

The instructions in this section are primarily supplementary to the previous chapters in Leviticus. They are concerned with the practices and procedures of the priests in handling the sacrificial offerings rather than with the responsibilities of the ordinary Israelites in presenting their sacrifices. The passage recalls prior instructions, such as those given in Exodus 29:38–46, but expands and goes beyond those instructions considerably. It also deals with what are referred to as the perquisites and prebends of the priests—that is, the portions of the sacrifices that go to the priests as partial compensation for their priestly services, and also to members of their families. However, the section closes by providing stern warnings with regard to carelessness and laxity in following these instructions, including the possibility of being cut off from the people and from God.

Other ancient Near Eastern documents also provide instructions concerning the care with which priests were to carry out their activities. The Hittite document Instructions to Priests and Temple Officials actually draws a comparison between divine and human masters. It asks the question:

> [Are] the mind of man and god somehow different? No! In this which is [concerned]? No! The mind is one and the same. . . . Is the mind of the god somehow different?[2]

The understanding here is that human masters expect their servants to carry out dutifully the instructions given to them. In the same way, the deity expects his priests to follow all the prescribed regulations meticulously. The document goes on to note that human masters will punish their servants who fail to carry out their duties responsibly; it also notes that the punishments will extend to their servants' families. Similarly, the document says

> if, however, someone angers the mind of a god, does the god seek it (revenge) only from him alone? Does he not seek it from his wife, [his children,] his descendants, his family, his male and female servants, his cattle, his sheep and his grain? He utterly destroys him with everything. Be very afraid of a god's word for your own sake.[3]

The idea is that even as the priest's household benefits from the compensation the priest receives, the priest's family will also suffer the punishment that will be executed on the priest if he fails to carry out his duties responsibly and diligently. Among the various transgressions against which this document warns are: priests taking beyond what is allowed for their perquisites, failure to present proper sacrifices properly, failure to carry out the rituals at the appointed times, and failure to protect the holiness and sanctity of the temple.

EXPLAIN the Story

In commentaries, this passage is regularly understood to be dealing with instructions for priests rather than laity. However, there are two important qualifications to be made to his generalization:

1. While it is true that the priests seem to be the primary addressees, there are nevertheless instructions here for the laity as well, particularly in three sections: 7:11–21, 22–27, and 28–36.

---

2. "Instructions to Priests and Temple Officials," *COS* 1.83:217.
3. Ibid., 218.

2. Even for the passages where the instructions are primarily for the priests, it is important to note that these instructions are not hidden away in a kind of secret manual for the priest's eyes only. Rather, all Israel is to be aware of them. Milgrom expresses this well:

> There can be no esoteric doctrine hidden away in priestly archives: "the Torah commanded us by Moses is the heritage of the congregation of Jacob" (Deut 33:4).[4]

If the priests do not carry out the instructions precisely as God directs, the repercussions are not for the priests alone but for their families, their households, and, indeed, for the entire people of Israel. The laity have a vested interest in the priests' diligent performance of their duties. It is not just the priests who will be punished for not following correct procedures; the people will experience the results as well, perhaps even to the point of being cut off from God. So even the laity have a role to play here.

This passage may be broken down into the following sets of regulations:

6:8–13[6:1–6] (Burnt Offering)
6:14–23[6:7–16] (Grain Offering)
6:24–30[6:17–23] (Sin Offering)
7:1–10 (Guilt Offering)
7:11–21 (Fellowship Offering)
7:22–27 (Prohibition against Consumption of Blood and Fat)
7:28–38 (The Priests' Portions)

The Burnt Offering (6:8–13)

The burnt offering spoken of in these verses is not the one brought by individual Israelites but rather one offered for the entire community each morning and evening (Exod 29:42; Num 28:1–8). This offering is to be kept burning on the altar at all times, but it is especially prescribed that it must be kept burning throughout the night till morning. Several reasons have been suggested for this requirement. Three of the most plausible suggestions are that:

1. This commandment anticipates the narrative in chapter 9 of how, when the newly ordained priests began their ministry and offered their first burnt offering, fire came out from the presence of the Lord and set

4. Milgrom, *Leviticus 1–16*, 618.

the burnt offering on fire. So, the perpetually burning burnt offering is seen as being one with, and a continuation of, the fire that came from God himself. This was also argued by John Calvin, who said that in this way all subsequent "offerings should be burnt with heavenly fire."[5] Additionally, Gorman points out that as the morning and evening burnt offerings mark out the day, it serves as a reminder of the "foundational act of creation" in Genesis 1:3–5, with light being called out of darkness, and even provides "one means for Israel to participate in the ongoing order of creation and creative activity of God."[6]

2. The perpetually burning offering symbolizes the continuing validity and divine acceptance of the offerings on Israel's behalf. It simultaneously reminded the Israelites of their sinfulness and need of atonement and forgiveness, and of how God had been propitiated and had accepted these offerings as atonement.
3. The light and the smoke from the perpetually burning offering, at the very center of the camp, was a constant reminder that God had taken up residence with the Israelites; he was ever present among them. His "camp fire" was always burning and assured the Israelites that he was still in their midst, and this called for continued worship from the Israelites as well.[7]

I believe it may well be the case that all three suggestions are correct.

The Grain Offering (6:14–23)

The grain offering described here, like the burnt offering, refers to a community offering rather than that of individuals. It is important to note the amount of attention paid to the priests' consumption of the grain offering. If the grain offering is presented on behalf of the priest, no one may eat of it. But for the regular grain offering, several directions are given for the priestly consumption of the offering. While on the one hand the grain offering serves as a perquisite for the priest, a measure of compensation for his services, it is important to note that there is more at stake here than just taking care of the priest. As Levine notes, the priests' consumption of the grain offering "was considered indispensable to the efficacy of the ritual."[8] The same thing is true for the sin offering and the guilt offering. We will examine the reason for this in the commentary for chapter 10 (see Explain the Story, pp. 146–47).

5. Calvin, *Last Four Books of Moses*, 2:364.
6. Gorman, *Divine Presence*, 45.
7. On this, see Tidball, *Message of Leviticus*, 98.
8. Levine, *Leviticus*, 37.

The Sin Offering (6:24–30)

Again, it seems that the main concern in this passage is the consumption of the offering by the priest. As with the grain offering, the meat of the sin offering provided food for the priest, as well as for any males in his family. Also, as with the grain offering, the sin offering was to be eaten in the courtyard of the tabernacle. However, as is the case with the grain offering, the priestly consumption of the sin offering goes beyond simply providing food for the priest. It also contributes to the efficacy of the sacrifice. We will look at why this is the case in the commentary for chapter 10, but by way of anticipating the answer to be given there, I call attention to Ross's comments that the priest was to consume the meat of the sin offering "as a sign that the sacrifice was accepted and that forgiveness was complete."[9] In the commentary on chapter 10, however, I will argue that this is not simply a sign but that the consumption actually contributes to the efficacy of the offering (see Explain the Story, pp. 146–47).

The Guilt Offering (7:1–10)

As with the previous passages on the grain and sin offerings, this passage deals primarily with the perquisite for the priest and the consumption by the priest and the male members of his family. Verses 6–7 are especially significant. After mentioning that the priest or any male in his family may eat from the meat of the guilt offering (actually, the officiating priest "must" do so, and the male in his family "may" do so), the text goes on to note that this is true for both the sin and the guilt offerings, and for the "priest who makes atonement with them." Again, this suggests that there is some connection with the atonement accomplished by these offerings and the priestly consumption of them.

In addition to the perquisite of the meat of the guilt offering, the text notes in verse 8 that the hide of the sacrificed animal also belongs to the priest.[10] Milgrom calls attention to several ancient Near Eastern texts where the hides of the sacrificial animals are variously distributed—in some texts to the priests, in other texts to the offerer.[11] Noordtzij has argued that even in this detail the priestly reception of the hide is symbolic of the atonement, since the offerer's person (as well as his sin) has been transferred to the hide of the animal.[12]

---

9. Allen P. Ross, *Holiness to the Lord: A Guide to the Exposition of the Book of Leviticus* (Grand Rapids: Baker Academic, 2002), 169; Hartley, *Leviticus*, 98; Derek Kidner, *Sacrifice in the Old Testament* (London: Tyndale, 1952), 21.

10. George Athas has suggested to me that the hide could have been used personally by the priest for clothing or other leather items, or perhaps even sold for income (personal communication, 2018).

11. Milgrom, *Leviticus 1–16*, 411.

12. Noordtzij, *Leviticus*, 81.

The Fellowship Offering (7:11–21)

This passage on the fellowship offering indicates that in the relatively brief instructions given for all the sacrifices there may be a number of details that are left out and that the instructions in any one place may be incomplete. For the fellowship offering in particular, we learn here that, in addition to the animal offering that was already mentioned in chapter 3, loaves of bread are to be presented as well, some unleavened and some with leaven. It is perhaps a bit of a surprise for us that leavened loaves of bread could be presented. But these loaves were for the priest in particular (not to be placed on the altar[13]) and were perhaps symbolic of the "entirety of the produce of the land."[14]

The meat of the fellowship offering had to be consumed either on the day of its presentation or the next day. It could not be eaten on the third day. There are two interesting things to note here. First, if any of the meat was eaten on the third day, the sacrifice was rendered invalid. Second, if the sacrifice was reckoned to be invalid, it was not credited to the offerer. This highlights the fact that even though the fellowship offering was not a required offering and was not an atoning offering at the same level as were the sin and guilt offerings, it was nevertheless a kind of propitiatory offering, one that was meant to please or placate the deity; it could, in some respect, be reckoned as credited to the offerer's account. It is not clear exactly how this credit or non-credit would have been reckoned. Was there a record kept in a ledger at the tabernacle/temple? Or was this reckoning done in heaven? In any case, the sacrifice had to be offered and the meat eaten in such a way that pleased the Lord.

Prohibition against Consumption of Blood and Fat (7:22–27)

This prohibition had already been given in 3:17. The prohibition against drinking blood is absolute. But verse 25 suggests that the prohibition against eating fat may have been limited to animals eligible for sacrifice. In other words, if the Israelites killed animals for food that would not have been offered in sacrifice (such as deer), it is possible that in those cases there would be no prohibition regarding the consumption of the fat. But this is a disputed interpretation.

The Priests' Portions (7:28–38)

Though there have already been several references in these two chapters to the priestly share of the offerings, these last verses address the issue with more focus, especially with regard to the fellowship offering. Though it is not

---

13. Milgrom, *Leviticus 1–16*, 414.
14. Hess, "Leviticus," 640.

completely clear in the text, Milgrom suggests that the offerers themselves are to present their offerings in such a way that the priests' share is already separated from what is to be offered on the altar.

For the first time in the book we come across the term "wave offering." While most modern translations render the Hebrew *tenufah* as "wave offering," some more recent commentators, as well as some translations (NRSV, NJPS), think it should be rendered as "elevation offering"—that is, it is not waved in some kind of horizontal back and forth or side to side motion, but simply lifted up to the LORD in one simple, vertical motion.[15] This understanding seems preferable.

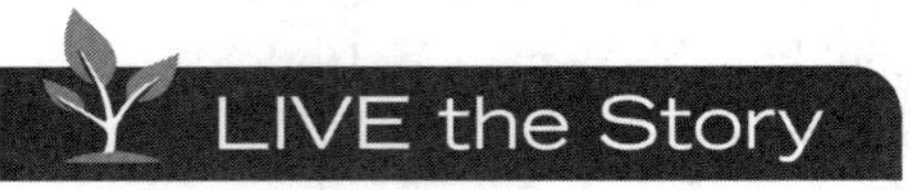

Caring for Those Whose Work Is Related to the Gospel

No doubt with our present passage in the back of his mind, the apostle Paul argues that those who dedicate their time to the ministry and propagation of the gospel should be compensated for their labor.

> Don't you know that those who serve in the temple get their food from the temple, and that those who serve at the altar share in what is offered on the altar? In the same way, the Lord has commanded that those who preach the gospel should receive their living from the gospel. (1 Cor 9:13–14)

The ministers and leaders of our church and parachurch organizations who, in dedicating themselves to the work of the ministry, have set aside regular and perhaps more lucrative ways of earning a living should be properly compensated for their labor in the work of the ministry. It is right and appropriate that we should cheerfully, and not begrudgingly, do all we can to make sure that our ministers and Christian workers are well taken care of so that they do not have to be concerned about their livelihoods. This section of Leviticus teaches us that those who benefit spiritually from those engaged in ministry should share monetarily with those so engaged.

The Need for an Educated Ministry *and* an Educated Laity

Seminaries exist because there was a recognized need that the church's ministers should have a good understanding of biblical literature, theology, church

15. Milgrom, *Leviticus 1–16*, 461–73.

history, practical theology, and so on. So, to a certain extent, despite some of the problems with the term "laity," there should be a kind of clergy/laity distinction, at least with regard to expertise and the professional exercise of ministry. Nevertheless, as we have seen in this present passage, even though the instructions are addressed to the priestly personnel, these instructions were not placed in a secretive private manual to which only the priests had access but instead were canonized in Scripture and were either read by or read aloud to ordinary Israelites. In this way even the laity were engaged in at least a measure of oversight of the priests to make sure the duties were performed diligently as commanded. After all, their sacrifices, their atonement, their forgiveness of sins, and their purification were all at stake based on the priest's diligence in carrying out his assigned ritual tasks. In the same way today, lay Christians in the church, to a certain extent, have oversight of the leaders in the church and should be educated in matters biblical and theological to the point where they can at least recognize overt departures from the biblical narrative and correct theology. The laity, too, have a role to play in assuring that the church is being faithful in its understanding of Scripture, maintenance of correct doctrine, and the ethical and responsible exercise of ministry.

The Diligence Required in the Exercise of the Ministry

One of the interesting things in this passage is the care that has to be exercised on the part of the priest *after* the sacrifice itself. The same diligence that is required in the presentation and offering of the sacrifice has to be present *post-sacrifice*. This highlights the seriousness and gravity of all the instructions given in these chapters. Tidball puts it appropriately and eloquently:

> The God of Israel was not to be worshipped in any slipshod manner, with rituals being hastily thrown together at the last minute according to the fancy of either the priest or the people. . . . The responsibilities of those who lead worship under the new covenant are no less than those of the priest of old.[16]

Wenham also appropriately notes that

> spontaneity and lack of preparation are equated with spirituality. Lev. 6–7 denies this: care and attention to detail are indispensable to the conduct of divine worship. God is more important, more distinguished, worthy of

16. Tidball, *Message of Leviticus*, 97.

> more respect than any man; therefore we should follow his injunctions to the letter, if we respect him.[17]

The reason for this meticulous attention to detail required of priests and people was that these services and offerings were done in obedience to a holy God. And this God is certainly no less holy today than he was when these instructions were first given.

Eternal Fire, Eternal Light, Eternal Presence, Eternal Hope

One of the most enjoyable things about camping is the campfire. There is a kind of campground sociology to which the lighting of multiple campfires contributes. There is something reassuring, comforting, unifying, even exciting, knowing that all around you are other campers, sitting around a campfire, eating, singing, telling stories, and just having a good time. But every good evening eventually has come to an end. As you get ready to retire for the night into your tent and begin to put out your campfire, and your fellow campers begin to do the same, it can actually be a bit of a letdown—all those campfires, one by one being extinguished till there are only one or two burning, and eventually none.

For forty years the Israelites wandered through the wilderness. Every night was a camping night. Every night was a campfire night.[18] But eventually they would put those fires out and retire to their tents. Perhaps an Israelite might exit their tent during the night to be met, especially on moonless nights, by deep darkness. But if they looked toward the center of the camp, they would see smoke rising, and perhaps even the flames that were causing the smoke, from the altar of burnt offering in the courtyard of the tabernacle. Corresponding to the lights of the golden lampstand that burned throughout the night inside the covered tabernacle proper, the fire on the altar of burnt offering in the uncovered courtyard was never allowed to go out. So on the darkest night, outside their tents, the Israelites could look toward the center of the camp where the tabernacle was and be assured by the fire and smoke rising from the altar of burnt offering that their God, their Creator, their King, was present in the camp.[19] God was with them. He dwelled among them. His tent was set up just like their tents were set up. The King was in residence.

---

17. Wenham, *Leviticus*, 128.

18. It is clear in the biblical text that Israelites did have campfires at their tents. It is less clear what they used for fuel and how plentiful and readily accessible that fuel would have been.

19. Of course, it should be noted that there was also the cloud above the tabernacle, which at night had the appearance of fire (Num 9:15–16).

The smoke and flames assured the Israelites that God had taken up residence among them. Though he was in his tent, he was not sleeping there; rather, he was keeping vigil over them, just as he had done earlier on the night of the first Passover (Exod 12:42). And this God would protect them from their enemies and would go with them and lead them into battle.

Perhaps even more than this went through their minds. Perhaps the flames reminded them that this God was a holy God, a consuming fire. Additionally, they knew that the smoke and flames were rising from the altar of burnt offering. They knew this was the place where they brought their sacrifices to be slaughtered and then offered on the altar. And they were reminded that if they offended this holy God, he had also provided a means of atonement for them. He had blessed them with livestock, and he had designated that the blood of an animal they offered from their herds or flocks could atone for their sins, and they would be forgiven.

The smoke and flames reminded them of God's eternal presence among them, his protection, his holiness, and the mercy of God in providing atonement for them and forgiveness of their sins. They also knew that the fire burning on that altar had come directly from God himself.

Interestingly, a number of these themes come together in the lyrics of a song that some have even suggested should replace "The Star Spangled Banner" as the United States's national anthem. During the Civil War, Julia Ward Howe wrote the very popular "Battle Hymn of the Republic." The second verse is as follows:

> I have seen Him in the watch-fires of a hundred circling camps,
> They have builded Him an altar in the evening dews and damps;
> I can read His righteous sentence by the dim and flaring lamps:
> His day is marching on.

The "watch-fires of a hundred circling camps" refers to the campfires of the Union Army soldiers. The vision of all these campfires seems to have raised a vision in Howe's imagination that they collectively constituted an "altar" for God (even as the Israelites would have been reminded by the flames and smoke of the altar of burnt offering). The "righteous sentence" recalls the idea of the judgment of God, one that is in accord with his righteousness, his holiness. Perhaps thoughts very similar to these were in the minds of the Israelites as they saw the smoke and flames rising from God's campfire.

Earlier in this chapter, I called attention to Gorman's observation that the rituals of the morning and evening burnt offerings, as well as the fact that the fire of the altar of burnt offering had to be kept burning perpetually, served to tie the prescribed rituals of Leviticus to the act of creation in Genesis. Gorman remarks, "The construction of the day is the foundational act of creation (Gen 1:3–5)."[20] In some way the Israelites, as they offered the morning and evening offerings and kept the altar fire burning through the night, participated with God in the "ongoing order of creation,"[21] in this way creating a "new day" in the life and history of Israel.[22]

Similarly, light, candles, and candlesticks have from earliest times played an important part in the rituals of the Christian church. There are the Christmas Eve services where all the lights are turned off in the church except for the candles held by the congregants as they sing—usually "Silent Night," with its reference to "love's pure light," "radiant beams" from Christ's "holy face," and the darkness dispelling "with the dawn of redeeming grace." There are the Tenebrae services, usually on Maundy Thursday, during which the shadows darken, corresponding to the Light of the world beginning to be extinguished, as the "hour and power of darkness" (Luke 22:53, NRSV) seems to have conquered "love's pure light." And I remember, as a small boy, anxiously awaiting that night every year when, from the front porch of the house where my family lived, we could watch a part of the Easter Vigil of the Greek Orthodox Church directly across the street. We knew that at some point during this special night-before-Easter service, around midnight, the people in the church would exit and circle around the church, carrying lit candles and singing, and then return to the doors of the church and finally reenter. I did not know what they sang as they circled the church, but I have since discovered that perhaps among the words they sang that night were the following:

> *The angels in heaven, O Christ our Savior, sing of Thy resurrection. Make us on earth also worthy to hymn Thee with a pure heart.*
>
> *Let God arise, let his enemies be scattered; let those who hate him flee from before his face!*
>
> *Christ is risen from the dead, trampling down death by death, and upon those in the tombs bestowing life.*
>
> *This is the day which the Lord has made, let us rejoice and be glad in it!*

---

20. Gorman, *Divine Presence*, 45.
21. Ibid., 45.
22. Balentine, *Leviticus*, 65–66.

The light that shines in the darkness reminds us that the "hour and power of darkness" will not reign forever. The ancient Israelites, upon seeing in the middle of the night the smoke and flame from the altar, would have been reminded that the King is in residence, that one to whom they would sing when they broke camp

> Rise up, Lord!
> May your enemies be scattered;
> may your foes flee before you. (Num 10:35)

Today, as we participate in these rituals, we join not just with one another but with the redeemed of all the ages, testifying that the darkness will not forever triumph and that the light will overcome the darkness. We do not simply testify to this truth, but we participate in it. By these rituals we join in the act of world construction, envisioning an alternative reality to what the rest of the world calls reality. We participate in the establishing of the kingdom as the day of the Lord marches on. Eternal fire, eternal light, eternal presence, eternal hope.

CHAPTER 7

Leviticus 8:1–36

LISTEN to the Story

8:1 The LORD said to Moses, 2 "Bring Aaron and his sons, their garments,
the anointing oil, the bull for the sin offering, the two rams and the basket
containing bread made without yeast, 3 and gather the entire assembly at
the entrance to the tent of meeting." 4 Moses did as the LORD commanded
him, and the assembly gathered at the entrance to the tent of meeting.

5 Moses said to the assembly, "This is what the LORD has commanded
to be done." 6 Then Moses brought Aaron and his sons forward and
washed them with water. 7 He put the tunic on Aaron, tied the sash
around him, clothed him with the robe and put the ephod on him.
He also fastened the ephod with a decorative waistband, which he tied
around him. 8 He placed the breastpiece on him and put the Urim and
Thummim in the breastpiece. 9 Then he placed the turban on Aaron's
head and set the gold plate, the sacred emblem, on the front of it, as the
LORD commanded Moses.

10 Then Moses took the anointing oil and anointed the tabernacle and
everything in it, and so consecrated them. 11 He sprinkled some of the
oil on the altar seven times, anointing the altar and all its utensils and
the basin with its stand, to consecrate them. 12 He poured some of the
anointing oil on Aaron's head and anointed him to consecrate him. 13 Then
he brought Aaron's sons forward, put tunics on them, tied sashes around
them and fastened caps on them, as the LORD commanded Moses.

14 He then presented the bull for the sin offering, and Aaron and his
sons laid their hands on its head. 15 Moses slaughtered the bull and took
some of the blood, and with his finger he put it on all the horns of the
altar to purify the altar. He poured out the rest of the blood at the base
of the altar. So he consecrated it to make atonement for it. 16 Moses also
took all the fat around the internal organs, the long lobe of the liver, and
both kidneys and their fat, and burned it on the altar. 17 But the bull with

its hide and its flesh and its intestines he burned up outside the camp, as the LORD commanded Moses.

[18]He then presented the ram for the burnt offering, and Aaron and his sons laid their hands on its head. [19]Then Moses slaughtered the ram and splashed the blood against the sides of the altar. [20]He cut the ram into pieces and burned the head, the pieces and the fat. [21]He washed the internal organs and the legs with water and burned the whole ram on the altar. It was a burnt offering, a pleasing aroma, a food offering presented to the LORD, as the LORD commanded Moses.

[22]He then presented the other ram, the ram for the ordination, and Aaron and his sons laid their hands on its head. [23]Moses slaughtered the ram and took some of its blood and put it on the lobe of Aaron's right ear, on the thumb of his right hand and on the big toe of his right foot. [24]Moses also brought Aaron's sons forward and put some of the blood on the lobes of their right ears, on the thumbs of their right hands and on the big toes of their right feet. Then he splashed blood against the sides of the altar. [25]After that, he took the fat, the fat tail, all the fat around the internal organs, the long lobe of the liver, both kidneys and their fat and the right thigh. [26]And from the basket of bread made without yeast, which was before the LORD, he took one thick loaf, one thick loaf with olive oil mixed in, and one thin loaf, and he put these on the fat portions and on the right thigh. [27]He put all these in the hands of Aaron and his sons, and they waved them before the LORD as a wave offering. [28]Then Moses took them from their hands and burned them on the altar on top of the burnt offering as an ordination offering, a pleasing aroma, a food offering presented to the LORD. [29]Moses also took the breast, which was his share of the ordination ram, and waved it before the LORD as a wave offering, as the LORD commanded Moses.

[30]Then Moses took some of the anointing oil and some of the blood from the altar and sprinkled them on Aaron and his garments and on his sons and their garments. So he consecrated Aaron and his garments and his sons and their garments.

[31]Moses then said to Aaron and his sons, "Cook the meat at the entrance to the tent of meeting and eat it there with the bread from the basket of ordination offerings, as I was commanded: 'Aaron and his sons are to eat it.' [32]Then burn up the rest of the meat and the bread. [33]Do not leave the entrance to the tent of meeting for seven days, until the

days of your ordination are completed, for your ordination will last seven days. [34]What has been done today was commanded by the LORD to make atonement for you. [35]You must stay at the entrance to the tent of meeting day and night for seven days and do what the LORD requires, so you will not die; for that is what I have been commanded."

[36]So Aaron and his sons did everything the LORD commanded through Moses.

Listening to the Text in the Story: Biblical Texts: Exodus 28:1–29:46; 30:22–33; 39:1–31; 40:12–15; Ancient Near Eastern Texts: The *Zukru* Festival; Establishing a New Temple for the Goddess of the Night; The Installation of the Storm God's High Priestess

This chapter has to do with the purification and dedication of the tabernacle and its furniture, as well as the ordination of Aaron and his sons to the priestly office. The biblical passages in Exodus listed above provide background for the present chapters in Leviticus, as they introduce us to the priestly garments, the Urim and Thummim, the consecration of the priests, the sacrifices to be offered in this consecration, the anointing oil, and the anointing of the tabernacle and its furnishings.

The ancient Near Eastern texts listed above all contain parallel accounts of ritual actions comparable to those contained in the biblical account of the anointing of the tabernacle, its furnishings, and the priestly personnel.

Leviticus 8 describes how both oil and blood are utilized in the anointing process. Similarly, in The *Zukru* Festival we read for one particular ritual,

> Total: four calves and forty sheep for the consecration.
>
> After eating and drinking they rub all the stones with oil and blood.[1]

> After eating and drinking they anoint the upright stones with oil and blood.[2]

The ordination of Aaron and his sons is a seven-day process. Similarly, in Establishing a New Temple for the Goddess of the Night, the dedication and consecration of the temple was carried out over seven days, and there is also

1. "The *Zukru* Festival," *COS* 1.123:433.
2. "The *Zukru* Festival," *COS* 1.123:433

reference to the use of blood to purify the both the temple and the image of the goddess.[3]

Perhaps the text that bears the most correspondences to Leviticus 8 is a text from Emar referred to as The Installation of the Storm God's High Priestess.[4] It is the only ancient Near Eastern extrabiblical text in which there is a specific reference to a priestly figure being anointed with oil.[5] The installation is a seven-day process within a larger festival. Additionally, there are offerings, clothing in priestly garb, and the priestess's first performance of sacrifices.[6] This text is dated between approximately the fourteenth and twelfth centuries BC, which would argue for the antiquity of the procedures in this chapter.[7]

Samuel Balentine and others have cogently argued that this chapter is structured heptadically—that is, on a series of sevens, which also reflects the relationship the chapter has to the creation account:

> The transfer of authority from God to the priests comprises seven steps, each one propitiously marked by Moses' faithful enactment of what "the Lord has commanded" (vv. 4, 9, 13, 17, 21, 29, 36). . . . The seven-step process that "creates" a consecrated priesthood recalls, enacts, and ritually extends God's seven-day process of creating a world that is blessed with the possibility of being "very good." That possibility, from the priestly perspective, is part of an ongoing process. Its journey toward completion is marked by interlinked intervals of sacred "sevens": seven divine speeches that create the world (Gen. 1:1–2:4a); seven acts of obedience through which Moses completes the sanctuary (Exod. 40:19–32); seven divine speeches setting forth instructions for the holy sacrifices (Leviticus 1–7); and now seven consecrated acts that enable ordinary persons to become priests, holy stewards of sacred hopes and visions (Leviticus 8). Inside this heptadic world of ritual enactment, the ordination of Aaron and his sons

---

3. "Establishing a New Temple for the Goddess of the Night," *COS* 1.70:173–77

4. "The Installation of the Storm God's High Priestess," trans. Daniel Fleming (*COS* 1.122: 427–31).

5. Richard S. Hess, *Israelite Religions: An Archaelogical and Biblical Survey* (Grand Rapids: Baker Academic, 2007), 113.

6. For a convenient summary of this installation, see Gane, "Leviticus," 1:298.

7. Hess, *Israelite Religions*, 114; Gerald A. Klingbeil, *A Comparative Study of the Ritual of Ordination Found in Leviticus 8 and Emar 369* (Lewiston, NY: Mellen, 1998).

> is a major move founded on the hope that the world of God's creation can in fact be all that God created it to be.[8]

I find this to be an attractive and mostly correct analysis of the chapter and its relationship to Genesis 1 and Exodus 40, though it is not entirely as precise and symmetrical as he suggests. For example, even though Balentine argues that the seven acts are marked off by the phrase "what the LORD has commanded," there are actually ten references in the chapter to the LORD's commands. Additionally, the seven "acts" that Balentine points out are not uniform in their wording. Thus, alternatively to his proposed seven-act structure, it would also be possible to analyze the passage as having fewer acts or more acts, perhaps even as many as thirteen separate acts.

This possibility notwithstanding, the narrative's connections to the creation and tabernacle-related narratives in Exodus are still valid. The tabernacle is, in many respects, the new garden of Eden, and Aaron (with his sons) is the new Adam, appointed to "work and keep" (*'abad* and *shamar*) the tabernacle (Num 3:7–8; 18:5–6; Ezek 44:14), even as Adam was appointed to "work and keep" (*'abad* and *shamar*) the garden (Gen 2:15).[9] Boyce notes that there is much more attention given to the ordination of the priests and the performance of their first duties in Leviticus 8–9 than there is to the creation of the world in Genesis 1–2: "It took seven days to create the world. Likewise, it takes seven days to ordain a priest."[10] This serves to highlight what we have mentioned before: rituals are acts of world construction. The rituals in Leviticus are acts of creation that mirror the creative acts in Genesis 1–2.

The Assembly

As was noted in the last chapter, the assembly of regular Israelites, the laity, have a vested interest in what takes place in the courtyard of the tabernacle. It was important for the assembly to witness the ordination process and to be assured that Aaron and his sons were, indeed, legitimately qualified and appointed to the priestly office. We will see, at the end of chapter 9 below, that the fire that will come out from the presence of the LORD when these newly ordained priests offer their first sacrifices will testify to the authority of these priests and validate their ministry in the eyes of the congregation.[11]

---

8. Balentine, *Leviticus*, 70–71.
9. Beale, *The Temple and the Church's Mission*, 66–70.
10. Boyce, *Leviticus and Numbers*, 34.
11. Ross, *Holiness to the Lord*, 209.

The Priestly Rite of Passage

The rituals of this chapter mark a rite of passage for the priest. He is undergoing a change of status from common to holy. Commentators refer to what happens to the priests as an act of dedication—they are being dedicated to the Lord. But dedication is probably too weak a word. They are actually being offered to the Lord. Moses "brought Aaron and his sons forward" (Lev 8:6). The word "brought" is the Hebrew *qarab*, the same word that has been used before in the book to describe how the Israelites "brought" their sacrifices to the Lord. The priests are envisioned as offerings made to the Lord. As such, they cross a border that changes their status from common to holy. Interestingly, later in Numbers 8:11, the Levites are regarded as a wave or elevation offering to the Lord.

The High Priest's Clothing

We will not be able to look at the individual articles of clothing that the high priest was to wear; these have already been detailed in Exodus 28.[12] We can note, however, the close correlation between the priestly garb and the materials used in the construction of the tabernacle, suggesting that the one who will work in and guard the holiness of the tabernacle must dress in a way that corresponds to the holiness of tabernacle and even participate in that holiness.[13] Boyce suggests that this is also supposed to recall the garden of Eden scene, after the fall, when Adam's insufficient attire in the presence of God was replaced with God-authorized proper attire; the one who would "draw close to the Lord of the universe must put on some reflectively royal clothes."[14] The priest's clothing "contributed to the splendor and majesty of the worship of Yahweh at the tent of meeting. They also bore witness to his endowment with authority to minister on behalf of the people before the great and holy God."[15] Kleinig argues that the clothing was not merely symbolic but actually "conferred that holy office on the priest."[16]

In this connection, Nancy Erickson has recently argued that, analagous to Egyptian cultic rituals, the clothing that the Israelite high priest wears, corresponding as it does to the *housing* of the tabernacle, contributes to a "role-play"

---

12. For further information on this, see the Exodus commentary in this series.

13. For an enlightening discussion of these correspondences, see Menahem Haran, *Temples and Temple-Service in Ancient Israel: An Inquiry into the Character of Cult Phenomena and the Historical Setting of the Priestly School* (Oxford: Clarendon, 1978), 165–74; Milgrom, *Leviticus 1–16*, 502–4, 548–49.

14. Boyce, *Leviticus and Numbers*, 33.

15. Hartley, *Leviticus*, 112.

16. Kleinig, *Leviticus*, 198.

in which the priest, in essence, represents Yahweh.[17] This dovetails nicely with the understanding of Jonathan Klawans that the high priest, in his actions, is the *imago dei*, the image of God[18] (see more on this in the commentary on Leviticus 10 (Explain the Story, pp. 144–47).

The Anointing with Oil

Of special interest here is that both the tabernacle with all its furnishings and the high priest are anointed (it is not specifically stated that the regular priests are anointed). The same verb (*mashah*; see 8:10) is used to refer to the anointing of both. Even as the priest's clothing was reflective of the materials of the tabernacle, so his anointing is one with the tabernacle's as well. He is holy as the tabernacle and all its furnishings are holy.

Noordtzij has appropriately noted that in the case of the high priest, his anointing, while serving as an act of dedication and consecration, perhaps primarily indicates that they have been chosen for the office.[19]

The Offerings

Three offerings are made in this ordination process: a sin offering, a burnt offering, and an ordination offering. There is a question as to exactly what the sin offering accomplishes in this ordination process. In verse 15 the NIV translates the last sentence as, "So he [Moses] consecrated it [the altar] to make atonement for it." However, various commentators have argued that the last phrase should be translated "to make atonement upon it"; the altar is not being atoned for but consecrated so that atonement offerings can be made on it.[20] This latter view seems preferable. To consecrate (*qadash*; "make holy") would not normally be used to refer to purifying an object or atoning for it but for dedicating it for a particular usage—in this case, designating the altar as the place where atonement is to be made.

The Anointing with Blood

For the ordination offering Moses was directed to apply the blood of the ram to the lobe of Aaron's right ear, the thumb of his right hand, and the big toe of his right foot. Gorman notes that the same procedure is done with

17. My thanks to Nancy for sharing this paper with me, which she read at the 2020 Virtual Annual Meeting of the American Schools of Overseas Research, titled, "Dressing Up: Role-Playing in the *wpt-r* Ritual and a Contextualized View of the Biblical Priesthood" (19, November 2020).

18. Jonathan Klawans, *Purity, Sacrifice, and the Temple: Symbolism and Supersessionism in the Study of Ancient Judaism* (Oxford: Oxford University Press, 2006), 62–66.

19. Noordtzij, *Leviticus*, 96.

20. For example, Levine, *Leviticus*, 52; Milgrom, *Leviticus 1–16*, 524–25.

the skin-diseased persons in Leviticus 14 and argues that the procedure, in both cases, marks a rite of passage. For the skin-diseased person, it is the passage from a state representative of death to that of life. For the priest, it is the passage from the common to the holy, a passage that has its own death/life symbolism. The ritual effects "safe passage across the boundary between life and death."[21] Additionally, the priests who cross from common to holy, and thus now handle holy things, are also in the most danger for that very reason.

This is one of the few places in Scripture where the blood of an offering is applied to the human body. This recalls Exodus 24:8, where the people are sprinkled with the blood of the covenant. In conjunction with this, Sklar notes that the ordination offering was a fellowship offering that, like the offering in Exodus 24, was used in the making of covenants. This then connects with several passages where it is said that God has given the priesthood to Aaron (and the tribe of Levi) by covenant (Num 18:19; 25:13; Jer 33:21; Mal 2:4).[22]

The "Filling" of the Hands

The Hebrew term translated "ordination" in verses 22, 28, 29, 31, and 33 is *millu'im*. It comes from a verb that means "to fill" and perhaps came to mean "ordination" on account of the procedure described in verse 27, in which Moses put in the hands of Aaron and his sons portions of the ordination offering and the unleavened bread (i.e., he "fills" their hands) and had them raise these offerings up as an "elevation" (rather than "wave") offering to the LORD (for this distinction, see the commentary on Lev 7:28–38). Interestingly, back in Exodus 32 in the narrative of the golden calf, when Moses calls for Israelites to go throughout the camp and kill a number of those who were engaged in the idolatry, it is the Levites who respond to this order. After they carry out this command, Moses says to them (v. 29), "You have been set apart to the LORD today, for you were against your own sons and brothers, and he has blessed you this day." The phrase "you have been set apart" is more literally translated, "you have filled your hands." That is, Moses considered them as having been in some way ordained in their acts of obeying this command (see ESV, NRSV, which use the word "ordained"). In the present narrative, Moses is the one who has been performing all the actions. But now Aaron and his sons are called upon to perform the ritual of the elevation offering, and in their initial ritual action are ordained to the priesthood.

21. Gorman, *Ideology of Ritual*, 131–35.
22. Sklar, *Leviticus*, 147.

The Seven Days of Ordination

There is disagreement as to exactly what happens during the seven days of ordination, as the newly ordained priests do "what the LORD requires" (more literally, "you shall keep watch over the watch"; v. 35). It seems to me that what is happening is that, having performed their first official act with the elevation offering, now they are to perform their second official act as the "guardians of the holy," keeping watch over the tabernacle to guard it against all encroachments that would contaminate the tabernacle's holiness. It has been suggested that they may have performed daily sacrifices during this week. The parallel text in Exodus 29:35–37 does indicate that sin offerings were offered each day during this period. However, it appears that it was still Moses who was carrying out the priestly role in the offering of these sacrifices. The sacrifices were offered on behalf of Aaron and his sons but still performed by Moses.[23]

The Perils of the Priesthood

Being a priest has its perils; it is a hazardous occupation. The last thing Moses tells the priests in this chapter is that they must remain in the courtyard of the tabernacle for seven days, "so you will not die" (v. 35). As already noted, this ordination process is a rite of passage for the priest, a transition from the common to the holy, and one that is fraught with danger. On the other side of the ordination ritual, the dangers will not have lessened. Indeed, when we come to Leviticus 10 we will see just how the perilous it is to be a priest, with the deaths of Aaron's sons, Nadab and Abihu. The priesthood has its rewards, but the priests can also "incur the wrath of God more quickly and easily" than the ordinary Israelite.[24]

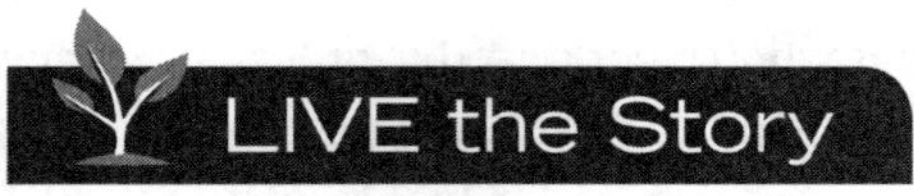

Christians have always believed that, in various ways, Christ fulfills the role of high priest, that believers constitute a "royal priesthood" (1 Pet 2:9), and that now, through no other mediator than Christ himself, we have direct and bold access to God. However, Christians have traditionally maintained that there is a distinction to be made between clergy and laity. While there may be some problematic connotations that come with that distinction, it seems to me that we should still understand that there are different and higher

---

23. See Milgrom, *Leviticus 1–16*, 538.
24. Hess, "Leviticus," 655.

expectations for those who are especially trained, prepared, and ordained to ministry and various leadership positions in the church. At the very least, it should be understood that "from everyone who has been given much, much will be demanded" (Luke 12:48) and those "who teach will be judged more strictly" (Jas 3:1). It seems right, then, that we should draw analogies between those who served in the priestly office in the Old Testament and those who serve as leaders in the Christian church. These assumptions are operative in the following suggestions for how we can "live the story."

Christ Fulfills and Perfects the Office of High Priest

One of the main themes in the New Testament book of Hebrews is that Jesus is our great high priest. The author of Hebrews was reliant on Leviticus for the brushstrokes with which he portrayed Christ as high priest. Briefly, the analogies are that Christ performs the work of atonement and provides purification from sin (Heb 1:3); Jesus, as one with the people, is himself holy and makes the people holy (2:11); he is a merciful and faithful high priest in his work of atonement for the sins of the people (2:17); he has ascended into heaven for us (correspondent to the holy of holies; 4:14; 6:19); he deals gently with weak and ignorant sinners (5:2); he was appointed high priest by God (5:4–6); and he, like the Old Testament priests, is a mediator between God and the people (9:15).

There are important differences as well. Christ's priestly work is in heaven rather than in a humanly made tabernacle or temple (Heb 4:14; 8:2; 9:11, 24). Christ did not sin; therefore, unlike the Old Testament priests, he did not have to offer sin offerings for himself (4:15; 7:26). He was not from the tribe of Levi but was appointed priest in the order of Melchizedek (5:10; 6:20; 7:1–17). He is a priest eternally (7:16–17, 23–25). He did not offer animal sacrifices but the sacrifice of his own body (9:12–14; 10:4–10). He offered himself as the full, final sacrifice, once and for all (9:25–28; 10:1, 10–14).

Beyond these fairly plain likenesses and differences, however, there is something else in Hebrews that lies just a bit deeper below the surface, relating in particular to Leviticus 8. A number of times Hebrews refers to Christ as having been "made perfect:"

> Son though he was, he learned obedience from what he suffered and, once made perfect, he became the source of eternal salvation for all who obey him and was designated by God to be high priest in the order of Melchizedek. (Heb 5:8–10)

> For the law appoints as high priests men in all their weakness; but the oath, which came after the law, appointed the Son, who has been made perfect forever. (Heb 7:28; see also 2:10)

These passages have proved puzzling for readers who ask the question, "How could the Son of God, who was already perfect, be made perfect?" Some have attempted to connect this perfecting process to one or another movement in Greek philosophy. However, others are convinced that what accounts for the language of perfection in these passages has to do with the narrative of the priests' ordination in Leviticus 8.

The Greek word translated "made perfect" in these two passages in Hebrews is *teleioō*. Interestingly, the Greek translation of the Old Testament, the Septuagint, uses the noun form of this same word (*teleiosis*) to translate the Hebrew word *millu'im*, which, as we saw above (Explain the Story, p. 119), is rendered in our English translations as "ordination." The author of Hebrews may have been influenced by the Septuagint translation of Leviticus 8 to use the verb *teleioō* to refer to Christ in these two verses. Rather than trying to say that Christ went from an imperfect state to a perfect state, or borrowing one or more concepts from Greek philosophy, he is perhaps using this term to make an analogy between the ordination of the priests in Leviticus 8 and what serves as the ordination for Jesus as high priest.

What makes this understanding most probable is the fact that in both passages in Hebrews, there is reference made to the idea of appointment. In Hebrews 5:8–10, once Christ is "made perfect" he is "designated" by God as priest in the order of Melchizedek. In 7:28, after saying that the law "appoints" priests who are weak, the verse goes on to say that God "appointed" the Son, who has been made perfect forever. On the one hand, the author of Hebrews can speak of Christ as a priest who offered himself as a sacrifice for our sins. On the another hand, he can, as he does in these passages, refer to Christ as one who, after being made perfect, is then appointed as priest. What this suggests, then, is that Hebrews understands Christ's offering of himself as a sacrifice to be equivalent to the ordination of priests in Leviticus 8. Even as the first priestly act of Aaron and his sons was that of lifting up an elevation offering to the LORD after Moses had "filled" their hands with this offering, which served as their ordination, so Christ's sacrifice of himself as an offering to God served as his ordination. Indeed, as Jesus says in John 17:19, it was by his death that he would be "consecrated" (ESV). Once he had performed this offering, he was "made perfect" (Heb 5:9; 7:28) and appointed as priest forever by his Father.[25] It was "fitting that God . . . should make the pioneer of [our] salvation perfect [*teleioō*] through what he suffered" (Heb 2:10). He has, indeed, been made perfect and appointed (ordained) to be our intercessory great high priest before God forever.

Ministers and Leaders in the Church Should Be Anointed

Not only has Christ been made perfect and appointed as great high priest, but he has also perfected those for whom he offered himself as a sacrifice for sin.

> For by one sacrifice he has made perfect forever those who are being made holy. (Heb 10:14)

The author of Hebrews does not go on to specifically make the connection between the perfection of believers and their becoming priests. However, without actually using the word "priest," the book does draw out the implication that we now have direct (though still mediated) access to God. We may approach the throne of God with confidence (Heb 4:16). Having been made perfect forever by Christ, we have a share in his ordination; we are priests alongside him. The law could not achieve this perfection for those who drew near to worship (10:1–2), but Christ has done so by his own perfect sacrifice (10:14). Therefore we now gain admission to the presence of God through Christ. We have been made holy (10:10). Like the high priest in the Old Testament, we may now "enter the Most Holy Place by the blood of Jesus" on the other side of the curtain that separated the holy place from the most holy place (Heb 10:19), something that even the regular priests were not allowed to do.

Of course, other places in the New Testament do make explicit the priesthood of all believers (e.g., 1 Pet 2:5, 9). But it is also appropriate to note the special role that attaches to those who are leaders in the church. For these leaders, it is right that we do something that corresponds to the anointing and ordination of Old Testament priests. There should be an assembly of the church to witness the laying on of hands by which we anoint and ordain ministers and leaders to the ministry of the gospel. It is, however, important to keep in mind Noordtzij's perspective, mentioned above (Explain the Story, p. 118), that we

25. For further discussion, see Kleinig, *Leviticus*, 204–5; Ross, *Holiness to the Lord*, 216–17; Mark F. Rooker, *Leviticus*, NAC 3A (Nashville: Broadman & Holman, 2000), 147. For a larger survey, see David Peterson, *Hebrews and Perfection: An Examination of the Concept of Perfection in the "Epistle to the Hebrews,"* SNTSMS 47 (Cambridge: Cambridge University Press, 1992).

do not so much dedicate these leaders to God in the ritual of ordination as recognize that they have been chosen by God to this office. As Milgrom notes with reference to the Old Testament priests, "It is God who is the author and executor of the priestly ordination."[26] In the same way, the church's role in the ordination of its leaders is not constitutive but recognitional. The church acknowledges and receives the gift that Christ has given to the church in its leaders. So, when the church assembly witnesses the ordination of its leaders, it recognizes that the leaders have been chosen by God and are a gracious gift of God to the church. As we have noted before, this ritual of ordination is an act of world construction. We envision an alternative reality in which we recognize that this world's view of leadership, with its political machinations and power plays, is not all there is. Rather, the church's leaders are a gift to the church from the risen, ascended, and exalted Christ (Eph 4:7–13).

On the other hand, the dedicatory understanding should not be discounted. Moses "brought" (*qarab*) to the LORD the priests who were to be ordained, even as the people brought their sacrifices to God. The priests played a part in their installation by lifting up their ordination offering to the LORD, symbolic of the fact that they are offering themselves to God. So today, even as Christ in his ordination "offered himself" to God (Heb 9:14), the leaders should understand that their lives are an offering to God. And even as Christ in his ordination offered himself to death, the leaders in the church must be willing to guard with their very lives the church that Christ purchased with his own blood (see Acts 20:28–31).

There Is a Special Danger for Those in Ministry

We noted above that this chapter highlights the danger that attaches to priestly ministry. Moses warns the priestly ordinands that they must not leave the entrance to the tent of meeting for the seven days of their ordination, "so you will not die" (Lev 8:35). As a number of commentators have noted, we may extrapolate from this that there is a danger factor that attends all aspects of priestly ministry. The priests lived in a danger zone as they handled the holy things of a holy God.

In a very real way, this danger factor applies to the entire church of Christ. Ananias and Sapphira died because they lied to the Holy Spirit about the offering they presented to the apostles (Acts 5:1–11), causing great fear for the church. Paul warns the Corinthians that some of those who had participated in the Lord's Supper unworthily had become sick, and some had even

26. Milgrom, *Leviticus 1–16*, 540.

died. Note that for both of these passages, punishment comes on those who have mishandled the "holy things" of God: offerings and the Lord's Supper. The author of Hebrews warns his readers:

> If we deliberately keep on sinning after we have received the knowledge of the truth, no sacrifice for sins is left, but only a fearful expectation of judgment and of raging fire that will consume the enemies of God. Anyone who rejected the law of Moses died without mercy on the testimony of two or three witnesses. How much more severely do you think someone deserves to be punished who has trampled the Son of God underfoot, who has treated as an unholy thing the blood of the covenant that sanctified them, and who has insulted the Spirit of grace? For we know him who said, "It is mine to avenge; I will repay," and again, "The Lord will judge his people." It is a dreadful thing to fall into the hands of the living God. (Heb 10:26–31)

Note again in this passage that the warning is for those who "have treated as an unholy thing the blood of the covenant" (v. 29). The problem is framed in terms of the mishandling of the holy.

While these passages deal with believers in general, as noted at the beginning of this section, the danger attaches in a heightened sense to those who are ministers and leaders in the church. Those who are entrusted with greater responsibility also have a greater degree of liability. Those who are teachers and leaders in the church will be judged more harshly (Jas 3:1). Paul realizes the need to guard himself in a disciplined manner so that he will not be disqualified (1 Cor 9:27). Those who are ordained as ministers and leaders in the church today must not become too familiar and cavalier in their handling of the holy things of God, realizing that the danger factor is, to a certain extent, heightened for them. Those who handle holiness must themselves be holy and must be diligent in maintaining that holiness.

There Is a Special Guarding Function for Those in Ministry

As mentioned above, the newly ordained priests were not only to stay at the entrance of the tent of meeting; they were actually to begin their role as *guardians of the holy*. They were told, in 8:35, to "watch the watch of the LORD" (author's translation). Kleinig captures this very well in his translation, "You shall do the sentry duty of the Lord."[27] To a large extent, the duty of the priests

27. Kleinig, *Leviticus*, 198.

was to guard the holiness of the LORD. Longman, strikingly, refers to this duty as that of being "God's bodyguards."[28] During their ordination week, the new priests were to perform this task as *security guards in training*. Their role was to guard against any encroachments on the divine holiness.

My translation for this passage, to "watch the watch of the LORD," attempts to capitalize on a redundancy in the Hebrew of this verse. The verb "watch" is *shamar*, often translated as "keep" or "guard." The noun "watch" is *mishmeret*, which is derived from the same verb, *shamar*. The *mishmeret*, then, refers to the task of guarding, watching, or (to use Kleinig's translation) the task of sentry duty.

Interestingly, when the Israelites celebrate the very first Passover in Egypt, and the death angel flies over all the homes in the land, another form of this same word (*shimmurim*) is used to refer to how the LORD "kept vigil that night" (Exod 12:42) over the Israelites to keep them from harm. Even as the LORD performed sentry duty to watch over his people, now the priests are called upon to guard the holy things of the LORD and to guard the people lest they endanger themselves by encroaching on the LORD's holiness.

The ministers and leaders of the church have a guarding role as one of their duties. The apostles are to guard against the teaching of the Pharisees and Sadducees (Matt 16:12). Paul tells the Ephesian elders to "[k]eep watch over yourselves and all the flock of which the Holy Spirit has made you overseers" (Acts 20:28); the next verses indicate that this guarding activity is to be against "savage wolves" and people "even from your own number [who] will arise and distort the truth (20:29–30). Therefore, they must "be on [their] guard!" (20:31). Finally, the author of Hebrews tells his readers to obey their leaders "who are keeping watch over your souls, as those who will have to give an account" (Heb 13:17 ESV). I once had a Greek teacher who was fond of translating this verse as "those who lay awake at night, watching over your souls." There is certainly a bit of interpretive license in this paraphrase, but it captures the thought dramatically. Ministers and leaders in the Christian church have a heavy responsibility laid on them: they are to guard the holiness of God and the purity of Christ's church, as those who will have to give an account of their guardianship.

Ministers Serve on the Basis of the Atonement

Ross perceptively calls attention to the role of the sacrifices that Moses offers for the priestly ordinands:

---

28. Longman, *Immanuel in Our Place*, 139, 147.

> Those who minister do so on the basis of the atonement. By identifying themselves with the atoning sacrifices, believers not only find salvation but also find release from the bondage of sin to serve the Lord.[29]

The author of Hebrews reminds us that the "law appoints as high priests men in all their weakness" (Heb 7:28). Therefore, before they could be ordained to their priestly office, they first had to have a sin offering provided for their own sins and had to regularly present sin offerings for themselves throughout their priestly ministry (Heb 5:3; 7:27; 9:7). It is important to remember that the high priest anointed and ordained in Leviticus is Aaron. Yes, golden calf Aaron! The only way he could have been ordained to the office of high priest was on the basis of the atonement.

In the same way, ministers and leaders in the church must constantly keep before them the realization that they only serve on the basis of the atonement. They do not serve because of their natural abilities, charisma, superior intellect, or the innate goodness of their character. They serve because Christ has shed his own blood for their souls. This is one of the reasons why Paul, when he ministered among the Corinthians (who seemed to attach so much importance to the power of personality and rhetorical skill as requirements in their leaders), was determined not to know anything but "Jesus Christ and him crucified" (1 Cor 2:2). Paul regarded as his most important qualification for ministry that he was "crucified with Christ," the one who loved him and gave himself for him (Gal 2:20). Christ's atonement for him and his identification with Christ in his crucifixion was Paul's entire life, his entire ministry. And so should it be for all leaders in the church of the crucified Christ. We are ministers because of Christ's atonement, and our ministries should be cross-shaped ministries. It is only in that cross that we may boast, and only in that cross that we may minister (Gal 6:14).[30]

---

29. Ross, *Holiness to the Lord*, 215.

30. For excellent discussions on the relationship between Christian ministry and the cross of Christ, see André Resner, Jr., *Preacher and Cross: Person and Message in Theology and Rhetoric* (Grand Rapids: Eerdmans, 1999); Andrew Purves, *The Crucifixion of Ministry: Surrendering Our Ambitions to the Service of Christ* (Downers Grove, IL: InterVarsity Press, 2007); D. A. Carson, *The Cross and Christian Ministry: An Exposition of Passages from 1 Corinthians* (Grand Rapids: Baker Books, 1993).

CHAPTER 8

Leviticus 9:1-24

LISTEN to the Story

9:1On the eighth day Moses summoned Aaron and his sons and the elders of Israel. 2He said to Aaron, "Take a bull calf for your sin offering and a ram for your burnt offering, both without defect, and present them before the LORD. 3Then say to the Israelites: 'Take a male goat for a sin offering, a calf and a lamb—both a year old and without defect—for a burnt offering, 4and an ox and a ram for a fellowship offering to sacrifice before the LORD, together with a grain offering mixed with olive oil. For today the LORD will appear to you.'"

5They took the things Moses commanded to the front of the tent of meeting, and the entire assembly came near and stood before the LORD. 6Then Moses said, "This is what the LORD has commanded you to do, so that the glory of the LORD may appear to you."

7Moses said to Aaron, "Come to the altar and sacrifice your sin offering and your burnt offering and make atonement for yourself and the people; sacrifice the offering that is for the people and make atonement for them, as the LORD has commanded."

8So Aaron came to the altar and slaughtered the calf as a sin offering for himself. 9His sons brought the blood to him, and he dipped his finger into the blood and put it on the horns of the altar; the rest of the blood he poured out at the base of the altar. 10On the altar he burned the fat, the kidneys and the long lobe of the liver from the sin offering, as the LORD commanded Moses; 11the flesh and the hide he burned up outside the camp.

12Then he slaughtered the burnt offering. His sons handed him the blood, and he splashed it against the sides of the altar. 13They handed him the burnt offering piece by piece, including the head, and he burned them on the altar. 14He washed the internal organs and the legs and burned them on top of the burnt offering on the altar.

15Aaron then brought the offering that was for the people. He took the goat for the people's sin offering and slaughtered it and offered it for a sin offering as he did with the first one.

[16]He brought the burnt offering and offered it in the prescribed way.
[17]He also brought the grain offering, took a handful of it and burned it on
the altar in addition to the morning's burnt offering.
[18]He slaughtered the ox and the ram as the fellowship offering for the
people. His sons handed him the blood, and he splashed it against the sides
of the altar. [19]But the fat portions of the ox and the ram—the fat tail, the layer
of fat, the kidneys and the long lobe of the liver—[20]these they laid on the
breasts, and then Aaron burned the fat on the altar. [21]Aaron waved the breasts
and the right thigh before the LORD as a wave offering, as Moses commanded.
[22]Then Aaron lifted his hands toward the people and blessed them.
And having sacrificed the sin offering, the burnt offering and the fellowship offering, he stepped down.
[23]Moses and Aaron then went into the tent of meeting. When they
came out, they blessed the people; and the glory of the LORD appeared
to all the people. [24]Fire came out from the presence of the LORD and
consumed the burnt offering and the fat portions on the altar. And when
all the people saw it, they shouted for joy and fell facedown.

Listening to the Text in the Story: Biblical Texts: Leviticus 8

This chapter continues the narrative begun in chapter 8. Aaron and his sons perform their first official sacrificial duties. In the previous narrative Aaron and his sons have only performed two official acts, including raising the elevation offering before the LORD, an action never performed by the regular Israelite, only by the priests; and (2) spending a week in the tabernacle courtyard guarding the sanctity of the holy things of the LORD. But now they will perform their first official duties with regard to the offering of sacrifices (for both themselves and the people) and the manipulation of the blood. For the first time Aaron will enter the tent of meeting, and, for the first time as a priest, he will pronounce a blessing on the people.

The Eighth Day

The narrative stresses that Aaron and his sons begin their priestly ministry on the "eighth day" (9:1), immediately after their seven-day ordination process.

Balentine draws a connection between this narrative and the creation account, arguing that the narrative in Genesis 3 is the eighth day after the seven-day creation.[1] The eighth day is emphasized in Israel's festival calendar. Kleinig notes the importance of the eighth day in the Old Testament:

> The eighth day is the first day of a new week. In ritual transactions the eighth day marks the inauguration of something new, a new way of life, the beginning of a clean or holy state after a period of purification or consecration. The original creation was completed within seven days, and so the eighth day in Scripture represents the start of God's new creation, his work of redemption. Circumcision took place on the eighth day to mark the start of the infant's new life as a member of God's covenant people.[2]

So it seems right to understand, against several commentators, that this eighth day is not to be understood as the conclusion of the seven-day installation process but rather the first day of a new beginning in the relationship between God and the priests and, through them, with the people of Israel.

Building toward a Theophany

There has already been a theophany recounted in Exodus 40 in which the glory of the Lord filled the tabernacle. But now, in Leviticus 9:4, there is the promise made of another theophany that will occur in response to the first offerings of the newly ordained priests. The whole chapter is building toward this appearance of the glory of the Lord. Sklar notes that all the people are gathered together "at the King's palace," where "the King himself was to appear."[3] There is excitement and great anticipation, but there is also drama: Will Aaron and his sons do everything just as they are supposed to? Will the King in fact appear? It will depend on the successful completion of the very first priestly sacrifices to be offered by Aaron and his sons.

As the Lord Commanded

This is exactly why, in this chapter as well as the previous one, there is much attention paid to the fact that Aaron and his sons performed the rituals "as the Lord commanded" (Lev 8:4, 9, 13, 17, 21, 29, 31, 35, 36; 9:7, 10). "The narrative therefore depicts the inauguration of the divine service as an exemplary

1. Balentine, *Leviticus*, 80.
2. Kleinig, *Leviticus*, 209.
3. Sklar, *Leviticus*, 149.

act of obedience by Moses, Aaron, and the people of Israel."[4] Tragically, an account of Aaron's sons doing that which the LORD did not command will come at the beginning of the very next chapter.

The Sacrifices

Aaron runs the sacrificial gamut in this narrative. He offers the sin offering (one for himself and one for the people), the burnt offering, the grain offering, and the fellowship offering. Except for the guilt offering, which was an individual rather than public offering, he offers the full range of sacrifices prescribed in chapters 1–7, including the wave (elevation) offering. So, on his first day of official duty, Aaron practically carries out the entire priestly sacrificial job description.

There are some minor differences between the prescription for the sin offering in Leviticus 4:3–12 and the execution of it here in this chapter. Gorman suggests that the differences are to be accounted for by understanding that the sin offering in this chapter should be recognized as a "founding ritual," which may depart in various ways from the regular procedure.[5]

We will, however, pay attention to one particularly significant difference.

The Bull Calf

Many commentators note that in Leviticus 4:3–12 the prescribed sin offering for the priest is a bull, but here in chapter 9 it is specified that the offering is to be a bull calf. While not all would agree, it seems that the reason for the difference, an understanding that goes back to the ancient rabbis, is that it is meant to recall the golden calf narrative in Exodus 32. Aaron is being purposefully reminded, as he provides an offering for his own sins, exactly how egregious his sins actually were. As Wright appropriately comments, "Indeed, it was only because of God's mercy that Aaron was even alive on this day, let alone entering on the privilege of high priesthood. Many others had died for their sin on that occasion."[6]

It is important to call attention to the purpose of chapters 8–9 at this point in the book. The tabernacle has already been erected and dedicated, and the glory of the LORD has already filled it. The prescriptions for the sacrifices have already been given in chapters 1–7. But there is a significant problem. There are as of yet no priests to offer those sacrifices. Chapters 8–9 are all about the ordination, installation, and divine approval of the priests who will move within the tabernacle precincts. Morales calls attention to the connection between this narrative, the creation account, and the fall of Adam:

4. Kleinig, *Leviticus*, 185–86.
5. Gorman, *Divine Presence*, 62.
6. Wright, "Leviticus," 134.

> While the tabernacle represents a new creation filled with the glory of God, there is as yet no new Adam for this new creation.[7]

> Anointed to the office of high priest, Aaron will play the role of the new Adam of this new creation within the drama of the tabernacle system of worship.[8]

Adam was the priest in the Edenic tabernacle/temple, but he failed as priest in the narrative in Genesis 3. Now a new garden of God has been built. God has once again taken up residence among his people. Who will serve as priest? Who will be the new Adam? Aaron had been designated and chosen as priest, but his sin in connection with the golden calf incident should have almost certainly disqualified him for the position. But God, in an incredible act of mercy and grace, not only did not have Aaron killed for his act of rebellion but affirmed his choice of Aaron as high priest. No wonder there is drama in this chapter as to whether Aaron will be able to successfully complete the assigned priestly task. And there is concern for the people as well. Aaron sacrificed not only for his own sins but also for the sins of the people, many of whom, almost certainly, had been among the golden calf worshipers. Would the sacrifices be accepted? The tension is great.

The Blessing

Some have suggested that this blessing may have consisted of the special priestly benediction referred to in Numbers 6:24–26. Though this is possible, it is by no means sure. What is important to note is the significance of the blessing at this point in the narrative. Aaron has offered the sacrifices, and he has apparently done so in accordance with the God-commanded prescriptions. When he lifts his hands to bless the people, he does so as a newly installed and apparently God-approved priest, one who is empowered to mediate between God and the people and to impart divine blessings to the assembled congregation.

The Entrance into the Tent of Meeting

We are not told exactly why Moses and Aaron enter the tent of meeting. Most likely, however, there is a kind of "hand off" taking place, with the full authority and responsibility over the work and guarding of the tabernacle now being transferred from Moses to Aaron. Indeed, when they exit the tent

---

7. L. Michael Morales, *Who Shall Ascend the Mountain of the Lord?: A Biblical Theology of the Book of Leviticus*, NSBT 37 (Downers Grove, IL: InterVarsity Press, 2015), 117.
8. Ibid., 118.

of meeting and together bless the people, it is immediately said that "the glory of the Lord appeared to all the people" (v. 23), almost as if the Lord is accompanying them as they exit and validating their ministry—in particular Aaron's, as he blesses the people a second time. Aaron has the imprimatur of the Lord upon him.

Fire from the Lord

We should probably understand that the appearance of the glory of the Lord mentioned in verse 23 is the fire that comes out from the Lord in verse 24, though it is at least possible that the glory and the fire should be seen as a two-stage appearance. In any case, this fire fulfills the expectations that were set up earlier in verses 4 and 6.

What is accomplished and signified by this fire? There are several answers to this question:

1. As opposed to some older rabbinical sources, Levine is correct to point out that this fire does not fall down from heaven on the sacrifice but from inside the tabernacle where God has now taken up residence.[9] That the fire comes out from inside the tent of meeting both assures the onlooking assembly that God has not only decided to dwell among them inside his royal tent, but that he is pleased to do so.
2. This fire is the one that is to be kept burning as commanded in 6:9–13. It will continually remind the Israelites that the Lord accompanies them: "The Tabernacle, in effect becomes a portable Sinai, an assurance of the permanent presence of the deity in Israel's midst."[10] Aaron's rod that budded and the jar of manna are placed either inside or beside the ark in the most holy place, out of view for the Israelites; but the fire on the altar would always be visible, available for the Israelites to "see, hear, and smell," assuring them of the Lord's presence.[11]
3. We are not to understand that this fire from the Lord actually lit the altar. Rather, Aaron had already lit the fire for the various sacrifices he offered that day. The fire from the Lord is added to the fire that Aaron had already lit and "makes quick work of the lot,"[12] so that the sacrifices are "vaporized in an instant."[13] In my opinion, Hartley extrapolates too

9. Levine, *Leviticus*, 58.
10. Milgrom, *Leviticus 1–16*, 574.
11. Gane, *Leviticus, Numbers*, 179.
12. Ross, *Holiness to the Lord*, 226.
13. Gane, *Leviticus, Numbers*, 179.

much when he suggests that this combination of humanly made and divinely made fire indicates "the synergistic nature of biblical faith, i.e., God and man working together,"[14] as if in some way humans are contributing to their own salvation. What is being indicated, however, is that Aaron's ritual performance has been validated; the sacrifices Aaron and his sons will offer on that altar will "meet with God's approval," and "every sacrifice offered on the altar will, with God's grace, also merit his acceptance."[15]

4. Morales, in accord with our citation from him above (p. 132), notes that there is an indication in this divine fire that comes out from the presence of the Lord that the Lord's purpose for his creation is being realized.[16] And Anderson states, "The moment of lighting the sacrificial pyre is the very apogee of the Torah."[17] Eden's light is being made to shine again.

The Response of the People

Initially, upon seeing this fire, the people "shout for joy," but then we are told that they "fell facedown" (v. 24). While these actions could be seen as simultaneous, I believe we should rather understand them to be successive. Bellinger theorizes:

> In response the people shouted for joy and then prostrated themselves as an indication of reverence and worship. This response suggests respect and awe, since if the devouring, fiery divine presence can consume what is on the altar, it can also consume the people.[18]

There is great joy because the Lord has manifested his presence among them. He has validated the ministry of his servant Aaron. He has accepted the sacrifice as atonement for their sins. But there is also prostration before the Lord. They recognize the distance between themselves as creatures and the Lord as creator. They recognize the gap between the holiness of the Lord and their own lack of holiness. And they also know that this fiery revelation from the Lord, as glorious and joy inducing as it is one day, can have disastrous effects another day. They may not have realized just how soon that day would come—that it would, in fact, be that very same day.

---

14. Hartley, *Leviticus*, 121.
15. Milgrom, *Leviticus 1–16*, 591.
16. Morales, *Who Shall Ascend*, 120.
17. Gary A. Anderson, "Biblical Origins and the Problem of the Fall," *ProEccl* 10.1 (2001): 22.
18. W. H. Bellinger Jr., *Leviticus and Numbers*, NIBCOT 3 (Peabody, MA: Hendrickson, 2001), 62.

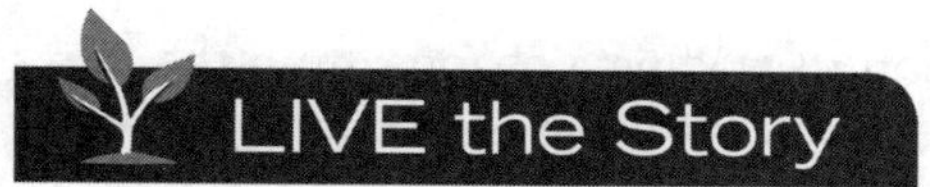

The Glory of God in the Death of Jesus Christ

George Knight strikingly remarks:

> The glory of God is made apparent to the mind of man, not just, as the Psalmist says, when "The heavens are telling the glory of God" (Ps. 19:1), but particularly at that *place* and *time* where sacrifice takes place. For it is primarily through sacrifice that the glory of God is revealed. No wonder the New Testament writers came to understand that the glory of God was most fully revealed at that *time* and *place* when Jesus submitted himself willingly to be the sacrifice, ultimate and *whole*, which God must exact for the sin of all mankind (John 13:31).[19]

The week before I completed the writing of this chapter, I preached a message in a local church, and I decided to preach from Leviticus 9. It was a bit of a gamble, but I decided to start off the message interactively and asked the members of the congregation that morning to tell me what reminded them most of the glory of God. The answers were fairly predictable: the majestic mountains, the beautiful blue sky, flowers, birds, crops, newborn babies, the stars, panoramic vistas, and another half-dozen answers. The gamble I took paid off in terms of providing a foil for the message. No one said anything close to "What reminds me most of the glory of God is the cross, the crucifixion, the death of Jesus Christ."

I also remember a scene from my early teen years and a conversation I had with my pastor and a few other members of the church. Someone raised the question as to where in the Bible we most see the glory of God, in the Old Testament or in the New Testament. Everyone answered that it was in the Old Testament: creation, the flood, the plagues on Egypt, the parting of the Red Sea, the thunder and lightning on Mount Sinai, the glorious theophanies, and so on. I believe I was the only one in the group who suggested that we see it more in the New Testament, and particularly in the death of Jesus Christ. Now, I'm not completely sure why I answered the way I did. But perhaps one factor in my answer was that I had become a Christian just two or three years before this conversation. When I became a Christian, someone gave me a pocket-sized copy of the Gospel of John. So, every day for the first few

19. George A. F. Knight, *Leviticus*, DSB (Louisville: Westminster John Knox, 1981), 56–57.

years of my Christian life, in addition to reading a chapter from the larger Bible, I read a chapter from that little Gospel of John. By the time of this conversation, I had already read John's Gospel two or three dozen times. And it is in John's Gospel that the author takes special pains to point out that it was in his death that Jesus would bring glory to God and that Jesus himself would be glorified. Almost from the beginning of this Gospel there is a special use of the term "hour" as a way of referring to the approaching death of Jesus. What surprises us, however, is that Jesus refers to this hour as the hour in which he would be glorified.

> "Woman, why do you involve me?" Jesus replied. "My hour has not yet come." (John 2:4)

> At this they tried to seize him, but no one laid a hand on him, because his hour had not yet come. (John 7:30)

> He spoke these words while teaching in the temple courts near the place where the offerings were put. Yet no one seized him, because his hour had not yet come. (John 8:20)

> Jesus replied, "The hour has come for the Son of Man to be glorified. (John 12:23)

> "Now my soul is troubled, and what shall I say? 'Father, save me from this hour'? No, it was for this very reason I came to this hour. Father, glorify your name!" (John 12:27–28)

> Jesus said, "Now the Son of Man is glorified and God is glorified in him. (John 13:31)

> After Jesus said this, he looked toward heaven and prayed:
> "Father, the hour has come. Glorify your Son, that your Son may glorify you. (John 17:1)

Additionally, Jesus refers to how he will be "lifted up" from the earth. The reader might be tempted to understand this as a reference to Jesus's ascension. There might indeed be a double entendre, a double-meaning, in the use of the term. But John makes at least the primary meaning explicit for us:

> "And I, when I am lifted up from the earth, will draw all people to myself." He said this to show the kind of death he was going to die. (John 12:32–33; see also 3:14; 8:28)

Knight, in the quotation above, shows how this narrative in Leviticus, and the glory of God being especially displayed at the point of sacrifice, prepares us for the message in the Gospel of John—that God is glorified in the death of Jesus Christ. Tidball rightly affirms this: "The true glory of God was manifested both in the life of Jesus and, paradoxically, even more in his death."[20] Indeed, if we were to ask the apostle Paul, "Where is the glory of God to be found?" his answer would be: "God's glory [is] displayed in the face of Christ" (2 Cor 4:6), and he would say that his only "boast" would be "in the cross of our Lord Jesus Christ" (Gal 6:14).

So how do we "live the story" of Leviticus 9? The answer, in large part, has to do with giving God great praise for what he has done in the atoning sacrifice of his Son.[21]

Amazing Grace and the Necessity of the Atonement

We saw above that Aaron's having to offer a bull calf rather than a full-grown bull was probably meant to remind him of the golden calf incident. Indeed, it is a wonder, at this point in the narrative, that he is even alive, much less now being ordained as high priest. The author of Hebrews reminds us that "the law appoints as high priests men in all their weakness" (7:28). In one respect, that is a good thing because, as again we read in Hebrews, "He is able to deal gently with those who are ignorant and are going astray, since he himself is subject to weakness" (Heb 5:2). A weak high priest is able to sympathize with weak people. A sinful high priest, who first has to sacrifice for his own sins (Heb 5:3), is able to sympathize with sinful people.

Ministers and leaders in the church today must constantly be aware of their own weakness and sinfulness. Unfortunately, in various parts of the world (and I am thinking here particularly of North America), a celebrity-pastor, celebrity-worship-leader syndrome has infected the Christian church. This syndrome tends to make the pastor or worship leader forget that they are weak and sinful. Correspondingly, not always but all too often, this celebrity syndrome is

---

20. Tidball, *Message of Leviticus*, 129.

21. For assistance in this task, see the excellent essays in Charles E. Hill and Frank A. James III, eds., *The Glory of the Atonement: Biblical, Historical & Practical Perspectives: Essays in Honor of Roger Nicole* (Downers Grove, IL: InterVarsity Press, 2004).

accompanied by a devaluation of the necessity of the cross and the atonement of Jesus Christ. After all, it is very hard for the message of the cross to coexist with the message of success, prosperity, power, and mega-this and mega-that.

A. W. Tozer, in a famous article entitled "The Prayer of a Minor Prophet," which was a reflection of Tozer's thoughts on the day of his own ordination to the ministry, penned these poignant words:

> And if in Thy permissive providence honor should come to me from Thy church, let me not forget in that hour that I am unworthy of the least of Thy mercies, and that if men knew me as intimately as I know myself they would withhold their honors or bestow them upon others more worthy to receive them.[22]

It is necessary for Christian leaders to remind themselves regularly that they are weak and sinful, and that they serve only by the grace of God, particularly the grace of the atonement and the blood of Jesus Christ.

The Necessity of Obedience, Especially in Worship

As wonderful as is the final scene of this chapter, with the people responding to the appearance of the glory of the Lord with fire by shouting for joy and falling down on their faces in worship, it is sobering to realize that just two verses later that same fiery glory will kill two of Aaron's sons. Nadab and Abihu, who went through the seven-day ordination process and assisted their father Aaron in the ritual acts on narrated in chapter 9, will die because they will, that same day, offer "unauthorized fire before the Lord, contrary to his command" (10:1).

It is no wonder, then, as mentioned above (pp. 130–31), that there are so many references in chapters 8–9 to Moses, Aaron, and Aaron's sons doing everything "as the Lord commanded." In particular, it is important to note that this obedience took place with reference to ritual and worship. I believe the lesson for us today is that, as best as we can discern, our worship should correspond to scriptural prescriptions for worship. As Longman states, "God does not leave it to human beings to define the type of worship they will offer him."[23]

Of course, in various ways, our worship today will not look like worship in ancient Israel, especially since the sacrificial system has been done away with because of Christ's final sacrifice. There isn't anywhere near the level of ritual detail provided in the New Testament as in the Old. So, I believe there can be

22. A. W. Tozer, "The Prayer of a Minor Prophet," in *God Tells the Man Who Cares* (Harrisburg, PA: Christian Publications, 1970), 88–89.

23. Longman, *Immanuel in Our Place*, 27.

considerable variety in the different styles of worship that exist in our churches. At the same time, I believe there are also some non-negotiables. Everything should be done in a "fitting and orderly way" (1 Cor 14:40). Worship should be done regularly and in such a way that people are "[spurred] on toward love and good deeds" (Heb 10:24). People should sing to the Lord and to one another in "psalms, hymns, and spiritual songs" (Eph 5:19, NRSV). The sacraments/ordinances should be observed. The word of God should be read. Instruction in the word should be given. People should confess their sins. There should be praises, prayers, and intercessions. Offerings should be taken. God's holiness should be emphasized. God's glory should be held before the people. The risen Christ should be celebrated. The Holy Spirit should be praised. Humility should be encouraged. And there should be no "star of the show" other than the Triune God. To reference Tozer again, he once said that worship was the "missing jewel" of the church.[24] We should not too casually consider ourselves to have rediscovered it. We should continually examine our worship practices to make sure that they are truly honoring to God.

A Potpourri of Christological Connections

Finally, I wish to call attention to a number of fascinating suggestions with regard to promising connections to Christ that can be made between Leviticus 9 and the New Testament, but do not have the space to discuss these fully.

Tidball has argued that in John's Gospel the author has "employed the language and thought of Leviticus 9 as a framework."[25] We explored some of that usage above (pp. 135–37) in the first point of this section. Ross maintains that Paul has utilized this chapter and other passages in Leviticus to structure the book of Romans.[26] Additionally, he argues that the Pentecost narrative in Acts 2:1–11 contains a number of parallels to the content of Leviticus 9.[27] Gane has helpfully constructed two charts in his commentary that show how Christ fulfills the priesthood ideal of this chapter, and how his priestly ministry contrasts with that of Aaron.[28] Several commentators have called attention to the eighth-day ritual of this chapter and the resurrection of Jesus on the day after the Sabbath—that is, the eighth day.[29] Kaiser draws the connection between the blessing that Aaron puts on the people at the end

---

24. A. W. Tozer, *Worship: The Missing Jewel of the Evangelical Church* (Harrisburg, PA: Christian Publications, n.d.).

25. Tidball, *Message of Leviticus*, 129; Hartley, *Leviticus*, 125.

26. Ross, *Holiness to the Lord*, 219, 229.

27. Ibid., 228.

28. Gane, *Leviticus, Numbers*, 181–182.

29. See, for example, Hartley, *Leviticus*, 209.

of this chapter and the blessing Jesus puts on the disciples at his ascension in Luke 24:50–52.[30] Finally, I call attention to Kleinig's fulsome discussion on Christ's fulfillment of this chapter.[31] He draws connections between this chapter and Christ's priesthood in the book of Hebrews. Also, fascinatingly, he discusses "five key events" in the Gospel of Luke that "relate to corresponding events in Leviticus 9."[32] The five events are (1) Zechariah's service in the temple in Luke 1:8–22; (2) the transfiguration "theophany" in Luke 9:28–36; (3) the establishment of the Lord's Supper in Luke 22:14–30; (4) the resurrection of Jesus on the "eighth day" and Christ's revelation of himself to the disciples on the Emmaus road in Luke 24:1–35; and (5) Christ's priestly blessing in Luke 24:50–51.

Christ is our great high priest. Unlike Aaron, who was weak and sinful, and had to sacrifice for his own sins, and was able to sympathize with the people, Christ, the strong Son of God, knew no sin and did not have to sacrifice for his own sins. Yet he came and subjected himself to weakness and suffering that he might be like his brothers and sisters and empathize with them in every way. He, rather than Aaron, is the true new Adam who has come to restore the Edenic glory to the church.

> Therefore, since we have a great high priest who has ascended into heaven, Jesus the Son of God, let us hold firmly to the faith we profess. For we do not have a high priest who is unable to empathize with our weaknesses, but we have one who has been tempted in every way, just as we are—yet he did not sin. Let us then approach God's throne of grace with confidence, so that we may receive mercy and find grace to help us in our time of need. (Heb 4:14–16)[33]

---

30. Kaiser, "The Book of Leviticus," in *NIB*, 1:1068.

31. Kleinig, *Leviticus*, 220–22.

32. Ibid., 220.

33. Coming out too late for me to interact with, as I was in the final editing stages of this commentary, was the second volume of Katherine Sonderegger's *Systematic Theology*, titled *The Doctrine of the Holy Trinity: Processions and Persons* (Minneapolis: Fortress, 2020). The volume is elegantly written, sublimely poetic in its style, deeply devotional, worshipful, and startlingly daring in its thesis. I have closed out this chapter by calling attention to the Christological connections, as I indeed do throughout this book. But Sonderegger helpfully cautions that all cannot be reduced to Christology. She argues that the very doctrine of the Trinity is to be seen as situated in ancient Israel's Scriptures, in particular in the book of Leviticus and in the sacrificial cultus. Throughout the book, but especially in the fifth chapter (pp. 355–484) and beginning with the final scene in verses 23–24 of Leviticus 9, she develops her argument. God himself is the one who gives Israel the sacrificial system. He provides the sacrifice. He sends out the flame that consumes the sacrifice. And then the smoke of the sacrifice returns to him as a pleasing aroma. This is God's own "self-offering," and, I would even say, his own self-propitiation. The inner holy life of the Trinitarian God—Father, Son, and Spirit—she maintains, is located in and on display in the sacrificial system. I have not done the thesis justice in this brief summary. The book is not the easiest of reads (she has many theological and philosophical conversation partners); but at the same time it is a delightful read. I highly commend this work to the reader who wants to delve into this more deeply. It is richly rewarding, and for me reading it was an act of worship.

CHAPTER 9

Leviticus 10:1–20

LISTEN to the Story

[10:1]Aaron's sons Nadab and Abihu took their censers, put fire in them and added incense; and they offered unauthorized fire before the LORD, contrary to his command. [2]So fire came out from the presence of the LORD and consumed them, and they died before the LORD. [3]Moses then said to Aaron, "This is what the LORD spoke of when he said:

"'Among those who approach me
  I will be proved holy;
in the sight of all the people
  I will be honored.'"

Aaron remained silent.

[4]Moses summoned Mishael and Elzaphan, sons of Aaron's uncle Uzziel, and said to them, "Come here; carry your cousins outside the camp, away from the front of the sanctuary." [5]So they came and carried them, still in their tunics, outside the camp, as Moses ordered.

[6]Then Moses said to Aaron and his sons Eleazar and Ithamar, "Do not let your hair become unkempt and do not tear your clothes, or you will die and the LORD will be angry with the whole community. But your relatives, all the Israelites, may mourn for those the LORD has destroyed by fire. [7]Do not leave the entrance to the tent of meeting or you will die, because the LORD's anointing oil is on you." So they did as Moses said.

[8]Then the LORD said to Aaron, [9]"You and your sons are not to drink wine or other fermented drink whenever you go into the tent of meeting, or you will die. This is a lasting ordinance for the generations to come, [10]so that you can distinguish between the holy and the common, between the unclean and the clean, [11]and so you can teach the Israelites all the decrees the LORD has given them through Moses."

[12]Moses said to Aaron and his remaining sons, Eleazar and Ithamar, "Take the grain offering left over from the food offerings prepared without yeast and presented to the LORD and eat it beside the altar, for it is most holy. [13]Eat it in the sanctuary area, because it is your share and your sons' share of the food offerings presented to the LORD; for so I have been commanded. [14]But you and your sons and your daughters may eat the breast that was waved and the thigh that was presented. Eat them in a ceremonially clean place; they have been given to you and your children as your share of the Israelites' fellowship offerings. [15]The thigh that was presented and the breast that was waved must be brought with the fat portions of the food offerings, to be waved before the LORD as a wave offering. This will be the perpetual share for you and your children, as the LORD has commanded."

[16]When Moses inquired about the goat of the sin offering and found that it had been burned up, he was angry with Eleazar and Ithamar, Aaron's remaining sons, and asked, [17]"Why didn't you eat the sin offering in the sanctuary area? It is most holy; it was given to you to take away the guilt of the community by making atonement for them before the LORD. [18]Since its blood was not taken into the Holy Place, you should have eaten the goat in the sanctuary area, as I commanded."

[19]Aaron replied to Moses, "Today they sacrificed their sin offering and their burnt offering before the LORD, but such things as this have happened to me. Would the LORD have been pleased if I had eaten the sin offering today?" [20]When Moses heard this, he was satisfied.

Listening to the Text in the Story: Biblical Texts: Leviticus 8–9; Ezekiel 24:15–24; Ancient Near Eastern Texts: Daily Ritual of the Temple of Amun-Re at Karnak

The narrative in Leviticus 10 picks up from the preceding account in chapters 8–9 of the ordination of the priests and their initial sacrificial duties. Unfortunately, the narrative takes a drastically disastrous turn. At the end of chapter 9, fire from the LORD had signaled the LORD's acceptance of the priestly rituals and their first attempts at making sacrificial offerings. The people had responded with shouts of joy and reverent worship. Now, just two first verses later, there is a ritual lapse on the part of Aaron's sons and fire from the LORD comes out and burns not the sacrifices but the sons of Aaron, Nadab and Abihu. An auspicious day has turned into an ominous one.

The Egyptian Daily Ritual text is informative about the use of incense in ritual worship in the ancient Near East. It provides details regarding ritual actions involving fire and incense, including various "spells" or "utterances" which are to be uttered during the performance. These actions consist of lighting the flame, taking hold of the incense bowl, putting it in its place in the censer arm, and adding the incense to the flame, and then the priest approaching the sacred place, the "holy of holies" in the temple where the deity resided.[1] While the actual content of these utterances is not especially important for us to look at, what is instructive is to recognize the cruciality of the precision employed in the preparation and offering of the incense. A holy deity had to be approached in the right way. The same was true for Israel's God.

EXPLAIN the Story

The narrative in the chapter is fairly straightforward. Aaron's sons, Nadab and Abihu, offer "unauthorized fire" before the LORD (v. 1). A fire comes out from the LORD and strikes them dead. Moses explains that this incident is actually the LORD bringing honor to himself and demonstrating himself to be holy. Two cousins are called upon to remove the dead bodies and take them outside the camp. The corpses, as Wenham says, are "treated like the useless parts of the sacrificial animals."[2] Aaron and his two remaining sons, Eleazar and Ithamar, are given instructions not to carry out external mourning rites for the two slain priests. Moses also communicates various instructions regarding the consumption of the food offerings. Moses, upon finding out that the goat of the sin offering had been completely burned up, inquires angrily of Aaron's sons why they had not eaten the meat of the sin offering as they had been previously instructed. Aaron responds and offers a reason as to why they had not done so. There are various suggestions as to exactly what Aaron's response means. I believe his response is best understood along emotional lines. The NIV's "such things as this have happened to me," is perhaps better captured on the emotional level by the NJPS "such things have befallen me!" Aaron and his sons have already had to deal with the burden of mourning inwardly but not outwardly. They felt that if they had tried to eat the sacrifice in that emotional condition, the LORD would not have been pleased. Moses was satisfied by this response.

1. "Daily Ritual of the Temple of Amun-Re at Karnak," trans. Robert K. Ritner (*COS* 1.34: 55–57).

2. Wenham, *Leviticus*, 158.

There are three additional interpretive issues to be addressed with this narrative.

What Was the Sin of Nadab and Abihu?

The NIV's "unauthorized" (v. 1) fire allows for a number of possibilities as to what the problem was with Nadab and Abihu's offering. Literally, the Hebrew word translated "unauthorized" (*zarah*) would be translated as "strange" or "foreign." Milgrom notes that among the ancient rabbis there were as many as twelve different suggestions, though he also notes that some of them are "pure flights of fancy."[3] Among the more plausible suggestions for what is referred to by this term are (1) fire taken from a place other than the fire that is already lit on the altar of burnt offering; (2) incense that has not been made according to the prescribed formula; (3) incense that was either taken from or made according to the formula for the worship of a foreign god; (4) Nadab and Abihu arrogating for themselves the act of offering this incense in the holy place, a duty which was reserved for the high priest; (5) or, even worse, the attempt to penetrate with the incense into the most holy place. These different suggestions are not necessarily mutually exclusive. I lean toward either or both of the first two suggestions.

What is important is to notice just how egregious this infraction was. It had been a remarkable day in the history of Israel. The priesthood had been instituted, the first priests had been ordained, they had successfully offered their first sacrifices, and the glory of the Lord had appeared to the people in a remarkable way. But then Nadab and Abihu managed to snatch defeat out of the jaws of victory. At the same time, we must note that this defeat, and the deaths of Nadab and Abihu, nevertheless resulted in the glory of the Lord and the display of his holiness. Whether it was the fire from the Lord that "consumed" the sacrifice in 9:24 or the fire from the Lord that "consumed" Aaron's sons (10:2), as Morales says, "both ceremonies . . . concluded the same, with God being glorified before the people."[4]

Why Were Aaron and His Sons Not Allowed to Engage in Mourning Rites?

Aaron and his remaining sons are told that they must not engage in the customary mourning rites for Nadab and Abihu. Later, in the commentary for Leviticus 21, we will come across general prohibitions for the priests with regard to mourning rites (pp. 275–86). There it is prescribed that priests must

3. Milgrom, *Leviticus 1–16*, 633–35.
4. Morales, *Who Shall Ascend*, 146.

not engage in mourning rites for regular Israelites, though they may do so in the case of a close family member. The high priest in particular is apparently not allowed to engage in any of the customary mourning rites, even for close relatives (though there is some ambiguity). In our current narrative, therefore, the restrictions would have already been operative for Aaron, but not for his sons. The question, then, raised by this account is why the restrictions for Aaron's sons, and perhaps for Aaron himself, go beyond the normal restrictions in Leviticus 21. Why were they not allowed to engage in the mourning rites on this occasion, even for their close relatives (sons and brothers)?

To answer this question, it is important to look at the narrative in Ezekiel 24:15–24. Ezekiel, of priestly descent, was a prophet among the Judahite exiles who had been carried to Babylon in 598 BC in one of the minor deportations of exiles. Part of the distressing message Ezekiel has for these exiles is that they will not be returning any time soon. Indeed, there is another larger exile yet to come, and many more exiles from Judah will be joining them. Additionally, his message for them is that the temple back in Jerusalem is going to be completely destroyed by the Babylonians.

One of the sign-acts Ezekiel is called upon to perform to reinforce this message is that of refraining from mourning rites when his wife dies. The Lord tells Ezekiel that his wife is going to die and that, when this occurs, Ezekiel is not to engage in the customary mourning rites, even for his own wife—even to the point of not shedding any tears. When this happens, the exiles ask Ezekiel what this strange action might mean. Ezekiel responds:

> The word of the Lord came to me: Say to the people of Israel, "This is what the Sovereign Lord says: I am about to desecrate my sanctuary—the stronghold in which you take pride, the delight of your eyes, the object of your affection. The sons and daughters you left behind will fall by the sword. And you will do as I have done. You will not cover your mustache and beard or eat the customary food of mourners. You will keep your turbans on your heads and your sandals on your feet. You will not mourn or weep but will waste away because of your sins and groan among yourselves. Ezekiel will be a sign to you; you will do just as he has done. When this happens, you will know that I am the Sovereign Lord." (vv. 20–24)

What ties these two incidents together is that they both occur in connection with judgment from God, a judgment connected to tabernacle/temple violations. In Leviticus 10 the judgment is against the offering of strange or foreign fire/incense in the tabernacle. In Ezekiel 24 the judgment is against the temple in Jerusalem for numerous violations that had occurred in the temple (Ezek 8–11), among them the use of censers and incense in illicit worship (Ezek 8:11). Even as Aaron and his sons are not allowed to engage in customary mourning rites for Nadab and Abihu, even as the priest Ezekiel is not allowed to do so for his wife as a sign-act, so the people will not be allowed to engage in mourning rites for the temple or for their sons and daughters back in Judah.

Why not? Because they must be in complete solidarity with God in his judgment. They must not, in their outward actions, give any indication whatsoever that they might be questioning the righteous judgment of God.

Jonathan Klawans has cogently argued that a large part of the priest's ritual actions is to be *imitatio Dei*, an imitation of the deity. He argues that the symbolism of the rites carried out by the priests indicates that the priests are actually replicating the actions of God. Every ritual the priest performs is to conform to the very actions and character of God.[5] Aaron and his remaining sons in Leviticus 10, and Ezekiel in his symbolic action in Ezekiel 24, must be in complete solidarity with God, not giving the slightest hint that that they might be in disagreement with God's view and his holy judgment. Yahweh himself, as much he might grieve over the punishment he has to inflict, nevertheless adopts a cold, stoic exterior; the priest must do so as well, and he must do so because he must give his "amen" to Yahweh's verdict—God's verdicts are righteous and just. Wenham captures the situation very well:

> The surviving priests, even though they were brothers, had to identify themselves entirely with God's viewpoint and not arouse any suspicion that they condoned their brothers' sins. Had they joined in the traditional customs of tearing their clothes, they might have been tempted in their grief to blame God for their brothers' deaths.[6]

Eating the Sacrifice to Make Atonement

When Moses inquires of Eleazar and Ithamar as to why they had not eaten the allotted priestly portion of the sin offering, he elaborates on his confusion by saying, "it was given to you to take away the guilt of the community by making atonement for them before the LORD" (v. 17). While some commentators are reticent to take the statement at what appears to be its face value, it seems

5. Klawans, *Purity, Sacrifice, and the Temple*, 62–66. Klawans argues that the priest imitates God with respect to examination of the sacrificial animal, blood manipulation, and consumption of the sacrifice.

6. Wenham, *Leviticus*, 157; Ross, *Holiness to the Lord*, 235; Nobuyoshi Kiuchi, *Leviticus*, ApOTC 3 (Downers Grove, IL: IVP Academic, 2007), 187; Gane, *Leviticus, Numbers*, 191.

that most recent commentators have acknowledged that, in some way, the priest's consumption of the sacrificial offering plays a part in the atonement process. The efficacy of the atonement is, in part, dependent on the priest eating his assigned portion of the offering. The text says that the priest "takes away" (Hebrew *nasa'*) the guilt (Hebrew *'awon*) of the community. I believe that "bear" rather than NIV "take away" is the more appropriate translation in this passage; as well, the word "guilt" could be alternatively translated as "iniquity," "culpability," or "punishment." In this case, I believe the text is saying that when the priest eats his designated portion of the sin offering, he bears the guilt and culpability that would have attached to the offerer. The burden would have been the offerer's, but now the burden is carried by the priest. This act of consuming the meat of the sacrificial offering plays an integral part in the complex act of atonement.[7] The priest, by virtue of this ritual action of eating the meat of the sin offering, is bearing the offerer's sin.

But the question has to be asked as to why this action is necessary. Why is the atonement process not complete with the slaughter, blood manipulation, and burning on the altar that has already occurred? The answer, I believe, is to be found in the work and thesis of Klawans: that the priest's actions are to be *imitatio Dei*, an imitation of God. The priest's role in ritual is to mirror the character, person, and even the actions of Yahweh himself. In the consumption of the meat of the sacrificial offering, this means two things. First, even as God metaphorically consumes the meat of the offering, the priest mirrors this by doing so literally. And second, even as I have argued in the commentary on the sin offering in Leviticus 4:1–5:13, God himself is portrayed as taking on himself the burden and guilt of the offerer's sin; so here in chapter 10, the priest, in imitation of God, eats of the sacrifice and takes on himself the burden and guilt of the offerer. The priest's bearing of sin and guilt is an imitation of God's bearing of sin and guilt. The priest is the human, flesh-and-blood representation of God's own person and actions in bearing the sin and guilt of his people.

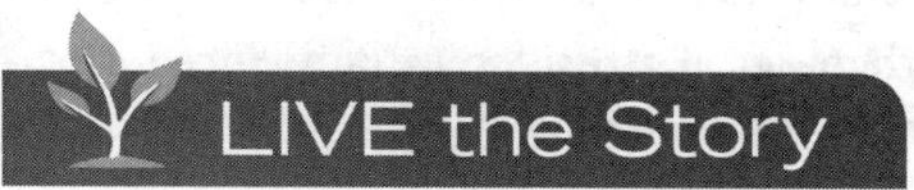

The Necessity of Obedience

Unfortunately, in some quarters of the church there has been a de-emphasis on the necessity of obedience in the Christian life. In the interest of emphasizing

7. For a more popularly oriented argumentation of this position, see Gane, *Leviticus, Numbers*, 190, 194–97; more academically, see Gane, *Cult and Character*, 91–105.

the grace of God, obedience has been denigrated in a way that neither Jesus nor Paul would ever have intended, almost as if the words "obey" and "obedience" do not occur in the New Testament.

We see in this narrative that Nadab and Abihu's action of offering unauthorized fire, which "the LORD did not command," stands in starkest contrast to Moses and the priests' obedience to "all that the Lord commanded," mentioned approximately fifteen times in chapters 8–9. The message could hardly be any clearer: obedience to the LORD's commands is essential.

This is no less the case in the New Testament. Jesus himself models obedience as he obeys the commands of his Father (John 10:17–18). Jesus expects his followers to do the same, and the evangelistic and missional work he commissions his followers to carry out is that of "teaching them to obey everything I have commanded you" (Matt 28:20). Aside from this, the words "obey" and "obedience" are used in the New Testament over forty times with reference to how God's people should relate to God. Additionally, a very strong case can be made that the necessity of obedience for Christians living in the new covenant is even greater than it was for the Old Testament saints under the old covenant. Obedience to God and to his Christ is an essential component of the Christian life.

The Reality and Righteousness of God's Judgments

Wenham calls attention to the unpalatability of this narrative for contemporary society and church. He notes that narratives like these

> are upsetting to the cosy bourgeois attitudes that often pass for Christian. In many parts of the Church the biblical view of divine judgment is conveniently forgotten or supposed to be something that passed away with the OT. Heine's famous last words, "God will forgive me, that's his job," have become the unexpressed axiom of much modern theology. This short story is therefore an affront to liberal thinkers. It should also challenge Bible-believing Christians whose theological attitudes are influenced by prevailing trends of thought more often than they realize.[8]

With regard to this point, the story of Ananias and Sapphira in Acts 5:1–11 is highly instructive. Hess has very nicely summarized the connections this story has to the Nadab and Abihu account.[9] Here I summarize and elaborate

8. Wenham, *Leviticus*, 153.
9. Hess, "Leviticus," 668.

on the correspondences to which he calls attention. Both narratives include the following features:

1. An unacceptable offering is presented.
2. The unacceptable act is perceived as intentional and not merely careless.
3. The guilty parties are suddenly struck dead.
4. Their corpses are carried away and buried.
5. The accounts narrate a sin and punishment that follow almost immediately upon a very positive scene (as I said earlier, snatching defeat out of the jaws of victory).
6. The texts draw attention to the glory that is given to God as a result of the judgment:

> In the Leviticus narrative God declares that in this incident he is "proved holy" and that he is honored [glorified] in the sight of all the people. (10:3)

> In the Acts narrative Luke writes that "Great fear seized the whole church and all who heard about these events." (Acts 5:11)

These correspondences demonstrate convincingly that the judgment of God has not simply been left behind in the Old Testament. Indeed, it could be cogently argued that God's expectations of obedience and his judgments are even more severe in the New Testament than they are in the Old. At the same time, it is also important to note that in neither Testament are we to understand that these instances of judgment constitute "regular fare." They can be quite exceptional. This caveat notwithstanding, these incidents still serve to remind the community that God will ultimately prove himself holy, gain glory for himself, and that he reserves the right to do so, no less in instances of judgment and wrath than in instances of salvation.

In Solidarity with the Holiness of God

The Old Testament priests had to be vigilant in their actions and discernment so that they might "distinguish between the holy and the common, between the unclean and the clean" and that they might "teach the Israelites all the decrees the Lord has given them through Moses" (Lev 10:10–11).

The command to Aaron and his sons to refrain from engaging in mourning rites for their disobedient sons and brothers reflects the attitude that Christians should adopt today with regard to false teachers and their teaching with respect to either doctrine or ethics, even should those teachers be numbered among friends or family. The harshness and severity of New Testament teaching in this area are quite stark. First, there are of course those passages that rail against false teachers (Matt 7:15; 24:11–13, 24; Acts 20:28–31; 2 Cor 11:12–15; Gal 1:6–9; 2:4–5; 1 Tim 1:3–11; 2 Pet 2:1–22; 1 John 4:1–6). But second, there is the harshness of statements in the New Testament, especially from Jesus himself, relativizing devotion to friends and family. Jesus says in one place, "Anyone who loves their father or mother more than me is not worthy of me; anyone who loves their son or daughter more than me is not worthy of me" (Matt 10:37). And when told on one occasion, in a place where he was ministering, that his mother and brothers had come to see him, he replied, "My mother and brothers are those who hear God's word and put it into practice" (Luke 8:19–21).

There must indeed be compassion and inward mourning when friends, family, and colleagues depart from scriptural norms in their doctrinal and ethical teaching. But there must be no hint of this sympathy in our external actions, lest we seem to be in some way siding with them against the Lord. Christians and Christian leaders, no less than the priests in the Old Testament, are responsible to "purify ourselves from everything that contaminates body and spirit, perfecting holiness out of reverence for God" (2 Cor 7:1) and to ensure that God in his holiness is worshiped "acceptably with reverence and awe, for our 'God is a consuming fire'" (Heb 12:28–29).

The Priest Who Bore Our Sins in His Own Body

Jesus proves to be the priest who stands in great contrast to Nadab and Abihu. He carries out the commands and ordinances of the LORD blamelessly. He is the one whose great concern was to do the will of his Father (John 4:34; 5:19, 30; 7:16–18, 28–29; 14:10, 24; Heb 10:7). He is the appointed and ordained priest who not only sanctified himself (John 17:19) but also carried out his priestly role blamelessly and without sin (Heb 4:15; 7:27; 9:14). Also, unlike Nadab and Abihu, though he did indeed give himself over to death for the sins of the people, he is nevertheless the priest who lives for ever and ever and therefore has a permanent priesthood (7:24), precisely because of his sinlessness and "the power of an indestructible life" (7:16).

But he is also the priest who, like the Old Testament priests who were to eat the sacrificial offering and in this way atone for the sins of the people, fulfilled that role as the priest who truly, fully, and finally bore the sins of the people in his own body (Matt 8:16–17; Heb 10:5–10; 1 Pet 2:24; 3:18; 4:1). He did this not merely in a symbolic ritual but in actuality. The sacrificial system in the Old Testament provides a rich, multiperspectival set of images by which we can understand the atonement that has been accomplished in Christ, as he is not only the fulfillment of the tabernacle, the temple, their rituals, and even their furniture but also of priest and sacrifice. Our response can only be one of great praise and adoration.

CHAPTER 10

Leviticus 11:1–47

LISTEN to the Story

[11:1]The LORD said to Moses and Aaron, [2]"Say to the Israelites: 'Of all
the animals that live on land, these are the ones you may eat: [3]You may eat
any animal that has a divided hoof and that chews the cud.
[4]"'There are some that only chew the cud or only have a divided hoof,
but you must not eat them. The camel, though it chews the cud, does
not have a divided hoof; it is ceremonially unclean for you. [5]The hyrax,
though it chews the cud, does not have a divided hoof; it is unclean for
you. [6]The rabbit, though it chews the cud, does not have a divided hoof;
it is unclean for you. [7]And the pig, though it has a divided hoof, does not
chew the cud; it is unclean for you. [8]You must not eat their meat or touch
their carcasses; they are unclean for you.
[9]"'Of all the creatures living in the water of the seas and the streams
you may eat any that have fins and scales. [10]But all creatures in the seas or
streams that do not have fins and scales—whether among all the swarming
things or among all the other living creatures in the water—you are to
regard as unclean. [11]And since you are to regard them as unclean, you must
not eat their meat; you must regard their carcasses as unclean. [12]Anything
living in the water that does not have fins and scales is to be regarded as
unclean by you.
[13]"'These are the birds you are to regard as unclean and not eat because
they are unclean: the eagle, the vulture, the black vulture, [14]the red kite,
any kind of black kite, [15]any kind of raven, [16]the horned owl, the screech
owl, the gull, any kind of hawk, [17]the little owl, the cormorant, the great
owl, [18]the white owl, the desert owl, the osprey, [19]the stork, any kind of
heron, the hoopoe and the bat.
[20]"'All flying insects that walk on all fours are to be regarded as unclean
by you. [21]There are, however, some flying insects that walk on all fours
that you may eat: those that have jointed legs for hopping on the ground.

22Of these you may eat any kind of locust, katydid, cricket or grasshopper.
23But all other flying insects that have four legs you are to regard as unclean.
24"'You will make yourselves unclean by these; whoever touches their
carcasses will be unclean till evening. 25Whoever picks up one of their
carcasses must wash their clothes, and they will be unclean till evening.
26"'Every animal that does not have a divided hoof or that does not
chew the cud is unclean for you; whoever touches the carcass of any of
them will be unclean. 27Of all the animals that walk on all fours, those that
walk on their paws are unclean for you; whoever touches their carcasses
will be unclean till evening. 28Anyone who picks up their carcasses must
wash their clothes, and they will be unclean till evening. These animals
are unclean for you.
29"'Of the animals that move along the ground, these are unclean for
you: the weasel, the rat, any kind of great lizard, 30the gecko, the monitor
lizard, the wall lizard, the skink and the chameleon. 31Of all those that
move along the ground, these are unclean for you. Whoever touches them
when they are dead will be unclean till evening. 32When one of them dies
and falls on something, that article, whatever its use, will be unclean,
whether it is made of wood, cloth, hide or sackcloth. Put it in water; it
will be unclean till evening, and then it will be clean. 33If one of them falls
into a clay pot, everything in it will be unclean, and you must break the
pot. 34Any food you are allowed to eat that has come into contact with
water from any such pot is unclean, and any liquid that is drunk from such
a pot is unclean. 35Anything that one of their carcasses falls on becomes
unclean; an oven or cooking pot must be broken up. They are unclean,
and you are to regard them as unclean. 36A spring, however, or a cistern
for collecting water remains clean, but anyone who touches one of these
carcasses is unclean. 37If a carcass falls on any seeds that are to be planted,
they remain clean. 38But if water has been put on the seed and a carcass
falls on it, it is unclean for you.
39"'If an animal that you are allowed to eat dies, anyone who touches
its carcass will be unclean till evening. 40Anyone who eats some of its
carcass must wash their clothes, and they will be unclean till evening.
Anyone who picks up the carcass must wash their clothes, and they will
be unclean till evening.
41"'Every creature that moves along the ground is to be regarded as
unclean; it is not to be eaten. 42You are not to eat any creature that moves

along the ground, whether it moves on its belly or walks on all fours or on many feet; it is unclean. [43]Do not defile yourselves by any of these creatures. Do not make yourselves unclean by means of them or be made unclean by them. [44]I am the LORD your God; consecrate yourselves and be holy, because I am holy. Do not make yourselves unclean by any creature that moves along the ground. [45]I am the LORD, who brought you up out of Egypt to be your God; therefore be holy, because I am holy.

[46]"'These are the regulations concerning animals, birds, every living thing that moves about in the water and every creature that moves along the ground. [47]You must distinguish between the unclean and the clean, between living creatures that may be eaten and those that may not be eaten.'"

Listening to the Text in the Story: Biblical Texts: Genesis 1:14–30; 7:1–9; 8:20; Leviticus 5:2, 7:19–21; Ancient Near Eastern Texts: Instructions to Priests and Temple Officials

Leviticus 11 deals with the distinctions the Israelites are to make with regard to clean and unclean animals. The chapter also provides regulations concerning contact with the carcasses of dead animals, whether clean or unclean, and what the remedies are for making such contact.

There are only a few passages in the texts leading up to this chapter that make any reference to the concept of distinctions between clean and unclean food, and there are no indications in those references as to what the criteria for these distinctions are. Noah, in Genesis 7, is commanded to take both clean and unclean animals onto the ark. Upon exiting the ark in Genesis 8, he sacrifices some of the clean animals and birds to Yahweh as a burnt offering. We are not told in those texts, however, which animals are clean and unclean. Then, in Leviticus 5:2 and 7:19–21, reference is made to how Israelites might defile themselves by coming into contact with unclean animals though, again, which animals are unclean are not specified. But now Leviticus 11 will provide the criteria. We will find in the exposition below that the Genesis 1 account of creation will assist in identifying these criteria.

Among the ancient Near Eastern texts, there is nothing that approximates the systematic nature of the distinctions made in this chapter; rather, they are more ad hoc or haphazard. The dietary regulations in the surrounding civilizations tended to focus on (1) particular localities rather than an entire populace, (2) what kinds of food can be offered to deities, (3) restrictions on the diets of priests versus commoners, (4) prohibitions on the consumption of animals considered sacred, and (5) restrictions for only specified periods of time. For example, a Hittite text, Instructions to Priests and Temple Officials, stipulates that pigs or dogs should not be allowed to enter rooms where sacred bread is stored but contains no laws preventing their consumption.[1] So Israel's dietary laws seem to be more systematic and encompassing, though the rationales for the system even today still seem elusive to biblical scholars.

EXPLAIN the Story

The chapter divides nicely into several sections:

Land animals (vv. 1–8)
Water animals (vv. 9–12)
Sky animals (vv. 13–19)
Flying insects (vv. 20–23)
Carcasses of unclean animals (vv. 24–25)
Summative and additional statements about land animals (vv. 26–31)
Provisions for dealing with the impurities caused by contact with the carcasses of unclean animals as well as the carcasses of clean animals that were not slaughtered (vv. 32–40)
Further summative statements regarding land animals (vv. 41–45)
Summative statements pertaining to all the dietary laws (vv. 46–47)

The most perplexing problem for scholars in dealing with this material is the rationale for the dietary laws. The distinctions between the clean and unclean animals are fairly clear. But the question is whether there is some overarching principle that explains why those distinctions serve as the criteria to separate clean from unclean.[2]

Several rationales have been offered in the history of interpretation. One suggestion is that the rationale is hygienic. The clean animals are "safe" for consumption, and the unclean animals are not. However, this rationale is favored by very few scholars today. Some of the unclean animals would actually

1. "Instructions to Priests and Temple Officials," *COS* 1.83:217–21.

2. Due to the nature of this commentary, space precludes comment on the identification of all the species mentioned in this chapter, for some of which there is no precise certainty. The reader is referred to more technical commentaries for discussion, especially Milgrom (*Leviticus 1–16*) and Hartley (*Leviticus*).

be healthier to eat than those that are deemed clean. Moreover, it is hard to tell how the various distinctions, such as divided hooves and chewing the cud, could serve as indicators of clean animals and thus healthy food. Additionally, if God gave these laws to the Israelites to ensure dietary health, it is hard to explain why he would have lifted the restrictions in the New Testament.

Another suggestion has been that the prohibited animals are the ones that would have been used in the idolatrous sacrificial worship of Israel's neighbors. However, that the calf is a clean animal yet is used for sacrifice in the Canaanite Baal cult seems to indicate that this cannot be the rationale.

A third suggestion is that the dietary laws in this chapter, as well as many of the purity laws in the following chapters, are in fact quite arbitrary. They were imposed on the Israelites by God simply to demonstrate whether the people would serve the LORD in observing the laws without having an explained rationale. This suggestion has a certain amount of merit, but such an explanation should be adopted as a last resort if no other logical rationale can be uncovered.

In my opinion, the work of the anthropologist Mary Douglas has, at the very least, set the discussion in the right direction.[3] She has convincingly argued that the rationale has to do with an animal's suitability for its creational and environmental context. In Douglas's words, for animals to be clean they must "conform to the class to which they belong."[4] It is only as an animal conforms to its creational context and class that it can serve as a symbol of wholeness, completeness, separateness, and, therefore, holiness.

Two charts will help us better understand Douglas's proposed rationale. The first chart represents the "framework hypothesis" for understanding the six days of creation in Genesis 1. Notice that the chart arranges the days of creation into panels, in which days one–three correspond to days four–six, respectively. As was noticed even in ancient times, the first three days of creation are actually days of separation. On day one God separates light from darkness, day from night. On day two God separates sky (waters above) from sea (waters below). And then on day three God further separates sea (waters below) from dry land. These three days of separation take the situation of chaos described in Genesis 1:2, "formless and empty" (Hebrew *tohu wabohu*; English equivalent something like "topsy-turvy"), and deal in particular with the "formlessness" half of that word pair. God separates light from dark, sky from sea, and then sea from land. This "separating" work is in fact an integral factor in the concept of holiness.

---

3. Mary Douglas, *Purity and Danger: An Analysis of Concepts of Pollution and Taboo* (London: Routledge & Kegan Paul, 1966).

4. Ibid., 53.

GOD'S DIVIDING AND ORDERING OF HIS CREATION

Day One	Day Four
Light (Day) from Darkness (Night)	Sun Moon and Stars
Day Two	**Day Five**
Waters Above (Sky) from Waters Below (Seas)	Birds Fish
Day Three	**Day Six**
Seas from Land	Animals and Humans

DIETARY LAWS OF LEVITICUS 11

Sea Animals—Clean	Sea Animals—Unclean
Fish that have fins and scales; that is, creatures that are appropriately conformed (equipped) to the environment in which they are found.	Animals that do not have fins and scales; that is, creatures that are not appropriately conformed (equipped) to the environment in which they are found.
Sky Animals—Clean	**Sky Animals—Unclean**
Birds that have wings and two legs; that is, animals that are supposed to be in the sky. As well, they must eat things birds are supposed to eat.	Animals that, though having wings, also dive and swim, making them not fully birdlike. Perhaps also that they are carnivorous, carrion eating, or fish eating; that is, they do not eat what birds are supposed to eat. It may also be that they are found to be guilty of violating the laws having to do with drinking blood.
Land Animals—Clean	**Land Animals—Unclean**
Animals that are four-legged and either hop, jump or walk.	Animals that are not four-legged and that move in some other way than hopping, jumping, or walking (such as crawling, swarming, or flying).
Further restricted to animals that, like cattle and sheep (the normal pastoral animals), have hooves and chew the cud.	Further specified as animals that, unlike cattle and sheep (the normal pastoral animals), do not have hooves or chew the cud. It is further specified that four-legged animals that have paws (literally "hands") are unclean; that is, animals that have human hands or use their "hands" for walking.
Flying insects that have jointed legs; that is, they hop.	Flying insects that do not have jointed legs; that is, they do not hop.

Days four–six have to do with rectifying the "emptiness" of verse 2. Now that God has separated the world into three realms—sky, sea, and land—he fills those realms with inhabitants. On day four God makes the sun, moon, and stars to rule over the day and night. On day five God creates the flying animals to inhabit the sky and the sea animals to inhabit the sea. On day six God creates the animals that "move along the ground" (1:24) to inhabit the land. To anticipate the next chart, note that the sky animals properly inhabit the sky, the sea animals properly inhabit the sea, and the land animals properly inhabit the land.

Now we look at the second chart. This chart outlines the substance of Douglas's proposal and also incorporates a number of additional explanatory factors. With regard to the sea animals, the primary delineating factor is that they must have fins and scales to be clean. Sea animals that have fins and scales *conform to the class to which they belong*. To put that another way, for a sea animal to properly qualify as a sea animal, it has to be a fish! Sea animals that are not fish tend to transgress their assigned boundaries, like, for example, amphibious creatures. The objection could be raised that there are other sea animals that do not have fins or scales and get along very well in the sea! But it is important to note that Douglas's classification is one that is not so much about practicalities but about symbolics. Fish, having fins and scales, serve as the symbolic paradigm for what is counted as clean among the sea creatures.

With regard to sky animals, the primary delineating factor is that for a sky animal to be clean, it has to have wings and two legs. Sky animals that have wings and two legs *conform to the class to which they belong*. To put that another way, for a sky animal to properly qualify as a sky animal, it has to be a bird! Additionally, the sky animals that are specifically prohibited can all be classified as carnivorous and carrion eating. And, of course, the meat they eat still has the blood in it. By eating meat that still has the blood, and by eating the meat of dead animals, these birds transgress the law on two counts. The birds the Israelites eat have to be law-observing birds! Additionally, it should be noted that though these birds have two feet, they use their talons to catch prey instead of simply using them for walking.

With regard to land animals, the clean animals are the ones that are four-legged and either hop, jump, or walk. They are truly land animals; they *conform to the class to which they belong*. Animals that employ some other means of locomotion, such as crawling or swarming, or that have more than four legs are not properly land animals. Additionally, the animals must be ones that have divided hooves and chew the cud. This last provision might serve to restrict the number of animals that may be slaughtered for food to those that conform to the normal pastoral animals: cattle, sheep, goats, and oxen. Thus there would be no carnivorous animals. With these restrictions in place, it might seem superfluous to indicate that animals that walk on their paws are unclean, but it actually serves to reinforce the principle. The "paws" (Lev 11:27) referred to here are literally "palms" or "hands." These animals use their legs/feet not just for walking but also use them like human hands; they transgress their boundaries.

With regard to insects, a more literal translation of verse 20 is "all swarming things that fly and go on all fours." Insects appear to belong to two different spheres: they fly, being somewhat birdlike, but they have four legs, being somewhat land-animal like. Additionally, they swarm—a locomotive method which is indeterminate and could belong to either sphere. However, swarming creatures like locusts, which have jointed legs that allow them to hop (like birds), are recognized by the text as separating themselves from the other swarming insects and are therefore considered to be clean.

Douglas's proposal has brought various reactions, from outright rejection to practically wholesale adoption, as well as various levels of agreement with added considerations.[5] In my opinion, her basic proposal serves quite well but does indeed need supplementation, some of which I incorporated in my description above. The value of Douglas's proposal comes in how she relates her ideas to the theme of holiness in Leviticus, uses the creation story in Genesis 1, and sees this idea playing out in the minds of the Israelites. She argues:

> If the proposed interpretation of the forbidden animals is correct, the dietary laws would have been like signs which at every turn inspired meditation on the oneness, purity and completeness of God. By rules of avoidance holiness was given a physical expression in every encounter with the animal kingdom and every meal. Observance of the dietary rules would thus have been a meaningful part of the great liturgical act of recognition and worship which culminated in the sacrifice in the Temple.[6]

Additionally, it should also be recognized that meals consisting of meat would not have been all that frequent for most Israelites and probably occurred only on special, perhaps primarily ritual, occasions.[7] This would have reinforced for the Israelites the necessity of living lives in conformity to God's

5. See, in particular, Walter Houston, *Purity and Monotheism: Clean and Unclean Animals in Biblical Law*, JSOTSup 140 (Sheffield: JSOT Press, 1993).

6. Douglas, *Purity and Danger*, 58.

7. Edwin B. Firmage, "Zoology (Fauna)," *ABD* 6:1120.

holiness, as well as reinforcing the idea of God's complete sovereignty over every sphere of their existence.

In addition to giving criteria for distinguishing between clean unclean animals, the chapter gives rules for how to deal with the contamination contracted by coming into contact with the corpses of either unclean animals or clean animals that died by some means other than ritual slaughter. For persons, the basic idea was that contact with a corpse rendered the person unclean until evening, which meant primarily that they could not participate in any tabernacle ritual observances. When evening came, they would wash themselves and their clothes and would become ritually clean again. The same was also true for household articles. For cooking utensils, the rules varied in accordance with the porousness of the utensil. A clay pot or oven was regarded as too porous to be cleaned from contamination and had to be broken; apparently less porous utensils, such as those that were fire-glazed, only needed to be washed. The water in household utensils was considered subject to contamination, but not larger bodies of water such as pools or ponds. Dry seeds that came into contact with corpses remained clean, but seeds that had been watered and presumably already in the process of germination were unclean. While it is not out of the question that these rules deal, at least in part, with hygienic considerations, the main issue is not so much hygienic as ritual defilement.

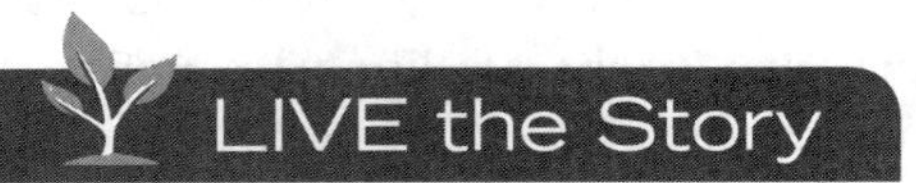

Dietary Laws, Christ, and the New Testament People of God

"So, does God really care all that much about lobsters, shellfish, and menstruating women?" I was once asked this question by a biblical scholar who wanted to demonstrate that God really was not behind the Old Testament dietary laws. We'll get to the menstruating women question when we come to Leviticus 15. But what do we do with these dietary laws, especially in light of the New Testament's apparent abrogation of them? Is there any value in these dietary law codes for New Testament Christians today? To borrow a phrase from the apostle Paul as he was addressing a different but related issue, "Much in every way!" (Rom 3:2)

In an interchange with the Pharisees and teachers of the law in Mark 7, Jesus seems to do away with the dietary laws, declaring "all foods clean" (v. 19, in apparent tension with his statement in Matt 5:17–20 with regard to the law's eternality). And, God seems to do away with them as well in Acts 10. But it is important to note the context and symbolic rationale in each case. In Mark

7 the context is that of human-made rules that had been added to the actual prescriptions of the laws. Even though he declares "all foods clean," Jesus also stresses in verses 8 and 13 the necessity of upholding the "commands of God" and how these human-made rules were in fact serving to "nullify the word of God." Interestingly, immediately after this interchange with the Jewish religious leaders, Jesus departs for the region of Tyre, where he performs a miracle for a gentile, a Syro-Phoenician woman. Also interestingly, in the dialogue between them Jesus introduces a dietary motif into the conversation by remarking how it is not right "to take the children's bread and toss it to their dogs" (v. 27), to which the woman cleverly responds by extending the metaphor with a remark about how even the dogs eat the crumbs that fall from the table.[8]

What is interesting to note about these two juxtaposed stories is how the dining motif connects two incidents. Declaring all foods clean in the first story prepares the way for the use of the dining motif in the second story as a way of highlighting the faith of a gentile. These two incidents in Mark 7, then, prepare the way for what happens in Acts 10, where we again find the motif of God declaring impure foods to be clean to serve as symbol of the gentiles becoming, by faith, Christians and full members of the people of God.

The dietary laws were given so that, in keeping them, Israel would be holy even as God was holy (Lev 11:45). They were also given so that Israel might distinguish themselves from the nations. Jesus does not by any means provide a critique of these laws. Indeed, neither Jesus in Mark 7 nor God in Acts 10 abrogates the dietary laws per se. Rather, what they do is declare all foods clean. In a context in which Jewish religious leaders had added human-made regulations to the law, and in a context in which the gentiles were being made to jump through multiple hoops in order to become part of the people of God, this cleanness declaration served to dramatically signify the full inclusion of believing gentiles in the people of God. This declaration did not render the law invalid for gentiles, as we will see when we come to Leviticus 17–18 and the use made of the laws there in Acts 15. Rather, paradoxically, in declaring all foods to be clean, and, symbolically, all believing gentiles, the commands of God are upheld and the word of God is rendered fully valid—not nullified.[9]

8. Notice that in another prominent miracle Jesus performs for a gentile, he again introduces a dining motif into the conversation: "Many will come from the east and the west, and will take their places at the feast with Abraham, Isaac and Jacob in the kingdom of heaven. But the subjects of the kingdom will be thrown outside" (Matt 8:11–12).

9. Coming out too late for me to interact with in this commentary is Matthew Thiessen's excellent volume, *Jesus and the Forces of Death: The Gospels' Portrayal of Ritual Purity within First-Century Judaism* (Grand Rapids: Baker Books, 2020). In his discussion of Mark 7:19 (pp. 187–95) Thiessen also argues, but on different grounds than I have, that Jesus was not abrogating the dietary laws.

The first time in Leviticus where we come across the prescription to "be holy" is in this chapter (11:44). While we, today, since all foods have been declared clean, do not observe the dietary laws, we still stand under the command to be holy. Indeed, this holiness must manifest itself in every area of our lives. We must do everything to the glory of God. Interestingly, one way to do this is directly related to the idea of eating and drinking: "So whether you eat or drink or whatever you do, do it all for the glory of God" (1 Cor 10:31). It is significant that, right after saying this, Paul then adds in verse 32: "Do not cause anyone to stumble, whether Jews, Greeks or the church of God." To be holy, to seek to bring God glory, relates directly to how we treat others. Indeed, this is one of the reasons why all foods were declared clean, to facilitate welcoming and showing love to gentile believers. It is enlightening to see how greatly New Testament ethics are related to the dining motif. We are to eat and drink to the glory of God (1 Cor 10:31–32). We are not to destroy those for whom Christ died by asserting our dietary rights (Rom 14:15). Shabby treatment of poorer brothers and sisters at church love feasts violates the covenant with God and merits condemnation and destruction (1 Cor 11:17–34). We are not to embarrass our dining hosts by squeamishness about what we are served (1 Cor 10:25–30). To wish for someone to be well fed but not do anything to feed them is to possess a dead rather than a living faith (Jas 2:14–17). As we take care to bring glory to God, even in matters of eating and drinking, we show ourselves as holy, even as God is holy.

Even as Douglas argues that the observance of the dietary laws would have, at every meal, "inspired meditation on the oneness, purity and completeness of God,"[10] our common meals can do so today as well. Every meal becomes an occasion for glorifying God by thanking him for his marvelous provision. Every meal becomes an opportunity to mirror God's holiness in our fellowship, love, and treatment of our brothers and sisters and those who are less fortunate. And every meal becomes an anticipation of that great day to which Leviticus 11, and indeed the entire book of Leviticus, points: the great wedding banquet of the Lamb, people coming from east and west to sit down to eat with Abraham, Isaac, and Jacob—and God himself dwelling in the midst of the redeemed people of the world, people who are holy even as he is holy.

---

10. Douglas, *Purity and Danger*, 58.

CHAPTER 11

Leviticus 12:1–8

LISTEN to the Story

12:1The LORD said to Moses, 2"Say to the Israelites: 'A woman who becomes pregnant and gives birth to a son will be ceremonially unclean for seven days, just as she is unclean during her monthly period. 3On the eighth day the boy is to be circumcised. 4Then the woman must wait thirty-three days to be purified from her bleeding. She must not touch anything sacred or go to the sanctuary until the days of her purification are over. 5If she gives birth to a daughter, for two weeks the woman will be unclean, as during her period. Then she must wait sixty-six days to be purified from her bleeding.

6"'When the days of her purification for a son or daughter are over, she is to bring to the priest at the entrance to the tent of meeting a year-old lamb for a burnt offering and a young pigeon or a dove for a sin offering. 7He shall offer them before the LORD to make atonement for her, and then she will be ceremonially clean from her flow of blood.

"'These are the regulations for the woman who gives birth to a boy or a girl. 8But if she cannot afford a lamb, she is to bring two doves or two young pigeons, one for a burnt offering and the other for a sin offering. In this way the priest will make atonement for her, and she will be clean.'"

Listening to the Text in the Story: Biblical Texts: Genesis 1:27–28; 3:16; 35:16–20; 1 Samuel 4:19–22; Ancient Near Eastern Texts: A Hittite text labeled Ritual K

Among Israel's neighbors, a number understood the process of childbirth as resulting in impurity. In some of these texts, the similarities and the differences are quite telling. For example, in a Hittite ritual text (simply denominated as Ritual K by one translator and editor), when a mother gives birth, an offering is to be made on the seventh day. If the child is a boy, there is a purification ritual carried out in the third month; if the child is a girl, the ritual is performed in the fourth month.[1] Noticeable similarities to the biblical text are that there is some kind of ceremony that takes place approximately one week after the birth and that the purification time is longer for the girl than for the boy. Notable differences are that in the Hittite text the ritual at the end of the first week is an offering, whereas in the biblical ritual there is the eighth-day circumcision; additionally, in the Hittite text both mother and child are purified, whereas the biblical text only explicitly mentions the mother's purification.

The biblical texts I listed above may contribute to our understanding of why something that should be seen as a great blessing and something even commanded by God—childbirth—renders the mother as in some way impure. I will reserve this discussion for the next section.

EXPLAIN the Story

The text and procedures are very straightforward. After giving birth, the mother will be ritually unclean for seven days, just as during her menstruation period (15:19–24), which simply means that she cannot have contact with sacred objects nor go to the tabernacle. On the eighth day, if the newborn is a boy, he is circumcised.[2] Afterwards, it will take an additional thirty-three days for the mother to be purified from her bleeding. If the newborn is a girl the initial period is fourteen days, followed by an additional sixty-six days. When this time period is over, she must present at the sanctuary a lamb for a burnt offering and a pigeon or dove for a sin offering. The priest will make atonement for her, and then she will be ritually clean. If she is too poor to bring a lamb, she may bring another pigeon or dove for the burnt offering. Despite the simplicity of the procedure, there are several questions the text raises, two of which will be discussed here:

1. Why are the days of purification longer for the mother who gives birth to a girl rather than a boy? Again, it is to be noted that this is mirrored in the birth ritual texts of other ancient Near Eastern countries. One suggestion is that a newborn girl is also capable of some vaginal

---

1. See the discussion in Gary M. Beckman, *Hittite Birth Rituals*, 2nd rev. ed., StBoT 29 (Wiesbaden: Harrassowitz, 1983), 132–47; Milgrom, *Leviticus 1–16*, 764. Milgrom also refers to Egyptian, Persian, and Greek texts.

2. This is the only mention of circumcision in the book of Leviticus. See the other commentaries in this series (Genesis and Exodus) for the meaning and significance.

bleeding, and this would require a longer purification time. Against this, however, is that it is only the mother who is to be purified, not the child. Another suggestion is that the longer wait time reflects the perception that the birth of a girl renders the mother more ritually impure than the birth of a boy. While this is possible, the suggestion has not drawn universal assent. There is no real consensus among the commentators, and perhaps it is safest to simply say that the reason is not yet known.[3]

2. The more important question to be asked is why there is need for purification at all and why, when the mother is finally permitted to go to the tabernacle again, she must present a burnt offering and sin offering, both of which are expiatory offerings. While in the history of the interpretation of this passage it has been argued that the offerings are necessary because of some sin on the woman's part in the birth process, most modern commentators reject this suggestion. It must be remembered that the preferred modern designation for the sin offering is rather "purification offering" and that most commentators understand that, in many cases, the sin/purification offering is dealing only with ritual impurity, for which there was no actual personal sin causing the impurity.

I propose an answer to this question that both agrees with the understanding of perhaps a majority of modern commentators but also brings a sin dimension into play. Many, if not most, modern commentators argue that the resulting impurity from childbirth is due to the "death" element in the delivery of a child. The bleeding that necessarily occurs in childbirth brings the mother into contact with the realm of death. The act of childbirth is an act in which the realms of life and death intersect. It is this contact with death that renders the mother impure and necessitates the rites of purification, including the burnt and sin offerings.

This explanation is compelling, but it also raises the question as to why death is defiling. This is where I believe the sin connection comes into play. The possibility of maternal death in the act of childbirth, greatly reduced in our more medically advanced societies, was much greater in ancient times. There are two recorded instances of a mother's death in childbirth in the Old Testament. Rachel dies while giving birth to Benjamin (Gen 35:16–20), and the wife of Phinehas dies in giving birth to a son whom she names Ichabod (1 Sam 4:19–22). These examples highlight the nexus between death and life.

3. George Athas, in personal communication (2018), has suggested that the reason might be that "the mother has given birth to someone who will also be capable of menstruation and childbirth herself in later life." This certainly seems plausible.

But according to the creation narrative in Genesis 1–3, this nexus was never supposed to exist. The act of giving birth, commanded in Genesis 1:28 ("be fruitful and increase in number"), takes on a threatening element on account of the fall by the pronouncement to the woman in Genesis 3:16, "I will make your pains in childbearing very severe; with painful labor you will give birth to children." Significantly, the word "increase" in 1:28 and the phrase "very severe" in 3:16 both derive from the same root in Hebrew (*rabah*). That which was meant to be only a blessing now becomes fraught with great pain and danger. It becomes the place where life and death meet.

Commentators are certainly correct to note that the sin offering is, in a number of cases, commanded to be offered where there is no suggestion that the particular individual has sinned, which is the reason why many suggest that the sin offering is better named as the purgation or purification offering. At the same time, it must be remembered that, according to the Pentateuchal narrative, the reason why impurities exist is on account of sin. Therefore, even where an individual presents a sin offering and there is no real question of some personal sin on the part of the individual, nevertheless, to borrow a phrase from Genesis 4:7, "sin is crouching at [the] door." Sin is always in the background. Boda, referring to the necessity of presenting sin offerings for the purity offenses in chapters 12–15, states it well:

> This meant that, even when they were seeking to rectify something as mundane as a moldy house or bodily discharge, they were reminded of a theological-symbolic world that was threatened by sin.[4]

Even in the act of childbirth—a life-giving act that has paradoxically become fraught with danger—sin and death present themselves. The purification offering is required because the mother, in giving life, has come into contact with death. But the purification offering is indeed a sin offering because this contact with death is the result of the sin of the first parents.

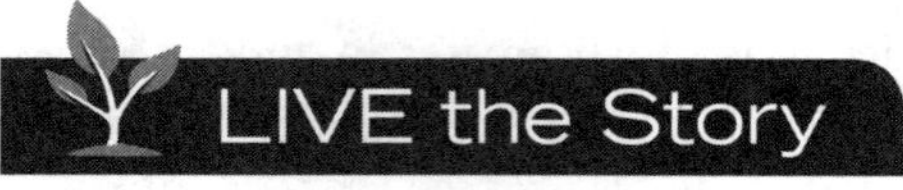

There are five significant implications to be derived from the subject matter of this chapter:

4. Boda, *Severe Mercy*, 74.

1. I once had a professor[5] in Bible college who told his class of "preacher boys," "Men, always be thankful for your mothers. Remember, she went down into the very jaws of hell to give you life." I do not recall if he tied this bit of advice to any particular biblical text, but he would certainly have been justified in doing so. The command and blessing of Genesis 1:28, the curse of Genesis 3:16, the stories of Rachel and the unnamed wife of Phinehas dying in giving birth, and multiple references in the Bible to the pain of childbirth all serve to remind us that the act of childbirth is a place where joy and pain, life and death, meet together. The text in Leviticus reminds us, additionally, that it is also a place where impurity invades the world of purity. This should serve as a sober reminder for Christians living in the modern medical world that, despite the tremendous advances in obstetrics, the birth process still has a measure of danger attached to it. It should also serve to remind us that even the joyous occasion of childbirth has been marred by the effects of the fall. Sin is always present. Childbirth should, of course, be a time of great rejoicing in a safe delivery and a new life that has come into the world. But it should also serve as a time of reflection and recognition that this world is not quite what it was meant to be.
2. The New Testament seems to recognize this danger as well. In one of the most difficult verses to interpret in the New Testament, Paul says, "But women will be saved through childbearing—if they continue in faith, love and holiness with propriety" (1 Tim 2:15). The different approaches to the interpretation of this verse are legion, and I certainly cannot go into a full-scale discussion here. I will say that, from a biblical-theological perspective, taking into account the creation-fall context already referred to in verses 13–14, I believe Paul is in fact referring to the dangers involved in giving birth. His statement that the woman will "be saved" could be interpreted either spiritually or physically, either absolutely or more generally.[6] At the very least, I believe Paul is indicating to his readers that the act of childbirth should engender—in mothers in particular and, indeed, in all of us—a renewed commitment to live lives of faith, love, and propriety and, in accord with the specific concerns of Leviticus, lives of holiness.
3. In Luke 2:21–24, after narrating the account of the birth of Jesus, Luke records that

5. Thomas G. Lawrence, beloved by all his students.

6. For this basic understanding that the passage is about the danger of childbirth itself, see Craig S. Keener, *Paul, Women and Wives: Marriage and Women's Ministry in the Letters of Paul, With a New Preface* (Grand Rapids: Baker Academic, 2004).

> on the eighth day, when it was time to circumcise the child, he was named Jesus, the name the angel had given him before he was conceived.
>
> When the time came for the purification rites required by the Law of Moses, Joseph and Mary took him to Jerusalem to present him to the Lord (as it is written in the Law of the Lord, "Every firstborn male is to be consecrated to the Lord"), and to offer a sacrifice in keeping with what is said in the Law of the Lord: "a pair of doves or two young pigeons."

Several commentators have called attention to Luke's emphasis on how different characters in the nativity story, as well as other places in the Gospel, performed certain duties in accordance with the Law of the Lord. It was important for Luke to recount, especially in the nativity narrative, that the birth of Christ was in accordance with Scripture. In Luke's nativity account we see this with Zechariah, Elizabeth, Mary, Joseph, Simeon, and Anna (1:5–6, 38, 59–64; 2:21–24, 25–27, 36–37, 39, 41). At the other end of Luke's Gospel we see it with the women who were going to anoint Christ's body (23:56). The bookends of the Gospel of Luke present us a Christ whose life is framed, not only by his own obedience to the law but even by the obedience of other characters in the narrative. Christ's life began in accordance with the law, and Christ continued to live in accord with that same law. At least in part, this is what Paul emphasized when he said that "when the set time had fully come, God sent his Son, born of a woman, born under the law" (Gal 4:4–5). As John Calvin said, it was not just Christ's death that accomplished our salvation, but it was accomplished by "the whole course of his obedience."[7] Indeed, Christ came to fulfill the law.

4. It is important to keep the covenantal context in mind here. According to Genesis 17, circumcision was a sign of the covenant. The signs of the Old Testament covenants were always "death signs" that symbolized the curse of the covenant.[8] In Genesis 17 Abraham is called upon to swear his covenant loyalty with the rite of circumcision. The curse is spelled out in verse 14:

> Any uncircumcised male, who has not been circumcised in the flesh, will be cut off from his people; he has broken my covenant.

---

7. Calvin, *Institutes of the Christian Religion*, 2.xvi.4:507.

8. This concept will be more fully explained in the commentary on Lev 26 below (pp. 346–48, 353–57).

There is a kind of punning going on here, with the terms "circumcised" (*mul*) and "cut off" (*karat*) acting as synonyms. We could, with justification, capture the import of this verse if we translated it this way:

> Any *uncut* male, who has not been *cut* in the flesh, will be *cut* off from his people; he has broken my covenant.

So in Luke 2, when Jesus is circumcised he is receiving the sign of the covenant. And unlike faithless Israel in the Old Testament, which horribly and repeatedly violated the covenant, Jesus as the new Israel perfectly keeps the covenant. Indeed, it is his very sinlessness, his complete and perfect obedience to the demands of the covenant, that qualifies him to be the one who can, by his own death, provide forgiveness and redemption for those who have broken the covenant.

Most interestingly, this circumcision, this covenantal cutting of Jesus's flesh when he is born, anticipates what will happen to him when he is crucified, concerning which Jesus, on the eve of his crucifixion, holds up the cup before his disciples in the upper room and declares:

> This cup is the new covenant in my blood, which is poured out for you. (Luke 22:20)

It is this connection between Christ's covenantal circumcision and his covenantal death that led the biblical theologian Geerhardus Vos to write strikingly:

> It is rightly observed that the blood of the Savior's circumcision is as much atoning blood for us as is the blood shed on Golgotha.[9]

5. Finally, it is also important to note that the book of Hebrews calls attention to how the Old Testament sacrifices, though they certainly served their purpose in their context, could not ultimately provide the needed purification from sin: "It is impossible for the blood of bulls and goats to take away sins" (Heb 10:4). This applies as well to the doves or pigeons that Joseph and Mary offered for purification. Rather, it was that little boy (whom they circumcised on the eighth

---

9. Geerhardus Vos, *Reformed Dogmatics*, ed. and trans. Richard B. Gaffin, Jr., 5 vols. (Bellingham, WA: Lexham, 2014), 3:192.

day and consecrated to the Lord on that trip to the temple) who by his death would ultimately provide the purification/sin offering for their redemption. He, rather than the priest before whom Joseph and Mary presented their sacrifices that day, would be the true high priest, who "after he had provided purification for sins . . . sat down at the right hand of the Majesty in Heaven" (Heb 1:3), who made "atonement for the sins of the people" (Heb 2:17), who "sacrificed for their sins once for all when he offered himself" (Heb 7:27), who "was sacrificed once to take away the sins of many" (Heb 9:28), and who has "appeared once for all at the culmination of the ages to do away with sin by the sacrifice of himself" (Heb 9:26). It was this high priest who, not by the sacrifice of bulls, lambs, goats, pigeons, or doves but by the sacrifice of his own body and his own blood, has procured our salvation, our redemption, and our purification from sin.[10]

---

10. The reader may also want to look at a blog article I wrote on this topic, Jerry Shepherd, "Leviticus and Christmas (2)," *The Recapitulator*, 5 January 2017, http://www.therecapitulator.com/leviticus-and-christmas-2/.

CHAPTER 12

Leviticus 13:1–14:57

LISTEN to the Story

13:1The LORD said to Moses and Aaron, 2"When anyone has a swelling or
a rash or a shiny spot on their skin that may be a defiling skin disease, they
must be brought to Aaron the priest or to one of his sons who is a priest.
3The priest is to examine the sore on the skin, and if the hair in the sore has
turned white and the sore appears to be more than skin deep, it is a defiling
skin disease. When the priest examines that person, he shall pronounce them
ceremonially unclean. 4If the shiny spot on the skin is white but does not
appear to be more than skin deep and the hair in it has not turned white,
the priest is to isolate the affected person for seven days. 5On the seventh
day the priest is to examine them, and if he sees that the sore is unchanged
and has not spread in the skin, he is to isolate them for another seven days.
6On the seventh day the priest is to examine them again, and if the sore has
faded and has not spread in the skin, the priest shall pronounce them clean;
it is only a rash. They must wash their clothes, and they will be clean. 7But
if the rash does spread in their skin after they have shown themselves to the
priest to be pronounced clean, they must appear before the priest again.
8The priest is to examine that person, and if the rash has spread in the skin,
he shall pronounce them unclean; it is a defiling skin disease.

9"When anyone has a defiling skin disease, they must be brought to
the priest. 10The priest is to examine them, and if there is a white swelling
in the skin that has turned the hair white and if there is raw flesh in the
swelling, 11it is a chronic skin disease and the priest shall pronounce them
unclean. He is not to isolate them, because they are already unclean.

12"If the disease breaks out all over their skin and, so far as the priest
can see, it covers all the skin of the affected person from head to foot,
13the priest is to examine them, and if the disease has covered their whole
body, he shall pronounce them clean. Since it has all turned white, they
are clean. 14But whenever raw flesh appears on them, they will be unclean.

[15]When the priest sees the raw flesh, he shall pronounce them unclean. The
raw flesh is unclean; they have a defiling disease. [16]If the raw flesh changes
and turns white, they must go to the priest. [17]The priest is to examine
them, and if the sores have turned white, the priest shall pronounce the
affected person clean; then they will be clean.

[18]"When someone has a boil on their skin and it heals, [19]and in the
place where the boil was, a white swelling or reddish-white spot appears,
they must present themselves to the priest. [20]The priest is to examine it,
and if it appears to be more than skin deep and the hair in it has turned
white, the priest shall pronounce that person unclean. It is a defiling skin
disease that has broken out where the boil was. [21]But if, when the priest
examines it, there is no white hair in it and it is not more than skin deep
and has faded, then the priest is to isolate them for seven days. [22]If it is
spreading in the skin, the priest shall pronounce them unclean; it is a
defiling disease. [23]But if the spot is unchanged and has not spread, it is only
a scar from the boil, and the priest shall pronounce them clean.

[24]"When someone has a burn on their skin and a reddish-white or
white spot appears in the raw flesh of the burn, [25]the priest is to examine
the spot, and if the hair in it has turned white, and it appears to be more
than skin deep, it is a defiling disease that has broken out in the burn. The
priest shall pronounce them unclean; it is a defiling skin disease. [26]But if
the priest examines it and there is no white hair in the spot and if it is not
more than skin deep and has faded, then the priest is to isolate them for
seven days. [27]On the seventh day the priest is to examine that person, and
if it is spreading in the skin, the priest shall pronounce them unclean; it
is a defiling skin disease. [28]If, however, the spot is unchanged and has not
spread in the skin but has faded, it is a swelling from the burn, and the
priest shall pronounce them clean; it is only a scar from the burn.

[29]"If a man or woman has a sore on their head or chin, [30]the priest is
to examine the sore, and if it appears to be more than skin deep and the
hair in it is yellow and thin, the priest shall pronounce them unclean; it
is a defiling skin disease on the head or chin. [31]But if, when the priest
examines the sore, it does not seem to be more than skin deep and there
is no black hair in it, then the priest is to isolate the affected person for
seven days. [32]On the seventh day the priest is to examine the sore, and if
it has not spread and there is no yellow hair in it and it does not appear to
be more than skin deep, [33]then the man or woman must shave themselves,

except for the affected area, and the priest is to keep them isolated another seven days. [34]On the seventh day the priest is to examine the sore, and if it has not spread in the skin and appears to be no more than skin deep, the priest shall pronounce them clean. They must wash their clothes, and they will be clean. [35]But if the sore does spread in the skin after they are pronounced clean, [36]the priest is to examine them, and if he finds that the sore has spread in the skin, he does not need to look for yellow hair; they are unclean. [37]If, however, the sore is unchanged so far as the priest can see, and if black hair has grown in it, the affected person is healed. They are clean, and the priest shall pronounce them clean.

[38]"When a man or woman has white spots on the skin, [39]the priest is to examine them, and if the spots are dull white, it is a harmless rash that has broken out on the skin; they are clean.

[40]"A man who has lost his hair and is bald is clean. [41]If he has lost his hair from the front of his scalp and has a bald forehead, he is clean. [42]But if he has a reddish-white sore on his bald head or forehead, it is a defiling disease breaking out on his head or forehead. [43]The priest is to examine him, and if the swollen sore on his head or forehead is reddish-white like a defiling skin disease, [44]the man is diseased and is unclean. The priest shall pronounce him unclean because of the sore on his head.

[45]"Anyone with such a defiling disease must wear torn clothes, let their hair be unkempt, cover the lower part of their face and cry out, 'Unclean! Unclean!' [46]As long as they have the disease they remain unclean. They must live alone; they must live outside the camp.

[47]"As for any fabric that is spoiled with a defiling mold—any woolen or linen clothing, [48]any woven or knitted material of linen or wool, any leather or anything made of leather—[49]if the affected area in the fabric, the leather, the woven or knitted material, or any leather article, is greenish or reddish, it is a defiling mold and must be shown to the priest. [50]The priest is to examine the affected area and isolate the article for seven days. [51]On the seventh day he is to examine it, and if the mold has spread in the fabric, the woven or knitted material, or the leather, whatever its use, it is a persistent defiling mold; the article is unclean. [52]He must burn the fabric, the woven or knitted material of wool or linen, or any leather article that has been spoiled; because the defiling mold is persistent, the article must be burned.

[53]"But if, when the priest examines it, the mold has not spread in the fabric, the woven or knitted material, or the leather article, [54]he shall order

that the spoiled article be washed. Then he is to isolate it for another seven days. [55]After the article has been washed, the priest is to examine it again, and if the mold has not changed its appearance, even though it has not spread, it is unclean. Burn it, no matter which side of the fabric has been spoiled. [56]If, when the priest examines it, the mold has faded after the article has been washed, he is to tear the spoiled part out of the fabric, the leather, or the woven or knitted material. [57]But if it reappears in the fabric, in the woven or knitted material, or in the leather article, it is a spreading mold; whatever has the mold must be burned. [58]Any fabric, woven or knitted material, or any leather article that has been washed and is rid of the mold, must be washed again. Then it will be clean."

[59]These are the regulations concerning defiling molds in woolen or linen clothing, woven or knitted material, or any leather article, for pronouncing them clean or unclean.

[14:1]The LORD said to Moses, [2]"These are the regulations for any diseased person at the time of their ceremonial cleansing, when they are brought to the priest: [3]The priest is to go outside the camp and examine them. If they have been healed of their defiling skin disease, [4]the priest shall order that two live clean birds and some cedar wood, scarlet yarn and hyssop be brought for the person to be cleansed. [5]Then the priest shall order that one of the birds be killed over fresh water in a clay pot. [6]He is then to take the live bird and dip it, together with the cedar wood, the scarlet yarn and the hyssop, into the blood of the bird that was killed over the fresh water. [7]Seven times he shall sprinkle the one to be cleansed of the defiling disease, and then pronounce them clean. After that, he is to release the live bird in the open fields.

[8]"The person to be cleansed must wash their clothes, shave off all their hair and bathe with water; then they will be ceremonially clean. After this they may come into the camp, but they must stay outside their tent for seven days. [9]On the seventh day they must shave off all their hair; they must shave their head, their beard, their eyebrows and the rest of their hair. They must wash their clothes and bathe themselves with water, and they will be clean.

[10]"On the eighth day they must bring two male lambs and one ewe lamb a year old, each without defect, along with three-tenths of an ephah of the finest flour mixed with olive oil for a grain offering, and one log of oil. [11]The priest who pronounces them clean shall present both the one to be cleansed and their offerings before the LORD at the entrance to the tent of meeting.

[12]"Then the priest is to take one of the male lambs and offer it as a guilt

offering, along with the log of oil; he shall wave them before the LORD as a wave offering. [13]He is to slaughter the lamb in the sanctuary area where the sin offering and the burnt offering are slaughtered. Like the sin offering, the guilt offering belongs to the priest; it is most holy. [14]The priest is to take some of the blood of the guilt offering and put it on the lobe of the right ear of the one to be cleansed, on the thumb of their right hand and on the big toe of their right foot. [15]The priest shall then take some of the log of oil, pour it in the palm of his own left hand, [16]dip his right forefinger into the oil in his palm, and with his finger sprinkle some of it before the LORD seven times. [17]The priest is to put some of the oil remaining in his palm on the lobe of the right ear of the one to be cleansed, on the thumb of their right hand and on the big toe of their right foot, on top of the blood of the guilt offering. [18]The rest of the oil in his palm the priest shall put on the head of the one to be cleansed and make atonement for them before the LORD.

[19]"'Then the priest is to sacrifice the sin offering and make atonement for the one to be cleansed from their uncleanness. After that, the priest shall slaughter the burnt offering [20]and offer it on the altar, together with the grain offering, and make atonement for them, and they will be clean.

[21]"If, however, they are poor and cannot afford these, they must take one male lamb as a guilt offering to be waved to make atonement for them, together with a tenth of an ephah of the finest flour mixed with olive oil for a grain offering, a log of oil, [22]and two doves or two young pigeons, such as they can afford, one for a sin offering and the other for a burnt offering.

[23]"On the eighth day they must bring them for their cleansing to the priest at the entrance to the tent of meeting, before the LORD. [24]The priest is to take the lamb for the guilt offering, together with the log of oil, and wave them before the LORD as a wave offering. [25]He shall slaughter the lamb for the guilt offering and take some of its blood and put it on the lobe of the right ear of the one to be cleansed, on the thumb of their right hand and on the big toe of their right foot. [26]The priest is to pour some of the oil into the palm of his own left hand, [27]and with his right forefinger sprinkle some of the oil from his palm seven times before the LORD. [28]Some of the oil in his palm he is to put on the same places he put the blood of the guilt offering—on the lobe of the right ear of the one to be cleansed, on the thumb of their right hand and on the big toe of their right foot. [29]The rest of the oil in his palm the priest shall put on the head of the one to be cleansed, to make atonement for them before the LORD. [30]Then he shall

sacrifice the doves or the young pigeons, such as the person can afford, [31]one as a sin offering and the other as a burnt offering, together with the grain offering. In this way the priest will make atonement before the Lord on behalf of the one to be cleansed."

[32]These are the regulations for anyone who has a defiling skin disease and who cannot afford the regular offerings for their cleansing.

[33]The Lord said to Moses and Aaron, [34]"When you enter the land of Canaan, which I am giving you as your possession, and I put a spreading mold in a house in that land, [35]the owner of the house must go and tell the priest, 'I have seen something that looks like a defiling mold in my house.' [36]The priest is to order the house to be emptied before he goes in to examine the mold, so that nothing in the house will be pronounced unclean. After this the priest is to go in and inspect the house. [37]He is to examine the mold on the walls, and if it has greenish or reddish depressions that appear to be deeper than the surface of the wall, [38]the priest shall go out the doorway of the house and close it up for seven days. [39]On the seventh day the priest shall return to inspect the house. If the mold has spread on the walls, [40]he is to order that the contaminated stones be torn out and thrown into an unclean place outside the town. [41]He must have all the inside walls of the house scraped and the material that is scraped off dumped into an unclean place outside the town. [42]Then they are to take other stones to replace these and take new clay and plaster the house.

[43]"If the defiling mold reappears in the house after the stones have been torn out and the house scraped and plastered, [44]the priest is to go and examine it and, if the mold has spread in the house, it is a persistent defiling mold; the house is unclean. [45]It must be torn down—its stones, timbers and all the plaster—and taken out of the town to an unclean place.

[46]"Anyone who goes into the house while it is closed up will be unclean till evening. [47]Anyone who sleeps or eats in the house must wash their clothes.

[48]"But if the priest comes to examine it and the mold has not spread after the house has been plastered, he shall pronounce the house clean, because the defiling mold is gone. [49]To purify the house he is to take two birds and some cedar wood, scarlet yarn and hyssop. [50]He shall kill one of the birds over fresh water in a clay pot. [51]Then he is to take the cedar wood, the hyssop, the scarlet yarn and the live bird, dip them into the blood of the dead bird and the fresh water, and sprinkle the house seven

times. [52]He shall purify the house with the bird's blood, the fresh water, the live bird, the cedar wood, the hyssop and the scarlet yarn. [53]Then he is to release the live bird in the open fields outside the town. In this way he will make atonement for the house, and it will be clean."

[54]These are the regulations for any defiling skin disease, for a sore, [55]for defiling molds in fabric or in a house, [56]and for a swelling, a rash or a shiny spot, [57]to determine when something is clean or unclean.

These are the regulations for defiling skin diseases and defiling molds.

Listening to the Text in the Story: Ancient Near Eastern Texts: By the Hand of Madi-Dagan, the Scribe and *Apkallu*-Priest; Purifying a House: A Ritual for the Infernal Deities; Namburbi Rituals

These two chapters deal with the identification of and ritual prescriptions for dealing with surface diseases, blemishes, or discolorations on skin, fabrics, and walls of houses. There are numerous references to skin afflictions in ancient Near Eastern literature, but to date only one of these texts seems to deal with the problem in any substantial way by ritual prescription. By the Hand of Madi-Dagan, the Scribe and *Apkallu*-Priest is a thirteenth-century text from Emar that has a number of correspondences with these two chapters.[1] Much like Leviticus 13–14, the text pays attention to blemishes, especially discolorations. For example, the text indicates what should be done if the blemish in the skin is white, yellow, red, black, or dark green. If the spot in the skin is yellow or red, it is regarded as being inflicted by the god Sin. Additionally, part of this text corresponds to Leviticus 14, in that two partridges are employed. One partridge is burned; the other is rubbed over the "patient's" body and then released to fly away. One significant difference, however, is that the ritual at Emar appears to be a healing ritual, but the ritual in Leviticus 14 is only a purification ritual; no healing is performed.

There are also several ancient Near Eastern texts that deal with mold in the walls of a house. One text, Purifying a House: A Ritual for the Infernal Deities, calls upon various deities to rise up from the underworld to clean a house of

1. Akio Tsukimoto, "'By the Hand of Madi-Dagan, the Scribe and *Apkallu*-Priest'—A Medical Text from the Middle Euphrates Region," in *Priests and Official in the Ancient Near East*, ed. Kazuko Watanabe (Heidelberg: Winter, 1999), 187–200; Yitzhaq Feder, "Behind the Scenes of a Priestly Polemic: Leviticus 14 and Its Extra-Biblical Parallels," *JHebS* 15 (2015), https://doi.org/10.5508/jhs.2015.v15.a4.

its impurities and carry them down to the underworld. But there is nothing in the text about any kind of priestly examination of the house.[2]

A closer correspondence to Leviticus 14:33–57 is provided by an Akkadian text that deals with a Namburbi (incantation) ritual that specifically refers to fungus and discolorations. The fungi are examined, and the various discolorations indicate exactly who in the house will suffer punishment to be inflicted by the gods (if the fungus is either green or red) or whether the owner of the house will actually prosper (if the fungus is black). Scraping of the walls is prescribed, as well as a purification ritual that, like the ritual in Leviticus 14 dealing with a person's skin disease, involves the use of birds.[3]

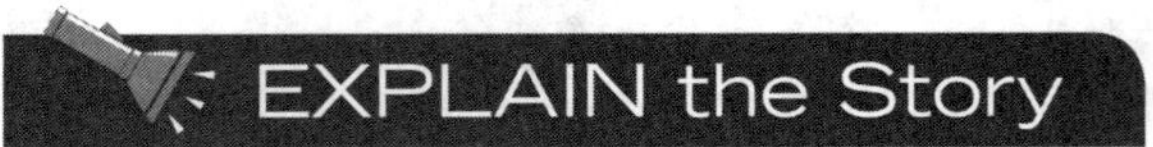

EXPLAIN the Story

The content of these two chapters divides into four basic sections:

13:1–46—Skin Diseases
13:47–59—Fabric Mold
14:1–32—Purification Rituals for Those Healed
14:33–57—House Fungus (and concluding statement)

Aside from the fact that these four passages are connected by the same basic theme—surface blemishes in the skin, fabric, or walls of a house—there are two Hebrew words that tie these passages together more specifically. The first is *tsara'at*, which occurs thirty times in these two chapters and which, in older translations, was rendered as "leprosy"; more recent translations have something more akin to the NIV's "defiling skin disease." This same word, *tsara'at*, also occurs in the sections dealing with fabric and house mold and is in fact translated as "mold" in those sections. In the NIV for these two chapters, then, *tsara'at* is translated as "defiling skin disease," "skin disease," "disease," "defiling disease," "defiling mold," and "spreading mold." So, literarily, *tsara'at* ties these four sections together as all dealing with variations of the same basic affliction.

We should also note at this point that, since the same word can be translated as "skin disease" and "mold," the term does not of itself mean "leprosy." While there is still a minority of scholars who believes that the main referent of the term is leprosy, most scholars today believe that the term actually describes

2. "Purifying a House: A Ritual for the Infernal Deities," *COS* 1.68:168–71.
3. Samuel A. Meier, "House Fungus: Mesopotamia and Israel (Lev 14:33–53)," *RB* 96 (1989): 184–92.

a variety of skin diseases, though some, like Milgrom, believe that the term "scale disease" would be an encompassing term for the skin-related infections.[4] Others believe that perhaps psoriasis comes the closest to the biblical description. Among those who believe that the term refers to a variety of skin diseases, some believe that at least one of those diseases could be what is more technically referred to as leprosy (Hansen's disease), while there are others who believe leprosy is not referred to at all. We do not need to come to any firm conclusions on this issue for this commentary.[5]

A second Hebrew word that ties these passages together is *nega'*, which occurs seventy-eight times in the Hebrew Bible, sixty-one of those occurrences being in these two chapters. In these two chapters NIV variously translates it as part of the phrase "defiling skin disease," as well as "sore," "affected person," "affected area," "mold," and "spoiled." Elsewhere in the Hebrew Bible it is variously translated as "disease," "plague," "assault," "flogging," "disaster," "affliction," "wound," and "scourge." Most important for our context in Leviticus is that the most recent prior use of the term in the Torah is in Exodus 11:1, in which *nega'* refers to the last "plague" that God will bring on the Egyptians, the death of all their firstborn sons.

The extensive usage of these two terms, *tsara'at* and *nega'*, casts an ominous shadow over the content of these two chapters. For *tsara'at*, Milgrom notes:

> Throughout the ancient Near East, disease is considered the work of supernal, malevolent forces. Scale disease, in particular, stands out as a prime means of divine punishment.[6]

Indeed, it has to be admitted that the Old Testament contributes to and seems to confirm this understanding. Among those whose contraction of skin disease is attributed to divine punishment are Miriam (Num 12:9–15); Uzziah (2 Chr 26:19–21); and Gehazi (2 Kgs 5:27; see also the curse in 2 Sam 3:29).

For the second term, *nega'*, the ominous shadows are deepened further by its occurrences in these chapters. Again, Milgrom states, "In the Bible, God is always the author of *nega'*. . . . It is invariably a divine punishment."[7] In the Bible, when a *nega'* occurs, it is always God who has caused it to occur. Indeed, when we see one particular place in these two chapters where the terms *nega'*

---

4. Milgrom, *Leviticus 1–16*, 775–76, 786, 816–20.

5. For some representative discussions besides that of Milgrom, see Wenham, *Leviticus*, 195–97; Hartley, *Leviticus*, 187–89; Sklar, *Leviticus*, 181–82; Kaiser, "Leviticus," 1094–95.

6. Milgrom, *Leviticus 1–16*, 820.

7. Ibid., 776; Levine, *Leviticus*, 76.

and *tsara'at* appear immediately juxtaposed to each other, this understanding is highlighted:

> When you enter the land of Canaan, which I am giving you as your possession, and *I* [Yahweh] put a spreading mold (*nega' tsara'at*) in a house in that land. (14:34; emphasis added)

I highlighted the first-person pronoun "I" in this verse to call attention to the fact that it is Yahweh himself who has put this "spreading mold" (*nega' tsara'at*) in the house. The LORD is the one who has put it there, and he is the one who provides the instructions as to what to do on account of it. It could well be that this verse should be understood as the default setting for all the occurrences of *tsara'at* in these two chapters. If there is an infection in someone's skin or mold in a piece of fabric or the wall of a house, it was the LORD who put it there.

This understanding, prevalent in the ancient Near East and well evidenced in the Old Testament, that defiling skin diseases were among the punishments that God could bring on people—coupled with the fact that *nega'* has such strong "punishment from God" associations in the Old Testament—introduces a dilemma for us in understanding these chapters. On the one hand, if these two chapters were indeed to be understood as God bringing these afflictions on the Israelites on account of their sins, that would be entirely consonant with the rest of the Old Testament. Levine declares, "Generally speaking, all disease was regarded as a punishment from God for some wrongdoing. In the case of *tsara'at* specifically, there was a tradition that it represented a punishment from God for acts of malice."[8]

On the other hand, there are certainly no explicit statements in this chapter that the skin-diseased person or the person whose clothing or house has become infected with mold has sinned against God. It is also possible that Leviticus 14:34, even if it does serve as a default setting for these chapters, may simply mean that all occurrences of skin disease and mold are under the sovereign control of God. Additionally, the detail into which these chapters go as to the diligence of the priest's examination of skin, clothing, and houses, as well as the description of the purification procedures, seems to put in place the expectation that, for the greater majority of the maladies in this chapter, the people will be healed of their skin eruptions, they will not have to throw away their clothes, and they will not have to tear down their houses.

8. Levine, *Leviticus*, 75.

However, even if the situation might not be that serious, it would not mean the persons could presume this to be the case. When they were afflicted with the skin disease, they could not simply assume, "it's probably nothing," and decide not to go to the priest so that he could carry out the prescribed examination. Of course, as Milgrom notes, "The reluctance of persons stricken with a skin eruption to report it to a priest and face quarantine and possible banishment is quite understandable."[9] Indeed, it still needed to be understood that these were matters of life and death. When people presented themselves before the Lord at the tent of meeting, they had to be in a state of cleanness. It was not just a concern for the skin-diseased person himself or herself. If there were ritual contagion in the community, this could prove to be fatal for those who came to present themselves before the Lord in the tabernacle precincts if they had unwittingly come in contact with someone who was skin diseased. This is why the skin-diseased person had to be quarantined outside the camp:

> If he were to remain in the community, people might be with him under the same roof and be unaware of it and then enter the sanctuary or east sacred food. And it is this fatal contact between the impure and the sacred that had to be avoided at all costs.[10]

So, ultimately, the attitude this chapter was intended to foster in the Israelites was one that was hopeful in the gracious love and kindness of their covenant God but also cognizant of his holiness and therefore not presuming on that grace.

Leviticus 13:1–46

This section deals with various kinds of skin afflictions, such as boils, burns, and the onset of baldness, some of which just seem to occur naturally as well as those that might occur for more specific reasons. The priest's responsibility in all these cases is to determine whether the sore in the skin is one that makes the person clean or unclean. If the person is definitely determined to be unclean, they must dwell outside the camp until such time as they become clean again. Those whose status the priest cannot immediately determine must go through quarantine periods until the priest is able to make a definitive pronouncement. The priest's role here is that of a monitor. He diagnoses, but he does not prescribe what might be done for a cure. He is not a doctor.

9. Milgrom, *Leviticus 1–16*, 776.
10. Ibid., 805–6.

The potential seriousness for these various cases of skin disease is the possibility that the disease might eat away the skin. When Miriam is punished for her actions in questioning her younger brother Moses's authority, she is afflicted with a disease that turns her skin white as snow. Aaron begs Moses to not hold her sin against her, "Do not let her be like a stillborn infant coming from its mother's womb with its flesh half eaten away" (Num 12:12). Notice the connection this description has with death. To be afflicted with this disease, which eats one's skin away, is to be in danger of entering death's realm. It is as if death itself had reached back from its domain into life in order to claim a new victim. In Job 18:13, Bildad describes the plight of the sinner who has contracted an affliction that "eats away parts of his skin." Then, metaphorically borrowing from the imagery of mythology, he states, "Death's firstborn devours his limbs." Gane strikingly refers to this condition as the "Blight of the living dead."[11] This is the fear that these potentially devastating skin conditions could cause in the afflicted.

Note that there are two conditions described here—whiteness of the skin and the flesh apparently being eaten away. The whiteness of the sore (or of the hair in the sore) is a sign that alerts the priest that the person is in fact unclean. However, paradoxically, for a person whose skin has turned completely white (the *tsara'at* covers them from head to foot), the priest is to pronounce the person clean. Probably what is meant by this is that even though their skin is completely white, the flakiness has vanished and there are no open sores or raw flesh.

Having referred to the passage in Job in which Bildad describes this dreadful skin condition as an incontrovertible sign that the afflicted person is a sinner, I need to point out this is one of the very understandings that the book of Job is attempting to challenge. The book of Job does not by any means overturn the concept of what has been referred to as "retribution theology," the idea that God does indeed punish people for their sins. This remains true. What the book does challenge, however, is that we can take for granted that this retribution aspect is always operative. It may be that there are other reasons why the person is being afflicted. Indeed, in the book itself, Job has been afflicted not because he is a great sinner but, on the contrary, because God has put him on display as a showcase saint! This is why it is important to note that there is no explicit suggestion in Leviticus 13–14 that the skin-diseased individual is being punished by God. That could indeed be the case, but it is not explicit. The priest pronounces certain individuals to be ceremonially

11. Gane, *Leviticus, Numbers*, 238.

or ritually unclean; he does not pronounce them to be sinners. On the other hand, we must note that there is still a sin connection with these skin diseases, even with those who have not "merited" these afflictions. We will discuss this further below.

One last thing to note is that the living conditions of those who are pronounced unclean, "outside the camp" (13:46), reflects the larger motif of exile in the Old Testament. Wenham notes:

> To live outside the camp was to be cut off from the blessings of the covenant. It was little wonder that when a man was diagnosed as unclean he had to go into mourning. He experienced a living death; his life as a member of God's people came to an end. . . . As Adam and Eve experienced a living death when they were expelled from Eden, so every man who was diagnosed as unclean suffered a similar fate.[12]

To this I would add that Israel's future exiles, of course, fit into this picture as well. Leviticus would prove to be informative but sober reading for the exiled communities in Babylon as well as the returning communities in the restoration from exile.

Leviticus 13:47–59

Again, note that the same Hebrew word, *tsara'at*, translated in the first part of the chapter as "defiling disease," is in this section translated as "mold." Also note that the NIV translation, "woven or knitted material," is probably better rendered "warp or woof," which refers respectively to the longitudinal and transverse threads in a garment or the materials on the loom.[13]

The only other thing I would note for this passage is a remark by Calvin, with respect to how God has even subjected garments to various corruptions, that God "has surrounded the human race with rottenness, in order that everywhere our eyes should light on the punishment of sin."[14] Radner notes that Calvin's comments here remind us that though we should not tie every punishment to personal sin, yet, as the Book of Common Prayer states, "in the midst of life we are in death."[15] Sin and death constitute the milieu in which we live in this world.

---

12. Wenham, *Leviticus*, 201.
13. For additional discussion on this, see Wenham, *Leviticus*, 202; Milgrom, *Leviticus 1–16*, 809–10.
14. Calvin, *Last Four Books of Moses*, 2:18.
15. Radner, *Leviticus*, 143.

Leviticus 14:1–32

This passage has to do with the purification, atonement, and restoration process for those who had been declared unclean as the result of the examination process in 13:1–46. The other individuals who have been examined by the priest and even quarantined as part of the inspection process did not have to do anything by way of a ritual nature to be ceremonially qualified to present themselves at the tabernacle, other than simply washing their clothes.

The skin-diseased person has to go through a two-movement, multi-act process to be purified and ultimately declared ceremonially clean. The two movements are from outside the camp to inside the camp and then from inside the camp to the tabernacle courtyard. The ritual actions are performed outside the camp, inside the camp, and then finally at the tent of meeting. As well, the person to be purified is declared to be ritually pure at each one of these locations. Gane helpfully notes that the first two of these declarations essentially mean "pure enough for this stage."[16] It is only at the end of the entire process that the restored person is finally a "happy camper."[17]

Four different ritual acts are performed involving the deaths of sacrificial animals:

1. On the first day, outside the camp, there is the ritual involving two birds—one of which is killed, the other of which is released—reminiscent of the two goats to be used on the Day of Atonement (Lev 16). Most likely, the death of the one bird is symbolic of the death that the diseased person had been facing.[18] The live bird symbolically carries away the impurity of the diseased person. Wild birds are perhaps chosen for this ritual so that the released bird will not return to the camp and bring the impurity back into it. The live bird, along with cedar wood and some scarlet yarn (probably chosen because of their red color) and hyssop is dipped into the blood of the killed bird. The cedar wood, scarlet yarn, and hyssop are then used to sprinkle the to-be-cleansed person with the blood, who is now declared to be clean. The live bird is then released, and the person then shaves off all their hair and bathes in water. The person may now return and enter the camp.
2. On the eighth day of the process (after the person has on the seventh day shaved and bathed a second time), a guilt offering is made in the courtyard of the tabernacle. There is debate among commentators as to why

16. Gane, *Leviticus, Numbers*, 247.
17. Ibid., 247.
18. Gorman, *Divine Presence*, 86; Wenham, *Leviticus*, 208–9.

a guilt offering should be made on this occasion, since the guilt offering is actually a reparation offering and is usually made when there has been some violation against the LORD's holy things (see the commentary on 5:14–6:7). One common suggestion is that the reparation is to make up for the lack of offerings that the diseased person would have brought had they not been forced to live outside the camp. Another possibility is that the reparation is for the damage done by the skin disease to the body of the diseased person, who is made in the image of God—the person himself or herself is reckoned to be one of the "holy things" (*sancta*) of the Lord.[19] Alternatively, the reparation may be to compensate the priest for the extra duties he has had to perform in the rituals.

Also, some of the blood from this offering is put on the right ear lobe, right thumb, and right big toe of the one to be cleansed. This is quite similar to the ceremony for the priest's ordination (see the commentary on Leviticus 8; Explain the Story, pp. 115–20). The similarity between these cases is probably to be accounted for by the "rite of passage" concept. The priest is moved from the status of "commoner" to that of a holy priest. The skin-diseased person is moved from the realm of death to the realm of life.[20]

3. The second sacrifice on the eighth day is the sin offering. Again, there is no explicit statement in these chapters that the diseased person has sinned. Nevertheless, it is important to reiterate what I argued in the commentary for Leviticus 12: to come into contact with the realm of death is to come into contact with sin as well (Explain the Story, pp. 165–66). Therefore, a sin/purification offering is needed.
4. Finally, the third sacrifice on the eighth day is a burnt offering presented along with a grain offering. With this, the formerly skin-diseased person is now declared to be completely clean.

One last thing to note is that the eight-day process is undoubtedly meant to recall the eight-day process of creation, the eight-day process of the priest's ordination, and the eight-day process of the major Israelite festivals. To slightly amend and add to a statement of Boyce that I cited in the commentary on chapter 8 (Explain the Story, p. 116), we can say that it takes eight days to create the world, eight days to ordain a priest, and eight days to restore a person from the realm of death to the realm of life.

19. Hartley, *Leviticus*, 197.
20. Balentine, *Leviticus*, 77, 111.

Leviticus 14:33–57

Two things are to be noted with regard to this passage:

1. Unlike what takes place with skin diseases and more along the lines of what happens with fabric mold, actual measures are put into place to try to get rid of the mold from a house (scraping, removal of stones, etc.). This suggests that though hygienic concerns with fabric and stone are by no means the main concern, they are not entirely absent either. Perhaps there was also medical attention for the skin-diseased persons as well, though there is no record of such in the text.
2. For house mold, there was a two-bird purificatory ritual procedure to be employed, almost identical to the one to be performed for the skin-diseased person. The fact that this kind of attention was paid to the purity of Israelite homes reinforces Sklar's contention that "such a focus on keeping their own homes ritually pure would have been a constant reminder for them to make sure the Lord's home remained ritually pure."[21]

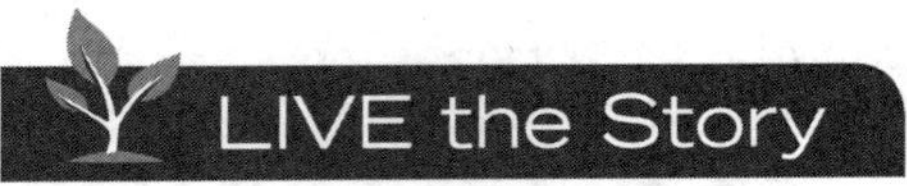

The Relationship between Sickness and Sin

As noted earlier, throughout the ancient Near East sickness in general, and skin disease in particular, was regarded as punishment from God for sins that the afflicted person had committed. As we also noted, the biblical text reinforces this conception. This is not the entire biblical picture; part of the lesson communicated by books like Job and Ecclesiastes is that this biblical picture of sickness as punishment is a general one, and we should not always "reason backwards" to assume that the afflicted person is necessarily suffering because of some sin in their life.

On the other hand, we must also acknowledge that the connection between sickness and sin is still there. Sklar argues, referencing Paul's warning in 1 Corinthians 11:29–30, that even today believers should examine their lives to see if there is indeed a possible connection between their illness and sin in their lives.[22] I remember one of my seminary classes with my beloved professor, Raymond Dillard, in which he said something along these lines (my rough paraphrase):

---

21. Sklar, *Leviticus*, 195.
22. Ibid., 188.

> Sometimes when there is some tragedy or sickness that comes into our lives, we go to God in prayer and ask, "Lord, is there some sin in my life that you have brought this affliction upon me?" If we were more honest and more aware of our sinful condition, we would ask that question quite differently: "Lord, for which one of my many sins have you brought this affliction upon me?"!

I do not believe we will usually be able to discern some direct connection between sickness and particular sins in our lives. At the same time, we must confess that when there is sickness in our lives, the sickness is indeed occurring in the life of a sinner. The sickness can still serve as a general reminder that we are sinful persons who live in the midst of sinful persons (cf. Isa 6:5). Sickness and disease are symptomatic of the sinful human race. Whether or not our sickness may be directly connected to some personal sin, we nevertheless live in a world that, because of sin, has been "subjected to frustration," and is in "bondage to decay" (Rom 8:20–21). Sickness can always serve as a general reminder of the sinful and cursed world in which we live. Indeed, it is telling that in Matthew 9:2–8 (Mark 2:5–12; Luke 5:20–26) Jesus, before he heals a paralyzed man who has been brought to him, pronounces that the man's sins are forgiven. While there is nothing in the text that indicates this man was afflicted because of his own personal sin, Jesus's words nevertheless seem to draw the connection between sin and sickness.

The Lengths to Which Our Great High Priest Went to Redeem Us

When the priest goes outside the camp to perform a purification ritual for the one who had previously been declared unclean, this is the only place in the book of Leviticus where the priest goes outside the camp as part of a "reclamation" project. On all the other occasions the priest takes the carcass or ashes of a sacrificial animal to dispose of them and rid the camp of impurity. But this is the only occasion on which the high priest goes outside the camp in order to bring a person who had been declared unclean back into the camp. This is analogous to what Karl Barth has referred to as "The Way of the Son of God into the Far Country."[23] Barth's title for this section of his *Church Dogmatics* capitalizes on both the parable of the Lost Sheep and the parable of the Prodigal Son in Luke 15. Jesus is the one who has gone outside the camp, into the "far country," to redeem that which was lost. It is not likely that the author of Hebrews was thinking of Leviticus 14:3 when he referred

---

23. Karl Barth, *Church Dogmatics*, 4 vols. (New York: T&T Clark, 1956), 14:157–210.

to the animal carcasses that were taken outside the camp and burned (Heb 13:11–13), but rather to other passages in Leviticus. Nevertheless, there is still an analogy between the priest, who goes outside the camp to reclaim the person whom he had declared unclean, and the work of Christ, as both priest and victim who "suffered outside the city gate to make the people holy through his own blood" (Heb 13:12). Christ has gone to extravagant lengths to procure our redemption.

Balentine has argued for a particular implication of the fact that both the priest and the one to be cleansed from their impurity go through a ritual in which blood is applied to person's right ear lobe, right thumb, and right big toe. He wonders whether there might be some sympathetic bond between the priest and the one to be cleansed:

> Because the priest and the person healed of skin disease are the only examples of persons who receive this particular daubing rite, we may be permitted to wonder if perhaps there is a subtle and peculiar connection between priesthood and suffering. Is it the case that only those who have traveled the life-scarring road from being condemned and ridiculed to being restored and embraced can really know what it means to minister to the afflicted?[24]

Balentine acknowledges the speculative nature of his suggestion. Nevertheless, it is intriguing and certainly falls into line with the declaration of the author of Hebrews that a priest must be one who is able to sympathize with those to whom he ministers. Of course, Jesus filled that role to the uttermost (Heb 2:10–11, 14, 17–18; 4:15–16; 5:1–3)

Elliott calls attention to a number of commentators through the centuries, especially in the ancient and medieval church, who conceived of Christ as one who was "accounted a leper" in his mediatorial and redemptive work.[25] While this could certainly be drawn out in a more fancifully allegorical direction, there is nevertheless a measure of exegetical justification for this. In my opinion, Kleinig is correct to indicate that Isaiah 53:4, 8 points in this direction.[26] In verse 4 the "we" group in the passage consider the Servant of the Lord to be one who been "punished" by God. The term "punished" in this verse is the verb *naga'*, which is the verbal form of the noun *nega'*, which, as we saw earlier, is used throughout Leviticus13–14 to refer to the "affliction" of the

24. Balentine, *Leviticus*, 112.

25. Mark W. Elliott, *Engaging Leviticus: Reading Leviticus Theologically with Its Past Interpreters* (Eugene, OR: Cascade, 2012), 127, 134, 138.

26. Kleinig, *Leviticus*, 301.

skin disease. This "we" group in Isaiah 53 was wrong in that they considered the Servant figure to be one who was punished by God for his own sins. But they were not wrong in understanding that God was the one afflicting the Servant. So, in verse 8, when it says that it was for the "transgression of my people" that he was punished, we come across that word, *nega'*, again, this time with the correct understanding that the Servant figure was stricken on account of transgressions that were not his own. So, the same word used to describe the affliction of the unclean person in Leviticus 13–14 is used to describe the suffering and strickenness of the Servant of the LORD. Kleinig correctly states:

> Therefore the Suffering Servant would heal people with unclean diseases by being afflicted for them and with them. He would take on their sickness and impurity and give them his purity and health. The Servant would be stricken even unto death (Is 53:8–9) and give his life as a reparation offering (Is 53:10). By doing so he would justify the many sinners and make intercession for them (Is 53:11–12).[27]

It should come as no surprise, then, that Matthew understands Christ's healing ministry in terms of Isaiah 53 and Christ's atoning work on the cross:

> When evening came, many who were demon-possessed were brought to him, and he drove out the spirits with a word and healed all the sick. This was to fulfill what was spoken through the prophet Isaiah:
>
> "He took up our infirmities
> and bore our diseases." (Matt 8:16–17)

Finally, I call attention to one more way this passage may connect to the story of Christ's redemption. It has become common within some streams of Christian interpretation and preaching to refer to the "scarlet thread of redemption" that runs through the Bible. This can take quite a fanciful turn in the attempt to find a type of Christ in "every stick, wood, tree"[28] in the Old Testament. Even in the early church (in the Epistle of Barnabas, for example) we find attempts to understand the scarlet rope that Rahab hung out the window (Josh 2:18–21) as a type of Christ. Many of the attempts to find this "scarlet thread" in the Old Testament are quite dubious.

---

27. Ibid., 301.
28. A phrase used by Karlfried Froehlich in his *Biblical Interpretation in the Early Church* (Philadelphia: Fortress, 1980), 13, to describe the allegorical interpretation of Justin Martyr.

On the other hand, most commentators understand the cedar wood and scarlet yarn used in the purificatory rite for the diseased person to have been chosen precisely because of their red color, corresponding to the red blood to be shed in the purification ritual. At the very least, this seems to indicate that there was indeed emphasis placed not only on the death of the sacrificial victims but also on the blood shed in that sacrifice and its use as a means of purification throughout the sacrificial system.

When we come to the New Testament, then, we should take care that we do not, like some theologians have done, take the references to the blood of Christ as being no more than a metaphorical way of referring to the death of Christ. There is no doubt, in his institution of the Lord's Supper, that Christ chose wine to symbolize his blood because the redness was reflective of the blood he was to shed. And there are over thirty passages in the New Testament that refer to the blood of Christ, specifically as the means of redemption. Within these thirty-plus references, a number of them refer specifically to the idea of cleansing, sanctification, purification, and sprinkling (Heb 9:14; 10:29; 12:24; 13:12; 1 Pet 1:2, 19; 1 John 1:7; Rev 7:14). To be sure, there is a level of metaphor in these New Testament references to the blood of Christ. But, in the light of the importance attached to blood in the Old Testament sacrificial system, even to the point of incorporating materials like cedar wood and scarlet yarn, whose redness corresponds to the blood, I believe we should recognize that we lose important theological perspectives if we try to eliminate the significance of these blood references in the New Testament texts. We are, indeed, cleansed, purified, and made holy through the blood of Christ.[29]

A Wholistic Salvation

Passages like Leviticus 13–14 serve to remind us that God in Christ is not simply concerned about the salvation of our souls but also the redemption of our bodies. This is why Christ did not only come preaching the good news of the kingdom; he also performed the good news of the kingdom. His miraculous healings of bodily diseases served as indicators of what he intended to ultimately accomplish in his work of redemption. In particular, he healed people from their skin diseases (whether or not these should be understood as leprosy). These healings served to identify him as the Messiah, and they also served to foreshadow the complete wholeness and salvation that will eventually be fulfilled at the consummation of the kingdom.

When asked by John the Baptist whether he really was the Messiah, part of

29. See more on this in the commentary on Leviticus 17 (Live the Story, pp. 231–35).

Jesus's reply to John was that "those who have leprosy are cleansed" (Matt 11:5). On two different occasions when Jesus healed individuals of their skin disease, he specifically told them to go to the priest as a testimony to them. Among other things, this was probably to indicate that he was not simply a skin-disease "monitor" but a skin-disease healer. This all points forward to the ultimate design for God's creation. The healing of the skin-diseased person was a mini-fulfillment and sign of God's great macro-design for the healing of his creation. The creation that had been "subjected to frustration" and brought into decay, a creation in which such a thing as sickness, skin disease, and leprosy existed, would finally "be liberated from its bondage to decay and brought into the freedom and glory of the children of God" (Rom 8:20–21). Indeed, on the day when our salvation will be complete, we who are the children of God will experience fully not only the salvation of our souls but also "the redemption of our bodies" (Rom 8:23).

But it is also important to remember that when Christ was here on the earth, he not only healed the diseased but sent out his disciples to do the same (Matt 10:1–8). This becomes our mandate to "live the story." We must not preach the gospel in word only but in word and deed. This means that we should not consider acts of mercy, kindness, and healing to be merely secondary or nonessential aspects of communicating the gospel. Wright captures this well when he says:

> Christian medical mission and compassionate ministry among the sick (including especially those whose sickness has been socially devastating, such as leprosy sufferers, and more recently AIDS sufferers) have always been powerful signs of the reign of God, precisely because they manifest the reign of one who himself was "despised and rejected by men, a man of sorrows, and familiar with suffering . . . one from whom men hide their faces" (Is. 53:3).[30]

So it is important to conduct these healing missions not simply as preparation for the gospel but as an integral part of the gospel itself, as both a sign and foretaste of the coming of the kingdom of God.

But there is also a social aspect to this compassionate ministry. Gorman notes that the diseased person who was forced to live outside the camp experienced a "social death."[31] Calvin refers to how the skin-diseased person was

30. Wright, "Leviticus," 141.
31. Gorman, *Divine Presence*, 85.

"accounted dead whom the leprosy had banished from the holy congregation."[32] So, again, Wright indicates the importance of the "re-socialization" aspect of the individual's restoration:

> The cleansing rituals were lengthy, significant and public. They provided not only subjective assurance to the sufferer that all was now well, but also objective social legitimation of his or her return to the community, and especially to its worship. They amounted to the celebration of new life as the person was restored from virtual death to the land of the living and to communion with God.[33]

Christ redeems us from sin and the effects of sin. He went to extravagant lengths to do so, in providing this wholistic salvation. And he has also committed to us this ministry of reconciliation, both to God and to one another. This is all entailed in what we should mean when we communicate the gospel in word and deed, saying, "Be reconciled to God" (2 Cor 5:20).

Special Note: Leviticus 13–14 and COVID-19

I submitted the manuscript for this commentary a good bit before the world was hit with COVID-19. After the devastating disease struck, a number of individuals, knowing that I had written a commentary on Leviticus, asked me to comment on the possible relationship between these chapters and this dread disease. So I wrote a four-part series of blog articles on this under the main heading, "Leviticus, Leprosy, and Lent—in the Light of the Corona Virus Crisis" attempting to answer a number of questions that were raised. These articles may be accessed by following the links in the footnote below.[34]

32. Calvin, *Last Four Books of Moses*, 2:26.

33. Wright, "Leviticus," 141.

34. The four articles, in order, are as follows: Jerry Shepherd, "Leviticus, Leprosy, and Lent—in the Light of the Coronavirus Crisis (Part 1)," *The Recapitulator*, 22 March 2020, http://www.therecapitulator.com/leviticus-leprosy-and-lent-in-the-light-of-the-corona-virus-crisis-part-1/; Jerry Shepherd, "Leviticus, Leprosy, and Lent—in the Light of the Coronavirus Crisis (Part 2)," *The Recapitulator*, 25 March 2020, http://www.therecapitulator.com/leviticus-leprosy-and-lent-in-the-light-of-the-coronavirus-crisis-part-2/; Jerry Shepherd, "Leviticus, Leprosy, and Lent—in the Light of the Coronavirus Crisis (Part 3)," *The Recapitulator*, 4 April 2020, http://www.therecapitulator.com/leviticus-leprosy-and-lent-in-the-light-of-the-coronavirus-crisis-part-3/; Jerry Shepherd, "Leviticus, Leprosy, and Lent—in the Light of the Coronavirus Crisis (Part 4)," *The Recapitulator*, 9 April 2020, http://www.therecapitulator.com/leviticus-leprosy-and-lent-in-the-light-of-the-corona-virus-crisis-part-4/.

CHAPTER 13

Leviticus 15:1–33

LISTEN to the Story

[15:1]The LORD said to Moses and Aaron, [2]"Speak to the Israelites and
say to them: 'When any man has an unusual bodily discharge, such a
discharge is unclean. [3]Whether it continues flowing from his body or is
blocked, it will make him unclean. This is how his discharge will bring
about uncleanness:

[4]"'Any bed the man with a discharge lies on will be unclean, and anything he sits on will be unclean. [5]Anyone who touches his bed must wash
their clothes and bathe with water, and they will be unclean till evening.
[6]Whoever sits on anything that the man with a discharge sat on must wash
their clothes and bathe with water, and they will be unclean till evening.

[7]"'Whoever touches the man who has a discharge must wash their
clothes and bathe with water, and they will be unclean till evening.

[8]"'If the man with the discharge spits on anyone who is clean, they
must wash their clothes and bathe with water, and they will be unclean
till evening.

[9]"'Everything the man sits on when riding will be unclean, [10]and
whoever touches any of the things that were under him will be unclean
till evening; whoever picks up those things must wash their clothes and
bathe with water, and they will be unclean till evening.

[11]"'Anyone the man with a discharge touches without rinsing his hands
with water must wash their clothes and bathe with water, and they will be
unclean till evening.

[12]"'A clay pot that the man touches must be broken, and any wooden
article is to be rinsed with water.

[13]"'When a man is cleansed from his discharge, he is to count off
seven days for his ceremonial cleansing; he must wash his clothes and
bathe himself with fresh water, and he will be clean. [14]On the eighth day
he must take two doves or two young pigeons and come before the LORD

to the entrance to the tent of meeting and give them to the priest. [15]The priest is to sacrifice them, the one for a sin offering and the other for a burnt offering. In this way he will make atonement before the LORD for the man because of his discharge.

[16]"'When a man has an emission of semen, he must bathe his whole body with water, and he will be unclean till evening. [17]Any clothing or leather that has semen on it must be washed with water, and it will be unclean till evening. [18]When a man has sexual relations with a woman and there is an emission of semen, both of them must bathe with water, and they will be unclean till evening.

[19]"'When a woman has her regular flow of blood, the impurity of her monthly period will last seven days, and anyone who touches her will be unclean till evening.

[20]"'Anything she lies on during her period will be unclean, and anything she sits on will be unclean. [21]Anyone who touches her bed will be unclean; they must wash their clothes and bathe with water, and they will be unclean till evening. [22]Anyone who touches anything she sits on will be unclean; they must wash their clothes and bathe with water, and they will be unclean till evening. [23]Whether it is the bed or anything she was sitting on, when anyone touches it, they will be unclean till evening.

[24]"'If a man has sexual relations with her and her monthly flow touches him, he will be unclean for seven days; any bed he lies on will be unclean.

[25]"'When a woman has a discharge of blood for many days at a time other than her monthly period or has a discharge that continues beyond her period, she will be unclean as long as she has the discharge, just as in the days of her period. [26]Any bed she lies on while her discharge continues will be unclean, as is her bed during her monthly period, and anything she sits on will be unclean, as during her period. [27]Anyone who touches them will be unclean; they must wash their clothes and bathe with water, and they will be unclean till evening.

[28]"'When she is cleansed from her discharge, she must count off seven days, and after that she will be ceremonially clean. [29]On the eighth day she must take two doves or two young pigeons and bring them to the priest at the entrance to the tent of meeting. [30]The priest is to sacrifice one for a sin offering and the other for a burnt offering. In this way he will make atonement for her before the LORD for the uncleanness of her discharge.

[31]"'You must keep the Israelites separate from things that make them

unclean, so they will not die in their uncleanness for defiling my dwelling place, which is among them.'"

[32]These are the regulations for a man with a discharge, for anyone made unclean by an emission of semen, [33]for a woman in her monthly period, for a man or a woman with a discharge, and for a man who has sexual relations with a woman who is ceremonially unclean.

Listening to the Text in the Story: Ancient Near Eastern Texts: Instructions to Priests and Temple Officials

The uncleanness referred to in this chapter is a temporary ceremonial or ritual uncleanness. This simply means that the person who had become unclean was not allowed to enter the tabernacle courtyard or present offerings to the Lord until such time as they had become ritually clean again. Similar concerns are expressed in ancient Near Eastern texts. For example, in the Hittite text Instructions to Priests and Temple Officials, we find the following:

> Whoever sleeps with a woman and his superior (or) his supervisor presses (him), let him say so. However, if he does not dare tell (his superior), let him tell a fellow servant. He still must bathe. However, if he intentionally delays, and without bathing he forces his way near the gods' sacrificial loaves (and) libation vessel (while) unclean, and his fellow servant knows about him, and he appears to him (!): If he conceals (it), but afterward it becomes known, it (is) a capital offense for them and both must die.[1]

This text concerns a member of the temple staff (a kitchen attendant) who has just recently had sex with his wife. This does not disqualify him from carrying out his duties, but he must become ritually clean again by bathing before he does so. The same would be true not simply for temple personnel but for any person who wanted to enter the temple precincts. Notice that the actual uncleanness, of itself, is a minor matter. Simply bathing removes the uncleanness. But if the person approaches the holy things in the state of uncleanness, then it becomes a matter of life and death.

One significant difference between this Hittite text, as well as throughout the ancient Near East, and the biblical prescriptions is that Leviticus uniquely

1. "Instructions to Priests and Temple Officials," *COS* 1.83:220.

prescribes a waiting period after bathing, "until evening" (vv. 5, 6, 7, 8, etc), which, for practical purposes, probably resulted in no approach to the tabernacle precincts till the following morning.[2]

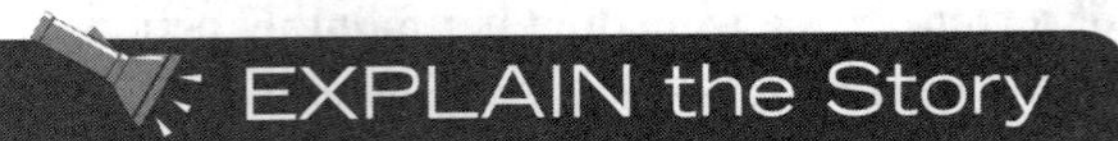

EXPLAIN the Story

This chapter has to do with male and female genital discharges, both normal and abnormal. As many commentators have pointed out, the substance of this chapter appears to have a chiastic (X-pattern) structure to it, though it is neither perfectly so nor symmetrical in terms of the length of each element. Some see the reference to sexual intercourse in verse 18 as being at the center of the chiasm, though this fails to deal with the reference to sexual intercourse in verse 24. My own modified version of the chiasm is as follows:

A Abnormal male discharges (vv. 2–15)
  B Normal male discharges (vv. 16–17)
    (reference to sexual intercourse in v. 18)
  B[1] Normal female discharges (vv. 19–24)
    (reference to sexual intercourse in v. 24)
A[1] Abnormal female discharges (vv. 25–31)

Indeed, the chiastic arrangement could be laid out in a more detailed version; for example, both of the sections that deal with abnormal discharges make reference to cleansing rituals as well. But the simpler chiastic arrangement above is sufficient, and it also demonstrates that verse 18 is not really at the center.

Abnormal Male Discharges (vv. 2–15)

This section, the lengthiest of the four, deals with abnormal genital discharges. NIV's "bodily" and "body" in verses 2–3 is a translation of the Hebrew *basar*, which means "flesh" or "body" but in these verses may be a euphemism for penis (though subsequent occurrences of the word in the chapter probably refer to the whole body). Various suggestions have been made as to the cause of the discharge, usually settling on gonorrhea. It is more likely, however, that several maladies are described here, including gonorrhea, coming under the broader classification of urethritis.

2. See Milgrom, *Leviticus 1–16*, 933; Hess, "Leviticus," 711–12.

Those who come into contact with this person will be unclean, but only for a short period of time. They simply need to bathe, and they are unclean until evening. After that, they can again enter the tabernacle precincts. The man himself, once he is healed of the discharge, must wait a week, at the end of which he may be ceremonially cleansed after washing his clothes and bathing. For the ceremonial cleansing, he is to take two doves or pigeons to the tabernacle, one for a sin offering and the other for a burnt offering. The priest sacrifices these, resulting in atonement for the man. Again, as discussed previously in the commentary on Leviticus 12 (Explain the Story, pp. 165–66), and 13–14 (Explain the Story, pp. 180–81), that atonement is needed does not necessarily indicate that the man has committed a specific sin that caused the discharge, though that is still a possibility. Rather, the atonement has to do with the fact that all such maladies have a sin-and-death connection; therefore, atonement is needed for purification from having come into contact with the realm of death and also of sin. The atonement purifies the individual and ransoms them from death.

Normal Male Discharges (vv. 16–18)

The concern here is with the normal emission of semen, specifically during sexual intercourse. Presumably, this would cover nocturnal emissions as well (see Deut 23:10). Again, there is nothing about either one of these situations that is sinful. But, then, why are they considered unclean, and why the need for bathing and the passage of time (an evening) before they can be considered clean again? Balentine provides a credible answer:

> Moreover, because the procreative act involves a loss of semen for the man and a loss of blood for the woman, it brings both man and woman dangerously close to the sphere of death. In effect, both partners in the sexual union lose some of their own life, symbolized by the loss of vital fluids, in creating a new life.[3]

Sklar helpfully points out that the "impurity resulted because of the seminal emission, not because sex was viewed as negative or sinful."[4]

Beyond this particular rationale, others have noted that a regulation regarding emissions as causing impurity would also have effectively "desacralized" the sexual act, indicating that, unlike some other ancient Near Eastern religions,

3. Balentine, *Leviticus*, 119; Gorman, *Divine Presence*, 92.
4. Sklar, *Leviticus*, 202.

cultic or sacred prostitution would not be seen as legitimate in the worship of Yahweh nor permitted in the tabernacle precincts.[5]

Normal Female Discharges (vv. 19–24)

In keeping with the chiastic structure of the chapter, the concern here is the normal monthly menstruation. Again, especially because there is the loss of vital bodily fluid, the same concerns as mentioned for verses 16–18 above are operative here. However, since it involves the loss of blood in particular, the woman has a longer waiting period for her ceremonial purification. It is unclear as to whether the seven-day waiting period begins at the onset of the menstruation or at the end of it, though it appears that most commentators think it begins at the onset. It is to be noted that, even though anyone who touches her or touches anything she has sat on will be unclean till evening, the woman is not actually isolated; apparently, she can still carry out her normal activities. Also, aside from the fact that her monthly period is longer, thus requiring the longer purification time than is the case with the man's seminal emission, in neither case is there any ceremonial cleansing required.

As is the case with the man's seminal emission during intercourse, there is a corresponding regulation with regard to intercourse during menstruation. If a man has sex with a menstruating woman, he is unclean for seven days. One problem with this, however, is that in an apparently corresponding passage (Lev 20:18), the penalty for both of them is "to be cut off from their people;" that is, death. We will look at this more closely in the commentary for chapter 20 but will simply note for now that the answer may involve the intentionality of the act.

Abnormal Female Discharges (vv. 25–30)

As is the case for the abnormal male discharges, there are a variety of medical problems that could be in view here, all of them capable of causing a discharge. What is important to note is that there is no difference for the male and female with regard to the description of the malady or the description of the ceremonial cleansing. In both cases, after the healing of the discharge there is the seven-day waiting period followed by the presentation of two doves or pigeons for a sin offering and a burnt offering on the eighth day for atonement. Indeed, in the entire chapter there has been no difference between male and female, other than the longer purification period for the menstruant due to the nature of the case.

5. Hartley, *Leviticus*, 211; Kleinig, *Leviticus*, 322–23.

A Couple of Observations

First, unlike the protocol for cleanliness issues in chapters 13–14, there is no priestly inspection and diagnosis. Very private, intimate parts of the male and female bodies are concerned here. On the one hand, this indicates Yahweh's lordship of every area of Israelite life. On the other hand, unlike the cases in chapters 13–14, the Israelites are likely on their honor as far as reporting goes. As Kleinig observes, "the main actors in this legislation are the Israelites. They are required to attend to their own diagnosis and treatment."[6] It will truly serve as a test of whether the Israelites believe that God is holy.

Second, these are life and death issues, not in themselves but as they relate to the danger involved if Israelites present themselves at the tabernacle in a ritually unclean state. A major reason for these instructions is that the Israelites should know what makes them unclean in this area so that when they present themselves before the LORD they will not die. Furthermore, these instructions are not simply about the preservation of individual Israelites; they are about the preservation of the community.

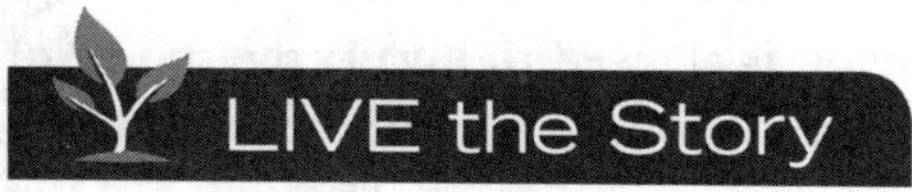

Christianity, Judaism, and Impurity

One very important lesson to be learned from this chapter is that we should not exaggerate the differences between Christianity and ancient Judaism. Of the four scenarios in this chapter, for one of them the impurity lasts only for part of a day and for another one it lasts only a week. For the other two scenarios, the impurity lasts for only as long as the discharge itself is not healed. In none of the four cases is the person to be put in isolation or considered to be an outcast from society. And for all four cases, while their impurity can indeed be communicated to other people, those other people are considered to be unclean only for part of a day. So it is wrong for Christians to argue that when Christ came, he put an end to a very oppressive and overly cruel system of purity rules and regulations. The Jewish scholar Amy-Jill Levine, a professor of New Testament and Jewish studies, has eloquently spoken against misguided Christian attempts to make "Jesus' Jewish context represent everything we don't like—sexism, elitism, militarism, you name it—and then depict Jesus as the one Jew to stand against his oppressive culture."[7]

---

6. Kleinig, *Leviticus*, 318.

7. Amy-Jill Levine, "Getting Judaism, and Jesus, Wrong," *HuffPost*, 17 January 2014, http://www.huffingtonpost.com/amyjill-levine/getting-judaism-and-jesus_b_4617731.html.

In fact, Richard Hess has observed that, in the story in Mark 5:24–34 of Jesus healing the woman with the bleeding disorder, "it is not clear that this text abolishes the laws of purification. . . . There is no abolition of the law with Jesus (Mt 5:17)."[8] The relationship between the Old Testament law and the Christian is a very complicated issue, and there is no space to settle that issue here. I do believe that, ultimately, the New Testament trajectory moves toward the abandonment of the purity laws, probably on account of the gentile mission of the church. But I also believe that Hess is correct to argue that the story of the woman with the bleeding disorder is not there for the purpose of contributing to this abrogation, nor for picturing the purity laws as oppressive, nor as being especially oppressive against women. In this particular narrative Jesus did not abrogate the law; rather, he healed the unclean woman.[9]

The Lord's "Unreasonable" Intrusion into Our Lives

George Knight recalls a saying attributed to the nineteenth-century figure, the Viscount Melbourne, William Lamb, who is said to have remarked, "Things have come to a pretty pass when religion is allowed to invade the sphere of private life."[10] By contrast, Boyce has called attention to the radical intrusiveness of Yahweh into the private life as reflected in Leviticus 15:

> One cannot but stand amazed at the way this legislation requires the synagogue's and the church's intrusion into even the most intimate areas of God's people's lives. There is indeed no area of our lives so "secular" or "profane" (the reader of Lev. 15 must conclude) that our response to it has no chance of reflecting God's glory.[11]

Even if the laws of physical and ritual purity have been abrogated, the concept of ethical and moral purity has not; the Lord is still the "Divine Intruder" in the life of the Christian. There is no room in the Christian life for the attitude expressed by the person who responded to a question by saying, "Yes, I am a Christian, but I try not to let it interfere with the way I live." Rather, the Lord's claim on the life of the Christian is both pervasive and absolute.

---

8. Hess, "Leviticus," 714.
9. Most recently on this issue, see Thiessen, *Jesus and the Forces of Death*.
10. Knight, *Leviticus*, 82.
11. Boyce, *Leviticus and Numbers*, 51.

Bodily Purity

At the same time, it is not completely right to say that spiritual purity has nothing to do with physical purity. Several commentators have argued that the laws regarding intercourse in Leviticus 15 have at least some investment in the concept of sexual restraint. We will see more about this in Leviticus 18 and 20, but even for this chapter it is good to note that the "Divine Intruder" is concerned about physical, sexual purity. This concern corresponds to the two motivations we noted earlier for the purity laws in Leviticus 15: so that we will not die and so that we will not contaminate the larger body of believers to whom we belong. As Rooker notes, the apostle Paul "often closely associates uncleanness . . . with fornication."[12] And passages like 1 Corinthians 6:12–20 remind us that sexual immorality is not only a sin against human bodies, but it is also a sin against the body of Christ. Indeed, Marion Soards has argued that the words "body" and "temple" in this passage should not be taken to refer to the individual but the church as corporate body and temple.[13] Whatever the case may be, it is important to see that there is indeed an analogy being employed. Gerstenberger remarks that

> the God of the cultic events—so say his temple servants—has provided a set of rules that must be observed even to the smallest detail. These rules are more strict than the court etiquette of the oriental kings.[14]

Sklar uses this royalty motif throughout his commentary on Leviticus, arguing that the rules in Leviticus are for the purpose of preserving royal protocol, and the concerns with discharges in this chapter are concerned with the possible defilement of the "Lord's holy palace."[15] Today, the Lord's holy palace, his temple, is the church, and by maintaining sexual purity we preserve the royal protocol and avoid defiling his church.

So the references to sexual purity in this chapter, as well as the ones we will be looking at in Leviticus 18 and 20, certainly have their New Testament counterparts. Indeed, the marriage bed is to be kept "undefiled" (Heb 13:4, NRSV).

At the same time, it is also important to note that sex is nowhere considered inherently sinful in the Bible. Balentine appropriately assesses the situation in Leviticus: "That Israel's priests viewed the sexual sphere as a matter of

12. Rooker, *Leviticus*, 207.
13. See Marion L. Soards, *1 Corinthians*, NIBCNT (Peabody, MA: Hendrickson, 1999), 133–35.
14. Gerstenberger, *Leviticus*, 208.
15. Sklar, *Leviticus*, 201.

ritual concern indicates neither a unique nor a repressive attitude toward the importance, worth, and enjoyment of sex."[16] And, as the anthropologist Mary Douglas notes, ancient societies that came up with all kinds of ritual rules regarding sex no more indicates a negative attitude toward sex than does a modern culture's numerous food regulations indicate a disapproval of food![17]

Jesus Takes Our Impurity

Finally, Christ is the one who not only heals us of our impurities, but he does so by taking our impurities on himself. I have already argued in the commentary Leviticus 4–5 (Explain the Story, pp. 76–77) and 10 (Explain the Story, pp. 146–47), with reference to the sin offering, that the sacrificial animal, the priest, and even the very tabernacle itself bear the ritual impurities of the Israelites. The story of the woman with the bleeding disorder in Mark 5 also corresponds to this understanding. Her reaching out and touching Jesus would have rendered him unclean. Above I referred to the position of Richard Hess that Jesus, in healing this woman, was not abrogating the purity laws. Indeed, Hess goes on to argue that Jesus was actually fulfilling these laws, and fulfilling them in his own body:

> If Jesus is truly the sacrifice for the sins of the world, then his acceptance of this uncleanness in his own body would be part of taking upon himself the suffering and sin of the world and redeeming it. . . . Jesus thus reverses the effects of sin and uncleanness.[18]

Tidball concurs with this understanding:

> At Calvary, Jesus, the pure one, was made impure; there "God made him who had no sin to be sin for us"; there, his wounds brought about our healing. His life-giving and life-restoring ministry is possible because he became the sacrifice that removed all our impurities and made us clean.[19]

Likewise, Kleinig remarks:

> According to Lev 15:25–27 and the teaching of the rabbis, her touch would have rendered Jesus ritually unclean. But by her touch the purity

16. Balentine, *Leviticus*, 119.
17. Mary Douglas, *Leviticus as Literature* (Oxford: Oxford University Press, 2000), 178–79.
18. Hess, "Leviticus," 714.
19. Tidball, *Message of Leviticus*, 169.

of Jesus was also conveyed to her. He took on her impurity in exchange for his purity.[20]

Jesus, as the full and final sacrifice, as the priest who is greater than the Aaronic priests, and as the one who offered the temple of his body to be "torn down"—but then raised up again in three days—has forever removed our sins and impurities from us by taking them upon himself and bearing them in his own body. Because he was raised from the dead, we are indeed healed and even given eternal life in him; we no longer need to fear the words in Leviticus 15:31, "lest they die" (NRSV).

20. Kleinig, *Leviticus*, 324.

CHAPTER 14

Leviticus 16:1–34

LISTEN to the Story

16:1The LORD spoke to Moses after the death of the two sons of Aaron
who died when they approached the LORD. 2The LORD said to Moses:
"Tell your brother Aaron that he is not to come whenever he chooses
into the Most Holy Place behind the curtain in front of the atonement
cover on the ark, or else he will die. For I will appear in the cloud over the
atonement cover.

3"This is how Aaron is to enter the Most Holy Place: He must first
bring a young bull for a sin offering and a ram for a burnt offering. 4He
is to put on the sacred linen tunic, with linen undergarments next to his
body; he is to tie the linen sash around him and put on the linen turban.
These are sacred garments; so he must bathe himself with water before he
puts them on. 5From the Israelite community he is to take two male goats
for a sin offering and a ram for a burnt offering.

6"Aaron is to offer the bull for his own sin offering to make atonement
for himself and his household. 7Then he is to take the two goats and
present them before the LORD at the entrance to the tent of meeting. 8He
is to cast lots for the two goats—one lot for the LORD and the other for
the scapegoat. 9Aaron shall bring the goat whose lot falls to the LORD and
sacrifice it for a sin offering. 10But the goat chosen by lot as the scapegoat
shall be presented alive before the LORD to be used for making atonement
by sending it into the wilderness as a scapegoat.

11"Aaron shall bring the bull for his own sin offering to make atonement for himself and his household, and he is to slaughter the bull for his
own sin offering. 12He is to take a censer full of burning coals from the
altar before the LORD and two handfuls of finely ground fragrant incense
and take them behind the curtain. 13He is to put the incense on the fire
before the LORD, and the smoke of the incense will conceal the atonement
cover above the tablets of the covenant law, so that he will not die. 14He is

to take some of the bull’s blood and with his finger sprinkle it on the front of the atonement cover; then he shall sprinkle some of it with his finger seven times before the atonement cover.

15“He shall then slaughter the goat for the sin offering for the people and take its blood behind the curtain and do with it as he did with the bull’s blood: He shall sprinkle it on the atonement cover and in front of it. 16In this way he will make atonement for the Most Holy Place because of the uncleanness and rebellion of the Israelites, whatever their sins have been. He is to do the same for the tent of meeting, which is among them in the midst of their uncleanness. 17No one is to be in the tent of meeting from the time Aaron goes in to make atonement in the Most Holy Place until he comes out, having made atonement for himself, his household and the whole community of Israel.

18“Then he shall come out to the altar that is before the LORD and make atonement for it. He shall take some of the bull’s blood and some of the goat’s blood and put it on all the horns of the altar. 19He shall sprinkle some of the blood on it with his finger seven times to cleanse it and to consecrate it from the uncleanness of the Israelites.

20“When Aaron has finished making atonement for the Most Holy Place, the tent of meeting and the altar, he shall bring forward the live goat. 21He is to lay both hands on the head of the live goat and confess over it all the wickedness and rebellion of the Israelites—all their sins—and put them on the goat’s head. He shall send the goat away into the wilderness in the care of someone appointed for the task. 22The goat will carry on itself all their sins to a remote place; and the man shall release it in the wilderness.

23“Then Aaron is to go into the tent of meeting and take off the linen garments he put on before he entered the Most Holy Place, and he is to leave them there. 24He shall bathe himself with water in the sanctuary area and put on his regular garments. Then he shall come out and sacrifice the burnt offering for himself and the burnt offering for the people, to make atonement for himself and for the people. 25He shall also burn the fat of the sin offering on the altar.

26“The man who releases the goat as a scapegoat must wash his clothes and bathe himself with water; afterward he may come into the camp. 27The bull and the goat for the sin offerings, whose blood was brought into the Most Holy Place to make atonement, must be taken outside the camp; their hides, flesh and intestines are to be burned up. 28The man who burns them must wash his clothes and bathe himself with water; afterward he may come into the camp.

[29]"This is to be a lasting ordinance for you: On the tenth day of the seventh month you must deny yourselves and not do any work—whether native-born or a foreigner residing among you—[30]because on this day atonement will be made for you, to cleanse you. Then, before the LORD, you will be clean from all your sins. [31]It is a day of sabbath rest, and you must deny yourselves; it is a lasting ordinance. [32]The priest who is anointed and ordained to succeed his father as high priest is to make atonement. He is to put on the sacred linen garments [33]and make atonement for the Most Holy Place, for the tent of meeting and the altar, and for the priests and all the members of the community.

[34]"This is to be a lasting ordinance for you: Atonement is to be made once a year for all the sins of the Israelites."

And it was done, as the LORD commanded Moses.

Listening to the Text in the Story: Biblical Texts: Leviticus 1–15; Ancient Near Eastern Texts: Temple Program for the New Year's Festivals at Babylon; Uḫḫamuwa's Ritual Against Plague

This chapter deals with the purification of God's sanctuary and the removal of sin and impurity not only from the sanctuary but also from the Israelite people. The chapter is set against the backdrop of the preceding instruction and narrative in the book. The sacrificial ritual in the chapter assumes acquaintance with the previously described sacrifices in chapters 1–6. Also, the first verse seems to indicate that the content of the chapter constitutes, in some measure, a response to the Nadab and Abihu incident in chapter 10.

The concerns of this chapter were also the concerns of other ancient Near Eastern peoples. The ritual texts of Israel's neighbors prescribed ways in which the sanctuaries of the gods were to be purified and also prescribed "elimination rituals" for removing impurities from the people. Two examples will demonstrate this.

First, from Babylon, the Temple Program text, which represents rituals probably going back to the third millennium BC, describes a ritual for the cleansing of the temple. The instructions prescribe what the priest is to do at each New Year's festival:

On the fifth day of the month Nisannu, four hours of the night (remaining?), the *urigallu*-priest shall arise and wash with water from the Tigris and Euphrates. [He shall enter into the presence of the god Bel, and] he shall . . . a linen *gadalū* in front of the god Bel and the goddess Beltiya. He shall recite the following prayer [to Bel]. . . .

After the recitation has been recited, he shall open the doors. All the *ēribbīti*-priests shall (then) enter and perform their rites in the traditional manner. The *kalū*-priests and the singers (shall do) likewise.

When it is two hours after sunrise, after the trays of the god Bel and the goddess Beltiya have been set, he shall call a *mašmašu*-priest to purify the temple and sprinkle water, (taken from) a cistern of the Tigris and a cistern of the Euphrates, on the temple. He shall beat the kettle-drum inside the temple. He shall have a censer and a torch brought into the temple. [He(?)] shall *remain* in the courtyard; he shall not enter the sanctuary of the deities Bel and Beltiya. When the purification of the temple is completed, he shall enter the temple Ezida, into the sanctuary of the god Nabu, with censer, torch, and *egubbū*-vessel to purify the temple, and he shall sprinkle water (from) the Tigris and Euphrates cisterns on the sanctuary. He shall smear all the doors of the sanctuary with cedar *resin*. In the court of the sanctuary, he shall place a silver censer, upon which he shall mix aromatic ingredients and cypress. He shall call a slaughterer to decapitate a ram, the body of which the *mašmašu*-priest shall use in performing the *kuppuru*-ritual for the temple. He shall recite the incantations for exorcising the temple. He shall purify the whole sanctuary, including its environs, and shall remove the censer. The *mašmašu*-priest shall lift up the body of the aforementioned ram and proceed to the river. Facing west, he shall throw the body of the ram into the river. He shall (then) go out into the open country. The slaughterer shall do the same thing with the ram's head. The *mašmašu*-priest and the slaughterer shall go out into the open country. As long as the god Nabu is in Babylon, they shall not enter Babylon, but stay in the open country from the fifth to the twelfth day (of the month Nisannu). The *urigallu*-priest of the temple Ekua shall not view the purification of the temple. If he does view (it), he is no (longer) pure. After the purification of the temple, when it is three and one-third hours after sunrise, the *urigallu*-priest of the temple Ekua shall go out and call all the artisans. They shall bring forth the Golden Heaven from the treasury of the god Marduk and (use it to?) cover the temple Ezida, the sanctuary of the god Nabu, from (its) . . . to the foundation of the temple.[1]

1. "Temple Program for the New Year's Festivals at Babylon," trans. A. Sachs (*ANET*, 332–33).

Apart from the obvious differences from the rituals preformed on the Israelite Day of Atonement (including worship of multiple deities), there are also various similarities to the Day of Atonement. The temple is purified by a high priest, who prepares by bathing and dressing in linen. He and the attendant priests perform the various purification rites involving censers, sprinkling (variously water/oil/blood), and sacrificial animals. The animal's body is disposed of. And, to some degree, the priest and the one who slaughters the animals become impure and must stay out in the open country for a seven-day (purification?) period.

There are several Hittite texts that have more in common with what has been referred to as the "scapegoat" element in the Day of Atonement ritual. The scapegoats in these texts are variously persons, bulls, dogs, mice, or rams. One example is a text known as the Uḫḫmuwa's Ritual Against Plague.

> Thus says Uḫḫamūwa, man of Arzawa. If in the land there is continual dying and if some god of the enemy has caused it, then I do as follows:
>
> They bring in one wether [a castrated ram] and they combine blue wool, red wool, yellow-green wool, black wool and white wool and they make it into a wreath and they wreathe the one wether and they drive the wether forth on the road to the enemy and they say to him (the god) as follows: "What god of the enemy has made this plague, now this wreathed wether we have brought for your pacification, O god! Just as a fortress is strong and (yet) is at peace with this wether, may you, the god who has made this plague, be at peace in the same way with the land of Ḫatti. Turn again in friendship to the land of Ḫatti." Then they drive the wreathed sheep into the enemy territory.[2]

While there are similarities to the scapegoat ritual of the Day of Atonement, it is significant that there is no hint in the biblical narrative that the goat is being sent into the wilderness to in any way appease a foreign deity or enemy god.

EXPLAIN the Story

There is some ambiguity in the chapter as to the exact order of the ritual actions performed in this chapter, as well as missing details that make it hard

2. "Uḫḫamuwa's Ritual Against Plague," trans. Billie Jean Collins (*COS* 1.63:162).

to reconstruct the ritual with precision. The following presents one possible chronology of actions:

Aaron brings a bull and a ram into the courtyard of the tabernacle.
He takes off his regular priestly clothing and bathes in water.
He puts on the linen clothing [these last two acts may take place inside the tabernacle or behind a screen somewhere in the courtyard].
He receives from the community two goats and a ram.
He casts lots for the two goats.
He slaughters the bull.
He takes coals from the altar of burnt offering in a censer, as well as some incense, enters the tabernacle, and then proceeds to enter the most holy place [this may have involved two trips, one to create the cloud of smoke and one to enter with the blood; also it is not exactly clear whether the coals come from the altar of burnt offering in the courtyard or from the altar of incense in the holy place].
He sprinkles some of the bull's blood on the atonement cover in the most holy place, as well as in front of the atonement cover.
He goes back out to the courtyard and slaughters one of the goats.
He reenters the tabernacle and the most holy place and performs the same blood applications with the goat's blood as with the bull's blood.
He performs additional sprinklings with the blood of the bull and the goat (perhaps mixed together) in the holy place.
He returns to the courtyard and places blood on the horns of the altar of burnt offering and then performs sprinklings of blood on the altar as well.
He places his hands on the live goat and confesses the sins of the Israelites, in this way placing all their sins on the live goat.
An appointed person leads the goat away into the wilderness.
Aaron enters the tabernacle, removes his linen clothes, bathes in water, and puts on his regular priestly clothing.
He returns to the courtyard and offers the burnt offerings for himself and the people, as well as offering on the altar the fat of the sin offerings.
The man who led the live goat into the wilderness washes his clothes, bathes, and returns to the camp.
Another man takes the hides, flesh, and intestines of the bull and the goat outside the camp and burns them.
This man washes his clothes, bathes, and returns to the camp.

There are a number of observations to make on the material in this chapter:

1. The mention of Nadab and Abihu in verse 2 and the warning that Aaron cannot enter the most holy place any time he wants seem to introduce the Day of Atonement as a contrastive response to the account of the death of Aaron's sons in chapter 10. Here in verse 12, Aaron is to enter the tabernacle with burning coals "from before the LORD," in contrast to the "unauthorized fire before the LORD" that Nadab and Abihu had offered (10:1).[3] Also, Nadab and Abihu were carried out of the tabernacle in their linen tunics (10:5), and Aaron must wear only a linen garment when he enters the most holy place.[4]
2. The dangers Aaron faces in this ritual are significant. The smoke from the burning coals he uses in the most holy place conceals the atonement cover from Aaron's view, reminiscent of the cloud on Mount Sinai,[5] which was intended to prevent a glimpse of God lest the onlooker die. Aaron brings incense in with him to placate God and avert his potential wrath.[6] Gorman has emphasized that in this chapter Aaron exists in a "liminal" state.[7] In this special ritual Aaron occupies a space between the holy and the impure as he confesses the sins of the people and actually bears them in his own person until he places them on the head of the live goat.[8]
3. The linen clothes that the priest is to wear during the ritual process contribute to the ambiguity. On the one hand, these clothes are sacred (holy). Linen is angels' clothing in Ezekiel 9:2–3 and Daniel 10:5–6. In the New Testament linen is associated with righteousness (Rev 19:8). On the other hand, in contrast to the priest's more ornate clothing, the linen, even though it was expensive material, seems to represent a special humility appropriate to the ritual that Aaron is about to perform; it appears more common than sacred. His ornate clothing makes him look regal, but in this linen dress "he looked more like a slave."[9] Perhaps part of what is being signified here is that, even though usually, according to royal protocol, the high priest is to wear ornate clothing, which reflects the royalty of the King he serves, the change to a simple linen garment reflects the fact that no servant should look too royal in the God's/

---

3. Bellinger, *Leviticus and Numbers*, 100.
4. Hess, "Leviticus," 718.
5. Gorman, *Divine Presence*, 96.
6. Milgrom, *Leviticus 1–16*, 1029–31; Wenham, *Leviticus*, 231; Levine, *Leviticus*, 104.
7. Gorman, *Divine Presence*, 98–99.
8. See Kiuchi, *Leviticus*, 297–98; Gane, *Leviticus, Numbers*, 283; Gane, *Cult and Character*, 245–46.
9. Wenham, *Leviticus*, 230.

King's immediate presence. On this special Day of Atonement, Aaron moves in this liminal space between holy and common, cleanliness and impurity, righteousness and sinfulness; it is in this position that he, in some way, bears the sins of the people.

4. In the commentary on the sin offering in Leviticus 4:1–5:13 (Explain the Story, pp. 76–77), I indicated my substantial agreement with Roy Gane in his understanding that the blood of the sacrificed animal actually transfers the sin of the offerer to the tabernacle itself. The offerer's sins are atoned for by the death of the sacrificial animal and the animal's blood being applied to the altar of burnt offering. The application of the blood to the altar is symbolic of the tabernacle as a whole absorbing the sin and guilt of the offerer, which in turn is symbolic of God himself bearing the guilt of the Israelites' sins. Correspondingly, Gane argues that on the Day of Atonement this process is reversed: the sins that have been atoned for throughout the year—becoming symbolically attached to the tabernacle and its furnishings—are removed from the tabernacle and atoned for by the death of the one goat and by the application of that goat's blood to the atonement cover. The live goat then carries off those sins into the wilderness. In essence, then, the Day of Atonement rituals are more concerned with the purification of the tabernacle than with atoning for the sins of individual Israelites; their sins have already been atoned for throughout the year, and they have already been pronounced forgiven for those sins.[10]
5. There is some debate among commentators as to what the Day of Atonement offerings have to do with sins that were not previously atoned for by the regular sin offerings throughout the year. Verses 16 and 21 refer, for the first time in the book, to sins of rebellion (*pesha'*) that are to be atoned for in addition to sins, uncleanness, and wickedness. Thus several commentators—and I tend to agree—have argued that, to various degrees, sins beyond those that would normally be atoned for throughout the year are also included on the Day of Atonement; this would include intentional sins and perhaps even sins considered to be of a "high hand."[11]
6. There is debate over the relationship between the goat to be slaughtered and the goat to be released into the wilderness. The two goats are introduced in verse 5 as "two male goats for a sin offering." After the lots are cast, the goat chosen by lot for the LORD is sacrificed as a "sin

10. Gane, *Leviticus, Numbers*, 277–88; Gane, *Cult and Character*, 129–43, 154–62, 217–41, 267–84.

11. Sklar, *Leviticus*, 211; Hartley, *Leviticus*, 240.

offering" (vv. 9, 15). But the live goat is not by itself referred to as a sin offering. It might be best therefore to regard the statement in verse 5 as in essence meaning that Aaron takes two male goats, one of which will be a sin offering proper. The live goat, since it is neither slaughtered nor designated "for the LORD," should not be thought of as a sacrificial sin offering per se. However, it still has its role to play in the atonement and propitiatory process—it bears the sins of the Israelites away into the wilderness, so it is still related to what the sin offering is meant to effect.

7. Perhaps the most controversial interpretive issue for the chapter is the actual symbolic nature of the live goat and what this live goat should be called. The Hebrew word translated by the NIV as "scapegoat" in verses 8, 10, 26, is *'aza'zel*. There are several theories—and no consensus—as to what this term designates and how it should be translated:

The term *'aza'zel* refers to the goat itself and is a compound word comprised of "goat" and "go away." Thus, it could be referred to as the "go-away-goat."

The term *'aza'zel* is by itself a term that means "removal," and thus it means "the goat that removes."

The term *'aza'zel* refers to a specific location in the wilderness or a general geological formation such as a cliff, a mountain, or rocky ground.

The term *'aza'zel* is a name for a wilderness-dwelling supernatural being, most likely a demon.

I believe that of these four options the first and fourth are the most likely candidates. And of these two, I am most inclined to the fourth one, for two reasons. First, the grammar in these verses puts the two goats parallel in a formulation with the same preposition: the first goat is *la-Yahweh* (for the LORD) and the second goat is *la-'aza'zel* (for *'aza'zel*). The most natural way to understand this parallel is to take it that both Yahweh and *'aza'zel* are named personal entities. Thus we should understand these two goats as one for Yahweh and one for Azazel. This is not an irrefutable argument, but it is the most normal way to understand the parallel construction.

Second, in the very next chapter there is a concern about how some of the Israelites have been making offerings to the "goat idols" (17:7; also rendered in some translations as "goat-demons"). Now, if this option is indeed the right one, one might question the wisdom of Yahweh instructing the Israelites to send an offering to the goat idol, Azazel, in the wilderness. However, this is not what would be happening. The live goat is not being sent to Azazel as an offering or some kind of appeasement. Rather, the picture is that of the live goat bearing the impurities and sins of the Israelites back to where they came from in the first place. Azazel is not being presented an offering; rather, he is being forced to receive back the impurities and sins for which he himself was responsible, reaping what he has sown. In some respects, an apt comparison is the account in Numbers 21:4–9, in which the LORD instructed Moses to make a bronze snake and put it on a pole to counter the plague of snakes he had sent against the Israelites. In the Day of Atonement ritual, Azazel reaps what he had sown; his evil returns to him.

8. This day was considered to be both a Sabbath day and a fast day. The people denied themselves (fasted). It was a day of mourning over sin yet also of great relief and satisfaction when the rituals came to a successful completion.

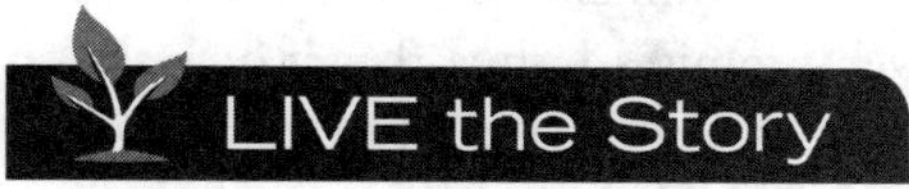

Outside the Torah, there is no explicit reference to the Day of Atonement in the rest of the Old Testament. Commentators have, however, suggested that there may be allusions to the day in various passages. In the next two sections, before going to the New Testament, we will look at some suggested allusions in the Old Testament.

The Day of Atonement in Isaiah 58

Shalom Paul has argued convincingly that Isaiah 58 should be interpreted against the background of the Day of Atonement.[12] The reference to the blowing of the trumpet in verse 1 recalls the trumpet blowing that was to take place on the Day of Atonement (Lev 25:9). The references to the people "humbling" themselves (vv. 4–5) recalls that on the Day of Atonement the people were to "deny" themselves (Lev 16:29, 31); the same Hebrew word (*'anah*) is translated "deny" in Leviticus 16:31 and "humble" in Isaiah 58:5. This humbling/denial certainly involved fasting; the phrase "the day of your fasting" in Isaiah 58:3 is probably a specific reference to the Day of Atonement.

---

12. Shalom M. Paul, *Isaiah 40–66: Translation and Commentary*, ECC (Grand Rapids: Eerdmans, 2012), 480–81.

The denial in Leviticus 16 was to entail abstaining from labor (v. 31). Yet in Isaiah 58 on the very day of their fasting the people are exploiting their workers (v. 3) and attending to their (business) affairs (v. 13).[13] Thus, at least part of the message in Isaiah 58 is that, on the very Day of Atonement itself, when the people should be lamenting and repenting of their sins, they are nevertheless engaged in activities that demonstrate that they are in reality still a very sinful and rebellious people (58:1). Their hypocrisy only serves to add to their sin and guilt—the exact opposite of what should have happened: their sin and guilt being atoned for, forgiven, and removed.

Zechariah, Atonement, and the Festival of Tabernacles

There are two possible allusions to the Day of Atonement in the book of Zechariah. First, in chapter 3 there is the scene in which Satan (or "the accuser") is making an accusation that the high priest Joshua is not worthy to serve in a priestly role, apparently on account of his sin and defilement that are symbolically represented by his filthy clothing. But Yahweh comes to the defense of the high priest and gives the command to clothe him in "fine" and "clean" clothing (vv. 4–5). Yahweh promises Joshua that if he walks in obedience and keeps Yahweh's requirements, then he will continue to serve as priest in the LORD's house. Then in verse 9 the LORD declares, "I will remove the sin of this land in a single day." These references to the changing of the high priest's clothing, the removal of sin, and the fact that it happens in a single day almost certainly are meant to allude to the Day of Atonement.[14]

Less certain, but still plausible as a Day of Atonement allusion, is that the promise of the removal of sin in a "single day" in Zechariah 3:9 anticipates a later passage in 13:1—"On that day a fountain will be opened to the house of David and the inhabitants of Jerusalem, to cleanse them from sin and impurity." Enhancing this possibility is that in chapter 14 there is an explicit reference to the Festival of Tabernacles and that both Jews and gentiles from the nations will celebrate this festival. This festival, as we will learn from Leviticus 23, begins just five days after the Day of Atonement. So it is possible that we have in Zechariah 13–14 both a textual and chronological reference to the Day of Atonement followed by the Festival of Tabernacles.

The day in 13:1 on which Yahweh cleanses his people from sin and impurity is the same day that is described in the immediately preceding verses in 12:10–14, in which Yahweh declares:

---

13. For the arguments that this is about conducting business, see Paul, *Isaiah 40–66*, 494–95.

14. Cogently argued by Mark J. Boda, *The Book of Zechariah*, NICOT (Grand Rapids: Eerdmans, 2016), 221, 225, 240–42, 259–61.

> And I will pour out on the house of David and the inhabitants of Jerusalem a spirit of grace and supplication. They will look on me, the one they have pierced, and they will mourn for him as one mourns for an only child, and grieve bitterly for him as one grieves for a firstborn son. On that day the weeping in Jerusalem will be as great as the weeping of Hadad Rimmon in the plain of Megiddo. The land will mourn, each clan by itself, with their wives by themselves: the clan of the house of David and their wives, the clan of the house of Nathan and their wives, the clan of the house of Levi and their wives, the clan of Shimei and their wives, and all the rest of the clans and their wives.

The people are cleansed from their sin and impurity because of Yahweh's appearance to them as the one they pierced. In a way not made explicit in Zechariah, but I believe hinted at, is that the "piercing" in 12:10 is connected to the cleansing from sin and impurity that takes place in 13:1. I believe, then, that Zechariah 3:1–9 and 12:10–13:1 look backward to the Day of Atonement and look forward to the New Testament revelation of Jesus as the one who is pierced for transgressions and whose atonement provides cleansing from sin and impurity.

Behold, the Goat of God, Who Takes Away the Sins of the World

At least in English, to call Jesus the "Goat of God" doesn't have the same ring to it as referring to him as the "Lamb of God." Yet, certainly, this title is appropriate as well. Jesus, in his death and crucifixion, brings together several sacrificial threads so that, in various respects, he fulfills all the sacrifices: Passover, burnt, grain, fellowship, sin, guilt, and so on. However, the question may be asked whether the New Testament presents us with any kind of fulfillment of the so-called scapegoat ritual of the Day of Atonement.

Several suggestions have been made for how we could see this. For example, in the trial scene before Pilate, Barabbas has been regarded by many as performing a scapegoat function. Recently, Hans Moscicke has intriguingly and cogently argued that for the Gospel of Matthew, besides Barabbas, the scapegoat imagery also extends to the crowds who cry out "Crucify him, Crucify him," who declare, "His blood is on us and on our children," and who will then suffer the destruction of Jerusalem in AD 70 and its aftermath.[15] Not only Barabbas, but also the crowd is the scapegoat.

---

15. Hans M. Moscicke, "Jesus, Barabbas, and the Crowd as Figures in Matthew's Day of Atonement Typology (Matthew 27:15–26)," *JBL* 139.1 (2020): 125–53.

While Moscicke's thesis is most likely correct, I find even more intriguing another way in which he proposes that the imagery might be construed. In this other alternate scenario, the crowd does not become the scapegoat; rather, the crowd constitutes the wilderness into which the scapegoat is released, or more pointedly, the crowd has become Azazel, the demon in the wilderness to whom the scapegoat returns the sins of the people. [16] If Barabbas is the scapegoat, then even as the scapegoat was sent into the wilderness to Azazel, so Pilate "released" Barabbas to the crowd (Matt 27:26).This accords with what I argued above, that the scapegoat returns the sins of people to the Azazel, the demon in the wilderness. However, in a kind of satirical parody of the Day of Atonement narrative, the crowd of people in the passion narrative have actually become the wilderness and/or Azazel.

These two scenarios, as Moscicke notes, are not necessarily exclusive of each other. We should allow for a certain amount of "slippage"[17] in the way Matthew creatively uses the imagery, now in one way, and then in another. In fact, in Matthew's narrative, Jesus, too, should be understood as the scapegoat. As Moscicke remarks,

> Matthew apparently cannot allow Jesus to be just one of the two goats, which functioned collectively to make atonement for sin (Lev 16:5). According to Andrei Orlov, "Despite the fact that the Barabbas episode assigns the scapegoat's features and functions to Barabbas [and the people, I would add], the broader context of the gospel attempts to simultaneously envision Jesus as both the immolated goat and the scapegoat."[18]

Indeed, not just in Matthew's Gospel, but also in John, even though he refers to the "*Lamb* of God, who takes away the sins of the world" (John 1:29, emphasis added), I believe we should recognize that scapegoat imagery is at play here as well. Jesus is the scapegoat who takes [carries] away the sins of the world. Furthermore, John's Gospel identifies the site of the crucifixion as "near the city" (19:20), implying that it was outside the city proper, a detail which should probably be seen as a corresponding parallel to the scapegoat ritual.

---

16. Ibid., 139–40.
17. Ibid., 145, 147.
18. Ibid., 152–53. The quotation is from Andre A. Orlov, *The Atoning Dyad: The Two Goats of Yom Kippur in the Apocalypse of Abraham*, Studia Judaeoslavica 8 (Leiden: Brill, 2016), 64.

Baptism and Wilderness

One (for the most part) overlooked connection to the Day of Atonement is the baptism and wilderness temptation of Jesus. Fleming Rutledge, in her justly praised volume on the death of Christ, calls attention to the proposed scapegoat connection, noting she was unable to find any corroborating literature.[19] However, among Leviticus commentators, John Kleinig has also argued for the scapegoat connection.[20] I would go further and argue that Jesus is here seen as the goat that was sacrificed *and* the goat driven into the wilderness.

First, in his baptism, since Jesus had no sins for which he needed to repent, his submission to the rite of baptism should be understood as an act of vicarious repentance for sinners. As he submits himself to be baptized, his death as vicarious sacrifice for sinners is anticipated and highlighted. It is to be noted that Jesus explicitly drew a connection between baptism and his approaching crucifixion: "But I have a baptism to undergo, and what constraint I am under until it is completed!" (Luke 12:50). Additionally, his baptism by John is one in which he "washes" by water, even as did the high priest on the Day of Atonement. Boyce suggestively remarks that in the light of the "stripping, washing, and clothing of the priest," the "baptism of Jesus takes on an added dimension. . . . The priest is not only preparing to approach the altar, but also to place himself upon it."[21]

Second, having gone through a ritual that corresponds to the sacrifice of the one goat in the Day of Atonement ritual, he is then "led" (Matt 4:1; Luke 4:1), or "driven" (Mark 1:12 [ESV, NRSV]) into the wilderness. There, even as the scapegoat encountered Azazel, Jesus now encounters Satan. Having provided purification for sins, he now returns those sins to Satan, the author of them, withstands all his temptations, and defeats the demon in the wilderness.[22]

The Day of Atonement and the Book of Hebrews

Hebrews deals significantly with Christ as both high priest and sacrifice, and much of its discussion on this topic is related to the Day of Atonement. In 1:3

19. Rutledge, *Crucifixion*, 248 n. 32.

20. Kleinig, *Leviticus*, 347 n. 35.

21. Boyce, *Leviticus and Numbers*, 57.

22. After I wrote this last section, I was delighted to find that Hans Moscicke had come to similar conclusions regarding the baptism and temptation narratives. See his now published dissertation, *The New Day of Atonement: A Matthean Typology*, WUNT 2.157 (Tübingen: Mohr Siebeck, 2020), esp. pp. 212–16. For other brilliantly suggestive articles see his "Jesus as Goat of the Day of Atonement in Recent Synoptic Gospels Research," *CurBR* 17.1 (2018): 59–85; idem, "Jesus as Scapegoat in Matthew's Roman-Abuse Scene (Matt 27:27–31)," *NovT* 62.3 (2020): 229–56; idem, "The Gerasene Exorcism and Jesus' Eschatological Expulsion of Cosmic Powers: Echoes of Second Temple Scapegoat Traditions in Mark 5.1–20," *JSNT* 41.3 (2019): 363–83.

the author states that Jesus sat down at the right hand of the Father after having provided purification of sins, indicating the finality of that purification, one that would most likely connect to the Day of Atonement (also 8:1). In 5:3 it is recalled that the high priest has to offer sacrifices for his own sins before he offers sacrifices for the sins of the people. This, of course, would have been true throughout the year, but most prominently in the very public ceremonies on the Day of Atonement. It is stressed in 6:19 that Christ has entered the "inner sanctuary behind the curtain" (of the heavenly temple), which took place only on the Day of Atonement.

In 7:23–28, though the passage talks about what happened in the tabernacle "day after day," it nevertheless emphasizes that, because Christ lives forever, he has a permanent priesthood. The instructions in Leviticus 16 are given not only to Aaron but to his son who will "succeed his father as high priest" (v. 32). Because Christ lives forever, there are not to be any successors. His priesthood is forever. And because this priest does not need to offer sacrifices for his own sins, the atonement that he effects for the people "saves completely those who come to God through him" (Heb 7:25) Therefore, the sacrifice of atonement that he makes is one that is done "once for all" (vv. 24–27). Furthermore, this high priest, in this once-for-all atonement, did not offer bulls and goats and rams; rather, "he offered himself" (v. 27).

In chapter 9 the author focuses on the Day of Atonement in verse 7, where the high priest enters the inner room only once a year—with blood, offered both for himself and for the people. But in verses 11–12 Christ enters with his own blood and obtains not just a temporal reprieve but an "eternal redemption." In doing so, Christ not only cleanses us from sin but also cleanses our consciences, removing all guilt, enabling us to "serve the living God" (v. 14). He does not need to present this offering "again and again," "with blood that is not his own" (v. 25). Rather, "he has appeared once for all at the culmination of the ages to do away with sin by the sacrifice of himself" (v. 26).

In chapter 10 we read that Christ has come into the world to provide what some have referred to as the "full and final sacrifice"[23] for sin: "we have been made holy through the sacrifice of the body of Jesus Christ once for all" (v. 10). Again, the author emphasizes that Christ's sacrifice was made "for all time," after which "he sat down at the right hand of God" (v. 12).

Finally, in chapter 13 the author seems to conflate the fact that the carcasses of sacrificed animals were burned outside the camp with the idea that

---

23. This is a phrase that I have heard in many different contexts, and that may have a much more ancient pedigree, but I have not been able to trace it back any further than Gerald Finzi's anthem, "Lo, the Full, Final Sacrifice," composed in 1946.

Christ "suffered outside the city gate to make the people holy through his own blood" (vv. 11–12). The comparison between the two is not perfectly symmetrical. However, the author may be employing a polemical argument in his formulation. He has just said in verse 10 that "We have an altar from which those who minister at the tabernacle have no right to eat." So the conflation in verses 11–12 may be an intentional part of his polemic: It is not just that the carcasses have to be taken outside the camp, but the sacrifice had to be made outside the camp as well. The cross of Jesus Christ, outside the city gate and outside the temple complex, has now made the altar in the temple forever invalid.[24] However, the suggestion that there is a reference in this passage to the scapegoat of Leviticus 16 seems unlikely.

Two observations are in order about this survey of the material in Hebrews. First, the author is not denigrating the Old Testament sacrificial system in itself. These sacrifices had been ordered by God. They served their function within the Israelite community in the Old Testament and served as a shadow of Christ's own sacrifice, of his high priestly work in the heavenly temple. The problem was not the system per se; rather, the problem was twofold. First, those who offered the sacrifices were priests who themselves were sinful and who, as finite human beings, were only temporary holders of their position. Second, the animals that were sacrificed could not truly and ultimately serve as substitutionary sacrifices for humans. Therefore, the sacrificial system was provisional but not without value in its own setting. As Hess articulately states, "The death of Christ did not nullify the OT sacrifices; instead, it gave them their complete value in that they participated as signs pointing to the fullness to come."[25] Unlike what is maintained by modern opponents of the idea of substitutionary atonement, it is important to maintain that Christ did not come to invalidate the Old Testament sacrificial system. Rather, he came to be its first ever and only perfect priest and to present its first ever and only perfect sacrifice. Therefore, he is also its last priest and its last sacrifice. He is the "full and final sacrifice."

Second, in continuity with the previous point, we should recognize that Christianity and Judaism have parted ways over the Day of Atonement. For Judaism, ever since the destruction of the temple in AD 70, repentance has replaced the sacrifices of the Day of Atonement. For Christianity, the death of Christ has, to the contrary, fulfilled, completed, and perfected the sacrifices of the Day of Atonement. Rutledge argues "that this is perhaps the major

---

24. For an extensive discussion of these verses, see William L. Lane, *Hebrews 9–13*, WBC 47B (Dallas: Word, 1991), 537–42.

25. Hess, "Leviticus," 729.

difference between Christianity and Judaism."[26] She notes that in the Jewish liturgy for the Day of Atonement it is declared, "Repentance will turn aside the severe decree."[27] However, it is important to note that not even in the Old Testament is repentance understood to be sufficient. And for Christianity—in the New Testament, and particularly in the book of Hebrews—it is not our repentance but the sacrifice of Christ that "turns aside the severe decree." Or, if one wishes to maintain that repentance is enough, then the Christian must answer that, yes, repentance is enough, but it has to be the vicarious repentance of Christ himself who, "through his flesh's own afflictions, becomes the true or perfect penitent."[28]

Boldness to Enter, and Boldness to Exit

How grateful, thankful, and worshipful Christians should be on account of what Christ has accomplished on our behalf by his sacrificial, substitutionary death on the cross for our forgiveness and our redemption. Worship itself is the practical result of what Christ has done by his great sacrifice for us. However, taking a clue from the book of Hebrews, we note two additional practical implications for Christians with regard to their practice of the Christian life.

First, Christ's sacrificial atonement should give his followers great boldness. On the one hand, like the Old Testament Israelites on the Day of Atonement, our response to the death of Christ should properly be one of solemnity, mourning, and repentance as we consider both the gravity of our sin and the cost Christ paid to provide forgiveness for our sins. Indeed, as in the Old Testament, our reflections on our sin and Christ's sacrifice should cause us to afflict or deny ourselves. Christians through the years have seen times in which they ponder these things to be especially appropriate occasions for fasting and other such practices. However, the author of Hebrews also sees a proper response to Christ's sacrifice to be a motivation to enter boldly, following Christ, into the most holy place itself (10:19–23). This certainly constitutes an invitation for intimacy with God and boldness in prayer and petition, with "full assurance" (v. 22), no longer troubled by a guilty conscience but fully confident that our sins have been forgiven, certain of the fact that God is for us.

Second, Christ's sacrificial atonement should also give his followers great boldness to exit. In the language of Hebrews, "Let us, then, go to him outside

26. Rutledge, *Crucifixion*, 172. See her larger discussion on pages 171–92.

27. More precisely, the formula is "Repentance, prayer, and righteousness will avert the severe decree."

28. Radner, *Leviticus*, 169.

the camp, bearing the disgrace he bore" (13:13). While sometimes the world and age in which we live regard us kindly and speak well of us, Jesus also points out that this might be an occasion for woe rather than congratulations (Luke 6:26). Indeed, Paul seems to regard persecution to be the default experience for those who would live lives of godliness and holiness (2 Tim 3:12). If we are not enduring ridicule, reproach, ostracization, and even persecution for our Christian faith, we have to examine ourselves and ask what our location actually is. Is it within the comfortable confines of the camp? Have we failed to "go to him outside the camp, bearing the disgrace he bore" (Heb 13:13)? Have we refused to join Christ where he actually is? Rather, our contemplation of the sacrifice of Christ should create within us great boldness to join him in harm's way, knowing full well that "here we do not have an enduring city, but we are looking for the city that is to come" (Heb 13:14).

CHAPTER 15

Leviticus 17:1–16

LISTEN to the Story

17:1The LORD said to Moses, 2"Speak to Aaron and his sons and to all
the Israelites and say to them: 'This is what the LORD has commanded:
3Any Israelite who sacrifices an ox, a lamb or a goat in the camp or outside
of it 4instead of bringing it to the entrance to the tent of meeting to present
it as an offering to the LORD in front of the tabernacle of the LORD—that
person shall be considered guilty of bloodshed; they have shed blood and
must be cut off from their people. 5This is so the Israelites will bring to
the LORD the sacrifices they are now making in the open fields. They
must bring them to the priest, that is, to the LORD, at the entrance to the
tent of meeting and sacrifice them as fellowship offerings. 6The priest is
to splash the blood against the altar of the LORD at the entrance to the
tent of meeting and burn the fat as an aroma pleasing to the LORD. 7They
must no longer offer any of their sacrifices to the goat idols to whom they
prostitute themselves. This is to be a lasting ordinance for them and for
the generations to come.'

8"Say to them: 'Any Israelite or any foreigner residing among them who
offers a burnt offering or sacrifice 9and does not bring it to the entrance
to the tent of meeting to sacrifice it to the LORD must be cut off from the
people of Israel.

10" 'I will set my face against any Israelite or any foreigner residing
among them who eats blood, and I will cut them off from the people.
11For the life of a creature is in the blood, and I have given it to you to
make atonement for yourselves on the altar; it is the blood that makes
atonement for one's life. 12Therefore I say to the Israelites, "None of you
may eat blood, nor may any foreigner residing among you eat blood."

13" 'Any Israelite or any foreigner residing among you who hunts any
animal or bird that may be eaten must drain out the blood and cover it
with earth, 14because the life of every creature is its blood. That is why I

have said to the Israelites, "You must not eat the blood of any creature, because the life of every creature is its blood; anyone who eats it must be cut off."

[15]"'Anyone, whether native-born or foreigner, who eats anything found dead or torn by wild animals must wash their clothes and bathe with water, and they will be ceremonially unclean till evening; then they will be clean. [16]But if they do not wash their clothes and bathe themselves, they will be held responsible.'"

Listening to the Text in the Story: Biblical Texts: Leviticus 1–16

As mentioned in the Introduction (pp. 4–7), perhaps the majority of scholars today believe that chapters 17–26 comprise a separate document, referred to as the "Holiness Code," which is more concerned with ethical than ritual purity, and has been incorporated within the book of Leviticus. There are valid reasons for such a suggestion, but it does not come without its problems. One of those problems has to do with the present chapter. While the majority opinion is probably that chapter 17 is part of the Holiness Code and goes with the following chapters, a strong case can be made that it goes rather with chapter 16, as it picks up themes, motifs, and catchwords that are present there, as well as prior material in the book. For example, chapter 16 talks about the scapegoat being sent out to Azazel in the wilderness. If indeed Azazel should be seen as some of kind of demonic presence in the wilderness, perhaps even envisioned as having a goat-like form, then chapter 17 connects with this as it prohibits sacrificing to and worshiping the goat idols. Additionally, the chapter reinforces the teaching found in the previous chapters that the blood and the fat from all the sacrifices belong only to the Lord and is not to be consumed by the people. And, of course, this chapter, as well as the entire Holiness Code, is dependent on the previous chapters when it even refers to the sacrifices at all. Furthermore, if there is a distinction to be made between ritual and ethical purity (a distinction that is problematic in several ways), then it seems odd that the first chapter of the Holiness Code, which is supposedly taken up with ethical purity, is almost wholly concerned with ritual and ceremonial purity. This is also the case with a number of sections in the chapters that follow.

So while the Holiness Code may be seen as a document with its own set of interests, there are valid reasons to question whether it ever had a separate existence, independent of the sixteen previous chapters. Rather, the book of Leviticus from the very start was concerned with both ritual and ethical purity. Rather than arguing whether chapter 17 should be seen as belonging with chapters 1–16 or chapters 18–27, it is better to understand the chapter as a "hinge linking the two halves of the book,"[1] halves that reinforce and complement each other, and that by design. Those who are ritually pure must also be ethically pure. Both are needed in order to be the holy people of God.

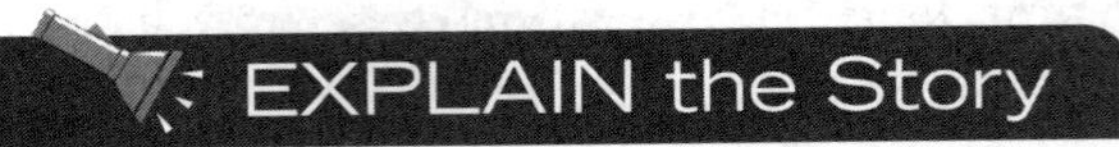

The basic content of the chapter is fairly straightforward. The LORD directs that no sacrifices are to be made in the open country but offered and slaughtered only at the tabernacle. The blood is to be splashed against the altar, and the fat is to be burnt as a pleasing aroma. No sacrifices are to be made to the goat idols or goat demons. These were demons who were thought to appear as goats, much like the satyrs of Greek mythology. Failure to obey in this matter will result in the person being cut off from the people of Israel. This rule applies to both Israelites and foreigners in the land. Additionally, the LORD will set his face against anyone who eats blood, and he himself will cut them off from the people. A rationale is supplied, in that the LORD has given the blood of the sacrificial animal to Israel as a means of atonement for their lives. Finally, rules are given prohibiting the Israelites from eating the meat of any animal that has been found dead or torn by wild animals.

Even though the instructions seem quite easy to understand, there are nevertheless some crucial interpretive issues.

What Is Being Prohibited?

A number of commentators argue that it is not only sacrificial slaughter that is being prohibited away from the tabernacle but all slaughter.[2] Thus, Israelites are prohibited from slaughtering any of their livestock only for food; all livestock must be presented at the tabernacle as an offering. Those who argue for this understanding also maintain that in Deuteronomy 12:13–15, 20–22, this original prohibition is then relaxed and the slaughter of animals for other than purely sacrificial purposes is allowed. They argue that the original prohibition would have worked well during the forty years in the wilderness, but once the Israelites were in the land, this prohibition would have been too restrictive

1. Wenham, *Leviticus*, 241.

2. Jacob Milgrom, *Leviticus 17–22: A New Translation with Introduction and Commentary*, AB 3 (New York: Doubleday, 2008), 1452–63.

on account of the greater distance between the tabernacle or temple and the homes of most of the Israelites living in the land.

This understanding is certainly possible and even plausible; there are other apparently altered laws in the Pentateuch that were changed in order to correspond to a settled existence in the land, as opposed to a more nomadic-like existence in the wilderness. However, in Leviticus, the verb for "slaughter" (NIV "sacrifice") in verse 3, *shahat*, is only used to refer to slaughter for sacrificial purposes. Therefore, it seems more likely that what is being prohibited is only sacrificial slaughter away from the tabernacle. The concern is that these sacrifices might be for deities other than Yahweh.

"Eating" Blood

The prohibition against eating blood had already been given in Leviticus 3:17; 7:26–27; it occurs again after this chapter in 19:26. This raises two interrelated questions. The first is why this prohibition is necessary; the second is why the verb in these prohibitions is "eat" rather than "drink."

One clue has to do with the fact that there is a similar prohibition against eating fat. In both of the previous places where the prohibition against eating blood is given, it is coupled with a prohibition against eating fat. In Leviticus 3:17 the prohibition is, "You must not eat any fat or any blood." Interestingly, in the immediately preceding verse (3:16) the declaration is made, "All the fat is the Lord's." In 7:26–27 eating blood is prohibited again. But it is preceded immediately by a prohibition against eating fat, in verses 23–25, and it is also specified that the fat that may not be eaten is the fat of an animal "from which a food offering may be presented to the Lord." A fair deduction from these passages is that one of the reasons why blood must not be eaten is the same as that given for the fat—it belongs to the Lord. We are not to understand from this that in some way blood constitutes food for God. Nevertheless, the blood belongs to him and should not be used for any other reason than that which he himself purposes.

A second, more explicit clue is in the text itself, when the Lord says that he has given the blood to the Israelites to make atonement for their sins and the blood is that which constitutes the life of the sacrificial animal. The Lord considers it objectionable to consume the blood that imparts life to the animal and provides atonement for the person who offers the animal.

Finally, Milgrom calls attention to the story in 1 Samuel 14:31–35, where King Saul's men pounce on the plunder they had taken in a battle with the Philistines. They kill the livestock they had taken, butcher them on the ground, and eat them, "together with the blood." However, the phrase is arguably more literally translated as "over the blood." Milgrom argues that this actually means that the men killed the animals, poured out the blood on the ground, and then ate the meat of the animals over the blood. Milgrom relates this action in particular to the worship of bloodthirsty underworld deities. In this act they were also performing a kind of divinatory rite in which they were attempting to consult these underworld deities to determine what their next actions should be in their war with the Philistines. And they were doing this instead of worshiping Yahweh and consulting him.[3]

Interestingly, Leviticus 19:26 uses the same language as 1 Samuel (literally, "do not eat over the blood") and is immediately followed by the command "Do not practice divination or seek omens." I believe this provides a clue as to one aspect of the problem in Leviticus 17. Milgrom himself believes that the situation described in verses 5–7 may be similar to that described in 1 Samuel. It refers to worshiping underworld goat idols, pouring out blood to them, and consulting the spirits of the dead. I also think that it is at least possible that the references to "eating the blood" in Leviticus 17 may be shorthand for "eating over the blood."

Thus there are three reasons why the Israelites are prohibited from eating or eating over the blood:

1. The blood belongs to the Lord, so it is not the Israelites' to eat.
2. It would be reprehensible to eat that which actually provides the life of an animal and provides atonement for one's life.
3. It can be taken for granted that one who "eats over the blood" is worshiping and consulting false deities in opposition to Yahweh, the one God of Israel.

It is no wonder, then, that Yahweh says he will set his face in opposition to the Israelite who does such a horrendous act.

What Does Leviticus 17:11 Mean?

For the life of a creature is in the blood, and I have given it to you to make atonement for yourselves on the altar; it is the blood that makes atonement for one's life.

A number of scholars have made various suggestions as to how this verse should be understood, in some tension with more traditional interpretations. Among their proposals are the following:

3. Ibid., 1490–93.

1. The verse is talking about the fellowship offering in particular and is not making a blanket statement about the atonement value of offerings in general.[4]
2. The specific atonement in view here is not atonement for sin in general but is specifically for the taking of the life of the animal.
3. It is not the death of the animal that provides atonement; rather, it is the life-force contained in the blood of the animal, which is released and in some (mystical?) way communicated to the offerer.
4. Rather than the last part of the verse being translated in terms of exchange (NIV "for one's life"), it should rather be translated in terms of agency (ESV "by the life"; similarly NET, NRSV, NJPS). That is, rather than "life" referring to the life of the offerer, it refers to the life of the animal, by which atonement is made.

I find the arguments given for the first three suggestions to be unpersuasive for the following reasons:

1. While the chapter does begin by talking about the fellowship offering in particular, probably the majority of scholars understand that, by this point in the chapter, things are being put in more general terms; the statement in verse 11 seems to be more gnomic or general in character. Additionally, while the fellowship offering does in fact have an expiatory or propitiatory element, the other offerings, particularly the sin and guilt offerings, are the primary atoning offerings.
2. There may be some element of truth in this understanding. It is certainly unfortunate that the lives of sacrificial animals have to be given up for the sins of the offerers; the very fact that a sacrifice has to take place is human sinfulness. Nevertheless, God has assigned the death of the animal along with the animal's blood as a means of atonement, and it is hard to understand that the act of sacrificial slaughter is one for which atonement has to be made. The slaying of the animal, while being a result of sin, is not in itself sinful since it is commanded by God.
3. There is no textual reason to understand that there is some kind of mystical or magical release of the life-force of the animal which is then communicated to the life of the offerer. Rather, Israel's sacrificial system is ritualistic and symbolic. The blood provides ransom and atonement for sin, and it purifies from ethical and ritual defilement. While the

4. Ibid., 1474. Milgrom is perhaps the primary advocate for this view.

verse does emphasize that the life of the animal provides atonement for sin, this should not be understood as a life that is released but as a life that is taken. To say that the animal's life provides atonement is shorthand for saying a "life given over to death." It is not the life of the animal per se that atones but the life that is sacrificed in death.

4. The fourth suggestion seems to me to be more exegetically supportable than the traditional rendering. The grammatical construction behind the last clause (the preposition *beth* attached to a word [in this case "life," *nephesh*], followed by the verb "atone") occurs a number of times in Hebrew Bible, and invariably the noun to which the preposition is attached indicates the instrument or means of atonement. So rather than indicating the idea of price or exchange—that is, "life for life"—the clause most likely is indicating that the life of the animal is the means by which atonement is accomplished. Nevertheless, the idea of exchange is still in the background. The life of the sacrificial animal is given as a ransom "for your lives" (more precise rendering of NIV "yourselves") on the altar. Indeed, Levine, who also understands the last clause as indicating agency or means, nevertheless also recognizes that exchange and substitution are communicated by the prior words in the verse as well as the larger context of Scripture:

> Basic to the theory of sacrifice in ancient Israel, as in many other ancient societies, was the notion of substitution. The sacrifice substituted for an individual human life or for the lives of the members of the community in situations where God could have exacted the life of the offender, or of anyone else, for that matter. Indeed, all who stood in God's immediate presence risked becoming the object of divine wrath. But substitution could avert the danger, with sacrificial blood being especially instrumental because it was the symbol of life.[5]

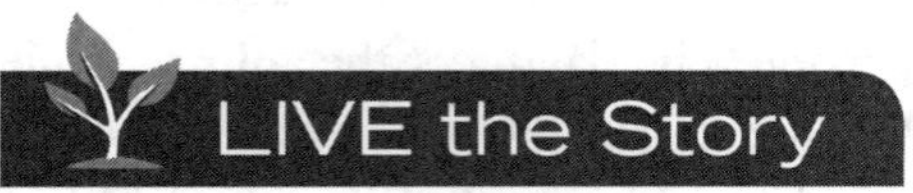

The Continuing Validity of Old Testament Law

The reader of the account of the Jerusalem Council in Acts 15 will perhaps be surprised at two things. The first is that even though there is an apparent relaxing of the demands of the law for gentile Christians in that they are

5. Levine, *Leviticus*, 115.

explicitly not required to be circumcised in order to become Christians or members of the church, there are still legal requirements laid upon them. There are certain requirements of the law of Moses that they are still required to obey. The second is the nature of these requirements. The reader may indeed have a *Sesame Street* moment ("three of these things are kind of the same") upon finding that the four requirements are to "abstain from food sacrificed to idols, from blood, from the meat of strangled animals and from sexual immorality" (v. 29; see also v. 20).

There are three major clues as to what is happening in this account. First, it should be noticed that the stated rationale for why the gentiles should be required to keep these requirements is that "the law of Moses has been preached in every city from the earliest times and is read in the synagogues on every Sabbath" (v. 21). The gentiles, and apparently in this case those who were already acquainted with Judaism, had had occasion to hear these laws read in the various synagogues located throughout the Greco-Roman world. These requirements would not have been a surprise to them and, in contrast to circumcision, would not have been seen as a burden to obey.

Second, the anomaly of the prohibition of sexual immorality being included with three dietary restrictions is most likely explained by the fact that, almost certainly, the laws contained in Leviticus 17–18 stand behind these prohibitions, as can be seen in the following comparison.

17:1–9 corresponds to "food sacrificed to idols"
17:10–14 corresponds to "blood"
17:13–16 corresponds to "strangled"[6]
18:1–30 corresponds to "sexual immorality"

Third, it is important to note the relatively high occurrence of the term "foreigner" in these two chapters and the declaration that these proscriptions apply to the foreigner as well:

17:8 "any foreigner residing among them"
17:10 "any foreigner residing among them"
17:12 "any foreigner residing among you"
17:13 "any foreigner residing among you"

6. "Strangled" would actually connect with two prohibitions. First, it would connect with the prohibition against eating blood, since strangulation would be a form of slaughter in which the blood was retained rather than being drained out. Second, it would come under the basic category of animals that had not been appropriately slaughtered, such as animals found dead or torn by wild animals.

17:15 "foreigner"
18:26 "the foreigners residing among you"

It would seem, then, that along with perhaps more pragmatic concerns regarding the desire to facilitate good relationships between Jewish and gentile Christians, these prohibitions were put in place by the Jerusalem Council in order to uphold the continuing validity of the Mosaic law in the life and conduct of the new Christian church. The relationship between Old Testament law and the Christian is a huge and complicated discussion. But, at the very least, the way in which the apostles utilized Leviticus 17–18 in the formulation of their decree, along with Jesus's own expressed declaration that he had not come to abolish the law but to uphold and fulfill it (Matt 5:17–20), should serve to warn against an all-too-easy dismissal of Old Testament law. Additionally, it should serve as a caution against those who argue that the Christian church today can, like the apostles in Acts 15, "relax" or "soften" Old Testament law and ethics in the name of relevance or cultural accommodation, especially in the area of sexual ethics.[7]

Hedging One's Bets in Worship

Wenham, commenting on this chapter, states, "Throughout history God's people have tended to forget that they owe exclusive allegiance to God."[8] He makes this remark in light of the warning against idolatry in this chapter. The warning is one that must be understood not simply against the polytheistic background of the ancient Near East. It needs to be understood against the polyolatrous background of the ancient Near East as well. Most people not only believed there were multiple deities (polytheism), but they also worshiped multiple deities (polyolatry). Though not necessarily unique in this respect, Israel's God demanded exclusive worship from his people. Indeed, one plausible translation of the first commandment in Exodus 20:3 is "You shall have no other gods in addition to me." Israel did not need to be monotheistic (believing there is only one god), but Yahweh did demand that his people be monolatrous (worshiping only one god), and that god was to be Yahweh.

It was the easiest thing to do in the ancient world to worship multiple deities. After all, what if the gods got into a battle against each other? And what if your

---

7. For one such caution, relating in particular to the same-sex relationship issue, see Bill T. Arnold, "Acts 15 Doesn't Mean What You Think It Means," *The Seedbed Blog*, 27 March 2014, http://seedbed.com/feed/acts-15-doesnt-mean-think-means/. Note that eating food sacrificed to idols and sexual immorality are also coupled together in Rev 2:14.

8. Wenham, *Leviticus*, 246.

god was one of the losers in the battle? Then you were in a bad position. The better strategy would be to hedge your bets so that you would be on good terms with several deities and never without an advocate in the pantheon of the deities. So, on one level it may seem surprising, but on another it may not, that God has to say in this chapter, "They must no longer offer any of their sacrifices to the goat idols to whom they prostitute themselves" (17:7). At the very same time that Yahweh is dwelling right in their midst, they are sacrificing to other gods.

It is yet more surprising that Paul needs to give the same warning in the New Testament:

> Therefore, my dear friends, flee from idolatry. . . . You cannot drink the cup of the Lord and the cup of demons too; you cannot have a part in both the Lord's table and the table of demons. Are we trying to arouse the Lord's jealousy? Are we stronger than he? (1 Cor 10:14, 21–22)

Nor should we think the Christian church of today is immune to the same phenomenon. Whether it be the syncretism that occurs in many parts of the world between Christianity and various pagan religions, the melding of Christianity with various godless philosophical movements, or even the celebrity worship of megachurch pastors, worship leaders, musicians, and so on that seems to have captured large swaths of the evangelical church, Christianity must be vigilant to avoid being drawn into making these idolatrous moves.

The Special Significance of the Blood of Christ

I still remember the uproar that arose among certain Christian groups over a Bible translation, released in the second half of the twentieth century, that regularly replaced New Testament references to the blood of Christ with such phrases as the "death of Christ" or the "sacrifice of Christ." Much of this uproar was over the top, too reactionary, and insufficiently appreciative of the target audience the translation was attempting to reach. Nevertheless, it is important to recognize that the New Testament does attach a special significance not simply to the death of Jesus but also to the shedding of Christ's blood. Fleming Rutledge well says that it is not just sacrifice but "specifically *blood* sacrifice" that "is central to the story of our salvation through Jesus Christ, and without this theme the Christian proclamation loses much of its power, becoming both theologically and *ethically* undernourished."[9]

---

9. Rutledge, *Crucifixion*, 233. The entire volume is invaluable reading, and her chapter, "The Blood Sacrifice" (pp. 232–83), from which this citation is taken, is especially rewarding.

In this light, then, it is instructive to note the different ways in which the New Testament authors highlighted the significance of the blood of Christ:

It is through the blood of Christ that the new covenant is established (Matt 26:28; 1 Cor 11:25).
We have forgiveness of sins through his blood (Matt 26:28; Eph 1:7).
The one who belongs to Christ must drink his blood in order to have eternal life (John 6:54–56).
The church has been bought by his blood (Acts 20:28; Rev 5:9).
The blood of Christ provides propitiation for sins (Rom 3:25).
We are justified by his blood (Rom 5:9).
We participate in the blood of Christ (1 Cor 10:16).
We have redemption through his blood (Eph 1:7; Heb 9:12; 1 Pet 1:18–19).
We have been brought near by his blood (Eph 2:13).[10]
We have reconciliation and peace through his blood (Col 1:20).
We have sanctification through his blood (Heb 9:13–14; 10:29; 13:12; 1 John 1:7; Rev 7:14).
Our consciences are cleansed by his blood (Heb 9:14).
By his blood we have confidence to enter the holy place (Heb 10:19).
By his blood Christ purifies the heavenly tabernacle (Heb 9:22–23).
The blood of Christ speaks to us a better word (Heb 12:24).
The resurrection of Jesus takes place by his blood (Heb 13:20).
We are saved by the sprinkling of the blood of Christ (1 Pet 1:2).
We are freed by his blood (Rev 1:5).
We overcome by his blood (Rev 12:11).

Without the Old Testament, and in particular the book of Leviticus, the significance the New Testament attaches to the blood of Christ would not be nearly so pronounced as it is.

"Without the Shedding of Blood There Is No Forgiveness"

When the author of Hebrews declares that "without the shedding of blood there is no forgiveness" (Heb 9:22), even though there is no direct quotation of an Old Testament passage here, there can be little doubt that this alludes to Leviticus 17:11. One question (or rather, objection) that has been raised, especially by those who would deny the teaching of penal substitutionary

10. Note that, in light of the background in Leviticus, the language of being "brought near" should be recognized as especially cultic or ritual in nature.

atonement, is whether this is really true. They note that there are several places in the Old Testament where atonement seems to be made without a blood sacrifice and that in the New Testament forgiveness is pronounced, especially in the Gospel narratives and Jesus's parables, without any reference to a blood sacrifice.

I have already, in the commentary above on Leviticus 5 (Explain the Story, pp. 77–78), dealt with the issue of the bloodless grain sacrifice being accounted as a sin offering. There are two other points that need to be made. First, in the Old Testament, even though there are several instances where atonement is said to be made by, for example, a monetary payment, simple intercession, burning of incense, and so on, it is important to recognize that the sacrificial system is still the *grounding* on which all acts of atonement are based.[11] For example, in Numbers 16:46–48, in the account of Korah's rebellion, Aaron stops a plague and effects atonement by taking his censer, putting incense in it, along with coals from the altar, and then hurrying to the assembly to make atonement for the people. But it is important to note that the altar from which he took those coals had already been made holy by the application of sacrificial blood. Atonement and forgiveness is still based on blood sacrifice.

Second, and similarly, the Jesus who several times in the Gospels declares to someone that their sins are forgiven is the same Jesus who, in the institution of the Lord's Supper, declares that his "blood of the covenant" is to be shed "for the forgiveness of sins" (Matt 26:28). The forgivenesses that Jesus proclaimed were proleptic and anticipatory, grounded in the shedding of his covenantal blood in his crucifixion.

"I Have Assigned"[12] . . . "God Presented Christ"[13]

While it is commonly recognized that Hebrews 9:22 is an allusion to Leviticus 17:11, what is perhaps not so commonly understood is that Romans 3:25 may be as well. In Leviticus 17:11 God states regarding the blood of the sacrificial animal, "I have given it to you to make atonement for yourselves on the altar." Other translations have opted to render the verb translated "given" in the NIV as "assigned" (NET, NJPS) or "appointed" (CSB). This alternative translation perhaps captures more accurately the legal character of this statement: "I have

11. On this point, see Jacob Milgrom, *Leviticus 23–27: A New Translation with Introduction and Commentary*, AB 3 (New York: Doubleday, 2001), 2335–36. Milgrom argues that even the sins that God forgave the Israelites in the exile were not fully expiated "without the requisite sacrifices" to be offered after the return from exile.

12. Lev 17:11, NJPS.

13. Rom 3:25.

assigned (appointed, designated) the blood to make atonement for your lives on the altar."

Similarly, the formal forensic nature of Paul's statement in Romans 3:25 should be recognized as well:

> God presented Christ as a sacrifice of atonement, through the shedding of his blood (NIV).
>
> Whom God put forward as a propitiation by his blood (ESV).
>
> God publicly displayed him at his death as the mercy seat (NET).

The similarity of style and substance suggests that Leviticus 17:11 was likely in the background of Paul's formulation when he described Christ, by means of his shed blood, as God's publicly appointed means for atonement and the forgiveness of sins.

"Participation in the Blood of Christ"

The radical nature of what God was doing in Christ when he made him and his blood the designated atonement for sin, as opposed to sacrificial animals and their blood, is also accompanied by a radical formulation regarding our union with Christ. Paul asks the question, "Is not the cup of thanksgiving for which we give thanks a participation in the blood of Christ?" (1 Cor 10:16).

The radical nature of this question was anticipated by the demand of Jesus in the Gospel of John:

> Jesus said to them, "Very truly I tell you, unless you eat the flesh of the Son of Man and drink his blood, you have no life in you. Whoever eats my flesh and drinks my blood has eternal life, and I will raise them up at the last day. For my flesh is real food and my blood is real drink. Whoever eats my flesh and drinks my blood remains in me, and I in them." (John 6:53–56)

These words, coupled with what Jesus does in the institution of the Lord's Supper—when he distributes the cup, referring to the wine as his blood and telling the disciples to drink it—is formally the exact opposite of the command in Leviticus 17, where the consumption of blood is absolutely forbidden. Of course, this command in John 6:53–56 is not a literal one; we drink wine (or grape juice) when we participate in the Lord's Supper. Nevertheless, the starkness of the metaphorical language serves to demonstrate that, while there is a proper continuity between the old and new covenants, there is a radical discontinuity as well. And that radical discontinuity is nowhere as starkly highlighted as when we consider that it is no longer the blood of the bulls and goats and lambs that is shed for our redemption. Rather it is the blood of God's very own Son that God has appointed as the means of atonement. Indeed, it is the very blood of God (Acts 20:28).

CHAPTER 16

Leviticus 18:1–30

LISTEN to the Story

18:1The LORD said to Moses, 2"Speak to the Israelites and say to them: 'I am the LORD your God. 3You must not do as they do in Egypt, where you used to live, and you must not do as they do in the land of Canaan, where I am bringing you. Do not follow their practices. 4You must obey my laws and be careful to follow my decrees. I am the LORD your God. 5Keep my decrees and laws, for the person who obeys them will live by them. I am the LORD.

6"'No one is to approach any close relative to have sexual relations. I am the LORD.

7"'Do not dishonor your father by having sexual relations with your mother. She is your mother; do not have relations with her.

8"'Do not have sexual relations with your father's wife; that would dishonor your father.

9"'Do not have sexual relations with your sister, either your father's daughter or your mother's daughter, whether she was born in the same home or elsewhere.

10"'Do not have sexual relations with your son's daughter or your daughter's daughter; that would dishonor you.

11"'Do not have sexual relations with the daughter of your father's wife, born to your father; she is your sister.

12"'Do not have sexual relations with your father's sister; she is your father's close relative.

13"'Do not have sexual relations with your mother's sister, because she is your mother's close relative.

14"'Do not dishonor your father's brother by approaching his wife to have sexual relations; she is your aunt.

15"'Do not have sexual relations with your daughter-in-law. She is your son's wife; do not have relations with her.

[16]"'Do not have sexual relations with your brother's wife; that would dishonor your brother.

[17]"'Do not have sexual relations with both a woman and her daughter. Do not have sexual relations with either her son's daughter or her daughter's daughter; they are her close relatives. That is wickedness.

[18]"'Do not take your wife's sister as a rival wife and have sexual relations with her while your wife is living.

[19]"'Do not approach a woman to have sexual relations during the uncleanness of her monthly period.

[20]"'Do not have sexual relations with your neighbor's wife and defile yourself with her.

[21]"'Do not give any of your children to be sacrificed to Molek, for you must not profane the name of your God. I am the LORD.

[22]"'Do not have sexual relations with a man as one does with a woman; that is detestable.

[23]"'Do not have sexual relations with an animal and defile yourself with it. A woman must not present herself to an animal to have sexual relations with it; that is a perversion.

[24]"'Do not defile yourselves in any of these ways, because this is how
the nations that I am going to drive out before you became defiled. [25]Even
the land was defiled; so I punished it for its sin, and the land vomited
out its inhabitants. [26]But you must keep my decrees and my laws. The
native-born and the foreigners residing among you must not do any of
these detestable things, [27]for all these things were done by the people who
lived in the land before you, and the land became defiled. [28]And if you
defile the land, it will vomit you out as it vomited out the nations that
were before you.

[29]"'Everyone who does any of these detestable things—such persons
must be cut off from their people. [30]Keep my requirements and do not
follow any of the detestable customs that were practiced before you came
and do not defile yourselves with them. I am the LORD your God.'"

Listening to the Text in the Story: Biblical Texts: Genesis 9:18–28; 11:27–31; 19:30–38; 20:12; 29:14–30; 35:22; Exodus 6:20; Ancient Near Eastern Texts: The Laws of Hammurabi; Hittite Laws; A Mesopotamian Omen; Middle Assyrian Laws; Egyptian Book of the Dead

The biblical texts listed above record actions that would have been regarded as violations of the prohibitions in this chapter: a homosexual act between father and son (depending on whether what Ham did to his father Noah was indeed a sexual act), marriage to one's half-sister, marriage to two sisters, marriage to one's aunt, incest between father and daughter, and having sex with one's father's concubine.[1] Indeed, Moses, the very one who was charged with communicating these statutes to the Israelites, was himself (and apparently his siblings, Aaron and Miriam, as well) the child of a marriage between a man and his father's sister. We will explore the relationship between the laws contained here and the prior patriarchal narratives later in this chapter.

A number of ancient Near Eastern texts contain proscriptions against a variety of sexual relationships. The texts selected above provide representative examples. The Laws of Hammurabi contain similar prohibitions to those of Leviticus, as well as additional ones:

> If a man should carnally know his daughter, they shall banish that man from the city.
>
> If a man selects a bride for his son and his son carnally knows her, after which he himself then lies with her and they seize him in the act, they shall bind that man and cast him into the water. . . .
>
> If a man, after his father's death, should lie with his mother, they shall burn them both.[2]

Perhaps it is the Hittite Laws that contain the greatest similarity to the laws of Leviticus 18:

> If a man has sexual relations with a cow, it is an unpermitted sexual pairing: he will be put to death. . . .
>
> If a man has sexual relations with a sheep, it is an unpermitted sexual pairing: he will be put to death. . . .
>
> If a man has sexual relations with his own mother, it is an unpermitted sexual pairing. If a man has sexual relations with (his own) daughter, it is an unpermitted sexual pairing. If a man has sexual relations with (his own) son, it is an unpermitted sexual pairing.

1. The last two instances are not specifically mentioned in the list of prohibitions, though we should almost certainly extrapolate from what is mentioned that these would have been proscribed as well.

2. "The Laws of Hammurabi," trans. Martha Roth (*COS* 2.131:345).

> If a man sleeps with his brother's wife, while his brother is alive, it is an unpermitted sexual pairing.[3]

By way of contrast, though the Hittite Laws also prohibit acts of bestiality with a pig or dog, other forms are permitted:

> If a man has sexual relations (lit. "sins") with either a horse or a mule, it is not an offence, but he shall not approach the king, nor shall he become a priest.[4]

Interestingly, there is variation with regard to statutes on homosexual acts. For example, the Mesopotamian Omens seem to look on homosexuality as praiseworthy:

> If a man has anal sex with a man of equal status—that man will be foremost among his brothers and colleagues.[5]

On the other hand, a Middle Assyrian text takes the opposite stance:

> If a man sodomizes his comrade and they prove the charges against him and find him guilty, they shall sodomize him and they shall turn him into a eunuch.[6]

Similarly, the Egyptian Book of the Dead contains a "negative confession" of righteousness in which the confessor maintains, "I have not copulated with a boy."[7]

The variations among the ancient Near Eastern texts (including Leviticus) are only to be expected, as each society expresses its own understanding of what counts as appropriate when it comes to sexual relationships. Nevertheless, whatever similarities and contrasts there are, it is important for the reader to understand that in Leviticus 18 the proscriptions are laid out specifically by the Lord through Moses to distinguish the Israelites from the other nations—and specifically from the Canaanite nations whom the Israelites were to displace from the promised land.[8]

---

3. "Hittite Laws," trans. Harry A. Hoffner, Jr. (*COS* 2.19:118).
4. Ibid., 118–19.
5. "Mesopotamian Omens," trans. Ann K. Guinan (*COS* 1.120:425).
6. Cited in Martha A. Roth, *Law Collections from Mesopotamia and Asia Minor*, WAW 6 (Atlanta: Scholars Press, 1995), 160.
7. "Book of the Dead," trans. Robert K. Ritner (*COS* 2.12:60). Ritner simply has "I have not copulated" in his translation but indicates that variant translations specify "with a boy."
8. For a fuller and excellent discussion of the ancient Near Eastern parallels, see Gane, "Leviticus," 1:309–11.

EXPLAIN the Story

The chapter begins in verses 1–5 with what is apparently meant to serve as an introduction to the specific sexual proscriptions contained in verses 6–23. The chapter concludes in verses 24–30 with summative, motivational, and reinforcing statements that expand on the introduction in verses 1–5. The following observations are important for understanding the content of this chapter:

1. The prohibitions serve to make a distinction between the Israelites and both Egyptians and Canaanites. This compares to other passages in the Old Testament in which the Israelites are warned about adopting the ways of the nations, both before and after their exodus and settlement in the land (e.g., Josh 24:14–15).
2. The Israelites are to abandon the ways of the nations, specifically because the God of Israel is the "LORD your God" (Lev 18:2). Their obedience will prove them to be the people of Yahweh. Their disobedience will prove the opposite.
3. The statement in verse 5, that the one who observes these statutes will "live by them," has to be read against the narrative and covenantal context that has already been established. Obedience to these laws does not establish the covenant nor make one qualified to enter into covenant with Yahweh or become a member of the people of God. Rather, this is a matter of covenantal maintenance. One obeys because one is already a redeemed member of the covenant community, and obedience ensures a life lived in the land under the blessing of Yahweh.
4. The overarching statement in verse 6, that "no one is to approach any close relative to have sexual relations," indicates the main concern of the chapter: incestuous relationships. This concern was especially relevant in light of the close proximity within which families would have lived. Several generations would have dwelt in close relationship with one another, with some estimates suggesting that a "household" could have consisted of "fifty to a hundred people" (not a single dwelling, but several dwellings in close proximity, something like what we might call a "compound" today).[9] Additional offenses other than incestuous ones are also dealt with in the chapter, but the initial concern is incest.

9. For more on this, see Hartley, *Leviticus*, 285–86.

5. We should not understand the chapter as providing a taxonomy of possible incestuous relationships, but rather a representative list. For example, the chapter does not explicitly prohibit sexual relations between father and either son or daughter, though such a relationship would certainly have been prohibited.
6. In this connection, we should also note that exceptions are not taken into account. For example, verse 16 prohibits sexual relations between a man and his brother's wife. Almost certainly the assumption here is that this is to be the case during the lifetime of the brother, since the institution of levirate marriage provided for a man to marry his brother's wife after the brother's death.
7. One of the main concerns of this chapter is that of honor. The NIV has consistently translated as "dishonor" a Hebrew phrase that, if rendered literally, would be "uncover the nakedness of." While the "dishonor" translation may seem overly interpretive, it probably does capture the concern. One dishonors or disrespects another person by having a sexual relationship with that person's legitimate spouse. Note that this dishonoring is not simply with regard to an elder. An older father can dishonor his son. A person can even dishonor himself (v. 10).
8. Several of the prohibitions (vv. 19, 21–23) seem to be unrelated to incest and purely familial concerns: sex with a menstruating woman, child sacrifice, homosexual acts, and bestiality. We will look more closely at the matter of sex with a menstruating woman in the commentary on Leviticus 20 below (Explain the Story, p. 269). The following paragraphs take the other three concerns in order.
9. It might seem that the prohibition against child sacrifice in verse 21 is out of place in this chapter. There are, however, several possible reasons for its inclusion, three of which I will give here. First, there is a linguistic connection between verses 20 and 21, with both verses using the word "seed." The relevant clause in verse 20, "Do not have sexual relations" is actually somewhat difficult to translate, but more literally would be something like "do not give your lying down for *seed*" (i.e., to implant seed). In verse 21, more literally, the first clause would be "Do not give of your *seed* to pass over to Molek" (author's translation). So the linguistic connection may account for both verses being placed together. They are both concerned with offspring. In verse 20 the concern is producing illegitimate children; in verse 21 the concern is sacrificing children to Molek.

   Second, the motivation in verse 21 is to avoid "profaning" the name of Yahweh. This is the first time this verb has been used in this chapter.

In a chapter in which the concern has been not to dishonor family members, now the concern is not to dishonor Yahweh by profaning his name. It also serves to demonstrate that if the Israelites were to sacrifice their children to Molek, they would not simply be sacrificing *their* children, they would be sacrificing Yahweh's children. Yahweh is profaned when *his* children are sacrificed to other gods.

Third, it is interesting that in a parallel passage in 20:5, Molek worship is referred to as "prostitution." Metaphorically, Molek worship is regarded, along with the other violations in this chapter, as a sexual aberration.[10]

10. Homosexual acts are forbidden in verse 22. There is a great deal of controversy surrounding this passage (as well as the parallel in 20:13), and, of course, there is the much larger biblical and theological discussion that has become particularly relevant today. I do not have the space here to go into all the interpretive arguments regarding this verse but will simply say that, as opposed to alternate suggestions that the prohibition has only to do with cultically related acts or acts between non-equals, I am convinced that the prohibition is rooted in creation theology and the concern here is the unnaturalness of the act itself. The implications will be fleshed out in the next section.
11. The last-mentioned prohibition is bestiality. We have already seen that most forms of bestiality were prohibited in the ancient Near East, though others were tolerated. There is no indication that there would have been any such tolerance on the part of Yahweh. We should also note that the deities of many of the pagan religions of the ancient Near East were depicted as engaging in incestuous and polyamorous acts and were also depicted as killing their own children and engaging in bestiality.[11] Yahweh, the holy one of Israel, was not such a deity, and his people must not be such a people either.
12. Finally, it is important to note the occurrence in this chapter of the Hebrew term *to'ebah*. The NIV translates it as "detestable." Other common renderings are "abomination" or "abhorrence." It is actually a noun "detestable thing," rather than an adjective. Though it occurs nearly eighty times in the Hebrew Bible and characterizes a number of violations, in the book of Leviticus the word only occurs six times—five times in this chapter and once in chapter 20. As a singular noun it

10. For further discussion, see Hartley, *Leviticus*, 289–90; Balentine, *Leviticus*, 159–60.
11. For more on this, see Hess, "Leviticus," 737–39.

occurs only in 18:22 and 20:13, both times in relation to homosexual acts. As a plural noun it occurs in 18:26, 27, 29, and 30 (NIV does not translate the occurrence in v. 27). So while the word is used four times in this chapter, apparently to refer to all the violations previously referred to in the chapter, it is interesting that only homosexual acts are specifically so identified. It is also worth mentioning that the occurrences of the term are clustered in the last few verses of the chapter. In other words, in terms of proximity, all the occurrences come after the more unique non-incestuous violations mentioned near the end of the chapter. It is at least possible that the use of the word *to'ebah* was triggered by these last violations—child sacrifice, homosexuality, and bestiality (which is also referred to as a "perversion"). It may be that, comparatively, these are more detestable than the violations listed in the first part of the chapter.

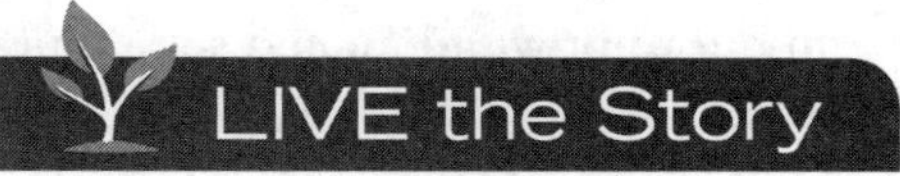

LIVE the Story

The Patriarchs and Leviticus 18

As noted earlier, the incest laws in Leviticus 18 provide a prescriptive contrast with the descriptive narratives contained in Genesis: Noah, Lot, Abraham, Jacob, Reuben, and even Moses's own father Amram were all involved in marriages or sexual relationships that would have been in violation of these laws. What are the implications of this for us today? I mention two things here.

First, this should cause us to better appreciate the narratival nature of the Scriptures. This is in fact one of the reasons why the name of the series to which this commentary belongs is The Story of God Bible Commentary. It would not be quite correct, without qualification, to say that the Bible is not a rule book, because there are indeed numerous laws and rules in the Bible, in both Testaments. But, with proper nuancing, it would be more correct to say that the Bible contains laws and rules that are set in a narratival context. And the narrative backdrop against which these laws and rules are set must be understood as progressively revelational in character. That is, God called individuals to follow him without necessarily giving them a full revelation of his ethical and moral will. While Old Testament narratives are not without ethical and moral lessons and implications, they are not moralistic. The early stories in the book of Genesis narrate how God was preparing a people for himself, and the individuals whom God used to form this people were fully imbedded in their own cultural contexts. For whatever reason, it was not until after God redeemed his people from the land of Egypt and led them out to the wilderness of Sinai that he gave them a fuller revelation of his will as contained in the laws given in Exodus through Deuteronomy. This also means that we should not necessarily read these laws as providing some kind of critique of the character of the patriarchs. The laws are corrective without at the same time being condemnatory.

Second, as we live out the story of God in our own lives today, or, better, as we live out our lives in the story of God, we should remember that we are playing out a dramatic script. Kevin Vanhoozer has eloquently argued that Christians today are called upon to live out their lives according to the Script(ure) (see Introduction: Reading from the Perspective of the Twenty-First Century, pp. 24–27). We are engaged in a dramatic performance of Scripture, one that attempts to be faithful to the authoritative canonical text yet one that is going to require a measure of improvisation as we both interpret and perform the Script(ure) in multiple and varied contexts. We will make mistakes in trying to maintain a proper balance in our improvisation, and sometimes those mistakes will be outright failures. Like the patriarchs, we are following the light of God's revelation while nevertheless embedded in our own respective cultures, and there will be times when it may be hard for us to determine precisely what that obedient following will look like in our particular cultural context. But we trust that the God who so patiently guided the patriarchs and our ancestors in the faith will, by his Spirit, guide us as well.

The Person Who Obeys God's Laws Will Live by Them

Obedience to the laws of God was not a prerequisite for entering into covenant with God or becoming part of the people of God. God did not give laws to Israel in order that they might become his people; rather, God gave the laws to those whom he had already constituted as his covenant people. He had already redeemed them from bondage in Egypt, and he had already brought them into a covenant relationship with himself. The laws were given to the Israelites that they might maintain their covenant relationship with God and enjoy long life before God, under his blessing and favor, in the land he gave to them.

This is no less the case in the New Testament. Paul, the great apostle of justification by faith apart from the law, was by no means trying to argue that Christians no longer had any responsibility to Old Testament law. However, one might think differently after reading two passages in which Paul quotes Leviticus 18:5—Romans 10:1–13 (v. 5) and Galatians 3:1–14 (v. 12). Some have read these passages in such a way that sees Paul setting observance of the law in opposition to faith, law in opposition to gospel. However, such a reading does not do justice to the rest of Paul's writings, in which he both quotes the law and encourages obedience to it.

It seems to me that in these two passages Paul is not setting up law in opposition to the gospel. Rather, he is simply pointing out that the law is not the gospel. Law and gospel serve two different purposes. The gospel is the good news of redemption in Christ Jesus. The law, on the other hand, is the gracious gift of God to assist the Christian in the process of sanctification and conforming to the image of Christ.[12]

Paul's citations of Leviticus 18:5 are for the purpose of showing the fallacy of the misuse of the law as a means to attain righteousness, to use the law for a purpose for which it was not intended. Paul does not always lay out his logic step-by-step, but it seems that the following paraphrase is a fair way to lay out what his intentions are in these two passages:

> If you think you can earn your salvation on the basis of obedience to the law, then you should know that this very same law says, "the person who does these things will live by them." If you, then, fail to keep all these laws, since you are trying to use the law to obtain salvation, you will not live, you will not inherit eternal life.

If the law is used as it was intended, then the promise of Leviticus 18:5 is held out before the Christian as a good and encouraging word. It holds out before us the promise of a life lived under the blessing and favor of God.[13] Two ancient church fathers understood this to be the case as well:

> Jerome: "The man who carries out the law will find life through it." Scripture did not say he will find life through it, in the sense that through the law he will live in heaven, but he will find life through it to the extent that what he merits, he reaps in the present world.

> John Cassian: For the law promises those who practice it not the rewards of the heavenly kingdom but the consolations of this life when it says, "The one who does these things shall live in them."[14]

---

12. This is often referred to as the "third use of the law."

13. For basically the same understanding among Leviticus commentators, see Rooker, *Leviticus*, 240–41; Wenham, *Leviticus*, 261; Sklar, *Leviticus*, 229; Kleinig, *Leviticus*, 391.

14. Both are cited in Joseph T. Lienhard, ed., *Exodus, Leviticus, Numbers, Deuteronomy*, ACCS 3 (Downers Grove, IL: IVP Academic, 2001), 187. The quotation from Jerome is from his "Homily 76" on Mark 1:13–31 in FC 57:137. The quotation from John Cassian is from his *Conferences* 3.21.5.2. in ACW 57:721–22. On this see also Wenham, *Leviticus*, 253; Kiuchi, *Leviticus*, 332.

Finally, I should also call attention to Cranfield's suggestion, in accordance with Karl Barth, that in Romans 10:5 the person of whom it is said that if they "do these things will live by them" is actually Jesus Christ himself. He is the one who has kept the law perfectly; he is the one who has life in himself; and he is the one who has given that life to those who are in solidarity with him.[15] While I am not necessarily convinced that this is specifically the case in this passage, I do believe, with the ancient church father Irenaeus, that Jesus "recapitulates" the entire Old Testament.[16] He fulfills the obedience to the law that Israel was supposed to have fulfilled but failed to do so. So, Jesus, by his life lived "under the law" (Gal 4:4), has indeed done what Israel did not do and what we cannot do. In this way we can see Jesus as the one who has fulfilled the law by his own obedience. And, of course, this would include the laws of Leviticus 18. Because he lives, we too shall live.[17]

The God Who Controls Our Sex Life

We have already observed that, in the book of Leviticus, Yahweh exerts his sovereignty over the entirety of Israelite existence. He is Lord over what the Israelites eat and over what they wear. And now, in this chapter, he is the Lord who is sovereign over sexual relationships. This sovereignty over all of life is not something that the Lord exercised only over the lives of the Old Testament Israelites; it continues into the life of the church and of individual Christians. Given the levels of sexual perversity that are so readily observable in the modern world, Gane's satirical comment is particularly apt: "If only Leviticus were not so relevant to modern life!"[18] Abraham Kuyper's famous words are appropriate as well: "There is not a square inch in the whole domain of our human existence over which Christ, who is Sovereign over all, does not cry: 'Mine!'"[19] And, for our purposes in this section, we note that God is authoritative and sovereign in the realm of human biology and sex. It is his because he created it.

Leviticus 18:22; 20:13, the New Testament, and the Church Today

The current debate regarding homosexuality and LGBTQ concerns has become a very divisive one in the church, even within evangelical circles.

15. C. E. B. Cranfield, *A Critical and Exegetical Commentary on the Epistle to the Romans*, ICC (Edinburgh: T&T Clark, 1979), 2:515–32.

16. The language of recapitulation can be found throughout Irenaeus's *Against Heresies* (*ANF* 1:315–567).

17. On this, see also Radner, *Leviticus*, 193, 196–99.

18. Gane, *Leviticus, Numbers*, 324.

19. Cited in James D. Bratt, *Abraham Kuyper: A Centennial Reader* (Grand Rapids: Eerdmans, 1998), 488.

In light of the clarity with which I believe Scripture speaks to this issue, I have been quite disappointed with much of the discussion in particular commentaries on Leviticus. Commentators, whose work I have consulted and used with great profit, when they address the interpretation and applicability of Leviticus 18:22 and 20:13 suddenly seem to abandon the responsible hermeneutical practices that they had employed throughout the rest of their commentaries. One such commentator even goes on at length in a section titled, "How Not to Read the Bible," to lecture those who believe these passages are condemning homosexual acts in general and are applicable today.

This is a huge debate, and I certainly cannot address all the issues raised in this debate. But in the points that follow I wish to simply address the interpretation and use of these verses in their original context, in the New Testament, and in the discussion today:

1. Attempts to argue that the proscriptions in Leviticus only have to do with Canaanite rituals that may have incorporated homosexual acts or presuppose some kind of imbalance of power simply do not work. There is no such suggestion in the context, and Gane has noted that the language employed in these verses is "devastatingly untechnical, leaving no room for ambiguity."[20] The wording of these verses certainly appears to be gnomic or general in character, and not confined to particularized situations.[21]
2. The late Jewish scholar, Jacob Milgrom, argued that, based on the context, the prohibition of same-sex acts is applicable only to Jews, only to males, only to relations with members of one's family, and only within the bounds of the land of Israel; it has nothing to do with any abhorrence with the act of itself but only with the wasting of seed (the male's semen).[22] However, as many scholars have observed in spite of their great respect for Milgrom's magisterial commentary, his arguments can only be seen as special pleading, and he does not apply this very narrow set of criteria to the other prohibitions in chapters 18 and 20.[23]

---

20. Gane, *Leviticus, Numbers*, 321.

21. See also, Jay Sklar, "The Prohibitions Against Homosexual Sex in Leviticus 18:22 and 20:13: Are They Relevant Today?," *BBR* 28.2 (2018): 165–98.

22. Milgrom, *Leviticus 17–22*, 1565–70, 1749–50, 1786–90.

23. For only a few of the critiques of Milgrom on this issue, see Gane, *Leviticus, Numbers*, 325–32; Tidball, *Message of Leviticus*, 226–27; Hess, "Leviticus," 744; Robert A. J. Gagnon, "A Critique of Jacob Milgrom's Views on Leviticus 18:22 and 20:13," 2005, *Rob Gagnon*, http://www.robgagnon.net/articles/homoMilgrom.pdf; Roy E. Gane, Nicholas P. Miller, and H. Peter Swanson, eds., *Homosexuality, Marriage, and the Church: Biblical, Counseling, and Religious Liberty Issues* (Berrien Springs, MI: Andrews University Press, 2012).

While there may be some validity with respect to the concern over the wasting of seed, it would seem that the proscription against homosexual acts has much more to do with the creation theology of the book of Leviticus. Homosexual acts are contrary to God's design; they are unnatural—that is, against nature.

3. There are three passages in particular in Paul's letters in which he mentions homosexual acts: Romans 1:24–27; 1 Corinthians 6:9–11; and 1 Timothy 1:3–11. In the last two passages Paul uses the word Greek word *arsenokoitēs* to refer to what the NIV has translated respectively as "men who have sex with men" and "those practicing homosexuality." Some have argued that Paul coined the term *arsenokoitēs*. We cannot be sure of this, but what does seem certain is that this term is derived from the Greek Septuagint's translation of Leviticus 18:22 and 20:13, which uses the words *arsenos* and *koitēs* in its rendering. The word that Paul has either coined or utilized, then, is based on the verses in Leviticus. Paul has brought these verses forward in his condemnation of homosexual acts.
4. The indictment in all three of these New Testament passages is quite serious. In the Romans passage, homosexual behavior is not only sinful in itself, but its proliferation is already indicative of the righteous judgment of God. The ones condemned in the larger context are not only those who engage in homosexual practice but also those who tolerate it and approve of it. In the Corinthians passage, those who engage in such practices are disqualified from inheriting the kingdom of God (note that the penalty in Lev 20:13 is death). In 1 Timothy, homosexual behavior is actually regarded as heretical, equivalent to false doctrine, and contrary to the gospel. Leviticus 18:22 and 20:13 are not only brought forward into the New Testament by the apostle Paul, but the violation of these prohibitions is determinative of one's eternal destiny. Gane, therefore, correctly states, "The answer for people enslaved by sexual perversion is not to tell them that they are OK. They are not."[24] To tell someone that their homosexual behavior is approved by God and is compatible with the Christian life is a serious and condemnable act of pastoral malpractice.
5. We should also note, with regard to the 1 Corinthians passage, that in the near context, in chapter 5 another prohibition from Leviticus 18 comes into play. Paul refers to a member of the church at Corinth who

24. Gane, *Leviticus, Numbers*, 329.

was guilty of "sleeping with his father's wife," (1 Cor 5:1), which would, of course, be a violation of the prohibition in Leviticus 18:8 and 20:11. It would seem that Leviticus 18 and 20 were very much operative in the apostle's thinking.

6. With regard to Jesus himself, one often hears in this debate that "Jesus never said anything about homosexuality." First, we should note that an argument from silence is especially tenuous, particularly in the light of the declaration in John 21:25. We should certainly not think that everything Jesus ever said has been recorded for us in the Gospels.
7. But, perhaps more importantly, while we have no record of Jesus explicitly mentioning homosexuality, it should certainly be understood that Leviticus 18 was in the background of several pronouncements in the Gospels. Space precludes any full discussion of these here; I refer the reader to the comprehensive work of Robert Gagnon and also to a couple of articles by Scot McKnight.[25] To give just one example, several times in the Gospels Jesus refers to "sexual immorality." The Greek word in these instances is *porneia*. To paraphrase McKnight, in these instances, if we had a hypertexted script of Jesus's speeches on these occasions, and we were to double-click on the link for the word *porneia*, we would be directed to Leviticus 18. As Gagnon notes, the term *porneia* in these instances is actually plural, "sexual immoralities," and "No first-century Jew could have spoken of *porneiai* (plural) without having in mind the list of forbidden sexual offenses in Leviticus 18 and 20 (incest, adultery, same-sex intercourse, bestiality)."[26]
8. Often the objection is raised that if we are going to enforce the prohibitions against homosexual acts, then we should also enforce the prohibitions against eating unclean food and wearing blended-material clothes, bring back sacrifices, and reinstitute all the ancient Israelite festivals. The problem with this objection, however, is that it fails to appreciate the biblical-theological reasons as to why, for example, the dietary laws have been abrogated and the sacrifices have been discontinued. And it fails to deal with the fact that the New Testament not only brings

25. Robert A. J. Gagnon, *The Bible and Homosexual Practice: Texts and Hermeneutics* (Nashville: Abingdon, 2001); Scot McKnight, "Did Jesus Talk about Homosexuality?," *Jesus Creed*, 6 April 2015, http://www.patheos.com/blogs/jesuscreed/2015/04/06/did-jesus-talk-about-homosexuality/; Scot McKnight, "What Is Porneia to a 1st Century Jew?," *Jesus Creed*, 4 April 2014, http://www.patheos.com/blogs/jesuscreed/2014/04/04/what-is-porneia-to-a-1st-century-jew/.

26. Gagnon, *Bible and Homosexual Practice*, 191.

forward the sexual prohibitions of Leviticus 18 but, if anything, actually doubles-down on them.

9. Finally, I must note that, in light of the above New Testament evidence, it is simply impossible to argue that there is some kind of biblical trajectory that would lead to a position where same-sex sexual relationships could be seen as legitimate within a Christian ethic. I call attention here to three authors within the last twenty-five years who have discussed the topic of homosexual acts in relation to other ethical debates. First, there is Richard Hays, who, in his book *The Moral Vision of the New Testament*, looked at the topics of violence, divorce and remarriage, anti-Judaism, and abortion.[27] Second, there is Willard Swartley, who wrote a volume titled *Slavery, Sabbath, War and Women*[28] and then followed it up over twenty years later with a volume discussing homosexuality.[29] Finally, William Webb wrote a book titled *Slaves, Women and Homosexuals*.[30] What all three authors, from very different denominational backgrounds, found was that, for a number of ethical issues (such as slavery, women in ministry, war, etc.) a case could be made for a trajectory that would lead to a more liberalizing understanding of the issue as one moves from the Old Testament to the New Testament. But all three also concluded that, for homosexuality, there is absolutely no evidence whatsoever for such a trajectory. Indeed, as I said above, if anything the New Testament is even more definitive in its prohibitive stance with regard to this issue than is the Old Testament. So Roy Gane is certainly correct:

> If we accept the biblical evidence, Christians everywhere are just as accountable to God for avoiding the practices listed in Leviticus 18 as the ancient Israelites were when the legislation was first given.[31]

---

27. Richard B. Hays, *The Moral Vision of the New Testament: Community, Cross, New Creation; A Contemporary Introduction to New Testament Ethics* (New York: HarperCollins, 1996).

28. Willard M. Swartley, *Slavery, Sabbath, War, and Women: Case Issues in Biblical Interpretation* (Scottdale, PA: Herald, 1983).

29. Willard M. Swartley, *Homosexuality: Biblical Interpretation and Moral Discernment* (Scottdale, PA: Herald, 2003).

30. William J. Webb, *Slaves, Women & Homosexuals: Exploring the Hermeneutics of Cultural Analysis* (Downers Grove, IL: InterVarsity Press, 2001).

31. Gane, *Leviticus, Numbers*, 328.

CHAPTER 17

Leviticus 19:1–37

LISTEN to the Story

19:1The LORD said to Moses, 2"Speak to the entire assembly of Israel and
say to them: 'Be holy because I, the LORD your God, am holy.

3"'Each of you must respect your mother and father, and you must
observe my Sabbaths. I am the LORD your God.

4"'Do not turn to idols or make metal gods for yourselves. I am the
LORD your God.

5"'When you sacrifice a fellowship offering to the LORD, sacrifice it
in such a way that it will be accepted on your behalf. 6It shall be eaten
on the day you sacrifice it or on the next day; anything left over until the
third day must be burned up. 7If any of it is eaten on the third day, it is
impure and will not be accepted. 8Whoever eats it will be held responsible
because they have desecrated what is holy to the LORD; they must be cut
off from their people.

9"'When you reap the harvest of your land, do not reap to the very
edges of your field or gather the gleanings of your harvest. 10Do not go over
your vineyard a second time or pick up the grapes that have fallen. Leave
them for the poor and the foreigner. I am the LORD your God.

11"'Do not steal.

"'Do not lie.

"'Do not deceive one another.

12"'Do not swear falsely by my name and so profane the name of your
God. I am the LORD.

13"'Do not defraud or rob your neighbor.

"'Do not hold back the wages of a hired worker overnight.

14"'Do not curse the deaf or put a stumbling block in front of the blind,
but fear your God. I am the LORD.

15"'Do not pervert justice; do not show partiality to the poor or favor-
itism to the great, but judge your neighbor fairly.

[16]"'Do not go about spreading slander among your people.

"'Do not do anything that endangers your neighbor's life. I am the LORD.

[17]"'Do not hate a fellow Israelite in your heart. Rebuke your neighbor frankly so you will not share in their guilt.

[18]"'Do not seek revenge or bear a grudge against anyone among your people, but love your neighbor as yourself. I am the LORD.

[19]"'Keep my decrees.

"'Do not mate different kinds of animals.

"'Do not plant your field with two kinds of seed.

"'Do not wear clothing woven of two kinds of material.

[20]"'If a man sleeps with a female slave who is promised to another man but who has not been ransomed or given her freedom, there must be due punishment. Yet they are not to be put to death, because she had not been freed. [21]The man, however, must bring a ram to the entrance to the tent of meeting for a guilt offering to the LORD. [22]With the ram of the guilt offering the priest is to make atonement for him before the LORD for the sin he has committed, and his sin will be forgiven.

[23]"'When you enter the land and plant any kind of fruit tree, regard its fruit as forbidden. For three years you are to consider it forbidden; it must not be eaten. [24]In the fourth year all its fruit will be holy, an offering of praise to the LORD. [25]But in the fifth year you may eat its fruit. In this way your harvest will be increased. I am the LORD your God.

[26]"'Do not eat any meat with the blood still in it.

"'Do not practice divination or seek omens.

[27]"'Do not cut the hair at the sides of your head or clip off the edges of your beard.

[28]"'Do not cut your bodies for the dead or put tattoo marks on yourselves. I am the LORD.

[29]"'Do not degrade your daughter by making her a prostitute, or the land will turn to prostitution and be filled with wickedness.

[30]"'Observe my Sabbaths and have reverence for my sanctuary. I am the LORD.

[31]"'Do not turn to mediums or seek out spiritists, for you will be defiled by them. I am the LORD your God.

[32]"'Stand up in the presence of the aged, show respect for the elderly and revere your God. I am the LORD.

33“ ‘When a foreigner resides among you in your land, do not mistreat
them. 34The foreigner residing among you must be treated as your native-
born. Love them as yourself, for you were foreigners in Egypt. I am the
LORD your God.

35“ ‘Do not use dishonest standards when measuring length, weight
or quantity. 36Use honest scales and honest weights, an honest ephah and
an honest hin. I am the LORD your God, who brought you out of Egypt.

37“ ‘Keep all my decrees and all my laws and follow them. I am the LORD.’ ”

Listening to the Text in the Story: Biblical Texts: Exodus 20:1–17

Exodus 20:1–17, which contains what has been traditionally referred to as the Decalogue, seems, at least to some measure, to be replicated in Leviticus 19. The correspondences can be seen in the following chart:

Commandment	Exodus 20	Leviticus 19
1	v. 3	
2	vv. 4–6	v. 4
3	v. 7	v. 12
4	vv. 8–11	vv. 3, 30
5	v. 12	v. 3
6	v. 13	v. 16
7	v. 14	
8	v. 15	vv. 11, 13, 35–36
9	v. 16	vv. 11, 16
10	v. 17	

The correspondences between Exodus 20 and Leviticus 19—not necessarily linguistically but certainly conceptually—are quite close for commandments 2, 3, 4, 5, 8, and 9. If, in Leviticus 19:16, NIV’s “endangering life” is a valid understanding of the Hebrew (more literally, “stand against the blood of your neighbor”), then the prohibition would certainly approximate the sixth commandment regarding murder. Some commentators regard Leviticus 19:20–22 and 29 as corresponding to the seventh commandment about adultery. However, while the content of these verses does describe sexual violations, they do not necessarily constitute adultery. Some suggest that Leviticus 19:9–10 and 17–18 correspond to the tenth commandment about coveting, but the correspondence is not very close. And though it could be argued that the "spirit" of the first commandment is present throughout the chapter, the connection is not made explicitly (though it is true that the mediums and spiritists in verse 31 would have been in the service of other gods). In conclusion, it has to be noted that while the laws in Leviticus 19:5–10, 14–15, 17–29, and 31–34 could be seen in some respect as deriving from the Ten Commandments, they do not really connect that closely with them. I believe it would be more correct to maintain that the chapter, though not a replication of the Ten Commandments, is nevertheless intentionally reflective of them. Supporting the intentionality of this correspondence is the fact that the preface to the Decalogue, "I am the LORD your God," is, with variations, replicated sixteen times in this chapter.

EXPLAIN the Story

The chapter presents a number of what appear to be miscellaneous and unstructured prescriptions for the Israelites to play out the holiness God expected of them. We will not be able to give sufficient attention to each prescription in this chapter, but the following observations place these prescriptions in proper perspective:

1. God's own holiness is the foundation of the holiness he expects from his people. But what does it mean to say that God is holy and that the people are to be holy? What is the relationship between God's holiness and that of the people?

   Early in the twentieth century Rudolf Otto, in his justly famous book *The Idea of the Holy*, argued that, originally, the concept of holiness had little to do with the moral and ethical content we attach to the term today (see the discussion on this in the Introduction: Holiness [pp. 16–17]. Rather, among most ancient peoples—including the ancient Israelites—holiness, for the most part, had to do with God's divinity,[1] transcendence, his otherness, his majesty, his awe-inspiringness, the *mysterium tremendum*.[2] Any moral or ethical content

1. This is generally recognized by Old Testament scholars; e.g, Boda, in his *Severe Mercy*, 51, says that "the term *holy* refers to what is divine and not created."
2. Otto, *The Idea of the Holy*; Gammie, *Holiness in Israel*, 5–8.

to the holiness was only derivative and, unfortunately, unduly began to replace the original understanding. Otto did not deny the ethical but did to a large extent downplay its significance.

As important as Otto's insights are for recovering this "otherness" aspect of holiness, many scholars have argued that the ethical was in fact integral to the concept of holiness from the beginning, and not merely derivative.[3] If God tells his people to be holy because he is holy, it is hard to understand how this human enterprise of *imitatio Dei*, this imitation of God, could be ethically and morally oriented unless God's own holiness was ethically and morally oriented as well. Leviticus 17–26 (especially its central affirmation, first expressed in Lev 19:2, that we are to be holy because God is holy) would seem to be founded on the understanding that God's own self-conception of his own holiness has an ethical content to it. When God's people do those things that are morally right, they are in fact imitating the holiness of God himself. Indeed, it is the duty of the people to imitate their God, in the same way it was understood throughout the ancient Near East that the royal court had a duty to imitate the king of the land.[4]

2. We have already noted that the phrase "I am the Lord" occurs sixteen times in this chapter. In addition to the role it plays in supplying a motivation for the people to imitate God in his holiness, it serves other purposes as well. Milgrom succinctly states two of those other purposes: "The author of the commandments is God, who will punish their violators."[5] The repetition reinforces in the minds of the original hearers that these laws are from God, and the omnipotence of Yahweh himself guarantees their enforcement.
3. One of the nine times in Leviticus in which the Lord reminds the Israelites that he brought them out of Egypt occurs in verse 36, and the affirmation is part of a sandwich structure that closes out the chapter:

> I am the Lord your God, who brought you out of Egypt.
> Keep all my decrees and all my laws and follow them.
> I am the Lord.

Yahweh's self-identification as God, and in particular the God who brought the Israelites out of Egypt, is the foundation on which the decrees

3. Kaiser, "Leviticus," 1132; Radner, *Leviticus*, 204–8.
4. Milgrom, *Leviticus 17–22*, 1604; Levine, *Leviticus*, 125.
5. Milgrom, *Leviticus 17–22*, 1612.

and laws stand and on which the obedience of the people is expected. To recognize this is vitally important, because it means that the Israelites were not expected to keep these laws in order to be become Yahweh's people or to be rescued from Egypt but because they were already his people and had already been rescued from Egypt. The Old Testament covenants, no less than the New Covenant, were built on the foundation of grace. Holiness is grounded in redemption. The Israelites were not to be holy in order to be redeemed but because they were already redeemed.

4. In a chapter that seems to be more ethically oriented, it might seem surprising, in verses 5–8, to come across laws relating to sacrifice—in particular the fellowship offering. There are two things to note. First, these more ritually related prescriptions, as well as those in verses 19, 21–28, and 31, may be located in this chapter precisely for the purpose of demonstrating that a holy people are to be holy in all things cultic as well as non-cultic. There is no separation between the cultic and the ethical. Second, it may well be, as Wright remarks, that the reason why the prescriptions occur here "in the midst of a chapter primarily devoted to social concerns is probably that the *fellowship offering* was the most social of all the sacrifices."[6]
5. The laws in verses 9–10 are significant in that, even though private charity was certainly encouraged throughout the Old Testament, there were nevertheless legal precepts dealing with the issue of poverty as well. As Wright puts it, "The relief of poverty in Israel, therefore, was built into economic and legal structures."[7] There were governmental programs in place to aid in relief of the poor.
6. There have been several interpretations of exactly what is meant by "as yourself" in verse 18. Without going into all of them, I simply note that the traditional understanding still seems to be the best one: you should care for your neighbor as you would care for yourself. It should also be noted that the commandment in this passage to love one's neighbor (vv. 17–18), in conjunction with the command in Deuteronomy 6:5, to love God with one's heart, soul, and strength, are commended by Jesus as the two greatest commandments (Matt 22:34–40). This proves that the old cliché about the Old Testament being a religion of externals, and the New Testament being a religion of internals, simply does not hold up. The design all along was that religion was to be a matter of the heart: "These commandments that I give you today are to be on your hearts" (Deut 6:6).

6. Wright, "Leviticus," 147.
7. Ibid., 147.

7. In verse 19 three mixtures are proscribed: mating two different animals, planting a field with two different seeds, and wearing clothes woven with two different materials. It has been generally assumed that such prohibitions are tied to the idea of holiness being a matter of separation and avoiding unnatural or unholy mixtures. Certainly for some mixture prohibitions, such as the dietary laws, this is the case. It has also been assumed that in a list of such prohibitions, they must all have the same motivation behind them. Such assumptions, however, are questionable for this particular passage.

    Milgrom argues that all the forbidden mixtures in this verse are prohibited not because they are profane or bad but because they are reserved for the divine, for Yahweh; in fact, they are holy.[8] Briefly, we can note that in the ancient Near East and also in the Bible hybrid creatures were portrayed as being among the divine or angelic beings (Ezek 1). In Deuteronomy 22:9, two kinds of seeds are forbidden in the same field because the result would be "made holy" (this, rather than NIV's "defiled" more accurately translates the verb *qadash* in this verse). The weaving together of two kinds of material was prescribed for the tabernacle curtains and priestly clothing (Exod 26:1, 31; 28:6, 15; 39:29). So the prohibition here is not given because these things are bad but because they are reserved for Yahweh—they are holy. In many respects, the Israelites were to imitate God by being holy as he is holy. But some areas of the divine holiness were not to be encroached upon. In this chapter, then, there are elements of both transcendence and immanence, distance and nearness, in the relationship between the human and the divine.

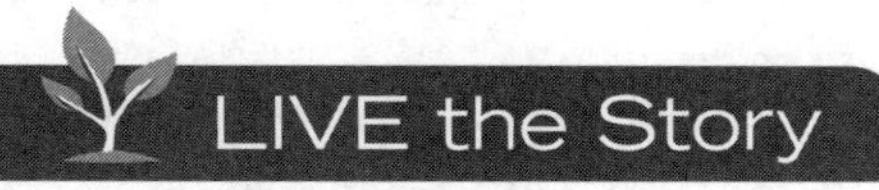

Leviticus 19, either directly or indirectly, appears to have been influentially informative for the theology and teaching of many of the New Testament authors, as well as of Jesus himself. We will look at four ways in which this influence plays out.

Ezekiel and Leviticus

While it is well recognized that the New Testament authors quoted, alluded to, and used passages in the Old Testament, what is perhaps not so well recognized

---

8. Milgrom, *Leviticus 17–22*, 1659–62. See also Gane, *Leviticus, Numbers*, 338; Kiuchi, *Leviticus*, 355–56; Sklar, *Leviticus*, 248.

is that the Old Testament authors also quoted, alluded to, and used other Old Testament passages.[9] Indeed, we have already seen this in Leviticus 19, as it alludes to and uses Exodus 20. Levine has well argued that Ezekiel 22:6–12, in its condemnation of both the Judahite leaders and the people, is literarily connected to and reflective of Leviticus 19.[10] This should not be a surprise in that Ezekiel was himself a priest. Indeed, much of the book of Ezekiel is reflective of the so-called Holiness Code in Leviticus 17–26. Ezekiel's famous question in Ezekiel 33:10, "How then can we live?" along with other passages (3:21; 18:9–32; 20:11–13, 21; 33:10–19, is certainly intentionally related to the declaration in Leviticus 18:5 that the one who keeps Yahweh's decrees and laws will live by them. In places Ezekiel seems to be almost a commentary on Leviticus.

The significance of this for the New Testament is that Ezekiel in the Old Testament and Jesus and the authors of the New Testament are addressing what are essentially similar audiences. For Ezekiel, it is the Babylonian exiles. For Jesus, it is the people of Galilee and Judah, who, though they are in fact living in the promised land, are actually still in exile ("O come, O come, Immanuel, and ransom captive Israel, that mourns in lonely exile here").[11] For the apostles and New Testament authors, the audience also includes the gentiles, those who were not the people of God but are now being called to become such. For each audience, the message is that the Lord is about to graciously redeem you and bring you back to himself and that obedience to the commands of the Lord is the path to life and blessing as a "kingdom of priests and a holy nation" (Exod 19:6). The book of Ezekiel contributes to the continuity between Leviticus and the New Testament. New Testament Christians can read Leviticus—as well as the refraction of Leviticus in the book of Ezekiel—and see themselves on those pages.

Be Holy Because I Am Holy–Yes, This Is a Word for Christians

This was a word for the Old Testament Israelites, and it is affirmed for New Testament Christians by Christ and the apostles:

> Be perfect, therefore, as your heavenly Father is perfect. (Matt 5:48)

---

9. For a fascinating scholarly introduction to this area, see Michael Fishbane, *Biblical Interpretation in Ancient Israel* (Oxford: Clarendon, 1985).

10. Levine, *Leviticus*, 125.

11. In line with this, George Athas has cogently argued that Dan 9 reinterprets Jeremiah's prophecy of a seventy-year exile (2 Chr 36:21; Jer 25:11–12; 29:10) as actually extending beyond the time of Israel's physical return to Jerusalem; see George Athas, "In Search of the Seventy 'Weeks' of Daniel 9," *JHebS* 9 (2009), https://doi.org/10.5508/jhs.2009.v9.a2.

> Be merciful, just as your Father is merciful. (Luke 6:36)

> But just as he who called you is holy, so be holy in all you do; for it is written: "Be holy, because I am holy." (1 Pet 1:15–16)

Yahweh's expectations for the Israelites were all-encompassing. We have already seen that he was to be Lord of every facet of their lives. He demanded and expected absolute and unquestioning obedience. Boyce says it well: "Surely the most exhilarating aspect of Leviticus in general, and the Holiness Code in particular, is the desire to claim all of life for God, or better, to show forth God's claim on the whole of our lives."[12] And Wright cleverly remarks, this holiness was to be on display "from the corners of your beard to the corners of your fields."[13] This is no less the case in the New Testament. Indeed, Jesus's expectations for his followers are even more stringent than those required of the Old Testament Israelites. And yet, I heard it again this morning from a preacher on a popular religious broadcast: "One of the myths of Christianity is that God demands perfection. And you cannot do anything to make God more pleased with you than he is right now." But that is neither the testimony of the Old Testament nor of the New. The goal is perfection. "Be perfect" does not merely mean, as some have suggested, "Be mature." The goal is holiness.

It is also important to acknowledge that the Scriptures do not take for granted that we know what holiness looks like. Therefore, we are provided with laws, statutes, and instructions as to how to be holy. It is for this reason that Leviticus 19 is well quoted and alluded to in the New Testament, and there are even places where longer passages in the New Testament give evidence of more than just casual interaction with Leviticus 19. For example, Luke Timothy Johnson has argued that the book of James gives evidence of "continuous and sustained use of Leviticus 19:12–18 in his letter."[14] He believes the following passages in Leviticus 19 are intentionally cited or alluded to in James:

Leviticus 19:12 (Jas 5:12)
Leviticus 19:13 (Jas 5:4)
Leviticus 19:15 (Jas 2:1, 9)
Leviticus 19:16 (Jas 4:11)
Leviticus 19:17 (Jas 5:20)

---

12. Boyce, *Leviticus and Numbers*, 75.
13. Wright, "Leviticus," 147.
14. Luke Timothy Johnson, "The Use of Leviticus 19 in the Letter of James," *JBL* 101.3 (1982): 399.

Leviticus 19:18 (Jas 5:9)
Leviticus 19:18 (Jas 2:8)

On account of these parallels, Johnson suggests that

> The emphasis of [James] 2:8, therefore, should be, "If you *really* keep the royal law, *according to the Scripture* (that is according to the dictates of the scripture), 'you shall love your neighbor as yourself,' you do well." For James, Lev 19:12–18 provides an accurate explication of that law of love which should obtain in the church.[15]

To put that another way, James does not take it for granted that we know what love of neighbor looks like; it needs an exposition.

To give another example, Kleinig remarks that "Christ and his apostles used Leviticus 19 to catechize the saints on what kinds of behavior either undermined or promoted their mutual participation in God's holiness."[16] He then gives a more expansive list of correspondences between Leviticus 19 and various New Testament passages.[17]

The point is that Christians should not trust their own instincts as a guide to what constitutes love and what constitutes holiness. Indeed, it is true that we walk according to the Spirit. But that same Spirit has given us the word in which the will of God is revealed to us and explicated for us. The Spirit always works with the word.

The Royal Law

It might surprise the reader to find out that the Old Testament verse most quoted in the New Testament comes from—of all places—Leviticus! Leviticus 19:18 is cited in Matthew 5:43; 19:19; 22:39; Mark 12:31, 33; Luke 10:27; Romans 13:9; Galatians 5:14; James 2:8 (and perhaps Rom 12:19).[18] This certainly suggests the importance of this commandment for Jesus and the apostles.

As mentioned earlier, James 2:8 apparently refers to this commandment, "love your neighbor as yourself," as the "royal law." There is debate whether the phrase "royal law" is referring to just this commandment or the entirety of Old Testament law. The debate may be academic, because even if the phrase

---

15. Johnson, "Use of Leviticus 19," 400.
16. Kleinig, *Leviticus*, 420.
17. Ibid., 420–21.
18. It is common to hear that Ps 110:1 is the most quoted verse, but you would have to add together its direct citations as well as indirect allusions to arrive at a total greater than the direct citations of Lev 19:18.

is referring to the entire law, the love-toward-neighbor commandment is nevertheless seen as a summary of the entire law with respect to one's attitude toward one's neighbor. Additionally, "royal law" probably is referring to the law as that which has been given by the king, pertains to the king, pleases the king, and constitutes those who keep this law as the loyal subjects of the king, thus being, indeed, a "royal priesthood."

One thing we should not do here is exaggerate the innovativeness of Jesus in his utilization of this law (Matt 5:43–48), nor of his apparent reformulation of this law in his giving of the golden rule (Matt 7:12). The Old Testament nowhere commands the Israelites to hate their enemies. Already in Leviticus 19, the love of neighbor commanded in verse 18 is extended to the foreigner in verse 34. And already in Exodus 23:4–5, 9, a benevolent and non-oppressive attitude toward one's enemy was demanded of the Israelites. Already, Rabbi Hillel had given his famous formulation: "What is hateful to you, do not do to your neighbor: that is the whole Torah, while the rest is commentary."[19] Contemporary, rabbinic literature had incorporated Leviticus 19:18 into their summaries of Old Testament law. And Goldingay even argues that Jesus is making explicit what is already implicit in the text:

> The First Testament gives examples of people loving their enemies, and when it tells people to love their neighbor (Lev 19:18), the context makes clear that the neighbor they are being bidden to love is the neighbor who is their enemy (people hardly need to be told to love the neighbor they get on with). So Jesus is making explicit something implicit in the commandment. Thus other Jewish teachers in Jesus' day could have accepted his teaching on the subject, as an exposition of the Scriptures. There was nothing shocking about it. One could say he is fulfilling or filling out or filling up the Torah by making explicit what the command implies, as well as by obeying it.[20]

In other words, Goldingay is arguing that the neighbor whom the Israelite is to love is actually a person they consider to be their enemy but against whom they are warned not to seek revenge or bear a grudge. However, even if this is the case, there does seem to be some evidence from various texts in the Dead Sea Scrolls that members of the Qumran community and other sectarian groups in the first century may not have understood it that way and may have

19. *Babylonian Talmud*, tractate *Shabbat* 31a.

20. John E. Goldingay, *Do We Need The New Testament?: Letting the Old Testament Speak for Itself* (Downers Grove, IL: IVP Academic, 2015), 31.

seen hatred of one's enemies as the corollary of loving one's neighbors.[21] But Jesus makes explicit that those who follow him must demonstrate an attitude of love toward one's enemies. Indeed, this is the appropriate attitude for the people of God to adopt.

Ritual, Law, Love, and Spiritual Formation

As noted above, this chapter is a challenge to those who would attempt to separate ritual from ethics in conceptualizing what it means to be holy. Ritual commands stand alongside so-called purely ethical ones, and apparently the author/editor did this intentionally. The ritual and ethical stand side by side, so that the Israelites (and we) should understand that "the call to holiness embraces every dimension of life, including the ethical and the cultic."[22] As Noordtzij remarks, when the ancient Israelites "endeavored to divorce the cultic sphere from the ethical, the prophets came forward in protest and emphasized the need to regard life as a unity."[23] Since the love commandments—to love God and to love neighbor—are to be regarded as a summary of the law, we may say that, respectively, love of God (ritual?) and love of neighbor (ethics?) go hand in hand in forming the holy people of God.

Over the last several decades there has been a great deal of attention paid to the concept of spiritual formation and the employment of a variety of spiritual disciplines. Along with this movement has come an increased attention to ritual. There has been a small but steady stream of what has been referred to as "evangelicals on the Canterbury trail," Christians who have gravitated toward churches that are more liturgical in their worship and more intentional in their use of spiritual disciplines for the purpose of spiritual formation.[24] I welcome these movements; as I have already said elsewhere in this commentary, a well-developed liturgy is world forming and helps us to see an alternative and true reality as opposed to the false narrative often put forward by contemporary society. Spiritual formation and the use of a variety of spiritual disciplines is helpful for our spiritual lives as we seek to be more conformed to the image of God's Son. Ritual also presents the benefit of introducing an aesthetic into our worship that is too often lacking in a great deal of evangelical worship

---

21. Craig L. Blomberg, "Matthew," in *Commentary on the New Testament Use of the Old Testament*, ed. G. K. Beale and D. A. Carson (Grand Rapids: Baker Academic, 2007), 28–29; and in the same volume, see Rikk E. Watts, "Mark," 218–19.

22. Hartley, *Leviticus*, 313.

23. Noordtzij, *Leviticus*, 192.

24. A now classic book which describes this movement is Robert Webber's *Evangelicals on the Canterbury Trail: Why Evangelicals Are Attracted to the Liturgical Church* (Waco: Word, 1985).

(as A. W. Tozer said many years ago, the worship of the liturgical churches is at least beautiful, while "our" services are often just ugly).[25]

But, as is always the case with ritual, the aesthetic, and the liturgical, there is the ever-present danger that we will look upon these as techniques that produce and guarantee spirituality in and of themselves. That is why the ritual must never be divorced from the so-called ethical, as if the ethical plays no part in spiritual formation. For me, to say "spiritual formation" is to say nothing less than "becoming holy." And to become holy, one must meditate on and obey the law of the Lord. We become holy by obeying God's commandments. Obedience to God's commandments is, perhaps, the most neglected spiritual discipline to be employed in the process of spiritual formation. We cannot be holy without it. Spirituality is not having warm feelings by which we feel close to God. Rather, spirituality is drawing near to God by keeping his commandments. As Radner remarks concerning what happens in Leviticus 19 after the command to be holy in verse 2,

> The relationship between holiness and the law becomes more evident in this light, and the immediate flow of commandments from Lev. 19:3 on, without explanatory connection to the initial call, seems absolutely natural: the keeping of the law is, in every aspect, an act of offering by which we draw near to God. *And the laws themselves are gifts from God, distinctive practices by which we are made close to him.*[26]

This is spiritual formation. This is being conformed to the image of God's Son. This is what it means to be holy.

25. A. W. Tozer, "God Tells the Who Man Who Cares" in *God Tells the Man Who Cares* (Harrisburg, PA: Christian Publications, 1970), 11.

26. Radner, *Leviticus*, 203, emphasis added.

CHAPTER 18

Leviticus 20:1–27

 LISTEN to the Story

20:1The LORD said to Moses, 2"Say to the Israelites: 'Any Israelite or
any foreigner residing in Israel who sacrifices any of his children to Molek
is to be put to death. The members of the community are to stone him.
3I myself will set my face against him and will cut him off from his people;
for by sacrificing his children to Molek, he has defiled my sanctuary and
profaned my holy name. 4If the members of the community close their
eyes when that man sacrifices one of his children to Molek and if they fail
to put him to death, 5I myself will set my face against him and his family
and will cut them off from their people together with all who follow him
in prostituting themselves to Molek.

6" 'I will set my face against anyone who turns to mediums and spiritists
to prostitute themselves by following them, and I will cut them off from
their people.

7" 'Consecrate yourselves and be holy, because I am the LORD your
God. 8Keep my decrees and follow them. I am the LORD, who makes
you holy.

9" 'Anyone who curses their father or mother is to be put to death.
Because they have cursed their father or mother, their blood will be on
their own head.

10" 'If a man commits adultery with another man's wife—with the
wife of his neighbor—both the adulterer and the adulteress are to be put
to death.

11" 'If a man has sexual relations with his father's wife, he has dishonored his father. Both the man and the woman are to be put to death; their
blood will be on their own heads.

12" 'If a man has sexual relations with his daughter-in-law, both of them
are to be put to death. What they have done is a perversion; their blood
will be on their own heads.

13“‘If a man has sexual relations with a man as one does with a woman, both of them have done what is detestable. They are to be put to death; their blood will be on their own heads.

14“‘If a man marries both a woman and her mother, it is wicked. Both he and they must be burned in the fire, so that no wickedness will be among you.

15“‘If a man has sexual relations with an animal, he is to be put to death, and you must kill the animal.

16“‘If a woman approaches an animal to have sexual relations with it, kill both the woman and the animal. They are to be put to death; their blood will be on their own heads.

17“‘If a man marries his sister, the daughter of either his father or his mother, and they have sexual relations, it is a disgrace. They are to be publicly removed from their people. He has dishonored his sister and will be held responsible.

18“‘If a man has sexual relations with a woman during her monthly period, he has exposed the source of her flow, and she has also uncovered it. Both of them are to be cut off from their people.

19“‘Do not have sexual relations with the sister of either your mother or your father, for that would dishonor a close relative; both of you would be held responsible.

20“‘If a man has sexual relations with his aunt, he has dishonored his uncle. They will be held responsible; they will die childless.

21“‘If a man marries his brother’s wife, it is an act of impurity; he has dishonored his brother. They will be childless.

22“‘Keep all my decrees and laws and follow them, so that the land where I am bringing you to live may not vomit you out. 23You must not live according to the customs of the nations I am going to drive out before you. Because they did all these things, I abhorred them. 24But I said to you, “You will possess their land; I will give it to you as an inheritance, a land flowing with milk and honey.” I am the Lord your God, who has set you apart from the nations.

25“‘You must therefore make a distinction between clean and unclean animals and between unclean and clean birds. Do not defile yourselves by any animal or bird or anything that moves along the ground—those that I have set apart as unclean for you. 26You are to be holy to me because I, the Lord, am holy, and I have set you apart from the nations to be my own.

[27]"'A man or woman who is a medium or spiritist among you must be put to death. You are to stone them; their blood will be on their own heads.'"

Listening to the Text in the Story: Biblical Texts: Leviticus 18

Leviticus 20 largely repeats the infractions of chapter 18 but attaches penalties to them. An important question to ask is why these two chapters are separated by chapter 19. This question is complicated by another question; that is, whether these two chapters are independent compositions. This second question is a very involved one, and I do not have the space to address it here.[1] With regard to the first one, Milgrom agrees with Mary Douglas, with slightly different argumentation and nuances, that chapters 18–20 constitute a chiasm and that chapter 19 in the middle (and not ch. 16!) is the center point of the book of Leviticus.[2] He even goes on to argue that chapter 19 is the center or "fulcrum for the entire Torah."[3]

Whether one agrees with Milgrom's understanding of Leviticus as comprised of two separate sources, P and H, and the entire book then being redacted by H, the idea that chapter 19 may be the center point of the book of Leviticus has a great deal of merit. In essence, then, chapters 18 and 20 (with their condemnation of pagan religion, Molek worship, and sexual degeneracy) properly frame chapter 19 with its central affirmation and imperative, "Be holy because I, the LORD your God, am holy" (19:2).

EXPLAIN the Story

The chapter begins by repeating and expanding on the prohibition against the offering of children to Molek. The "be holy" command is repeated in verse 7. The chapter goes on to repeat a number of the sexual prohibitions already given in chapter 18, but with specified penalties. Other prohibitions are added having to do with adultery and cursing one's parents. The chapter

1. For discussion on this issue, see Milgrom, *Leviticus 17–22*, 1765–68.

2. Milgrom, *Leviticus 17–22*, 1767–68. Douglas's understanding may be found in her article, "Poetic Structure in Leviticus," in *Pomegranates and Golden Bells: Studies in Biblical, Jewish, and Near Eastern Law and Literature in Honor of Jacob Milgrom*, ed, David P. Wright, David Noel Freedman, and Avi Hurvitz (Winona Lake: Eisenbrauns, 1995), 239–56; and also in her monograph, *Leviticus as Literature*.

3. Milgrom, *Leviticus 17–22*, 1768.

then provides motivations for obeying these commands, primarily that of being able to remain in the land of promise. The people are then reminded that they have been set apart from the nations and that they are not to defile themselves as the nations do, so that they may be holy. They are also reminded to keep the dietary laws. The chapter ends with warnings against mediums and spiritists. There are a number of important observations to make:

1. The prior prohibition against sacrificing children to Molek is greatly expanded in this chapter. The expansion has to do primarily with the community's responsibility—not to ignore such sacrifice when it happens but to report it—as well as with their duty to play their part in the execution by stoning. Sklar notes that the temptation to not assume these responsibilities could have been considerable. The responsibilities could entail informing on and stoning a close friend or relative. "Nevertheless, loyalty to the redeeming king was to come ahead of any earthly loyalty."[4]
2. Three times in the first six verses the LORD declares that he will set (Hebrew *natan*) his face against Molek worshipers, mediums, and spiritists. This language occurs especially in the priestly literature and in the book of Ezekiel, himself of priestly lineage. There are two special things to note about this language. First, there is a bit of punning taking place in that the person against whom the LORD will "set" (*natan*) his face is the person who has "put" (*natan*; NIV translates as "sacrifice") his children to Molek. Second, with regard to the word "face," despite the similarity of expression, there is a world of difference between the LORD setting his face against a person and the LORD "lifting up his face" on a person, as in the priestly blessing in Numbers 6:24–26. It is a terrible thing to have the LORD's face set against you.
3. The Hebrew word translated "children" in verses 2–4 is actually the word "seed" (Hebrew *zera'*). This use of this word reminds the reader, and perhaps intentionally so, of the great Abrahamic promises to make his seed great and numerous and to inherit the land of promise (Gen 12:7; 13:14–17; 15:5, 13, 18). To sacrifice one's seed to Molek was a flagrant covenantal violation, a horrible act of disrespect for the promises of the covenant. It is no wonder, then, that the LORD says that he will set his face against the man and his family and will cut them off from the people. They will have no seed, and they will be cut off from the covenant community.[5]

---

4. Sklar, *Leviticus*, 255.
5. See further the discussion in Hartley, *Leviticus*, 338.

4. There is disagreement among commentators with regard to the exact import of the "cutting off" mentioned in this passage. Is "cutting off" something that Yahweh does through the community's execution of the violator, or is it an additional action that Yahweh himself does after the community has acted? This raises the possibility that "cutting off" refers to the violator's being cut off from any possibility of a blessed existence in the next life.[6] The Old Testament portrayal of the afterlife is a murky one, so it is hard to make definite pronouncements in this area.[7] Still, I believe the possibility should be entertained.[8]
5. In verses 5–6 the LORD warns the people, in regard both to Molek worship and to consulting mediums and spiritists, that he will set his face against those who prostitute themselves in worshiping false gods. This is a common way in the Old Testament to depict following after other gods. But in this chapter it may be especially significant in that the worship of false gods is set alongside numerous sexual deviations. Levine, noting that Molek worship is set alongside sexual sins in chapter 18 as well, says that "What is common to both chapters is the assumed connection between pagan worship and sexual degeneracy—both are regarded as the causes of exile."[9]
6. Serving as a bridge between the prohibitions on pagan worship and sexual sins, verse 9 deals with cursing one's father or mother. Milgrom believes, correctly in my opinion, that verse 9 properly heads the list of sexual sins in that "dishonoring parents—that is, the breakdown of obligations to one's father or mother—is able to lead to the breakdown of relationships with the other members of the familial chain, including the sexual taboos."[10]
7. In verse 17 the sexual violation is described as a "disgrace." Interestingly, the Hebrew word here is *hesed*. This word, which occurs nearly 250 times in the Hebrew Bible, in the NIV is translated variously as "love," "kindness," "steadfast love," "loyalty," "faithfulness," and so on. However, scholars are convinced that the word in this verse is not actually the same word translated as "steadfast love" but a homonym

6. See, e.g., Wenham, *Leviticus*, 242, 278.

7. For a valuable survey, see Philip S. Johnston, *Shades of Sheol: Death and Afterlife in the Old Testament* (Downers Grove, IL: IVP Academic, 2002); see also Jon D. Levenson, *Resurrection and the Restoration of Israel: The Ultimate Victory of the God of Life* (New Haven: Yale University Press, 2006).

8. For an extensive discussion as to exactly what "cutting off" refers to, see Milgrom, *Leviticus 1–16*, 457–60.

9. Levine, *Leviticus*, 135.

10. Milgrom, *Leviticus 17–22*, 1744.

meaning "disgrace" or "shame" that occurs here and in only one other verse in the Hebrew Bible (Prov 14:34). I agree with a number of commentators who argue that the word is intentionally used here for satirical purposes. Sexual and marital relations are supposed to be built on faithfulness and steadfast love (*hesed*), but the illegitimate sexual relationships in this chapter are rather characterized by shame and disgrace (*hesed*). They constitute a distortion of the covenantal love that should exist in sexual and marital relationships.

8. A problem is raised by verse 18, in that a man having sexual intercourse with a menstruating woman results in both the man and the woman being "cut off from their people" (see above on p. 268), whereas the consequence for this violation in 15:24 is simply that the man will be unclean for seven days. It would seem that the difference between these two instances is intentionality. In 15:24 the problem is that during intercourse the woman's monthly flow "happens to come upon him" (my somewhat more literal translation). It is entirely possible that the man was unaware that the woman was menstruating or that the flow from the menstruation actually began during the intercourse. But in 18:19 and 20:18, the language suggests that the couple engaged in intercourse fully aware that the woman was menstruating. The intentionality warrants the severe penalty.
9. As noted earlier, perhaps the most prominent feature of this chapter is that penalties are now specified for the prohibited Molek worship and illegitimate sexual relationships such as had been listed in chapter 18; that penalty is death. In nine of the ten verses in this present chapter in which the NIV has "put to death," perhaps a better translation of the grammatical construction would be "shall surely" or "must be put to death" (vv. 2, 9, 10, 11, 12, 13, 15, 16, 27 [NIV does have "must" in v. 27]; the other occurrence, in v. 4, is a simpler construction). The assigning of the death penalty to these sexual violations indicates the seriousness with which the Lord looked on them. As a number of scholars note, the fact that these violations were considered to be capital crimes provides a contrast with other ancient Near Eastern law codes in which crimes involving economic loss were treated more harshly than religious and sexual violations and deviations from legitimate marital relationships.
10. Finally, and on a more positive note than the prior observations, in verse 8 we have the first of seven occurrences in the book of Leviticus of the clause, "I am the Lord, who makes you holy." The other occurrences, with slight variations, are found in 21:8, 15, 23; 22:9, 16, 32. The

people are to sanctify themselves. The people are to be holy by keeping the LORD's commands and avoiding uncleanness. The people are to be holy by keeping themselves from defilement. The people are to be holy through various ritual procedures. But, all importantly, the people will be holy because, ultimately, the LORD himself is the one who sanctifies them. The importance of this observation will be further explored in the next section.

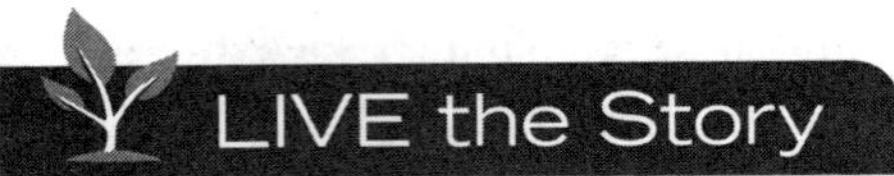

The Christian and Capital Punishment

Recently, an influential Christian theologian, in a critique of a book defending capital punishment, stated, "I am firmly convinced that no Christian who truly understands his or her faith can possibly defend the practice of capital punishment." The author then goes on to disparage any possibility that a Christian could possibly defend capital punishment, regarding such attempts as "crude" and completely lacking in any "biblical and theological sophistication." He states that "Christ repeatedly and explicitly forbids the application of such punishment." And, relevant to our chapter in particular, this theologian goes on to refer to "Leviticus 20, with its list of incredibly trivial capital crimes."[11]

Of course, the problem with this theologian's comments is that all of them founder on the actual evidence that is available to us from the biblical text. For example, we have these words of Jesus recorded for us in the Gospel of Matthew, in which he calls the Pharisees and teachers of the law to account for their hypocrisy:

> And why do you break the command of God for the sake of your tradition? For God said, "Honor your father and mother" and "Anyone who curses their father or mother is to be put to death." But you say that if anyone declares that what might have been used to help their father or mother is "devoted to God," they are not to "honor their father or mother" with it. Thus you nullify the word of God for the sake of your tradition. (Matt 15:3–6)

Rather than Jesus regarding the crime described in Leviticus 20:9 as trivial, he castigates the Pharisees for trivializing the law that God himself gave.

---

11. David Bentley Hart, "Christians and the Death Penalty," *Commonweal*, 16 November 2017, https://www.commonwealmagazine.org/christians-death-penalty.

He does not explicitly forbid the application of this capital punishment; rather, if anything, he seems to support it. Apparently, Jesus did not "truly understand his faith!"[12] Beyond this, there are many places in the Gospels, in Jesus's teachings, parables, and warnings of coming judgment, that demonstrate he regarded the penalty of death to be appropriate for a number of offenses that would have been regarded as capital crimes in the Old Testament.

In the rest of the New Testament, there is no hint whatsoever that capital punishment is in conflict with the character of God or his expectations of civil authorities. After listing a number of offenses, among them sins of a sexual nature, Paul refers to "God's righteous decree that those who do such things deserve death" (Rom 1:32). Paul also acknowledges that civil authorities, who implement justice with the sword, are in fact "God's servants, agents of wrath to bring punishment on the wrongdoer" (Rom 13:4). And, when it came to Paul's own personal experience with the Roman authorities, he acknowledged that if he was indeed guilty of the crimes with which he had been charged, execution would be the appropriate penalty (Acts 25:11). Additionally, there are at least three places in the New Testament in which God himself administers capital punishments for various offenses (Acts 5:1–11; 12:20–24; 1 Cor 11:29–30).

In terms of the current debate over the death penalty, there are, of course, a number of contextual considerations that must be taken into account in the contemporary discussion: corruption within the political and penal systems; the possibility of wrongful convictions; racial, ethnic, and class prejudice; and so on. We must also remember that the New Testament church is not the same as the Old Testament theocratic state. All of these factors, rightly, should be taken into account and could be used to form valid arguments against capital punishments. However, as far as the biblical data itself is concerned, there are no solid arguments whatsoever to be mustered against capital punishment per se.

The church, unlike the theocratic people of Israel in the Old Testament, is not a political entity but rather the pilgrim, wandering people of God. The church, rightly, does not carry out capital punishment, but neither should the church, on supposed biblical grounds, denigrate the right of the state to do so.

God, Holiness, and Sex

Leviticus 18 gives the prohibitions against certain sexual relationships, and Leviticus 20 delineates the penalties. As we noted above, perhaps the reason why these chapters are separated by chapter 19, is so that, by this sandwich

12. That Jesus would have been supportive of the death penalty for those who curse their parents is supported by the Jewish literature of the time period; see Watts, "Mark," 169.

structure, the command of Leviticus 19:2, "Be holy because I, the Lord your God, am holy," would be accentuated. If Leviticus 17–26 is to be considered as a Holiness Code, then it is in 19:2 that this formulation occurs for the first time there. Chapter 20, then, picks that up and employs a similar formulation in verses 7 and 26. If holiness, in the first sixteen chapters, was understood as being ceremonially and ritually related, the emphasis in chapters 17–26 takes on a marked ethical and moral character, yet in such a way that the ritual and ethical/moral are never divorced. The same is true in the New Testament. Regarding this connection, Kleinig notes that, for Christians in the New Testament, "Their lifestyle reflects their ritual status."[13] He goes on to explain:

> Like the book of Leviticus, the NT does not inculcate a system of natural ethics based on universal human values that promote harmony within the order of creation. Instead, the NT proclaims a system of liturgical ethics—the ethics of holiness—a heavenly lifestyle for God's people on earth. The NT presupposes that all Christians are involved in the Divine Service that is enacted by the church together with Christ in the heavenly sanctuary. They are all priests who serve together with Christ their High Priest (1 Pet 2:5; Rev 1:6; 5:10). They are also God's earthly sanctuary, the temple of the living God (1 Cor 3:16–17; 2 Cor 6:16).[14]

Since this is the case, it is no wonder then that the New Testament, just like Leviticus 18 and 20, places such importance on the connection between holiness and sexual morality. Among the most explicit passages in the New Testament in this regard are 1 Corinthians 5–6; Ephesians 5:3; 1 Thessalonians 4:3–8; 1 Timothy 1:8–11; Hebrews 12:14–17; 13:4 (less explicitly, but almost certainly having sexual morality in mind, are passages like 2 Pet 1:14–15). Not only do these passages make explicit the relationship between holiness and sexual morality, but several of them, apparently taking their cue from Leviticus 20, make explicit the punishment that God will bring to bear on the sexually immoral. Representative in this regard would be 1 Thessalonians 4:3–8 (I have highlighted especially pertinent words):

> It is God's will that you should be *sanctified*: that you should avoid *sexual immorality*; that each of you should learn to control your own body in a way that is *holy* and honorable, not in passionate lust like the pagans,

13. Kleinig, *Leviticus*, 440.
14. Ibid.

> who do not know God; and that in this matter no one should wrong or take advantage of a brother or sister. The Lord will *punish* all those who commit such sins, as we told you and warned you before. For God did not call us to be impure, but to live a *holy* life. Therefore, anyone who rejects this instruction does not reject a human being but God, the very God who gives you his *Holy* Spirit.

It is also important to note that God is by no means against sex; indeed, as Allender and Longman have exclaimed in the title of one of their books, *God Loves Sex* (!).[15] But as the subtitle goes on to note, sexual desire must be played out in the context of holiness. God loves sex, but he hates sexual immorality, which is contrary to holiness.

One last thing to note in this regard is that, in large part, the exhortations in these New Testament passages to sexual holiness are directed toward gentiles who, in their former way of life (ironically referred to as being "dead" in "transgressions and sins"; Eph 2:1–2), were caught up in the sexual immorality which the New Testament in several places associates with gentiles and pagans. But now, by God's great mercy, they have been joined to the holy people of God and are expected to live the same holy lives. The startling nature of this development is captured articulately by Jeffery Weima in commenting on 1 Thessalonians 4:1–12:

> What is surprising, however, even astonishing, is that Paul applies this standard of holiness to predominantly Gentile believers in Jesus at Thessalonica. The holiness that previously has been the exclusive privilege and calling of Israel has now also become God's purpose for Gentiles at Thessalonica who have "turned to God from idols to serve the living and true God." (1:9). The holiness that previously had been the characteristic that distinguished Israel from the Gentile nations has now become the boundary marker that separates Thessalonian Gentile believers from "the Gentiles who do not know God" (4:5), those who are "outside" God's holy people (4:12).[16]

Even as God's Old Testament holy people were promised an inheritance, the land of promise, now the largely gentile holy people of God in the New are also promised an inheritance "among all those who are sanctified"

15. Dan B. Allender and Tremper Longman III, *God Loves Sex: An Honest Conversation about Sexual Desire and Holiness* (Grand Rapids: Baker Books, 2014).

16. Jeffrey A. D. Weima, "1–2 Thessalonians," in *Commentary on the New Testament Use of the Old Testament*, ed. G. K. Beale and D. A. Carson (Grand Rapids: Baker Academic, 2007), 877.

(Acts 20:32), the right to "share in the inheritance of his holy people in the kingdom of light" (Col 1:12).

Jesus the Sanctifier

As mentioned above, Leviticus 20:8 is the first of seven occurrences in the book (variously worded) of the phrase "I am the LORD, who makes you holy." Though the Israelites are commanded to do those things that promote their holiness, the verse suggests that, ultimately, Yahweh himself is the one who makes the people holy.

Interestingly, in the New Testament Jesus takes on this role of bringing those who believe in him to a position of holiness. In Acts 26:18 Paul quotes Jesus as referring to gentiles who will have a place among those who are "sanctified by faith in me." It is significant here that Jesus says that the gentiles will be sanctified by faith in him. Both Moses and the priests could be said to sanctify, make holy, or consecrate persons in the Old Testament. But those persons were never sanctified because they put their faith in either Moses, Aaron, or another one of the priests. Here in Acts 26, however, Paul relates that the gentiles will be sanctified by faith in Christ. In John 17:19, Jesus says that he will sanctify himself, so that his apostles may be "truly sanctified." In 1 Corinthians 1:2 believers are sanctified "in Christ Jesus." In 1 Corinthians 1:30 Jesus himself becomes the sanctification for those who believe in him. In 1 Corinthians 6:11 believers are sanctified "in the name of the Lord Jesus Christ." In Philippians 1:1 the believers are holy "in Christ Jesus." In Hebrews 2:11 Jesus is the one who "makes people holy." In Hebrews 10:29 it is the blood of Jesus himself that sanctifies those who come to him. In Hebrews 13:12 Jesus suffered "to make the people holy through his own blood." If Yahweh is the one who sanctifies the people in the Old Testament, and Jesus is the one who sanctifies the people in the New Testament, then we have here an identification being made between Yahweh and Jesus, which constitutes one more important testimony to the belief of the New Testament authors in the deity of Christ. Jesus, as the Second Person of the Trinity, is the one who sanctifies those who put their faith in him.

CHAPTER 19

Leviticus 21:1–24

LISTEN to the Story

21:1The LORD said to Moses, "Speak to the priests, the sons of Aaron, and say to them: 'A priest must not make himself ceremonially unclean for any of his people who die, 2except for a close relative, such as his mother or father, his son or daughter, his brother, 3or an unmarried sister who is dependent on him since she has no husband—for her he may make himself unclean. 4He must not make himself unclean for people related to him by marriage, and so defile himself.

5"'Priests must not shave their heads or shave off the edges of their beards or cut their bodies. 6They must be holy to their God and must not profane the name of their God. Because they present the food offerings to the LORD, the food of their God, they are to be holy.

7"'They must not marry women defiled by prostitution or divorced from their husbands, because priests are holy to their God. 8Regard them as holy, because they offer up the food of your God. Consider them holy, because I the LORD am holy—I who make you holy.

9"'If a priest's daughter defiles herself by becoming a prostitute, she disgraces her father; she must be burned in the fire.

10"'The high priest, the one among his brothers who has had the anointing oil poured on his head and who has been ordained to wear the priestly garments, must not let his hair become unkempt or tear his clothes. 11He must not enter a place where there is a dead body. He must not make himself unclean, even for his father or mother, 12nor leave the sanctuary of his God or desecrate it, because he has been dedicated by the anointing oil of his God. I am the LORD.

13"'The woman he marries must be a virgin. 14He must not marry a widow, a divorced woman, or a woman defiled by prostitution, but only a virgin from his own people, 15so that he will not defile his offspring among his people. I am the LORD, who makes him holy.'"

[16]The LORD said to Moses, [17]"Say to Aaron: 'For the generations to come none of your descendants who has a defect may come near to offer the food of his God. [18]No man who has any defect may come near: no man who is blind or lame, disfigured or deformed; [19]no man with a crippled foot or hand, [20]or who is a hunchback or a dwarf, or who has any eye defect, or who has festering or running sores or damaged testicles. [21]No descendant of Aaron the priest who has any defect is to come near to present the food offerings to the LORD. He has a defect; he must not come near to offer the food of his God. [22]He may eat the most holy food of his God, as well as the holy food; [23]yet because of his defect, he must not go near the curtain or approach the altar, and so desecrate my sanctuary. I am the LORD, who makes them holy.'"

[24]So Moses told this to Aaron and his sons and to all the Israelites.

Listening to the Text in the Story: Biblical Texts: Leviticus 10; Ancient Near Eastern Texts: Nergal and Ereshgikal; The Great Hymn to Osiris; Enmeduranki and the Diviners

George Knight labels this chapter "The Odour of Death."[1] Aside from a few verses, this characterizes the chapter pretty well. Already, in Leviticus 10 when the priest-sons of Aaron, Nadab and Abihu, were put to death by fire from the LORD, their brothers who were priests, Eleazar and Ithamar, had been forbidden to engage in customary mourning rites. Additionally, they were forbidden to defile themselves by touching the corpses. For Israel, death and holiness were contrary categories. Of course, in Leviticus 10 the particular sin of Nadab and Abihu was a complicating factor. Nevertheless, the idea that holiness and death were diametrically opposed categories was certainly understood.

While there are a few Mesopotamian texts that also seem to oppose holiness and death, this does not seem to have been as much a concern as it was in Israel. In the Babylonian document Nergal and Ereshkigal, concerns are expressed over possible contact with the underworld: "If a man is chosen for death, and a ghost has seized him, you must purify everything," the concern being that death is defiling.[2] Additionally, the queen of the underworld, Ereshkigal, cannot ascend to the holy gods, and the gods cannot descend to

1. Knight, *Leviticus*, 131.
2. "Nergal and Ereshkigal," trans. Stephanie Dalley (*COS* 1.109:384).

the underworld, because that would bring life into defiling contact with death. However, such concerns are not often expressed in Mesopotamian texts.

Almost the opposite was the case in ancient Egypt, where the dead were venerated as gods and contact with death was actually contact with the holy. In The Great Hymn to Osiris, this deity who was variously and simultaneously regarded as the god of the afterlife, the underworld, and the dead, and who dwells in the "graveyard," was praised as "Lord of eternity," "Holy in White-wall," "Sanctified in the northern sky." Of his son Horus it was said, "Holy and splendid is his name."[3] Thus, unlike as was the case in Israel, in Egypt "because death was holy, tombs were temples where priests officiated."[4]

When it comes to the other major and overlapping focus of the chapter, physical defects barring men from the priesthood, this was much more prevalent in the ancient Near East. One representative text is Enmeduranki and the Diviners, in which a priest or diviner is barred from serving in this capacity if he is

> of impure descent, not without defect in body and limbs, with squinting eyes, chipped teeth, a cut-off finger, a ruptured testicle, suffering from leprosy, a eunuch.[5]

Whatever the reasons were in the larger ancient Near East, for Leviticus and Israel, these defects had the "odour of death" attached to them.

EXPLAIN the Story

The chapter deals with various things that would disqualify a priest, either permanently or temporarily, for service in the tabernacle. Verses 1–6 deal with corpse-contact defilements and various prohibited mourning practices. Verses 7–9 deal with two instances involving prostitution. Verses 10–12 return to the topic of corpse contamination with regard to the high priest. Verses 13–15 return somewhat to the topic raised in verses 7–9, with regard to whom a priest may marry. In verses 16–23 physical defects that would bar a priest from service are dealt with. Then, verse 24 states that Moses related these

3. "The Great Hymn to Osiris," trans. Miriam Lichtheim (*COS* 1.26:41–43).

4. Gane, "Leviticus," 1:318.

5. W. G. Lambert, "The Qualification of Babylon Diviners," in *Festschrift Für Rykle Borger Zu Seinem 65. Geburtstag Am 24. Mai 1994.*, ed. S. M. Maul (Groningen: Styx, 1998), 152.

instructions to Aaron and the entire community. Several observations and perspectives are important for understanding this chapter:

1. At this point in the larger narrative, the Israelites had been rescued from their bondage in Egypt only a little more than a year earlier. Their memory of the "gods of Egypt" was still fresh in their minds. We learn from Joshua 24:14 and Ezekiel 20:7–8 that the Israelites, just recently redeemed from Egypt, were still prone to worship the Egyptian deities. As we saw in the last section (p. 277), Egyptian worship was done in a context in which death and holiness were connected. While the dead were to be honored in Israel, they were not to be worshiped. So, for the priests in particular, strict rules were put in place to avoid even the barest hint that the worship of the tabernacle had any connection with a cult of the dead or with ancestor worship.
2. The restrictions against contact with a corpse and engaging in particular mourning rites are general and therefore not directly connected with the narrative in Leviticus 10, where Aaron and his remaining priest-sons were not allowed to come into contact with the corpses of Nadab and Abihu nor engage in the customary mourning rites for them on account of the manner in which they died. In the more general rules of the present passage, priests could temporarily come into contact with the corpses of their close relatives, as well as engage in limited mourning rites—but not the ones mentioned in verses 5–6. This temporary defilement could then be dealt with by a mandatory one-week waiting period (Num 19:11; Ezek 44:25–27) followed by purification rites.
3. Interestingly, both in this passage as well as in Ezekiel 44:25–27, the priest's wife is not listed as one of the relatives for whom a priest could allow himself to become ceremonially unclean. That both lists omit the priest's wife could indicate that the priest could not defile himself for her, perhaps because she is not a blood relative. However, two things seem to me to indicate that this is not an omission but rather a case in which it was simply taken for granted that a priest would make himself ceremonially unclean. First, though the priest's wife was not a blood relative, nevertheless a man and his wife were regarded as being one flesh (Gen 2:24). Second, in Ezekiel 24:15–27 there is the account in which Ezekiel is forbidden to carry out the customary mourning rites for his wife. This was to be symbolic of how, when the exiles in Babylon hear the news that back in Jerusalem the temple has been destroyed and many of their sons and daughters have been slain, they would not

be allowed to mourn. But, initially, when the people see Ezekiel not carrying out the customary mourning rites for his dead wife, they are puzzled that he is not doing so. If these rites had not been expected, the people would not have been confused. It seems more likely that in the present passage the priest becoming temporarily ceremonially unclean for his dead wife would have been taken for granted. The list then indicates for which actual blood relatives the priest could defile himself.

4. The reason for these rules about ceremonial defilement, as well as the rules regarding physical defects barring individuals from becoming priests, is that priests were responsible for handling the food offerings of the Lord. Sklar articulates this nicely:

> The Lord calls the priests to a special role as those who serve constantly in the courts of his palace. And since the Lord is a holy King, it is especially important that his palace servants maintain their holy status, not only so they can come near him, but also to communicate to his people how much he values holiness. If the palace servants desecrate their holy status, it would show that they thought little of their privileged position, and could suggest to others that the King cared little about holiness.[6]
>
> The reason is clear: like royal servants presenting food to a king, the priests *presented* the Israelites' *food offerings to the* Lord.[7]

God was the owner of the tabernacle.[8] As the owner and, of course, its greatly honored royal resident, it was his right to determine who had the right to be a member of his servant staff.

5. Priests were only allowed to marry virgins, and it was specifically noted that they could not marry widows, divorced women, or prostitutes. In particular, for prostitutes, there were probably at least two reasons for this prohibition. First, along with the requirement for marriage to a virgin and not to a widow or divorced woman, there would have been concern for the purity of the priestly line. Unlike the custom of Israel's neighbors, the priesthood in Israel was hereditary, open only to descendants of the line of Aaron. It was imperative then that the purity of the priestly lineage be preserved and the Aaronic descent be demonstrable.

---

6. Sklar, *Leviticus*, 263.
7. Ibid., 264.
8. Kleinig, *Leviticus*, 460.

Second, because of the associations in the ancient Near East between prostitution and the temple, associations which were detestable for Yahweh, there was the concern that the worship of Yahweh must not even have the hint of any connection with prostitution. For a considerable time in Old Testament scholarship, it was taken for granted that prostitution and other sexual acts played a role in the fertility cult of ancient Near Eastern religions, and these sexual acts were for the purpose of inducing the gods to engage in sexual activity, resulting in the fertility of families and crops. The evidence for this, however, is lacking. What does seem to be the case, at the very least, is that women could pay monetary vows they had made by providing sexual services in the vicinity of a temple, tabernacle, or shrine, thus contributing to the temple treasury. Additionally, sexual acts, some of which may have involved prostitution, as well as sexual orgies, do seem to have been connected with certain rituals and/or religious festivals.[9] It was appropriate, therefore, to proscribe marriage to a prostitute, especially since the priests' tents may have been in close proximity to the tabernacle/temple.

6. There are twelve physical defects that bar a man of Aaronic descent from being a priest. The number twelve probably indicates that the listed defects are not to be taken as either complete or exhaustive but representative. Additionally, the twelve are external, visible, surface defects. This indicates that the concern here is one of appearance. The servant staff of the king must appear to be sound in body.
7. It is usually noted by commentators that the twelve defects are parallel to the list in the next chapter of twelve physical defects that bar animals from being offered as sacrifices (22:17–25). The two lists of defects are not identical, though they do overlap. What ties these two lists together is the idea of food offerings. Animals that are to be given to the Lord as food offerings must be without blemish or defect. Likewise, those who handle and present these food offerings to the Lord must also be without defect.
8. As noted earlier, this chapter has the odor of death about it. While this is particularly true for the first part of the chapter and the fact that a priest must not defile himself by contact with corpses, so the latter part of this chapter partakes of the same odor. The physical defects are reminders of death. Among ancient peoples, these defects would have been taken

9. For a valuable discussion of this topic, see Karel van der Toorn, "Cultic Prostitution," *ABD* 5:510–13.

as evidence that death personified had, as it were, reached from Sheol back into the land of the living to strike people with various afflictions. So, to a large extent, the motivation for barring Aaronic descendants with physical defects from serving in the tabernacle was the same as to why priests were barred from having contact with the dead. Holiness and death are opposing categories.

9. However, as a descendant of Aaron, the person who had one or more of these afflictions was still allowed to eat from the holy food offerings. They could not, as it were, be members of the King's servant staff, but they could, by Yahweh's gracious provision, still be provided for by being allowed to eat of those very same offerings. This can be seen as a benevolence project put into place by the King who resides in the tabernacle.
10. Finally, in verse 24 these instructions were given to Aaron and his sons and to "all the Israelites." As we have noted elsewhere, the priestly service was not a mysterious, hidden service. The rules were made public so that the entire community would learn what the Lord's holy requirements were and could serve the important function of encouraging the priests—even holding them accountable for seeing that things were done in accordance with the Lord's holy statutes.

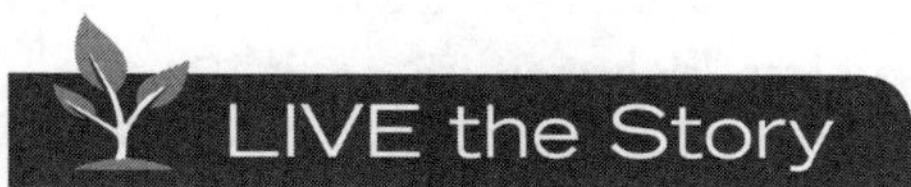

It is a common move among commentators to shift from the very material and physical subject matter of this chapter and move toward spiritual realities for application. We will do this as well. Indeed, not only the New Testament, but even the Old Testament make similar hermeneutical moves. However, we must not discount the material, physical, "bodiliness" of this chapter as we seek to understand the relevance of this text and to live our lives within God's story. So both the material and the spiritual will be emphasized in the points below.

Christ as Unblemished Priest

It is interesting that, even though Christ was not from the tribe of Levi, the first narrated revelation of the Christ in the New Testament was to a Levitical priest, Zechariah (Luke 1:5–22), even as he was carrying out his priestly duties. Zechariah's future son is referred to as the one who "will go on before the Lord" (1:17), the latter designation almost certainly referring to the Messiah. Interestingly, later in the chapter, when Mary and Zechariah sing their inspired prophetic songs, it is in Zechariah's song (Luke 1:67–79), rather than Mary's, that this "Lord" figure (1:76) is referred to as one who will provide "forgiveness of sins" (1:77), a particularly priestly concern. So, interestingly, even before he is born, a priest refers to Christ as the one who will provide his people with the forgiveness of their sins. A priest from the tribe of Levi, Zechariah prophetically pronounces that it will be the one for whom his son will prepare the way, one who will be from the tribe of Judah (1:69), who will provide the ritual forgiveness for his people, and who will have the requisite "holiness" (1:75) to do so. In a sense, we could say that the priestly mantle is being passed from the tribe of Levi to the Messiah from the tribe of Judah.

It is also interesting that the service Zechariah was performing in the temple was likely his last priestly service for a number of months, because once he became mute, he was now a priest with a defect and no longer allowed to perform priestly duties. His muteness is finally removed, but his first recorded action once this is done is to speak prophetically of the transference of the priesthood to the tribe of Judah and to David's Son, the priest without defect or blemish.

It is also important to note that there is a correspondence between the Nadab and Abihu incident in Leviticus 10 and Zechariah's lapse and lack of faith in Luke 1. Even as Nadab and Abihu, during their ordination to the priesthood, had done "everything the LORD commanded through Moses" (Lev 8:36), so Zechariah was one who was "righteous in the sight of God, observing all the Lord's commands and decrees blamelessly" (Luke 1:6). Yet, even as Nadab and Abihu "snatched defeat out of the jaws of victory" as they offered incense in the tabernacle with "unauthorized fire" (Lev 10:1), so Zechariah was in the act of offering incense when the angel Gabriel appeared to him, and, like Nadab and Abihu, he suffers a setback when he fails to believe the angel's words (Luke 1:8–22). Even the faithful priest Zechariah at one point proves faithless. The blemished Levitical priesthood is coming to an end. The unblemished priesthood of Jesus will soon take its place.

It is common, especially among more popularly oriented commentaries, to note that Christ lived his life in front of the priests (primarily Sadducees), whose responsibility it was to examine the sacrificial offerings to make sure they had no blemishes, and that, in essence, they "found no fault in him." Pilate's statements in Luke 23:4, 14, that he found no basis for a charge against Jesus, in at least some respect, echo the earlier narrative of Jesus's trial before the Sanhedrin in Matthew 26:59–60 and Mark 14:55–59; see also John 8:46). What should also be recognized, however, is that this declaration applies to Jesus not only as sacrifice without blemish but also as priest without blemish.

That Jesus is the unblemished, sinless priest is echoed also in the book of Hebrews (4:14–15; 7:23–28). Also, Hebrews 7:23–28 is especially important in light of the concerns with death in Leviticus 21. Jesus is the priest who has conquered death (see also Heb 7:16). Jesus is the unblemished, sinless priest who has not been corrupted by death (see Acts 2:31), and he therefore ever lives to perform his intercessory work for us.

Christ as Disfigured Priest

In order to carry out his work of redemption, atonement, and forgiveness as the unblemished, sinless priest, Christ also, ironically, becomes the priest who is disfigured. There are at least two passages, one in each Testament, where I believe this disfigurement comes into play with Christ's priestly work.

First, in the fourth Servant Song in Isaiah 52:13–53:12, the disfigurement of the Servant of the Lord is especially highlighted. It is said of the Servant that "his appearance was so disfigured beyond that of any human being and his form marred beyond human likeness" (52:14). His form was so appalling that as "one from whom people hide their faces he was despised" (53:3). The servant was "pierced" and "crush[ed]" (53:5, 10). Of course, what those who at first despised him come to find out is that it is this very disfigurement that will turn out for their redemption and salvation. The Servant's life given over to death will serve as salvation for them (53:5–6, 10–12). The Servant's poured out life will be reckoned as a guilt offering (*'asham*) for their sins (53:10). But the Servant is not only the sacrificed offering; he is also the sacrificing priest. He was active in his own sacrifice: "he poured out his life unto death"; "he bore the sin of many"; "he made intercession for the transgressors" (53:12). There is an exegetical question as to who the subject is for the verb "make" in 53:10. Is it Yahweh ("the Lord makes his life an offering for sin")? Is it the Servant's soul ("when his soul makes . . .")? Or is it the Servant himself ("when he makes himself . . .")? If it is this last one, then the Servant's active role in his own suffering is highlighted: he offers himself as a guilt offering. He fulfills the mission that has been given to him (Isa 42:1–7; 49:1–9) by offering himself as sacrifice for sin.

Further, there is the issue in 52:15 of whether the verb in the first sentence should be translated as "sprinkle" or "startle." Though the majority position today is that "startle" makes more sense in context, the traditional "sprinkle" translation still has considerable support.[10] If correct, this translation argues

10. For example, John Goldingay, *The Message of Isaiah 40–55: A Literary-Theological Commentary* (London: T&T Clark, 2005), 492–93, idem, *A Critical and Exegetical Commentary on Isaiah 40–55*, vol. 1, ICC (T&T Clark, 2006), 294–95.

for the Servant in Isaiah to be seen as a priestly figure who, in a bold figure of speech, sprinkles the nations (with water? with his own blood?) as a propitiation for their sins and as a priestly act of purification and sanctification.

The second passage is in Luke 23:34, when Christ cries from the cross, "Father, forgive them, for they do now know what they are doing." The previous night, at the institution of the Lord's Supper, Christ, when he distributed the cup, said to his apostles, "This cup is the new covenant in my blood, which is poured out for you" (Luke 22:20). Matthew adds the phrase, "for the forgiveness of sins" (Matt 26:28). So the night before he is crucified, Jesus tells his apostles that his blood will be shed for the forgiveness of sins. And then, his first words from the cross—after he has been beaten, scourged, and nailed to the cross (i.e., "disfigured")—are a prayer to his Father that he would forgive those who had done these things to him. Additionally, Christ, in effect, pronounces a word of forgiveness to the sin-confessing, repentant thief crucified beside him (Luke 23:43).

In conjunction with what we saw in the first point in this section (p. 282), the pronouncements of Zechariah and Jesus serve as bookends for the gospel of Luke. In Luke 1 a once-mute and therefore blemished priest in a prophetic song declares that the Messiah will provide salvation, redemption, and forgiveness of sins as an act of remembrance of the "holy covenant." Now, near the end of Luke's Gospel, Jesus, marred in form and disfigured in appearance as he is crucified, performs the priestly work of interceding for his crucifiers and even pronounces absolution to a repentant sinner, as the new covenant is established in his blood. Jesus, the disfigured priest, provides salvation and forgiveness for the sins of the world.

Christ as the Priest Who Heals All Blemishes

As mentioned before, while it is not wrong to transmute Old Testament references to physical defects to the realm of the ethical and the so-called spiritual, we must not discount the New Testament emphasis on redemption as having very much to do with the physical. Jesus came to heal not just soul and spirit but also the body. He heals the blind, the lame, the deaf, and the twisted and disfigured, and he also invites them to eat at his table (Luke 14:21).[11] Not only does he heal the living who are afflicted with bodily impairments, he even brings the dead back to life, and, of course, he comes into contact with

11. For the possibility that the list of defects in Luke 14:21 is linked to Lev 21, see David W. Pao and Edward J. Schnabel, "Luke," in *Commentary on the New Testament Use of the Old Testament*, ed. G. K. Beale and D. A. Carson (Grand Rapids: Baker Academic, 2007), 340.

the corpse to do so.[12] Elliott relates how the church father, Procopius of Gaza, regards Jesus, in John 11:35, as a "priest lamenting the corruption which underlay death."[13] So, again, Christ deals with both the concerns mentioned in this chapter: he heals disfigurements, and he conquers the realm of death. These miracles Jesus performed were all anticipatory signs of the final resurrection and the complete establishment of the kingdom, in which there will be no more death, no more disfigurement, no more pain (Rev 21:4).

Christ Is the Priest Who Sanctifies His Priestly Followers, Who Also Sanctify Themselves

Nevertheless, it is also true that Christ purifies and sanctifies in the realm of ethics and the spiritual. His followers constitute a "holy" and "royal" priesthood" (1 Pet 2:4–10), and Christ, the great high priest, sanctifies his "underpriests." Indeed, all of Christ's sanctification and purification of those who are in solidarity with him should be seen under this rubric.

However, though Christ himself is the one who sanctifies us, the New Testament also encourages Christ's believer-priests to sanctify themselves and to strive to live lives of holiness and purity. This was true of the Old Testament saints, and it is still true of New Testament saints.

It is precisely because we have been made into a holy and royal priesthood (1 Pet 2:4–10; Rev 1:6; 5:10; 20:6) that we should seek to maintain that status, as we "abstain from sinful desires, which wage war against your soul" (1 Pet 2:11–12). We are to live holy lives before the pagans so that God's name will not be profaned but glorified. Hartley remarks, "The priests of the new covenant are not to be unduly preoccupied with affairs of this life, which have the kiss of death on them."[14] Boyce suggests that Jesus's command in Matthew 8:22 (Luke 9:60), "Follow me and let the dead bury their own dead," is related to the prohibitions in Leviticus 21, but that, now, for the sacrifices Jesus demands from his followers,

> the motivation for such prescriptions has shifted from questions of ritual cleanliness (at least the initial reason for the priests' staying away from funerals) to those of ultimate loyalty ("No one who puts a hand to the plow and looks back is fit for the kingdom of God"; Luke 9:62).[15]

12. Ibid., 325.
13. Elliott, *Engaging Leviticus*, 223.
14. Hartley, *Leviticus*, 351.
15. Boyce, *Leviticus and Numbers*, 82.

Kleinig also draws a connection between the concern in Leviticus 21, that only those who are holy should be allowed to offer food offerings to God and to eat of that holy food, to passages in the New Testament that also refer to the Lord's table:

> As members of God's heavenly priesthood, Christians receive the holy food that comes from their Lord's Table (1 Cor 10:16–22). They eat the bread of God that comes down from heaven, the life-giving flesh of Christ (Jn 6:33, 51). Since they serve the living God they must not once again become involved in "dead works," deeds that defile and deaden their conscience (Heb 9:14). They are therefore required to separate themselves from every defilement of body and spirit (2 Cor 7:1). They are to avoid spiritism and all forms of contact with unclean spirits (1 Cor 10:14–22).[16]

So we have a beautiful vision, one in which we have our part to play in bringing to fulfillment: those who were formerly unholy, sinful, separate from God, crippled, lame, blind (Luke 14:21), now made into a holy priesthood, offering and eating of the holy food of their God. This is truly an anticipation of Rev 19:7–9 and the wedding supper of the Lamb, when all the attendees to that wedding will be clothed in fine linen, symbolic of the fact that because of God's mercy, they are now the holy people of God. They are those who have maintained their status as God's holy people by their righteous actions ("Fine linen stands for the righteous acts of God's holy people"; Rev 19:8). It is this for which we strive.

---

16. Kleinig, *Leviticus*, 455.

CHAPTER 20

Leviticus 22:1–33

LISTEN to the Story

22:1The Lord said to Moses, 2"Tell Aaron and his sons to treat with
respect the sacred offerings the Israelites consecrate to me, so they will not
profane my holy name. I am the Lord.

3"Say to them: 'For the generations to come, if any of your descendants
is ceremonially unclean and yet comes near the sacred offerings that the
Israelites consecrate to the Lord, that person must be cut off from my
presence. I am the Lord.

4"'If a descendant of Aaron has a defiling skin disease or a bodily discharge,
he may not eat the sacred offerings until he is cleansed. He will also be unclean
if he touches something defiled by a corpse or by anyone who has an emission
of semen, 5or if he touches any crawling thing that makes him unclean, or
any person who makes him unclean, whatever the uncleanness may be.
6The one who touches any such thing will be unclean till evening. He must
not eat any of the sacred offerings unless he has bathed himself with water.
7When the sun goes down, he will be clean, and after that he may eat the
sacred offerings, for they are his food. 8He must not eat anything found dead
or torn by wild animals, and so become unclean through it. I am the Lord.

9"'The priests are to perform my service in such a way that they do
not become guilty and die for treating it with contempt. I am the Lord,
who makes them holy.

10"'No one outside a priest's family may eat the sacred offering, nor
may the guest of a priest or his hired worker eat it. 11But if a priest buys
a slave with money, or if slaves are born in his household, they may eat
his food. 12If a priest's daughter marries anyone other than a priest, she
may not eat any of the sacred contributions. 13But if a priest's daughter
becomes a widow or is divorced, yet has no children, and she returns to
live in her father's household as in her youth, she may eat her father's food.
No unauthorized person, however, may eat it.

14“‘Anyone who eats a sacred offering by mistake must make restitution to the priest for the offering and add a fifth of the value to it. 15The priests must not desecrate the sacred offerings the Israelites present to the Lord 16by allowing them to eat the sacred offerings and so bring upon them guilt requiring payment. I am the Lord, who makes them holy.’”

17The Lord said to Moses, 18“Speak to Aaron and his sons and to all the Israelites and say to them: ‘If any of you—whether an Israelite or a foreigner residing in Israel—presents a gift for a burnt offering to the Lord, either to fulfill a vow or as a freewill offering, 19you must present a male without defect from the cattle, sheep or goats in order that it may be accepted on your behalf. 20Do not bring anything with a defect, because it will not be accepted on your behalf. 21When anyone brings from the herd or flock a fellowship offering to the Lord to fulfill a special vow or as a freewill offering, it must be without defect or blemish to be acceptable. 22Do not offer to the Lord the blind, the injured or the maimed, or anything with warts or festering or running sores. Do not place any of these on the altar as a food offering presented to the Lord. 23You may, however, present as a freewill offering an ox or a sheep that is deformed or stunted, but it will not be accepted in fulfillment of a vow. 24You must not offer to the Lord an animal whose testicles are bruised, crushed, torn or cut. You must not do this in your own land, 25and you must not accept such animals from the hand of a foreigner and offer them as the food of your God. They will not be accepted on your behalf, because they are deformed and have defects.’”

26The Lord said to Moses, 27“When a calf, a lamb or a goat is born, it is to remain with its mother for seven days. From the eighth day on, it will be acceptable as a food offering presented to the Lord. 28Do not slaughter a cow or a sheep and its young on the same day.

29“When you sacrifice a thank offering to the Lord, sacrifice it in such a way that it will be accepted on your behalf. 30It must be eaten that same day; leave none of it till morning. I am the Lord.

31“Keep my commands and follow them. I am the Lord. 32Do not profane my holy name, for I must be acknowledged as holy by the Israelites. I am the Lord, who made you holy 33and who brought you out of Egypt to be your God. I am the Lord.”

Listening to the Text in the Story: Biblical Texts: Leviticus 21; Ancient Near Eastern Texts: Instructions to Priests and Temple Officials

This chapter is a continuation of the material in the preceding chapter in two specific areas, including (1) the purity qualifications that priestly personnel must meet in order to handle and eat of the food offerings; and (2) the need for the sacrificial animals to be unblemished, with a representative list of twelve blemishes corresponding to the representative list of twelve bodily blemishes that would disqualify the priests for service in the tabernacle.

Other ancient Near Eastern texts also exhibit concern that priests and temple personnel must meet both hygienic and ritual qualifications to handle the food offerings of their deities. For example, in the Hittite document Instructions to Priest and Temple Officials, the following reconstructed passage expresses this concern and gives an analogy to demonstrate why the concern is important:

> Let those who make the daily bread be clean. Let them be washed and trimmed. Let (their) hair (?) and finger[nails] be trimmed. Let them be clothed in clean garments. I[f] (they are) [not], let them not prepare (them). Let those who normally [propit]iate the spirit and body of the gods prepare them. The baker's house in which they bake them must be swept and sprinkled down. . . . (Are) the mind of man and god somehow different? No! In this which (is concerned)? No! The mind (is) one and the same. When the servant stands before his master, he (is) washed. He has clothed (himself) in clean (clothes). He gives him (his master) either to eat or to drink. Since the master eats and drinks, (in) his spirit he (is) relaxed. He is favorably inclined toward him (the servant). When he (is) solicitous (?), (his master) does not find fault (with him). Is the mind of the god somehow different? If the servant at some point angers his master, either they kill him, or they injure his nose, eyes, (and) ears. Or he (the master) [will sei]ze him, (and) his wife, his children, his brother, his sister, his in-laws, (and) his family, whether his (master's) male or female slave. They (may) only call (him) over. They (may) do nothing to him. If ever he dies, he does not die alone. His family (is) also included with him.[1]

Notice that the analogy in this text indicates that the servant who displeases his master may be seized and put to death, and his family along with him. Similarly, the priests in Leviticus 22:9 are subject to death for performing their service to the LORD in a contemptuous manner.

---

1. "Instructions to Priests and Temple Officials," *COS* 1.83:217–18).

EXPLAIN the Story

The chapter basically consists of two major sections, including (1) regulations about the ritual and ceremonial purity that priests must possess to be able to handle and consume the LORD's offerings (vv. 1–16); and (2) regulations concerning the cleanliness required of sacrificial offerings, as well as a representative list of the blemishes that disqualify animals being given as such offerings (vv. 17–25). The chapter concludes with additional regulations concerning acceptable offerings, along with motivational statements (vv. 26–31). There are a number of observations to make:

1. The first half of this chapter is addressed to "Aaron and his sons" (v. 2), while the last half is addressed to "Aaron and his sons and all the Israelites" (v. 18), which is appropriate considering the subject matter of the two halves. However, as noted before, even passages dealing primarily with priestly regulations and behavior were made known to the people as a whole. The community had a vested interest in how the priests handled the sacrifices and offerings which they brought to the tabernacle.
2. In verse 2, the verb *nazar*, which the NIV translates as "treat with respect," would be more literally translated as the ESV has it, "abstain from." This results in the hyperbolic declaration that the priests must abstain from handling and consuming the food offerings the Israelites bring to the tabernacle. The intended effect is that the priests should regard the default position with regard to these offerings to be "do not handle, do not eat." This is, of course, impossible, for handling these offerings and then consuming them was the very duty of the priest! But the declaration strikingly reminds the priests that they must not touch or eat of these offerings unless they are ceremonially clean. Indeed, for verse 3, Milgrom argues that the verb "approach" (*qarab*) would be more appropriately rendered, in this context, as "encroach."[2] If the priest approaches the sacred offerings in a ritually impure state, he is actually encroaching on what does not belong to him. The NJPS translation of verse 2, "be scrupulous about the sacred donations," correctly captures the force of the command.
3. If the hyperbolic statement in verse 2 was not clear enough, the declaration in verse 3 that the priest who "encroaches" on these offerings in a

2. Milgrom, *Leviticus 17–22*, 1850.

ceremonially unclean state would be "cut off" (i.e., put to death) makes the import crystal clear (see also v. 9). Gorman remarks, "It is dangerous to stand in the holy place!"[3] And Gerstenberger aptly observes that "The x-ray physician is far more at risk than is the patient."[4] The priests were held to a more severe accountability than the lay members of the community.

4. Verses 4–8 list some representative states of uncleanness that would prohibit the priest from partaking of the sacred food offerings. For the most part, these states are temporary, lasting no longer than a day, and the impurities are considered to be washed away by bathing. For skin diseases and bodily fluid emissions, the purification times could, of course, be longer.
5. Members of the priest's family also had the privilege of eating from these food offerings. As Kleinig memorably puts it, "The presence of the sacred food in the home of the priest therefore made its table an extension of the Lord's table. His house became a holy place."[5] However, the family members had to meet the ceremonial cleanness qualifications that the priest had to meet. So, picking up on Gorman's statement above, we can say that for those members of the priest's family who were allowed to eat the sacred food offerings, and who by extension lived in a holy house, they too were living in a dangerous place!
6. Milgrom notes that part of the concern in verses 15–16 was that priests might manipulate things in such a way that they unduly increase the size of their proceeds from the sacred offerings, defrauding both God and the offerers. He refers to Hosea 4:8, in which Yahweh rails against priests who "feed on the sins of my people and relish their wickedness." Perhaps behavior like that of Eli's sons in 1 Samuel 2:12–16 was also in view.
7. In the latter half of the chapter, the concern has to do with quality control with regard to the sacrificial animals and the kinds of blemishes that disqualified animals from being offered as sacrifices. However, the text says that for one particular fellowship offering, the freewill offering, animals with some measure of deformity could in fact be offered (v. 23). This concession, however, was not granted for any of the other fellowship offerings or for any of the other categories of offerings. Nevertheless, it is possible that the concession with regard to freewill offerings may have led to the priests and/or the people becoming lax

3. Gorman, *Divine Presence*, 124.
4. Gerstenberger, *Leviticus*, 306.
5. Kleinig, *Leviticus*, 467.

with regard to the quality of sacrificial animals for other offerings for which no such exceptions were allowed. So this section dealing with defects and blemishes was needed.[6] Additionally, Malachi 1:6–14 witnesses to how the people in that prophet's day were not carelessly or ignorantly but intentionally flouting the law and offering blind, lame, and diseased animals in contempt of the Lord's table.

8. The list of twelve defects that disqualify potential sacrificial animals corresponds in number to the twelve defects that disqualify priests from serving in the tabernacle. The two lists are not to be considered as exhaustive but rather representative of the various kinds of disqualifying defects. While the two lists correspond in number, other correspondences are less precise. Both lists begin and end with the same defects: blindness and damaged testicles. In addition to these, there are several other common defects, but there is no real symmetry between the two lists. While there has been some attempt to make the lists resemble each other, there has been no attempt to make the two lists precisely identical. It is best, therefore, to take the two lists as representative but not exhaustive.
9. The question must still be asked as to why there was any effort at all to make the two lists resemble each other. The answer is probably to be found in the use of the number twelve. Both the priests and the sacrificial animals were intended to represent the people of Israel in their identity as twelve tribes. We already know that the high priest, as he wore the breastpiece with twelve stones engraved with the names of the twelve Israelite tribes (Exod 28:17–21; 39:10–14), bore upon his heart the Israelites as he ministered before the Lord. In the present chapter, then, it is likely that both the priests and the sacrificial animals, in their twelvefold purity, represent the goal that God has set before the Israelites. While not explicitly reaching this same conclusion regarding these two twelve-item lists, Milgrom understands that Israel's compliance in this area "will hasten its progress toward the divine goal, the attainment of holiness."[7] These two twelve-item lists—priests and sacrificial animals, free from defect and blemishes, both clean and sacred (holy)—represent both the example that the Israelites are to emulate and the goal toward which they are to strive to attain, not only ritually and ceremonially but also morally and ethically. They are to be holy as the priests and sacrifices are holy—and as Yahweh is holy.

6. Hartley, *Leviticus*, 359–60.
7. Milgrom, *Leviticus 17–22*, 1889.

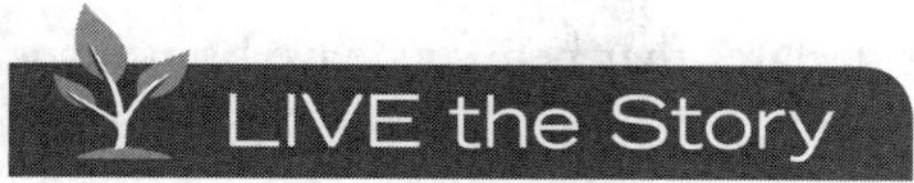

LIVE the Story

Wenham, commenting on chapters 21–22, notes that "There are indications within Lev. 21 that physical integrity was viewed as symbolic of moral integrity."[8] The importance of this observation is that already, within the book of Leviticus itself, there is a built-in slant toward a "spiritualizing" interpretation. When we draw lines from the ceremonial and ritual directives in the book toward a spiritual/moral/ethical application, we are continuing the trajectory begun by the book of Leviticus itself.

Purity and Holiness as the Goal for Christians and Leaders in the Church

That which began in the Old Testament, even in Leviticus itself, continues in the New Testament with regard to all Christians, especially Christian leaders. "There are echoes of these two chapters, therefore (though in a rather different tone), in the lists of qualifications for elders, overseers and deacons."[9] The language of purity, purification, sanctification, and holiness pervades New Testament statements regarding the kind of lives believers are to live. As mentioned elsewhere in this commentary, there are those who believe that the last eleven chapters of Leviticus constitute a Holiness Code that emphasizes (in a way that the first half of the book of Leviticus does not) that it is not only the priests but all the Israelites who, by their sacrifices, their rituals, and their obedience to God's commandments, can become holy. I am not convinced that the first half of Leviticus denies this possibility, but it does seem to be true that the second half of Leviticus emphasizes this in a way that the first half does not make explicit. Whether this is seen to be the goal of the entire book, or just of the putative Holiness Code, what is especially striking to note is that the New Testament regards the goal as having been accomplished. When Paul addresses his letters to those who are "saints" (e.g., Rom 1:7; 1 Cor 1:2; NIV uses the phrase "holy people" in these texts) and, in many other passages, refers to believers as saints (holy ones) and those who have been sanctified (made holy), he is declaring that the goal of the book of Leviticus has been met (though there is, of course, an "already but not yet" character to this sanctification).[10] If the goal of Leviticus is that the people might be

8. Wenham, *Leviticus*, 297.

9. Wright, "Leviticus," 151.

10. It must also be acknowledged that this is true of a limited number of places in the Old Testament as well (see, e.g., Pss 16:3; 34:9; Dan 7:18).

made holy, then the New Testament declares that believers have been made holy by the death of Christ, the one who has become to us our "holiness and redemption" (1 Cor 1:30).

Of course, because this is the "already" part of our sanctification, that means there is a "not yet" part, a progressive sanctification in which we engage now and that will one day come to its completion. So, even though we have been sanctified, we are also being sanctified, and we are working toward this goal (see Rom 6:19, 22; 2 Cor 7:1; 1 Thess 4:3; Heb 12:14; 1 Pet 1:15–16).

This striving for holiness must especially characterize those who are leaders in the church. Wright, as mentioned above, regards New Testament passages that describe the qualifications of leaders in the church to be echoing the emphases in Leviticus 21–22, especially such passages as 1 Timothy 3:1–13; Titus 1:5–9; and James 3:1.[11] One interesting connection here is that the emphasis in the 1 Timothy and Titus passages, that a leader must manage his own household well, echoes the requirements in Leviticus 21:7–9 and 22:10–13 regarding the ceremonial and ethical purity of the priest's household. This certainly highlights that leaders in the church are to be held to a higher standard. Interestingly, the exact opposite attitude sometimes characterizes church leaders: "It is one of the occupational hazards of the clergy to think that God's word applies to everyone else but them."[12]

John Calvin quaintly observes that "God is served amiss when He is served by halves, since He abominates a double heart."[13] God is best served with an undivided heart; how much more is this the case with those whom he has appointed leaders in his church.

Sacred Offerings—Spiritual Food

On the one hand, the subject matter of the first half of this chapter can be seen as spiritualized in the New Testament. First Corinthians 10:3–4 talks about spiritual food and drink. First Peter 2:2 speaks of "spiritual milk" by which we grow up in our salvation. Regarding this concept, Kleinig remarks:

> All Christians belong to the royal priesthood of God. As priests they receive the spiritual food and drink that the Lord provides for the sustenance of their faith. Many biblical passages speak of such food and drink in a spiritual sense or eschatologically (e.g., Mt 22:1–14; Lk 14:16–24). This spiritual food and drink are most holy things that they have from God.

11. Wright, "Leviticus," 151.
12. Tidball, *Message of Leviticus*, 266.
13. Calvin, *Last Four Books of Moses*, 2:378–79.

> Just as he sanctified the food for the Israelite priests and their families, so he consecrates this food and drink for those who are sanctified by his blood (Heb 10:29; 13:12).[14]

However, on more than just a spiritual or immaterial level, there is a material connection that can be drawn between the sacred food offerings spoken of in Leviticus 22 and the Christian's sacred meal, the Lord's Supper. In one respect the Lord's Supper, which commemorates Christ's sacrificial death that provides forgiveness of sins, can be seen as having a connection to the sin and guilt offerings. However, in this particular chapter the offerings under consideration are the fellowship offerings, the only offering from which the priest's family, and even the offerer of the sacrifice, could partake. They were truly "communion" offerings. Just as the priest had to take care that his family members were ceremonially clean when they ate of the offerings, so those who officiate the Lord's Supper must take care to "fence the table" by warning would-be participants of the solemnity of the meal, that taking of this meal unworthily is the same as drinking condemnation to oneself. Again, Kleinig aptly remarks, "The pastors who administer the Sacrament are to take care that they do not give what is holy to those who are unclean because they are unbaptized, impenitent, or heretics."[15]

Christ as Unblemished Sacrifice

In the Live the Story section for Leviticus 21 (pp. 281–83), we saw that Christ fulfills the type of the unblemished priest. But in fulfillment of this chapter's concern with the idea that the sacrificial animals should be without defect, we turn to what is perhaps the more familiar conceptualization of Christ as the unblemished sacrifice. Also, we saw in that same section that various figures (the Sanhedrin, Pilate, etc.) declared Christ, despite themselves, to be without fault, so here in this chapter it is important to recognize that the Gospels portray Christ as the Lamb of God, a lamb who survived the scrutiny of those figures and is to be seen as truly "a lamb without blemish or defect" (1 Pet 1:19).

Christ as Disfigured Sacrifice

This unblemished sacrifice, the spotless Lamb of God, is also the disfigured sacrifice, the one who took all our blemishes upon himself. He is the Lamb of God who took upon himself the blemishes and defects of those who confess:

---

14. Kleinig, *Leviticus*, 469.
15. Ibid., 470–71.

> We all, like sheep, have gone astray,
>   each of us has turned to our own way;
> and the LORD has laid on him
>   the iniquity of us all.
>
> He was oppressed and afflicted,
>   yet he did not open his mouth;
> he was led like a lamb to the slaughter. (Isa 53:6–7a)

As mentioned above, those who put their trust in Christ should strive to live lives of holiness in service to God. We also know that in this present life and in the midst of human frailty, we will fall short of that goal. Yet how wonderful it is to know that the Lamb in whom we have put our trust is also the one who has taken our blemishes and defects upon himself.

CHAPTER 21

Leviticus 23:1–44

LISTEN to the Story

23:1The LORD said to Moses, 2"Speak to the Israelites and say to them:
'These are my appointed festivals, the appointed festivals of the LORD,
which you are to proclaim as sacred assemblies.

3"'There are six days when you may work, but the seventh day is a
day of sabbath rest, a day of sacred assembly. You are not to do any work;
wherever you live, it is a sabbath to the LORD.

4"'These are the LORD's appointed festivals, the sacred assemblies you
are to proclaim at their appointed times: 5The LORD's Passover begins at
twilight on the fourteenth day of the first month. 6On the fifteenth day
of that month the LORD's Festival of Unleavened Bread begins; for seven
days you must eat bread made without yeast. 7On the first day hold a
sacred assembly and do no regular work. 8For seven days present a food
offering to the LORD. And on the seventh day hold a sacred assembly and
do no regular work.'"

9The LORD said to Moses, 10"Speak to the Israelites and say to them:
'When you enter the land I am going to give you and you reap its harvest,
bring to the priest a sheaf of the first grain you harvest. 11He is to wave the
sheaf before the LORD so it will be accepted on your behalf; the priest is to
wave it on the day after the Sabbath. 12On the day you wave the sheaf, you
must sacrifice as a burnt offering to the LORD a lamb a year old without
defect, 13together with its grain offering of two-tenths of an ephah of the
finest flour mixed with olive oil—a food offering presented to the LORD,
a pleasing aroma—and its drink offering of a quarter of a hin of wine.
14You must not eat any bread, or roasted or new grain, until the very day
you bring this offering to your God. This is to be a lasting ordinance for
the generations to come, wherever you live.

15"'From the day after the Sabbath, the day you brought the sheaf of
the wave offering, count off seven full weeks. 16Count off fifty days up to

the day after the seventh Sabbath, and then present an offering of new grain to the LORD. [17]From wherever you live, bring two loaves made of two-tenths of an ephah of the finest flour, baked with yeast, as a wave offering of firstfruits to the LORD. [18]Present with this bread seven male lambs, each a year old and without defect, one young bull and two rams. They will be a burnt offering to the LORD, together with their grain offerings and drink offerings—a food offering, an aroma pleasing to the LORD. [19]Then sacrifice one male goat for a sin offering and two lambs, each a year old, for a fellowship offering. [20]The priest is to wave the two lambs before the LORD as a wave offering, together with the bread of the firstfruits. They are a sacred offering to the LORD for the priest. [21]On that same day you are to proclaim a sacred assembly and do no regular work. This is to be a lasting ordinance for the generations to come, wherever you live.

[22]"'When you reap the harvest of your land, do not reap to the very edges of your field or gather the gleanings of your harvest. Leave them for the poor and for the foreigner residing among you. I am the LORD your God.'"

[23]The LORD said to Moses, [24]"Say to the Israelites: 'On the first day of the seventh month you are to have a day of sabbath rest, a sacred assembly commemorated with trumpet blasts. [25]Do no regular work, but present a food offering to the LORD.'"

[26]The LORD said to Moses, [27]"The tenth day of this seventh month is the Day of Atonement. Hold a sacred assembly and deny yourselves, and present a food offering to the LORD. [28]Do not do any work on that day, because it is the Day of Atonement, when atonement is made for you before the LORD your God. [29]Those who do not deny themselves on that day must be cut off from their people. [30]I will destroy from among their people anyone who does any work on that day. [31]You shall do no work at all. This is to be a lasting ordinance for the generations to come, wherever you live. [32]It is a day of sabbath rest for you, and you must deny yourselves. From the evening of the ninth day of the month until the following evening you are to observe your sabbath."

[33]The LORD said to Moses, [34]"Say to the Israelites: 'On the fifteenth day of the seventh month the LORD's Festival of Tabernacles begins, and it lasts for seven days. [35]The first day is a sacred assembly; do no regular work. [36]For seven days present food offerings to the LORD, and on the eighth day hold a sacred assembly and present a food offering to the LORD. It is the closing special assembly; do no regular work.

[37]("'These are the LORD's appointed festivals, which you are to proclaim as sacred assemblies for bringing food offerings to the LORD—the
burnt offerings and grain offerings, sacrifices and drink offerings required
for each day. [38]These offerings are in addition to those for the LORD's
Sabbaths and in addition to your gifts and whatever you have vowed and
all the freewill offerings you give to the LORD.)

[39]"'So beginning with the fifteenth day of the seventh month, after you
have gathered the crops of the land, celebrate the festival to the LORD for
seven days; the first day is a day of sabbath rest, and the eighth day also
is a day of sabbath rest. [40]On the first day you are to take branches from
luxuriant trees—from palms, willows and other leafy trees—and rejoice
before the LORD your God for seven days. [41]Celebrate this as a festival to
the LORD for seven days each year. This is to be a lasting ordinance for the
generations to come; celebrate it in the seventh month. [42]Live in temporary
shelters for seven days: All native-born Israelites are to live in such shelters
[43]so your descendants will know that I had the Israelites live in temporary
shelters when I brought them out of Egypt. I am the LORD your God.'"

[44]So Moses announced to the Israelites the appointed festivals of
the LORD.

Listening to the Text in the Story: Biblical Texts: Sabbath: Exodus 16:1–36; 20:8–11; 31:12–17; 35:1–3; Leviticus 16:31; 19:3, 30; Passover and Festival of Unleavened Bread: Exodus 11:1–13:16; 23:15; 34:18; Feast of Weeks: Exodus 23:16, 19; 34:22, 26; Day of Atonement: Exodus 30:10; Leviticus 16:1–34; Feast of Tabernacles: Exodus 23:16; 34:22; Ancient Near Eastern Texts: Six Months of Ritual Supervision by the Diviner (Emar 446)

The biblical texts listed above are the ones that narratively precede Leviticus 23 and relate information regarding the festivals listed in this chapter. These prior texts make no mention of the one-day Firstfruits celebration that was connected with the Festival of Unleavened Bread, nor do they mention the Festival of Trumpets. Two later passages also give festival calendar information, Numbers 28–29 and Deuteronomy 16, but neither one mentions the Firstfruits celebration. Numbers does refer to a "day of firstfruits," but this is the same as the Festival of Weeks. Numbers refers to the Festival of Trumpets, but not Deuteronomy.

In terms of the ancient Near Eastern context, there are many documents that provide information about the celebration of various festivals. Unique among these documents, however, is a thirteenth-century BC text denominated by one of its translators as Six Months of Ritual Supervision by the Diviner (also known as Emar 446).[1] Like Leviticus 23, it gives a calendar of religious festivals. The text is not especially quote worthy, and the tablet is damaged in a number of places, but some important points of comparison are as follows:[2] both texts

- deal with festival celebrations that take place in the fall and spring of the year;
- begin with a heading that identifies the content to follow;
- tie particular festival occasions to offerings of different grain crops as well as sacrificial animals;
- describe distinct celebrations that are nevertheless quite similar to each other and are clustered closely together at the same time of the year; and
- contain imbalances between the lengths of descriptions of some feasts versus that of others.

There are differences between these texts as well. The Emar text lists festivals in honor of a number of different deities, whereas in Leviticus 23 the festivals belong to and are celebrated in honor of Yahweh only. Also, there is a redemptive-historical or salvation-history dimension to the festivals in Leviticus 23 that is not particularly prominent in the Emar festivals.

Additionally, we note that the similarity between these two texts argues for the antiquity of the Leviticus material as coming from the second millennium BC rather than being a postexilic text.[3] We see reinforced here for us the book of Leviticus as a text that is truly situated in its second-millennium context. Yet we also see that God, in an act of accommodation, speaks to his people in this context and gives them forms of worship with which they would have already been to some extent familiar, as were the human authors of this text.

---

1. "Six Months of Ritual Supervision by the Diviner," *COS* 1.124:436–39.

2. For these comparisons I am dependent on Hess, "Leviticus," 781–92; Richard S. Hess, "Multiple-Month Ritual Calendars in the West Semitic World: Emar 446 and Leviticus 23," in *The Future of Biblical Archaeology: Reassessing Methodologies and Assumptions*, ed. James K. Hoffmeier and Allan Millard (Grand Rapids: Eerdmans, 2004), 233–53.

3. Bryan C. Babcock, *Sacred Ritual: A Study of the West Semitic Ritual Calendars in Leviticus 23 and the Akkadian Text Emar 446*, BBRSup 9 (Winona Lake, IN: Eisenbrauns, 2014).

Yet, God also truly reveals himself in this accommodation and expects his people to recognize him and worship him by means of these forms. These are the words of human beings living in a particular context and yet no less the words of God.

EXPLAIN the Story

There are two observations to be made with regard to the celebrations as a whole before making a few brief comments about each festival individually. First, Milgrom argues that chapter 23 is a logical extension of chapters 21–22. The preceding chapters dealt with the sanctification of place, and now in chapter 23 the focus shifts to sanctification of time.[4] Balentine remarks accordingly that the calendar, centering as it does on holy days, "commands us to tune our lives to sacred time, failing which there can be no order to anything else we do."[5] Gorman notes that the Israelites were being called to participate in ritual acts that were themselves acts of creation.[6] Not just Yahweh, but Yahweh's people are called upon to make "proclamations of holiness"[7] concerning these festivals. In so doing they image God himself; they are holy as he his holy.

Second, for the most part, these festivals had a narrative, dramatic character to them. By participating in them, the Israelites rehearsed the "mighty acts of God," a history of redemption. Commentators often point out that the festivals also have an agricultural flavor to them. This is certainly true and may have played a part in the timing of the festivals. But it is important to note that there would be no agricultural element if it were not for the overarching rubric of redemptive history. The reason Israel can be in the land and grow crops is because the Lord redeemed them with a mighty hand and brought them up from the land of Egypt. Even though the two major festivals, Passover/Unleavened Bread and the Feast of Tabernacles, are separated by six months, they both tell the same story. The Lord rescued his people from the land of Egypt, and he guided them in all their wilderness wanderings. The festivals belong to Yahweh; they are his sacred occasions. The people are to observe these festivals as a way of fulfilling the command, "Be holy because I, the Lord your God, am holy" (Lev 19:2).

4. Milgrom, *Leviticus 23–27*, 1978.
5. Balentine, *Leviticus*, 172.
6. Gorman, *Divine Presence*, 127.
7. Kleinig, *Leviticus*, 487.

Sabbath (v. 3)

The Sabbath is not one of the appointed festivals. In fact, it seems that there was no actual assembly that met on the regular Sabbath day. There were prescribed duties for the priests on the Sabbath, but there is no recorded prescription for ritual activity on the part of the people. To have it referred to as day of "sacred assembly" seems strange. It may well be that Kleinig and others are right when they argue that the Hebrew phrase is better rendered as "proclamation of holiness";[8] that is, the Sabbath day is proclaimed as sacred and holy, but no actual worship assembly takes place. The Israelites kept the day holy by refraining from work, not by any service of communal worship.

The question then arises as to why the Sabbath is even included in this chapter. Several non-exclusive reasons have been offered:

1. The "seven" pattern plays out significantly in the festivals: there are two seven-day festivals; two of the festivals are separated from each other by seven sevens of days; three of the festivals take place in the seventh month; and there were extra Sabbaths in the festivals.
2. The Sabbath could be seen as the "archetypal" holy day;[9] the festivals are "Sabbath-like."[10]
3. The Sabbath is the only overtly ritual commandment in the Decalogue, and the only one that specifically provides the motivation of imitating God for its observance; the Sabbath provides a theological foundation for the imitation of God to be executed in the festivals.[11]
4. The Sabbath belongs to Yahweh, and therefore serves as the prototype for the festivals, which also belong to Yahweh.[12]
5. Finally, Wright notes that the Sabbath "heads the list . . . partly because all the festivals participated in the sabbatical principle of the dedication of time and labour to God."[13]

Passover (vv. 4–5)

One of the oddities of the book of Leviticus is that a book that contains so much detail about sacrifice only contains one verse (v. 5) about the Passover. However, as noted in the commentary on chapter 3 (p. 58), the Passover

8. Ibid., 487, 502; Kiuchi, *Leviticus*, 420.
9. Kleinig, *Leviticus*, 502.
10. Rooker, *Leviticus*, 283.
11. Balentine, *Leviticus*, 174.
12. Levine, *Leviticus*, 155.
13. Wright, "Leviticus," 151.

should probably be considered a particular type of fellowship offering, so it is, in a way, referred to in that chapter. Also, in keeping with the "seven" patterning of the festivals, it should be noted that the Passover is celebrated on the fourteenth day of the first month—that is, two "sevens" into the new year.

Festival of Unleavened Bread (vv. 6–8)

The Festival of Unleavened Bread, like the Passover, receives only brief mention in this list, perhaps because in the narrative flow of the Torah both festivals were discussed at length in Exodus. But in this present passage the festival is described as being seven days in duration, and on two of the seven days (the first and last) no regular work is to be done. So again, the Sabbath provides a measure of patterning for this festival, and the regular weekly sabbath would also come during the festival, making three days that were to be celebrated as Sabbaths.

Firstfruits (vv. 9–14)

This single-day event is apparently not specifically referred to anywhere else in the Torah. The actual term for firstfruits, *bikkurim*, does not occur in this passage. In its other occurrences the term either refers to firstfruits in general, or it refers to the firstfruits of the next festival to be described in this chapter, the Festival of Weeks (vv. 15–22; *bikkurim* occurs in vv. 17 and 20). Most commentators, based on other passages in the Old Testament (Exod 9:31–32; Ruth 1:22; 2:23), maintain that this one-day firstfruits offering was a presentation of the firstfruits of the barley harvest and that the Feast of Weeks firstfruits offering was of the wheat harvest.

The exact time of this one-day event is not certain. Verses 11 and 15 indicate that the offering is to be made on the day after the Sabbath. But which Sabbath is this? The basic options are (1) a special non-regular Sabbath during the Feast of Unleavened Bread; (2) the regular seventh-day Sabbath that occurs during the week of the feast; (3) the first Sabbath after the conclusion of the feast; (4) an unspecified Sabbath that occurs sometime after the conclusion of the feast. Without going into all the arguments for and against these theories, I will simply say that I favor the second option. We will look at this again in the Live the Story section (see pp. 308–9).

Festival of Weeks (vv. 15–22)

As mentioned earlier, the firstfruits offering for this festival is probably the wheat harvest, as opposed to the first of the barley harvest presented seven weeks earlier. However, even though the firstfruits offerings are of different products, there appears to be some kind of symbolic relationship between them, since the Festival of Weeks occurs seven weeks plus one day (i.e., fifty days) after the prior firstfruits offering. What that significance might be we will explore in the Live the Story section (see pp. 308–10).

Since this Festival would have begun some fifty-plus days after the Passover, it has been associated with the giving of the law and establishment of the Mosaic covenant at Mount Sinai because, according to one understanding of Exodus 19:1, the Israelites arrived at Mount Sinai on the first day of the third month, which would be approximately six weeks after Passover on the fourteenth day of the first month[14] (see also 2 Chr 15:10–14).

Verse 22, the substance of which also occurs in Leviticus 19:9–10, may appear to be disconnected from the subject matter of this festival. However, it has been plausibly argued that it is repeated here to indicate that "in addition to making gifts of the harvest to Yahweh they need to express compassion toward the poor."[15]

Festival of Trumpets (vv. 23–25)

On the first day of the seventh month, trumpets were to be blown.[16] Rather than NIV's "commemorated," the Hebrew *zikkaron* is given its more proper nuance by other translations' "a memorial" (e.g., ESV, NET). The question, however, is who is doing the remembering. Consistent with other occurrences of the term in Leviticus, it is most likely that the trumpet blasts are a way of calling on Yahweh to remember his people with favor. It is a plea for the LORD to be gracious and merciful. The texts do not give us the specifics as to why this action on the first day of the seventh month was necessary. However, we should probably see a relationship here between this day and the Day of Atonement that was to come just nine days later. This "musical prayer"[17] was both a petition to Yahweh to be gracious and merciful to his people as the Day of Atonement was approaching and a reminder that they needed to be truly humble before God and penitent in light of the great solemnity attached to that day.

Day of Atonement (vv. 26–32)

See the commentary on chapter 16 in Explain the Story, pp. 208–13.

---

14. This, however, is not the usual understanding of the timing.

15. Hartley, *Leviticus*, 386–87.

16. There are no biblical data that would understand this day, in biblical times, as constituting a New Year's Day. The understanding of this day as Jewish New Year (*rosh hashanah*) is postbiblical.

17. Sklar, *Leviticus*, 284–85.

Festival of Tabernacles (vv. 33–43)

Prior to this chapter, the Festival of Tabernacles had only been briefly mentioned twice and was referred to as the Festival of Ingathering (Exod 23:16; 34:22). So, it was definitely an agricultural festival celebrating the successful completion of the harvest. But here in Leviticus it is referred to as the Festival of Tabernacles, a remembrance of the forty-year wilderness journey of the Israelites during which they lived in tents. The word here translated "Tabernacles" is not the same one that is used to refer to Yahweh's tabernacle. Rather it is the word *sukkot*, which refers to temporary shelters. The NIV translates this word as "Tabernacles" in verse 34 and translates it in verses 42–43 as both "temporary shelters" and "shelters." To remember this time period, the Israelites are to live in temporary shelters for the seven days of the festival. So, both of the seven-day festivals in the Israelite ritual calendar serve as reminders of the exodus, the redemption from the land of Egypt and the subsequent forty-year wilderness journey to the promised land.

In verse 40 the Israelites are instructed to gather branches from "palms, willows and other leafy trees—and rejoice before the Lord your God." Interestingly, the text does not indicate what they are to do with these branches. However, in Nehemiah 8:14–17 the branches are understood to be the construction material for the temporary shelters.[18]

This seven-day feast is expanded to an eighth day (v. 36), which is also referred to as a "day of sabbath rest" in verse 39. The NIV's "closing special assembly" in verse 36 translates the Hebrew *ʿatseret*, which is a word of uncertain meaning. Interestingly, the word is also used in Deuteronomy 16:8 to refer to an event that occurs on the seventh and last day of the Festival of Unleavened Bread. The exact purpose of this day is obscure. It may be that it provides a symmetrical symbolic, and perhaps even literary, balance to the firstfruits day that is associated with the Feast of Unleavened Bread.

The Church Calendar

For many churches/denominations, the church calendar is not of any great significance, and perhaps the only two events on that calendar are Christmas and Easter. But both the individual and congregational/communal experience can be enhanced by a deliberate attempt to follow the dramatic story of the life of Christ by giving attention to a church calendar. Even as the ancient

18. See Fishbane, *Biblical Interpretation*, 109–12.

Israelites were given a series of festivals and holy days by which to rehearse the redemptive deeds of Yahweh on their behalf, so the church can benefit from following the life of Christ in a calendar that recognizes that the life of Christ consisted of more than just his birth and resurrection. Of course, churches that are more liturgical already do this, with every Sunday assigned its particular place in the church year. Without necessarily adopting a full calendar, a church, as part of its congregational life and part of the spiritual formation of its members, who have been called to be conformed to the image of God's Son, can enhance that formation via the use of a church calendar shaped around the crucial events in the life of Christ. This could include remembering his:

Birth
Circumcision and purification/presentation in the temple
Visit from the Magi and flight into Egypt
Baptism
Temptation
Transfiguration
Determined journey to Jerusalem
Triumphal entry
Death and crucifixion
Resurrection
Ascension
Giving of the Spirit at Pentecost
Second coming

Various other events in the life of Christ could be added to the list, as well as the inclusion of the traditional preparatory periods of Advent and Lent.

There are several benefits to be derived from adopting such a calendrical structure:

1. Following such a calendar supports the church's confession that Jesus is Lord. It reinforces the church's profession of devotion to Christ.
2. As we focus our attention on the life of Christ in the liturgical calendar and trace his footsteps, it aids in the process and goal of sanctification: becoming holy as he is holy.
3. It provides a rich communal experience as the whole congregation is focused on a particular event in the life of Christ.
4. It turns one of evangelicalism's most pronounced faults on its head. Too often our contemporary worship services are too individual centered,

> or even too congregation centered. The lines we say or sing betray this. We say to God, "I'm so glad you're in my life," as if God was an optional plug-in that can enhance our lives and give them additional enrichment. We talk of making God relevant in our lives rather than realizing that the question is not "How can God fit into my life story?" but rather, "How does my life fit into God's story?"

In essence, such a practice can bring a rich biblical-theological, redemptive-historical, salvation-history perspective to our worship and spiritual formation, one that immerses our lives in the story of God and celebrates the great redemptive deeds of God in Christ. In so doing, we acknowledge his all-surpassing greatness, bow before his awesomeness, declare his holiness, and resolve to obey the command of Christ, seeking to be perfect/holy as he is perfect/holy.

Ephraim Radner has argued that the festivals in this chapter are a prefiguring of the life of Christ. As Radner puts it, "The full range of the Levitical festivals themselves is now refracted (not discarded) through the prism of his life."[19] As the ancient festivals were, for the Israelites, windows into the character, redemptive purposes, and acts of God, so in the New Testament these "pilgrimage" festivals highlight Jesus's own pilgrimage as he makes his way to Jerusalem to sacrifice himself during the Festival of Passover and Unleavened Bread.[20]

In what follows we will look at how the Israelite festivals are used figurally in the New Testament with reference to the life of Christ and his church.

Sabbath

As opposed to some construals of Jesus as being anti-Sabbath, it is important to note that this is definitely not the case in the New Testament. In the account of Jesus's confrontation with the citizens of Nazareth, Jesus went to the synagogue on the Sabbath, "as was his custom" (Luke 4:16). To be sure, he has differences with the Jewish leaders about what kinds of activity are permitted on the Sabbath; however, he does not disown the Sabbath but rather proclaims himself "Lord of the Sabbath" (Matt 12:8). He not only heals on the Sabbath, but Jesus's healing miracles are signs of his redemptive power; the Sabbath serves as a sign of Christ's redemptive work.[21] Additionally, the Sabbath serves as a sign of the eschatological rest into which those who trust in Christ will one day enter (Heb 4:9) and rest from all their labors.

19. Radner, *Leviticus*, 254.

20. Ibid., 238–39.

21. It is also possible that we are expected to understand, in the account of the Sabbath-day healing of the invalid in John 5:1–15, that Jesus also forgave the man's sins.

Passover

It is well known that the New Testament portrays Jesus as the "Lamb of God, who takes away the sin of the world" (John 1:29). Though John the Baptist does not specifically refer to Jesus as the Passover Lamb of God, most commentators understand this to be case. On one understanding of John's passion narrative, Jesus is crucified at the very time the Passover lambs are being slaughtered, further pointing to him, ironically, as the true Passover Lamb. John, in what may be a citation of Exodus 12:46 (John 19:36), understands Christ as the Passover lamb whose bones were not to be broken. Paul states that "Christ, our Passover Lamb has been sacrificed," and then urges his readers, "Therefore let us keep the Festival . . ." (1 Cor 5:7–8), referring to the Festival of Unleavened Bread. As we mentioned before, in keeping with the pilgrimage nature of the Passover festival, the Gospels portray Jesus as making a determined, deliberate pilgrimage to Jerusalem to sacrifice himself at the Passover Festival.

Festival of Unleavened Bread

This festival is never really mentioned in the Gospels in its own right, but it is always connected with the Passover, which was regarded as being the first day of the festival. So the typological connections that the New Testament draws seem to be with the Passover, rather than with the following festival. However, it is interesting to note that one redemptive event that does occur during the Festival of Unleavened Bread proper is Jesus's resurrection. The significance of this will come out more clearly in the next item.

Firstfruits

As mentioned earlier, there is some debate as to exact date of this offering of firstfruits. Of the various suggestions, I, as well as many commentators, maintain that it comes the day after the regular weekly Sabbath during the Feast of Unleavened Bread. If this is correct, in the New Testament this corresponds to the Sunday on which Christ arose from the dead. Very possibly, this understanding lies behind Paul's statement "Christ has indeed been raised from the dead, the firstfruits of those who have fallen asleep" (1 Cor 15:20). Paul sees Christ as the firstfruits, whose resurrection from the dead is a guarantee of the rest of the harvest: "Christ, the firstfruits; then, when he comes, those who belong to him" (1 Cor 15:23). Christ's resurrection on the day of the offering of the firstfruits is a guarantee that those who belong to Christ will also be raised from the dead.[22]

22. Richard B. Gaffin, Jr., *Resurrection and Redemption: A Study in Paul's Soteriology*, 2nd ed. (Phillipsburg, NJ: P&R, 1987), 34–36.

Furthermore, the date of the Festival of Weeks is determined by the date of the one-day offering of firstfruits, coming seven full weeks later (i.e., fifty days after the Sabbath). The Festival of Weeks—Pentecost—is itself a firstfruits festival (Exod 23:16, 19; 34:22, 26; Num 28:26). The time between the two firstfruits celebrations is itself ritually and symbolically significant. The earlier one serves as a guarantee of the later one. In the New Testament, then, Christ's resurrection on the first Sunday after the Sabbath of the Feast of Unleavened Bread anticipates what happens at Pentecost. His resurrection is inextricably tied to the birth of the church that takes place at Pentecost. Also, on the day of his resurrection Jesus appears to his apostles, breathes on them, and then says to them, "Receive the Holy Spirit" (John 20:22). Jesus's breathing on them and imparting the Holy Spirit to them is a symbolic anticipation of what will happen fifty days later on the Day of Pentecost when Peter declares:

> God has raised this Jesus to life, and we are all witnesses of it. Exalted to the right hand of God, he has received from the Father the promised Holy Spirit and has poured out what you now see and hear. (Acts 2:32–33)

So Jesus's resurrection on the Day of Firstfruits during the Feast of Unleavened Bread is a guarantee of the resurrection of all those who belong to him, the birth of the church on the Day of Pentecost, and the pouring out of the Spirit on the church.

Festival of Weeks (Pentecost)

As mentioned earlier, the Festival of Weeks (Pentecost) is itself a firstfruits festival. The offerings given on this occasion, as well as their acceptance, were an anticipation and guarantee of the full harvest yet to come. The pouring out of the Spirit on that day was a guarantee of the church's continued full possession of the Spirit in all times and places (see Acts 4:31; 8:15–17; 9:17; 10:44–47; 11:15–18; 19:2–6). Additionally, the three thousand converts that day were the firstfruits of a much greater harvest of converts to come.

F. F. Bruce has argued for another fascinating connection. In Acts 20:16, as Paul is making his last recorded journey to Jerusalem, the text says that "he was in a hurry to reach Jerusalem, if possible, by the day of Pentecost." Bruce notes that as he was making this journey, he was accompanied by a representative number of gentiles (Acts 20:4), converts from Paul's various missionary journeys. Bruce argues that Paul wants to be in Jerusalem by Pentecost so he can symbolically "offer" these gentiles to God as the firstfruits of his evangelistic work among them, a guarantee of a greater harvest of gentiles yet to come.[23] Bruce's understanding of Paul's desire is reinforced by Romans 15:16, where Paul declares that

> He [God] gave me the priestly duty of proclaiming the gospel of God, so that the Gentiles might become an offering acceptable to God, sanctified by the Holy Spirit.

The Christian church of the last two millennia, as well as all the converts and members yet to be added, especially in its gentile makeup, constitute the harvest of which the Festival of Weeks, Pentecost, was the firstfruits and guarantee.

Festival of Trumpets

If, as argued above (p. 304), the Feast of Trumpets was a prayer for God to remember his people and be gracious and merciful to them, especially in light of the Day of Atonement and judgment yet to come, then the references to the blowing of trumpets in the New Testament continue this motif. A trumpet is sounded when God sends his angels to gather his elect, when the saints are bodily resurrected, and when the saints are raised from the dead and the church is caught up in clouds to meet the Lord in the air (Matt 24:31; 1 Cor 15:52; 1 Thess 4:16–17). God remembers his people, raises them from the dead, and calls them to be with himself, rescuing them from the judgment to come. Additionally, the occasions of trumpet blowing in the book of Revelation are by and large comforting announcements, anticipatory of God's rescue of his saints and his pouring out of judgment on their oppressors (Rev 1:10; 4:1; 8:2–9:14; 10:7; 11:15–19).

Day of Atonement

See the commentary on chapter 16 (Live the Story, pp. 213–21).

Festival of Tabernacles

By the time of the New Testament, the Festival of Tabernacles had taken on distinctive covenantal and messianic overtones, as well as a number of additional rituals beyond those recorded in the Old Testament. It is against this background that three incidents in the Gospels are to be understood.

First, in John 7–8 two of Jesus's statements are of particular importance. In John 7:37–39 we read:

23. F. F. Bruce, *New Testament History* (Garden City, NY: Doubleday, 1969), 353–54.

> On the last and greatest day of the festival, Jesus stood and said in a loud voice, "Let anyone who is thirsty come to me and drink. Whoever believes in me, as Scripture has said, rivers of living water will flow from within them." By this he meant the Spirit, whom those who believed in him were later to receive.

It should be remembered that, to a considerable extent, the Festival of Tabernacles was an agricultural festival, referred to in Exodus as the "Festival of Ingathering." It was a time of thanksgiving for the completion of the full harvest as well as a time of prayer for the autumn rains for the next planting season in the spring. One of the practices that had attached to the festival by Jesus's day was a ritual pouring out of water on the altar; this occurred daily and, on the seventh day of feast, was done seven times. This poured out water was both an expression of thanksgiving for the rains that had provided the previous harvest and also a prayer for the rains that would provide the next harvest. This rain was also interpreted symbolically of spiritual blessings that God would pour out on his people, especially on the day of the Lord ushered in by the Lord's Messiah. So when Jesus, against this backdrop, stands up in the temple courts and calls people to come to him for the living water, he is making a messianic claim, consistent with his proclamation that the day of the Lord is at hand. Already in Zechariah 13–14 a complex association of messianic motifs was present: the day of the Lord, the Festival of Tabernacles, living water flowing out of Jerusalem, the provision of needed rains, victory over the oppressive enemies, and the full acknowledgement of Jerusalem and Judah as "holy to the LORD." Jesus claims and proclaims that all these motifs are now met in him. Also, when John interprets Jesus's pronouncement as having to do with the giving of the Holy Spirit, he is probably capitalizing on an association between water and spiritual blessings that was already present within Judaism.

Additionally, when Jesus at the same time refers to himself as the "light of the world" (John 8:12), he may well be making this claim against the backdrop of the special lighting of a large candelabrum that occurred on the first night of the festival. Thus Jesus again claims that the motifs of the Festival of Tabernacles are met in him.

Second, in Luke's account of the Transfiguration, he is unique among the Synoptic Gospels in mentioning that this event occurred on the eighth day after Peter's acknowledgement of Jesus as God's Messiah. Luke may have done this to evoke the picture of the Festival of Tabernacles as an eight-day feast. When Jesus is transfigured, Peter is reminded of the messianic motifs associated with the festival and wants to erect three shelters (i.e., huts, tabernacles). Though Luke remarks that Peter "did not know what he was saying" (Luke 9:33), Peter was not entirely void of understanding the implications of what he had just witnessed.

Third, several theologians and church historians have argued that the Feast of Epiphany in the early church was influenced by and seen in some respects as a continuation of the Festival of Tabernacles. The Feast of Epiphany is related not solely, but most particularly, to the visit of the Magi. A passage that might explain how the early church related the Festival of Tabernacles to the visit of the Magi is Zechariah 14:14–16:

> The wealth of all the surrounding nations will be collected—great quantities of gold and silver and clothing. . . . Then the survivors from all the nations that have attacked Jerusalem will go up year after year to worship the King, the LORD Almighty, and to celebrate the Festival of Tabernacles.

Notice in particular what this passage says about the gentiles. They will go up to Jerusalem, they will go there to celebrate the Feast of Tabernacles, they will go there to worship the divine King, and they will not go there empty-handed: they will bring gifts with them, including gold. Similarly, the Magi go to Jerusalem, they go there to worship the king, and they bring gifts with them, including gold. No doubt this passage in Zechariah had something to do with the connections the early church drew between the Feast of Tabernacles and the Feast of Epiphany.

Zechariah's prophecy finds one installment of its fulfillment in the visit of the Magi. But the installments continue as the gentiles enter the church of God on account of the great missionary journeys of the apostle Paul, and they continue even in our day as gentiles continue to come to Christ and are grafted into the Israel of God. Indeed, Zechariah's prophecy is not entirely unique but was in some ways already envisioned in the original intent of the Feast of Tabernacles:

> Celebrate the Festival of Tabernacles for seven days after you have gathered the produce of your threshing floor and your winepress. Be joyful at your festival—you, your sons and daughters, your male and female servants, and the Levites, the foreigners, the fatherless and the widows who live in your towns. For seven days celebrate the festival to the LORD your God at the place the LORD will choose. For the LORD your God will bless you in all your harvest and in all the work of your hands, and your joy will be complete. (Deut 16:13–15)

We (gentiles) have been grafted into the people of God. Though we celebrate the Feast of the Epiphany, we also have a right, as former foreigners but now a part of the very people of Israel, to own Israel's history as our history. Therefore, it was not some remote people with whom we have nothing to do; it was our very own ancestors who were redeemed from the land of Egypt. It was our ancestors who crossed the Red Sea. It was our ancestors who journeyed through the wilderness to the promised land, living in tents as they made their way. It was our ancestors who celebrated the Feast of Tabernacles. And we, who were formerly "excluded from citizenship in Israel and foreigners to the covenants of the promise, without hope and without God in the world," have now "been brought near by the blood of Christ" (Eph 2:12–13). We are the descendants of those ancient Israelites. So as we celebrate the Feast of Epiphany, we also celebrate the Feast of Tabernacles, and we come to the heavenly Jerusalem and worship the divine King. Our joy is made complete because of the Christ who dwells within us and because we have our dwelling in the place and the people who are known as the Israel of God.

CHAPTER 22

Leviticus 24:1–9

LISTEN to the Story

24:1The LORD said to Moses, 2"Command the Israelites to bring you clear oil of pressed olives for the light so that the lamps may be kept burning continually. 3Outside the curtain that shields the ark of the covenant law in the tent of meeting, Aaron is to tend the lamps before the LORD from evening till morning, continually. This is to be a lasting ordinance for the generations to come. 4The lamps on the pure gold lampstand before the LORD must be tended continually.

5"Take the finest flour and bake twelve loaves of bread, using two-tenths of an ephah for each loaf. 6Arrange them in two stacks, six in each stack, on the table of pure gold before the LORD. 7By each stack put some pure incense as a memorial portion to represent the bread and to be a food offering presented to the LORD. 8This bread is to be set out before the LORD regularly, Sabbath after Sabbath, on behalf of the Israelites, as a lasting covenant. 9It belongs to Aaron and his sons, who are to eat it in the sanctuary area, because it is a most holy part of their perpetual share of the food offerings presented to the LORD."

Listening to the Text in the Story: Biblical Texts: Bread of the Presence: Exodus 25:30; 35:13; 39:36; 40:23; Lampstand: Exodus 25:31–39; 26:35; 27:20–21; 37:17–25; Ancient Near Eastern Texts: Installation of the Storm God's High Priestess; Temple Program for the New Year's Festivals at Babylon

The biblical texts listed above are taken from passages in the book of Exodus in which either the instructions for the making of the lampstand and the table of the bread of the presence are given or the actual making of them is narrated.

Numerous ancient Near Eastern texts describe the furniture to be placed in the sanctuaries of the temple for the various deities. Many of them give directions for the care and feeding of the gods, for laying out loaves of bread before the gods, and even specify that there are to be twelve loaves. The Installation text specifies that these loaves are to be laid out daily.[1] The Temple Program for the New Year's Festivals at Babylon specifies that twelve "usual" loaves are to be set before the god Marduk during the New Year enthronement festival.[2] In most of these texts the loaves are to be set out daily rather than on the Sabbath day each week. One possible reason for the difference will be suggested in the next section.

EXPLAIN the Story

The Lampstand

The community is to bring the oil for the lampstand. The altar of incense is not referred to in this passage, but we know from Exodus 25:1–7 and 35:4–9 that the incense is also contributed by the community. It is possible, and likely, that the bread of the presence is also made from the grain offerings of the Israelites. If this is the case, it is noteworthy that for all three pieces of furniture in the holy place—the lampstand, the altar of incense, and the table of the bread of the presence—and the supply for them (oil, incense, and grain) are contributed by the community. The Israelite people have an important role to play in the daily service of the holy place in the tabernacle.

The lamps on the lampstand are to burn continually, meaning either that the high priest is to light them regularly each night or he is to keep them burning continuously. Perhaps against most commentators, I lean toward the latter understanding. The holy place was a covered area, and it is entirely possible that the light from the lampstand would have been desirable or necessary even during daylight hours.

On a practical level, the lampstand provides light for the holy place. But there are a number of possibilities for a symbolic significance. Almost certainly the tabernacle is to be seen as a microcosm of the universe. Correspondingly, the lamps on the lampstand would be representative of the lights of the heavens. Additionally, the seven-branched lampstand, with its almond-flower-shaped cups (Exod 25:33), is probably also to be seen as representative of the tree of life.[3] It is probably also the case that the light of the lampstand is symbolic of the

1. "The Installation of the Storm God's High Priestess," *COS* 1.122:428
2. "Temple Program for the New Year's Festival at Babylon," trans. A. Sachs (*ANET*, 334).
3. On this, see Longman, *Immanuel in Our Place*, 57. See also his larger discussion on the connections between the tabernacle and garden of Eden, where humans dwelt in God's presence.

eternal light of God, the light of God's countenance (Num 6:25, "the LORD make his face shine on you").

The Table

There are a number of linguistic correspondences between verses 1–4 (dealing with the lampstand and its olive oil) and verses 5–9 (dealing with the table and the bread of the presence), as can be seen in this list.[4]

"continually," "regularly" (*tamid*; vv. 2, 3, 4, 8)
"tend," "set out" (*'arak*; vv. 3, 4, 8)
"bring," "take" (*laqah*; vv. 2, 5)
"pure" (*tahor*; vv. 4, 6)
"clear," "pure" (*zak*; vv. 2, 7)
"lasting ordinance," "perpetual share" (*huqat 'olam*; v. 3; *hoq 'olam*; v, 9; notice also the "lasting covenant" in v. 8; *berit 'olam*)
"before the LORD" (*liphne yhwh*; vv. 3, 4, 6, 8)

These correspondences certainly suggest that the author/editor of this passage composed the text to highlight the correspondence between the light of the lampstand and the bread of the presence. Two passages, Exodus 25:37 and Numbers 8:1–4, indicate that the lampstand was to illuminate the area where the altar of incense and the table of the bread of the presence were located; some commentators suggest the light shone directly on the table. The symbolic effect may well be that the light of God, the light of his face, is seen to be shining directly on the twelve loaves of bread, representative of the tribes of Israel.[5]

The loaves were most likely large, round loaves, each one weighing between four and seven pounds. The NIV rightly translates, against prior understanding, that the loaves were not arranged in rows but in two stacks of six each. The NIV is perhaps correct that the incense was placed beside the loaves, but it is also possible that the incense was sprinkled on top of the loaves and then brushed off before being given to the priests to eat. Since the loaves were not actually consumed by the priests until one week after having been placed on the table we should probably understand that the bread was unleavened.

We should not think that the Israelites were supposed to understand that God actually ate the food of the sacrifices that were offered to him (see the

4. For these linguistic correspondences I am indebted to Hartley, *Leviticus*, 398.
5. For a fuller discussion of the symbolic significance, see Morales, *Who Shall Ascend*, 187–92.

commentary on chapter 1, Explain the Story, pp. 38–39). On the other hand, by the use of the imagery employed, the Israelites were actually encouraged in some way to conceptualize God as smelling the aroma and being presented with a meal. As Gane aptly describes it, "Talk about high-tension theological balance! The offering of bread (i.e., basic food . . .) walks a tightrope to demonstrate God's real Presence while simultaneously denying that he is just like a human being."[6] Earlier in this chapter we called attention to how most of the other ancient Near Eastern texts indicate that bread was set before their deities on a daily basis. But Israel's God is presented with bread once a week on the Sabbath day. Perhaps the reason for this difference was to emphasize that God did not actually consume the food that was set before him and was not dependent on it.[7] Indeed, in the end, the bread actually becomes food for the priests; ultimately, God feeds his priests rather than their being the ones who feed him. The priests are God's servants, but, as the one who resides in the tabernacle, God is the host.[8]

There are several non-exclusive possibilities for the symbolic significance of the loaves. The bread could serve to indicate the presence of God among his people. That there were twelve loaves of bread, and that the grain for this bread came from the contributions of the Israelites, indicates that the bread in some way represents the tribes and the people of Israel. The incense that was placed either on or beside the bread is referred to as a "memorial" portion, indicating that the bread served the purpose of being both a reminder and a plea for Yahweh to remember his people with favor.

Finally, the bread is referred to as a lasting covenant. As Kleinig remarks, as God's loyal covenant partners the Israelites were obligated to supply this bread to be laid on the table.[9] And the priests "ate the bread on the people's behalf . . . confirming the covenant with the Lord every time they did so."[10]

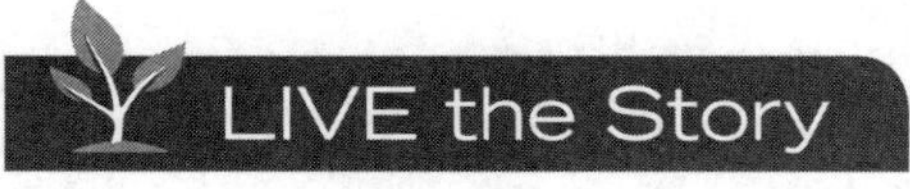

A Royal Priesthood?

Priests had several roles to play in the tabernacle ceremonies and rituals, which we have already described. But this present passage highlights another part of the

6. Gane, *Leviticus, Numbers*, 423.
7. Hess, "Leviticus," 796; Sklar, *Leviticus*, 289.
8. Kleinig, *Leviticus*, 518.
9. Ibid., 514.
10. Sklar, *Leviticus*, 289.

high priest's job description: servant to Yahweh. The high priest makes sure the lights on the lampstand are trimmed and kept lit. He makes sure there is bread on the table. And though it is not mentioned in this particular passage, we know from other texts that the high priest was to make sure the altar of incense was perpetually burning. So, to be more metaphorically precise, the high priest was God's butler, God's valet! He was to make sure the lights were on, food was on the table, and the aromatherapy was going. He was, to be sure, the chief butler, head of the servant staff, but a butler nevertheless. This highlights for us that, among other things, the tabernacle was God's residence. As Averbeck notes, "If there is a lamp burning, incense burning and bread on the table, then someone is 'home.'"[11] And it was not simply God's home; it was God's royal residence, and the high priest was servant to the King. The priest's duty was to make sure that the tabernacle was a welcome place for its royal resident to dwell.

Several times in the New Testament believers are referred to as priests (Rom 15:16; 1 Pet 2:5, 9; Rev 1:6; 5:10; 20:6). In several of these passages emphasis is laid on the royal nature of this priesthood, echoing the language of Exodus 19:6, where the Israelites are referred to—potentially, if they keep God's commandments—as a "kingdom of priests." Even though a few of these passages seem to emphasize the great honor that is attached to this royal priesthood, it is important to keep in mind that the royal character of this priesthood derives from the fact that it is a priesthood in the service of the King. We are a royal priesthood, but we are so because we are on the King's servant staff. There is a glory to the priesthood, but it is, nevertheless, a service occupation. Therefore, we should never think of ourselves as being the stars of the show. Our priestly service to God does not give us celebrity status. There is a menial, mundane character to our priestly work. The priesthood to which we have been called is a service occupation, and the service we render is to make sure that our individual lives and our churches are places where God is pleased to dwell by his Spirit.

In this vein, it is important to realize that this servant element is to be characteristic of our priesthood because it was characteristic of Christ's own priesthood. We exalt him as our great high priest, but Christ's ministry as priest, glorious as it is, is one that he performs "in service to God" (Heb 2:17). Indeed, he "remains a priest forever" in service to God (Heb 7:3, 24). Our own priesthood most resembles that of Christ when it is characterized by humble and obedient service to God.

11. Richard E. Averbeck, "Tabernacle," *Dictionary of the Old Testament: Pentateuch*, ed. T. Desmond Alexander and David W. Baker (Downers Grove, IL: InterVarsity, 2003), 815; Haran, *Temples and Temple-Service*, 218–19.

God as Host

We should also understand that since the tabernacle was God's home, ultimately, he was the actual host. One indication of this is that even though the loaves of bread were symbolically set out on the table as food for God, these loaves were eventually given by God to the priest for their consumption.[12] In the same way, even though we are priests who are in the employ of the divine King, ultimately, he is the one who hosts us.

Morales has argued that this passage shows that "the lampstand shining upon the bread of the presence offers a symbolic picture of the Sabbath: Israel basking in the light of God's blessed presence."[13] So even though it is the Israelites who bring oil for the light and grain for the bread, it is ultimately God, the consummate host, who shines the light of his face upon the Israelites, guiding them Sabbath to Sabbath—Sabbaths which, according to Jesus, "were made for man." The ceremonials and rituals of the tabernacle constitute the way in which the Israelites honored God. In turn, the whole sacramental system was a way in which God, as the royal host in the tabernacle, provided for and cared for his people. And so it is that, even today, we should give thanks to God that he has invited us to live in his temple, his church, and that he provides for us and cares for our needs.

Jesus, Light of the World, Bread of Life, the Everlasting Covenant

It is noteworthy that the two main symbols in this passage provide the background for two of Jesus's "I am" statements in the Gospel of John: "I am the light of the world" (John 8:12), and "I am the bread of life" (John 6:35, 48).

If indeed the tabernacle is a microcosm of the universe, and the lamps on the candlestick are symbolic of the light of creation and of the light of God's face shining on the Israelites, then it should not be surprising that Paul draws an explicit creational connection in 2 Corinthians 4:6:

> For God, who said, "Let light shine out of darkness," made his light shine in our hearts to give us the light of the knowledge of God's glory displayed in the face of Christ.

For Paul, the symbolism of the light of God's face shining on his people, pictured in the lamps on the lampstand, is now replicated in the

12. Kleinig, *Leviticus*, 518.
13. Morales, *Who Shall Ascend*, 187.

light of Christ's face shining on believers to give them the knowledge of God's glory.[14]

As for the bread of the presence and Jesus's declaration that he is the bread of life, these come to a dramatic point in the institution of the Lord's Supper. In all three Synoptic Gospels the account of the Lord's Supper has him declaring that the bread is his body (in John 6:51, he declares that the bread is his flesh). Additionally, the covenantal element of Leviticus 24:8 ("a lasting covenant") is replicated in that the Lord's Supper is explicitly a covenantal meal (Matt 26:28). In a number of ways, then, we can draw the lines from the table of the bread of the presence to the table of the Lord's Supper. The bread symbolizes the very body of the Lord; it is bread that the Lord has given for the life—the eternal life—of his people. The bread is covenantal bread, and in both cases God himself is the one who is the host at the table, inviting his people into covenant with him. Additionally, the bread of the Lord's Supper, just like the bread of the presence, is distributed to those who make up a royal priesthood. It is little wonder, then, that the Lord's Supper should also be referred to as the Eucharist, which, as often as we participate in this meal, gives us the opportunity to express our gratitude to our gracious King and host.

Jesus, the Divine King-Priest Who Eats the Bread with His Fellow Priests

The last thing to note here is the use that is made of this text in the passages in the Gospels that recount how Jesus's disciples went through a grain field on the Sabbath day and ate some of the kernels of grain (Matt 12:1–8; Mark 2:23–28; Luke 6:1–5). When the Pharisees accuse the disciples of violating the Sabbath, Jesus refers to the incident in 1 Samuel 21:1–6 in which David, on the run from Saul, stops at the house of God at Nob and requests that the priest Ahimelek provide him with some bread. Ahimelek does so, giving him the consecrated bread of the presence that has just been replaced by the new week's supply. Jesus even alludes to our present Leviticus passage by noting that the bread which Ahimelek gave David and his men was bread that was only lawful for the priests to eat. There are at least three ways in which these passages in the Gospels connect with Leviticus 24:1–9.

First, Jesus notes that even though the priest knew that the law specified that the bread of the presence was only lawful for the priests to eat, the priest made a decision to give that bread to David and his men. In this way the

14. Note that this is one of a number of passages in the New Testament in which Christ fulfills a role that was the sole prerogative of Yahweh in the Old Testament, giving support to the understanding that Paul regarded Christ as God.

priest legitimated the kingship of David over that of Saul.[15] Jesus, in essence, is using a "how much greater" argument in his reply to the Pharisees. If it was deemed lawful by the priest to give David and his men this bread, how much more lawful it must be in Jesus's case, since he is the one who is "greater than the temple" (Matt 12:6), and, as "Son of Man," is "Lord of the Sabbath" (Matt 12:8). The term "Son of Man," from its occurrences in the Psalms, Ezekiel, and Daniel, should be understood as a royal title. Jesus is "David's greater son," the true inheritor of the royal prerogatives. If David and his men were blameless in eating this bread, how much more are Jesus and his men not only blameless but legitimately exercising their royal rights.

Second, the priest is the authorized teacher and interpreter of the law. It was the priest's duty to distinguish between that which was clean and unclean, between that which was holy and that which was profane (or common). David's eating of the bread was not illegitimate because the priest, the official interpreter of the law, had ruled that David and his men were ritually clean (1 Sam 21:4).[16] Jesus's reasoning is that since he is greater than the temple, how much more ritually clean he and his men were to eat of the consecrated bread.

Indeed, in these passages in the Gospels (and many others), Jesus becomes the one who is himself the interpreter of the law. He arrogates for himself the role of authorized interpreter of the law. Jesus is the high priest, and, since he is the high priest, the consecrated bread is his bread to eat. The bread is his by priestly prerogative and by his interpretation of the text. How much more so it is legitimate for him and his disciples to eat a few raw kernels of uncooked grain. He shares the bread with his under-priests.

Finally, Jesus is not only the royal son of David, the king. He is not only the priest for whom these loaves of bread were a legitimate perquisite. But, by referring to himself as one who is greater than the temple, he must indeed be its truly royal resident. Jesus is King in residence in his tabernacle/temple. As Son of Man, he is Lord of the Sabbath. And when the loaves are spread out on the table of the bread of the presence each Sabbath, they are in fact his loaves by divine right. Jesus is king, Jesus is high priest, Jesus is greater than the temple. The only one who can be greater than the temple is the one who lives in the temple, Jesus, "very God of very God."

---

15. Watts, "Mark," 140.
16. Ibid., 141.

CHAPTER 23

Leviticus 24:10–23

LISTEN to the Story

24:10 Now the son of an Israelite mother and an Egyptian father went out
among the Israelites, and a fight broke out in the camp between him and
an Israelite. 11 The son of the Israelite woman blasphemed the Name with a
curse; so they brought him to Moses. (His mother's name was Shelomith,
the daughter of Dibri the Danite.) 12 They put him in custody until the
will of the LORD should be made clear to them.

13 Then the LORD said to Moses: 14 "Take the blasphemer outside the
camp. All those who heard him are to lay their hands on his head, and the
entire assembly is to stone him. 15 Say to the Israelites: 'Anyone who curses
their God will be held responsible; 16 anyone who blasphemes the name
of the LORD is to be put to death. The entire assembly must stone them.
Whether foreigner or native-born, when they blaspheme the Name they
are to be put to death.

17 "'Anyone who takes the life of a human being is to be put to death.
18 Anyone who takes the life of someone's animal must make restitution—
life for life. 19 Anyone who injures their neighbor is to be injured in the
same manner: 20 fracture for fracture, eye for eye, tooth for tooth. The one
who has inflicted the injury must suffer the same injury. 21 Whoever kills
an animal must make restitution, but whoever kills a human being is to
be put to death. 22 You are to have the same law for the foreigner and the
native-born. I am the LORD your God.'"

23 Then Moses spoke to the Israelites, and they took the blasphemer
outside the camp and stoned him. The Israelites did as the LORD commanded Moses.

Listening to the Text in the Story: Biblical Texts: Exodus 20:7; 21:23–24; Ancient Near Eastern Texts: Assyrian harem edicts; Laws of Hammurabi

The biblical background for the first part of this narrative is primarily the prohibition in Exodus 20:7 against misusing the name of the Lord. The Ten Commandments in Exodus 20 do not indicate what the penalties are for the violation of the commandments. But now that this violation has actually occurred in the camp, it must be determined what is to be done with the violator.

Several ancient Near Eastern texts contain similar prohibitions against blasphemy, as well as admonitions to reverence the names of the various gods. One that is strikingly similar is in what are referred to as the Assyrian harem edicts:

> [Should] either the wives of the king or the other women [of the harem] fight with each other, and during their quarrel utter/invoke the name of the/a god blasphemously, they will cut the throat of the one who has [reviled] the god Aššur.[1]

In the second half of this passage (24:18–20) there is the occurrence of what has been referred to as the *lex talionis* formulation—the law of talion (tooth)—"Eye for eye, tooth for tooth." This formula had already occurred in a variant form in Exodus 21:23–24:

> You are to take life for life, eye for eye, tooth for tooth, hand for hand, foot for foot, burn for burn, wound for wound, bruise for bruise.

Though not in either of these exact formulations, the *lex talionis* seems to have been an innovation that first occurred in the Laws of Hammurabi, also referred to as the Code of Hammurabi, in the eighteenth century BC. Varied formulations of this law exist throughout the ancient Near East. Some representative statements from the Laws of Hammurabi are given below. Note that the italicized term, *awilu*, refers to a person who is either of the same social class as the offender or of a more elite, noble class.[2]

> If an *awilu* should blind the eye of another *awilu*, they shall blind his eye.
>
> If he should break the bone of another *awilu*, they shall break his bone.
>
> If an *awilu* should knock out the tooth of another *awilu* of his own rank, they shall knock out his tooth.[3]

1. Cited in Milgrom, *Leviticus 23–27*, 2118.
2. Roth, *Law Collections from Mesopotamia and Asia Minor*, 268.
3. "The Laws of Hammurabi," *COS* 2.131:348.

Lesser penalties, usually of a monetary nature, were assigned if the injury was inflicted on a person of a lower class than the offender. The biblical formulations do not make an allowance for this class differential, though there are differences when it comes to injuries to slaves (Exod 21:26–27).

EXPLAIN the Story

The narrative in this passage is straightforward. A fight takes place between an Israelite man and a man who is half-Israelite and half-Egyptian. During the fight, the latter figure "blasphemes the Name with a curse" (v. 11). Some community members bring the man to Moses, who in turn inquires of the LORD as to what should be done to him. The LORD's decree is that the community is to put him to death by stoning. This then leads to the LORD giving additional laws clarifying what is to be done in situations where bodily harm has been inflicted on both persons and animals. We are then told that the community carried out the prescribed punishment. A number of important issues arise:

1. In a number of respects this narrative mirrors the story of Nadab and Abihu in Leviticus 10. There, Aaron's sons snatch defeat out of the jaws of victory when they offer strange fire before the LORD after the glorious priestly ordination that took place in chapters 8–9. The present narrative comes after the outlining of the celebratory festivals of chapter 23 and an ideal picture, in 24:1–9, of the high priest's duties in the holy place. In this narrative, however, it is not a priest who is the offender but a "lay" Israelite. Perhaps, then, the motivation behind these two accounts is that of indicating that both priests and people must jealously guard the holiness of the LORD to ensure the survival of the community. If priests or people fail in this duty, then ritual observance alone will not ensure that survival.
2. It is also interesting to note that the only other occurrences in Leviticus of the particular Hebrew verbal form translated "went out" (*yatsa'*) in verse 10 are located in 9:24 and 10:2 ("fire came out").[4] This is perhaps another signal from the author/editor that these two passages are intended to be read in light of each other. Kiuchi has also noted that the blasphemer "went out" among the Israelites to fight, and that the

4. Hess, "Leviticus," 797. There actually is one other occurrence, in 9:23; but it is in the same narrative as that of 9:24 and 10:2.

LORD, correspondingly, ordered that the blasphemer be taken "outside" the camp for the execution of his punishment.[5]

3. With regard to the connection between this narrative and the immediately preceding passage in 24:1–9, it should be noted that the divine name, Yahweh, occurs seven times in 24:1–9. So the juxtaposition of these two passages is both appropriate and striking in that the offender blasphemes the name of Yahweh.
4. It is unclear exactly what this particular blasphemy entailed, whether it was an actual curse pronounced against the LORD or a careless utterance of the divine name in the heated context of the fight, more like what we think of as "swearing" today. Verse 11 is more ambiguous than the NIV and other translations suggest. For example, one possible literal rendering might be no stronger than "he pronounced the name and cursed." However, there are two good reasons for thinking the violation here is actually a curse pronounced against the LORD. First, though verse 11 is ambiguous, verse 15 is less so: "Anyone who curses their God." In this light, it would seem that the blasphemer is not simply pronouncing the LORD's name carelessly and cursing the other man in the fight but that he is actually directing a curse at God. Second, other passages, like Exodus 22:28 ("Do not blaspheme God or curse the ruler of your people") where blaspheming God and cursing the ruler are set in parallel, certainly seem to suggest animosity toward God. For these and other reasons, it would seem that the cursing in this narrative is actually directed at Yahweh.
5. Why does the entire assembly have to be involved in executing the punishment and putting the blasphemer to death? The answer, in my opinion, is provided by the already-mentioned correspondence between this account and the narrative in chapter 10. If Aaron and his remaining priest-sons had engaged in mourning rites for Nadab and Abihu, it could have been taken as disapproval of Yahweh's executing of punishment. If the community had failed to stone the blasphemer, they could have been seen as being in solidarity with him, against the penalty imposed by Yahweh.
6. It is interesting that even though we are told the names of the blasphemer's mother and grandfather, we are not given the name of the blasphemer himself. Though the term is not used in this passage, this is part of what it means to be "cut off" from the LORD and from his

5. Kiuchi, *Leviticus*, 440.

people. Their name will not be remembered (cf. Deut 32:26; Ps 9:6). Also fittingly, the punishment fits the crime: the one who blasphemed the Name—his own name will not be remembered.

7. The penalty for this crime might seem harsh. But, as Sklar aptly reminds us, treason is a capital crime.[6]
8. This incident, similar to a few other narratives in the Torah, results in the giving of additional laws and ordinances (see Lev 10:1–11; Num 9:1–14; 27:1–11; 36:1–12). The laws here all have to do with violations concerning the taking of human life, the taking of animal life, and the infliction of permanent bodily injury on human beings. Almost certainly this suggests that the act of blasphemy is being put into the same category as these latter crimes. The use of the Lord's name in a blasphemous utterance, especially if it is not simply a careless expression but an actual curse pronounced against God, is in the same category as that of an attack on the very life of God. The blasphemy is an expression of one's desire to put Yahweh under a curse and indicates that the blasphemer, given the opportunity, would actually make an attempt on Yahweh's life.[7]
9. Rather than the barbaric and bloodthirsty law that the *lex talionis* is caricatured to have been, this principle, apparently first instituted in the Code of Hammurabi several hundred years before Moses, was put in place to ensure fair and equitable punishment relative to the violation. The biblical formulation of this law is even more equitable than previous formulations, for it makes no distinctions between various social classes in the law's application, though it still preserves distinctions when it comes to slaves and slave owners. The law's purpose was to make sure that the punishment was appropriate to the crime and that violators were not given excessive penalties.[8] The law also, to a large extent, sought to make sure that punishments for capital crimes and bodily injury were not simply executed according to personal vendetta.[9]
10. Finally, it should be noted that even though the *lex talionis* should not be caricatured as bloodthirsty or barbaric, many commentators in their zeal to demonstrate this have perhaps swung the pendulum too far and have argued that the law was never meant to be implemented literally.

6. Sklar, *Leviticus*, 291–92.
7. On this point, see Kleinig, *Leviticus*, 527–30.
8. For further discussion, see Hartley, *Leviticus*, 411–12; Wright, "Leviticus," 152; Gane, *Leviticus, Numbers*, 420, 424–28; Milgrom, *Leviticus 23–27*, 2119–28, 2133–40.
9. Hess, "Leviticus," 798.

They maintain that the penalties exacted for violations were most likely monetary. So they would argue, for example, that the phrase "eye for eye" might be better translated or understood along the lines of "the value of an eye for an eye." However, more recently several commentators have argued that the law's intention was literal, and it may well have been enforced literally in the ancient Near East and in the earliest biblical times. In particular, the formulation in verse 19, "Anyone who injures their neighbor is to be injured in the same manner," is difficult to be pressed into a monetary penalty (the Hebrew of the last half of the verse, more literally is, "just as he has done, so will it be done to him").[10] Thus Milgrom states that "[t]he upshot is that the talion formula in the ancient Near East is to be understood literally."[11] Certainly, over the centuries, in the later biblical period, and in rabbinic Judaism, these laws seem to have been relaxed. Milgrom also recognizes that, even originally, there was probably some imprecision in the way the law was applied.[12] But, while recognizing that there may be a difference between theory and original intention and the actual implementation over the centuries, Milgrom goes on to state, "Nonetheless, the plain meaning of the text cannot be altered: literal talion is intended."[13] In sum, whatever happened in the centuries that followed the giving of the *lex talionis*, the original intention of these laws, especially in the case of the loss of life or permanent bodily injury, should be understood as more literal than not.

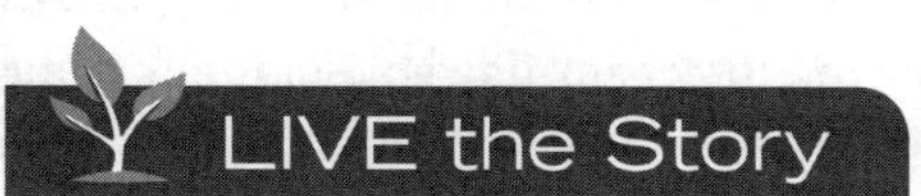

From Blasphemy to Speech Seasoned with Grace

Even though I believe the blasphemy in this passage is a curse directed against God rather than simply a careless use of his name, I also believe that all forms of the misuse of God's name are implicated in the prohibition in Exodus 20:7—and in the present narrative as well.[14] Correspondingly, in the New

10. See Gane, *Leviticus, Numbers*, 420.
11. Milgrom, *Leviticus 23–27*, 2136.
12. Ibid., 2133–34.
13. Ibid., 2138.
14. I need to mention here that I do believe the third commandment in Exod 20:7 and Deut 5:11 certainly does include blasphemy and what we traditionally think of as using God's name in a vulgar expression. So this passage in Lev 24:10–23 does indeed narrate a violation of that commandment. However, I have also been persuaded by Daniel Block's work that the specific and larger intention

Testament, when Jesus and the apostles make various pronouncements about blasphemy, oaths, idle words, and speech in general, they are extending the intention of the original prohibition in Exodus 20:7 to cover the entire area of honoring God in all of our communications. Beyond this, when we look at these pronouncements we are probably justified in concluding that the real culprit in all these concerns is not so much the speech act itself as it is the pride, arrogance, and deception that lie behind it.

Jesus warns against the swearing of oaths, referring to how the various things by which one could swear—heaven, earth, Jerusalem, or even the hair of one's head—are all things over which the swearer has no actual control (Matt 5:33–37; also Jas 5:12). Yet, the very act of swearing by these things implies that those who swear have, as it were, arrogated for themselves a supposed measure of sovereignty over these things, even over God himself. This should not be done, because it only comes from an arrogantly prideful heart.[15]

In Matthew 12:31–39 Jesus warns against blasphemy against himself and also against the Holy Spirit. He then goes on to extend the discussion to talk about how the words that proceed from our mouths are indications of what is in our hearts. He declares that all our empty (or idle, careless) words are ones for which we will have to give an account on the day of judgment.

A legitimate extension of this is Paul's words in Colossians 4:6, when he says that our speech should be "full of grace." Along with the majority of commentators, we should probably take "grace" here to refer to both the content and manner of our speech, full of the message of God's grace in Christ Jesus and also delivered in a gracious manner. This imperative for gracious speech, then, also leads to the mandate to "not let any unwholesome talk come out of your mouths" (Eph 4:29). Additionally, Paul says, "Nor should there be obscenity, foolish talk or coarse joking, which are out of place, but rather thanksgiving" (Eph 5:4).

Unfortunately today, various Christian leaders have decided that coarse, obscene, and profanity-laden speech is appropriate for Christian communication. They even go so far as to employ this speech in lectures, sermons, and various forms of social media. When challenged on this, they come up with

---

of the third commandment for the Israelites is that they are to live in such a way that their behavior honors rather than disgracing the name that has been placed upon them, the name of Yahweh (Num 6:24–27). See Daniel I. Block, "Bearing the Name of the Lord with Honor," in his volume of collected essays, *How I Love Your Torah, O LORD!: Studies in the Book of Deuteronomy* (Eugene, OR: Wipf & Stock, 2011), 61–72. Also, see more recently, Carmen Joy Imes, *Bearing Yhwh's Name at Sinai: A Reexamination of the Name Command of the Decalogue*, BBRSup 19 (University Park, PA: Eisenbrauns, 2018).

15. However, see the commentary on ch. 27 for legitimate use of the oath, pp. 361–63, 365–67.

very lame excuses as to why they are above Christ's directives in these areas. Such profanity and such excuses can only come from an attitude of superiority and pride. As Christ says, our words reveal our hearts, and those words will either acquit or condemn us (Matt 12:37). On the other hand, the use of the simple "yes" or "no" safeguards us from the pride of assuming that the God whose name we have used to utter a profanity is necessarily on our side and takes our point of view on a particular matter. Blasphemy does not get very good press in the Bible, and every Christian leader who decides to regularly use profane speech should remember the profanity-laden speech of one particular follower of Christ on the night of our Lord's betrayal (Matt 26:74).

From Stoning to Church Discipline and Excommunication

The church is not a political entity in the same way that the Israelite nation was in the Old Testament. Rather, the church is the pilgrim, wandering people of God. The church does not and should not seek to discipline its members by legal means, especially capital punishment. Nevertheless, the discipline that the church carries out in the New Testament, even that of excommunication, does seem to have a very public nature to it. Thus Paul, in 1 Corinthians 5:1–5, encourages the Corinthian church to carry out what amounts to an act of excommunication "when you are assembled and I am with you in spirit, and the power of our Lord Jesus is present" (v. 4). Thus, while not a capital punishment or a stoning, the public nature of the event is still comparable to the demand that the entire assembly be involved in the disciplinary act.[16] The reason would be the same: the congregation must not be seen as in some way objecting to the righteous judgment of the Lord against the excommunicant. They must not appear to be taking sides with the excommunicant against the Lord.

Jesus and the Lex Talionis

It is often claimed that, in Matthew 5:38–42 in the Sermon on the Mount, when Jesus said, "You have heard that it was said, 'Eye for eye, and tooth for tooth.' But I tell you . . . ," Jesus was repudiating the *lex talionis*. But such a conclusion can only result from a very flat and unnuanced reading of the text, as well as of the entirety of the Gospels and the rest of the New Testament. For example, elsewhere in this same sermon Jesus declares, "For in the same way you judge others, you will be judged, and with the measure you use, it will be measured to you" (Matt 7:2). This is simply the *lex talionis*

16. Roy E. Ciampa and Brian S. Rosner, "1 Corinthians," in *Commentary on the New Testament Use of the Old Testament*, ed. G. K. Beale and D. A. Carson (Grand Rapids: Baker Academic, 2007), 707.

stated in a different formulation, and there are other similar statements in the Gospels (e.g., Luke 6:37–38; 12:47–48). Indeed, many of Jesus's statements are founded on and validate the assumption that violators of the law and commandments should receive their measured punishments. For only a few representative passages from the Gospel of Matthew, see Matthew 7:19; 10:15, 32–33; 11:24; 12:32; 13:40–43, 49–50; 18:23–35; 21:43–44; 23:33–36; 25:14–30, 31–46; 26:24. Among passages in the rest of the New Testament that seem to assume the validity of measured punishment, see Acts 25:11; Romans 13:4–5; 1 Peter 2:13–14, 20.

With many commentators, I believe the best understanding of what Jesus is saying in Matthew 5:38–42 has to do with private revenge rather than civil, legally enforced justice.[17] Jesus's concern is not with the *lex talionis* per se but rather with an attitude which is all too ready, at the drop of a hat, to use the "eye for an eye" to pursue personal retaliation for perceived slights. In fact, such a correction in attitude is in line even with Old Testament statements, such as Leviticus 19:17–18; Prov 25:21–22 (cf. Rom 12:17–21). So we cannot even say that Jesus's ethic here is an innovation; it was already there in both Old Testament legal and wisdom texts. Jesus's words should also probably be applied, in measure, to legal recourse as well—even though we should also consider there to be a certain hyperbolic character to what Jesus says rather than taking them as an absolute prohibition. Today, in our own overly litigious society, the default position of the Christian should not be one that is bent on pursuing redress in the courts. Christians should differentiate between themselves and the rest of society by employing a higher ethic when it comes to their default setting for pursuing private revenge and legal recourse. Certainly this understanding, in part, stands behind Paul's words to the Corinthians as well (1 Cor 6:1–8). Christians are called to a higher standard.

17. See, representatively, the Leviticus commentaries by Balentine, Wright, Radner, Sklar, Tidball, Wenham, Hess, and Gane.

CHAPTER 24

Leviticus 25:1–55

LISTEN to the Story

25:1The LORD said to Moses at Mount Sinai, 2"Speak to the Israelites and say to them: 'When you enter the land I am going to give you, the land itself must observe a sabbath to the LORD. 3For six years sow your fields, and for six years prune your vineyards and gather their crops. 4But in the seventh year the land is to have a year of sabbath rest, a sabbath to the LORD. Do not sow your fields or prune your vineyards. 5Do not reap what grows of itself or harvest the grapes of your untended vines. The land is to have a year of rest. 6Whatever the land yields during the sabbath year will be food for you—for yourself, your male and female servants, and the hired worker and temporary resident who live among you, 7as well as for your livestock and the wild animals in your land. Whatever the land produces may be eaten.

8"'Count off seven sabbath years—seven times seven years—so that the seven sabbath years amount to a period of forty-nine years. 9Then have the trumpet sounded everywhere on the tenth day of the seventh month; on the Day of Atonement sound the trumpet throughout your land. 10Consecrate the fiftieth year and proclaim liberty throughout the land to all its inhabitants. It shall be a jubilee for you; each of you is to return to your family property and to your own clan. 11The fiftieth year shall be a jubilee for you; do not sow and do not reap what grows of itself or harvest the untended vines. 12For it is a jubilee and is to be holy for you; eat only what is taken directly from the fields.

13"'In this Year of Jubilee everyone is to return to their own property.

14"'If you sell land to any of your own people or buy land from them, do not take advantage of each other. 15You are to buy from your own people on the basis of the number of years since the Jubilee. And they are to sell to you on the basis of the number of years left for harvesting crops. 16When the years are many, you are to increase the price, and when the

years are few, you are to decrease the price, because what is really being
sold to you is the number of crops. 17Do not take advantage of each other,
but fear your God. I am the LORD your God.

18"'Follow my decrees and be careful to obey my laws, and you will
live safely in the land. 19Then the land will yield its fruit, and you will eat
your fill and live there in safety. 20You may ask, "What will we eat in the
seventh year if we do not plant or harvest our crops?" 21I will send you
such a blessing in the sixth year that the land will yield enough for three
years. 22While you plant during the eighth year, you will eat from the old
crop and will continue to eat from it until the harvest of the ninth year
comes in.

23"'The land must not be sold permanently, because the land is mine
and you reside in my land as foreigners and strangers. 24Throughout the
land that you hold as a possession, you must provide for the redemption
of the land.

25"'If one of your fellow Israelites becomes poor and sells some of
their property, their nearest relative is to come and redeem what they
have sold. 26If, however, there is no one to redeem it for them but later on
they prosper and acquire sufficient means to redeem it themselves, 27they
are to determine the value for the years since they sold it and refund the
balance to the one to whom they sold it; they can then go back to their
own property. 28But if they do not acquire the means to repay, what was
sold will remain in the possession of the buyer until the Year of Jubilee. It
will be returned in the Jubilee, and they can then go back to their property.

29"'Anyone who sells a house in a walled city retains the right of
redemption a full year after its sale. During that time the seller may
redeem it. 30If it is not redeemed before a full year has passed, the house
in the walled city shall belong permanently to the buyer and the buyer's
descendants. It is not to be returned in the Jubilee. 31But houses in villages
without walls around them are to be considered as belonging to the open
country. They can be redeemed, and they are to be returned in the Jubilee.

32"'The Levites always have the right to redeem their houses in the
Levitical towns, which they possess. 33So the property of the Levites is
redeemable—that is, a house sold in any town they hold—and is to be
returned in the Jubilee, because the houses in the towns of the Levites are
their property among the Israelites. 34But the pastureland belonging to
their towns must not be sold; it is their permanent possession.

35“‘If any of your fellow Israelites become poor and are unable to
support themselves among you, help them as you would a foreigner and
stranger, so they can continue to live among you. 36Do not take interest
or any profit from them, but fear your God, so that they may continue to
live among you. 37You must not lend them money at interest or sell them
food at a profit. 38I am the LORD your God, who brought you out of Egypt
to give you the land of Canaan and to be your God.

39“‘If any of your fellow Israelites become poor and sell themselves to
you, do not make them work as slaves. 40They are to be treated as hired
workers or temporary residents among you; they are to work for you until
the Year of Jubilee. 41Then they and their children are to be released, and
they will go back to their own clans and to the property of their ancestors.
42Because the Israelites are my servants, whom I brought out of Egypt,
they must not be sold as slaves. 43Do not rule over them ruthlessly, but
fear your God.

44“‘Your male and female slaves are to come from the nations around
you; from them you may buy slaves. 45You may also buy some of the
temporary residents living among you and members of their clans born
in your country, and they will become your property. 46You can bequeath
them to your children as inherited property and can make them slaves for
life, but you must not rule over your fellow Israelites ruthlessly.

47“‘If a foreigner residing among you becomes rich and any of your
fellow Israelites become poor and sell themselves to the foreigner or to a
member of the foreigner’s clan, 48they retain the right of redemption after
they have sold themselves. One of their relatives may redeem them: 49An
uncle or a cousin or any blood relative in their clan may redeem them.
Or if they prosper, they may redeem themselves. 50They and their buyer
are to count the time from the year they sold themselves up to the Year of
Jubilee. The price for their release is to be based on the rate paid to a hired
worker for that number of years. 51If many years remain, they must pay
for their redemption a larger share of the price paid for them. 52If only a
few years remain until the Year of Jubilee, they are to compute that and
pay for their redemption accordingly. 53They are to be treated as workers
hired from year to year; you must see to it that those to whom they owe
service do not rule over them ruthlessly.

54“‘Even if someone is not redeemed in any of these ways, they and
their children are to be released in the Year of Jubilee, 55for the Israelites

belong to me as servants. They are my servants, whom I brought out of Egypt. I am the LORD your God.

Listening to the Text in the Story: Biblical Texts: Exodus 21:2–11; 22:25; 23:10–11

The two main topics of this chapter are the Sabbath year (vv. 1–7) and the Year of Jubilee (vv. 8–55). The only previous passages in the Pentateuch relevant to these two topics are the ones indicated above from the book of Exodus. The Exodus 21 passage is not referring to a Sabbatical Year but to the year of a servant's release after having served for any six-year period, so it does not provide narrative background for Leviticus 25:1–7. It is possible that the servitude and release in this current passage (substantially repeated in Deut 15:12–18) relates to the subject matter of the Jubilee, but that relationship may only be tangential; the two passages may be referring to different situations and circumstances with reference to how the servitude came about.

Exodus 22:25 (cf. Deut 23:19–20), regarding not charging interest on loans to the poor, seems to correspond well to Leviticus 25:35–37. And Exodus 23:10–11 coheres with Leviticus 25:1–7 with regard to a Sabbath year rest for the land.

There are texts from other ancient Near Eastern civilizations, primarily Babylonian, in which there were royal decrees granting freedom for slaves, land return, and debt remission. However, these decrees were only issued on special occasions, such as a new king's accession to the throne; thus, they were only issued at the sovereign's pleasure. By contrast, the divine King of Israel established a regular calendrical Jubilee that was not put into effect at the whim of a human king.[1]

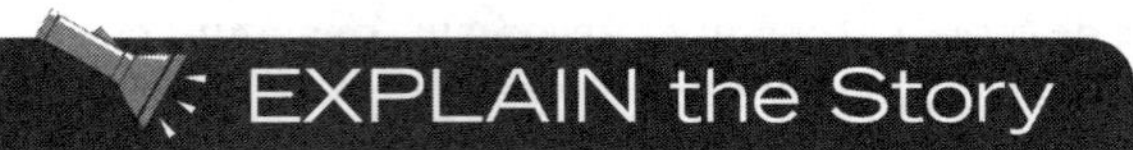

The Sabbath Year

In Exodus 20:8–11, the Sabbath is to be a day of rest for humans and animals. Now we are told that even the land itself is to have a Sabbath, a full year, in which it cannot be worked. It is almost as if the land has been personified.

1. For a survey of this material see Gane, "Leviticus," 1:322–23.

Yahweh looks after his creatures, and he looks after his land. Indeed, the Sabbath for the land is specifically a Sabbath for Yahweh. The instructions in verses 5–7 are a bit confusing and may seem contradictory. But the intention seems to be that, since there was no sowing done, the land was not to be harvested for commercial purposes—only for the immediate consumption of family, workers, and animals. We should probably assume that the poor would have been permitted to glean as well.

The Jubilee

The content of this passage is quite complicated, and there are a number of ambiguities and disputed interpretations. In a commentary of this sort, we cannot comment on all the specific details. I will try to give a basic understanding of the passage and then touch on some of the more important interpretive issues.[2]

First, it is important to look at the theological assumptions behind what happens in the Jubilee Year itself, as well as the intervening years between the Jubilees. The land belongs to Yahweh. Although the whole earth belongs to the Lord (Ps 24:1–2), the land that would come to be known as the land of Israel was already especially the Lord's before he called Abraham to leave his home country and family and go to the land which he would show him (Gen 12:1). When God brought the Israelites out of Egypt, it was his express intention to bring them to that same land that God had chosen for his own inheritance, where he would establish his holy dwelling (Exod 15:13–17). So, even when God distributes the land among the tribes and clans of the Israelites, he is really partitioning the land to a nation of tenants. The Israelites, who had been servants of Pharaoh, are now Yahweh's servants, and they are tenants whose responsibility is to work and keep Yahweh's land for him. Yet, at the same time, they are tenants who have been empowered by Yahweh to be, in some respect, owners of the land. They own this land not so much as private individuals but as members of tribes, clans, and extended households. They had been given, as it were, land grants from the Lord, with the specific mandate not to let the land pass into the possession of another tribe, clan, or household. So one of the reasons for the Jubilee laws is that the land should remain within these units.

Israel was primarily an agrarian society. As all farmers know, farming is not only hard work, but it is also fraught with risk. There are any number of reasons why crops can fail, including lack of rain, too much rain, other weather

2. I am especially indebted to Christopher Wright for his construal of the possible scenarios in this chapter. See Christopher J. H. Wright, "Jubilee, Year Of," *ABD* 3:1023–30; Wright, *Old Testament Ethics*, 198–210; see also Milgrom, *Leviticus 23–27*, 2191–93.

phenomena, various kinds of diseases, and swarms of locusts or other devastating insects. A farmer who is getting ready for the planting season may need to buy the seed for planting on credit. If the harvest fails that year, he would probably be unable to pay his debt; plus, he will need to again buy the seed for the new planting season on credit. If this cycle repeats, he may be forced to consider selling some of his land just to survive. So he finds someone who would be interested in purchasing a portion of his land. But the poor farmer is not actually allowed to sell the land; rather, he is selling the future harvests from the land. The amount that the purchaser pays for the land is determined by the number of harvests that can be expected until the next Jubilee Year. If there are, say, forty years until the next Jubilee, the purchaser pays an amount equal to the proceeds from forty harvests. The more years until Jubilee, the more the purchaser pays; the fewer years until Jubilee, the less the purchaser pays. Apparently, the entire amount is paid up front. One might think this would actually be a good deal for the poor farmer, because he has received a potentially huge lump sum payment. However, he has to use a considerable portion of that money to pay off his debts, and now he also has less land to farm and from which to earn profits.

This cycle might continue to repeat until the farmer has finally sold all his land. Again, he can use the money from the sale to pay his debts, but now he has no means by which to provide for himself and his family. He is reduced to the possibility of selling himself and his family, perhaps to the same person who purchased the land. On the one hand, this could be thought of as a form of slavery. However, verses 39–40 specifically prohibit an actual slave relationship; rather, they are to be regarded as "hired workers." This hiring may have also allowed for the paid wages to be applied to the reduction of the farmer's debt.

However, when the Year of Jubilee arrives, this temporary "land sale," which, to reiterate, is really a sale of a number of harvests, now comes to an end. The land again belongs to the farmer; indeed, we can say that he never actually lost title to the land. He and his family return to their full status as owners of the land, their indentured servitude comes to an end, and their debts are now considered paid in full.

Several purposes are served by this Jubilee Year arrangement. First, the person who purchased the land from the farmer may not have been of the same tribe or clan as the farmer, but no land was to pass from tribe to tribe or clan to clan. So in the Jubilee, the land returns not only to the farmer but to his own clan and tribe as well. The original land grants given by Yahweh are back in place as they were intended. A restoration has taken place. Second, the disparity between rich and poor, though it has not been eradicated, has nevertheless been seriously mitigated. "There will always be poor people in the land" (Deut 15:11); however, "there need be no poor people among you" (Deut 15:4). There will be poverty, but it will not be because of a flaw in the LORD's economic policy; rather, it will be because of the wickedness of the people's heart in their refusal to implement the policy. Third, the economics, if properly implemented, will also have an effect on the politics. The resulting balance which obtains among the tribes, the clans within each tribe, and between the poor and middle class versus a wealthier class will prevent the formation of an oppressive oligarchy in Israel, an oligarchy that the prophets railed against so vehemently.

Here are a few brief notes on some individual items and interpretive issues:

1. We do not know for certain what the term translated "Jubilee" (*yobel*) means. A popular understanding is that it comes from the word for "ram" and that it refers to a ram's horn. This is certainly possible, yet it is strange that the word for the "trumpet" that announces the Jubilee is not *yobel* but *shophar*. Among other suggestions are "bring," "produce," and "release."
2. The chapter also mentions that the proposed land sale can be prevented by a relative who could provide redemption for the farmer, even after the land sale occurs. However, it is possible that the entire clan/family/tribe is in the same dire straits.
3. Those who would assist the poor farmer by way of loans are prohibited from charging interest on those loans. This does not necessarily mean that interest could not be charged on other business or commercial loans. Whether such loans were allowed is a matter of debate; I tend to believe they were.
4. The legislation in Deuteronomy 15:1–11 seems to suggest that debts were also cancelled in the Sabbatical Years. If so, then the question arises as to why debt remission in the Jubilee Year is necessary. One possible solution to the apparent discrepancy is that for the Sabbatical Years in which the land lay fallow and could not be worked, the debt is not actually cancelled, but the debt repayment is deferred, something like a "payment holiday," and the repayment resumes the following year.[3]
5. It is interesting to note that the legislation in this chapter is intended to prevent the very kind of thing that happened in Genesis 47:13–26, in which the people of Egypt, on account of the famine, were forced to sell their land to Pharaoh and were reduced to servitude.

---

3. See the discussion in Hartley, *Leviticus*, 431.

6. Notice that there is a lack of romanticism in the way the poor are portrayed in this chapter. In verses 14–17 the warning is for both the seller (the poor farmer) and the purchaser not to take advantage of the other. This corresponds to the warning in Leviticus 19:15 not to show partiality to the poor or to the great; both constitute perversions of justice.
7. The use of the Hebrew word *yatsa'* in this chapter is significant, translated variously as "returned" (vv. 28, 33), "brought out" (vv. 38, 42, 55), and "released" (vv. 41, 54). Even as Yahweh "brought out" his people from their servitude in the land of Egypt, so the indentured Israelites are caused to go out—that is, "returned" or "released" from their servitude in the year of Jubilee. Yahweh again redeems his people, and it is an also an opportunity for the purchasers to image God as they release their indentured servants from their servitude.
8. It is especially appropriate that the proclamation of the Year of Jubilee takes place on the Day of Atonement. On the same day that rams are offered as a sin offering, the ram's horn is blown to proclaim Jubilee. On the same day that God's mercy is shown to the Israelites, not only does that divine mercy continue to be shown in the Jubilee, but also the Israelites are called upon to image God by showing that same mercy to their indentured servants.
9. Finally, I have twice, above, referred to "indentured servitude," which is a more accurate and appropriate way of labeling the practice in the Old Testament usually referred to as "slavery." While this indentured servitude in ancient Israel was certainly not as egalitarian as a modern-day employer-employee arrangement, neither was it the harsh system that we normally associate with slavery and the brutally inhumane practices of the master-slave relationship. Uniquely (or nearly so) in ancient Israel in the context of the larger ancient Near East, Israelite slaves (1) had particular legal rights, (2) were not to be subjected to harsh abuse, (3) had the final say in entering into a lifelong slave-master relationship, and (4) were not to be returned to an owner from whom they had run away. Indeed, for these indentured servants, to refer to them as slaves appears to be a mislabeling.[4]

   The situation with foreign slaves in Israel was definitely less liberal and thus constituted a true slavery, but it was also a bit murkier in that

4. For a helpful survey of slavery in the ancient Near East and the Old Testament, see Guenther H. Haas, "Slave, Slavery," *Dictionary of the Old Testament: Pentateuch*, ed. T. Desmond Alexander and David W. Baker (Downers Grove, IL: InterVarsity, 2003), 778–83. Also see Wright, *Old Testament Ethics*, 292–93, 333–37, 351–52.

there were nevertheless living among the Israelites foreigners and resident aliens who were free persons. In fact, the Israelites acquired some of their foreign slaves from these free resident aliens (v. 44). Also, it has been argued that the laws governing the indentured servitude of Israelites may have influenced the treatment of foreign slaves, even to the extent that foreign slaves may have been afforded many of the same rights as those enjoyed by members of the covenant community.[5] Specifically, with respect to the content of this chapter, whether and to what extent the slave-release laws of the Jubilee might have applied to foreign slaves is hard to determine, but the answer is probably in the negative.

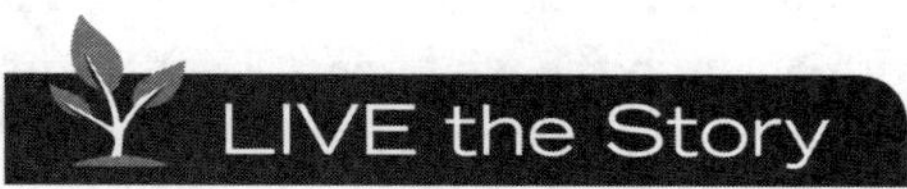

Before asking how we may "live the story," an appropriate question to ask is whether the ancient Israelites ever "lived the story." Despite the extensive and detailed instructions in this chapter, there is little to no evidence of the Jubilee being implemented in the subsequent history of Israel. When, in 2 Chronicles 36:21, the Chronicler concludes that during the exile, "The land enjoyed its sabbath rests; all the time of its desolation it rested, until the seventy years were completed in fulfillment of the word of the Lord spoken by Jeremiah" (Jer 25:11–12; 29:10), we perhaps should recognize that there were some ten to fifteen Jubilee Years included in that indictment as well.

So when, in Isaiah 61, the Servant of the Lord figure declares that he has been anointed to "proclaim good news to the poor," "freedom for the captives" "release from darkness," and the "year of the Lord's favor" (v. 1), we should understand that this message to postexilic Israel is intended to encourage them that the Jubilee Year was finally to be implemented. And when Ezekiel prophesies about what will happen in the "year of freedom," we should understand there a reference to the Jubilee Year ("freedom" in Ezek 46:17 is the Hebrew word *deror*, the same word translated as "liberty" in Lev 25:10).

All of this highlights the significance of what Jesus does and says in Luke 4 when, early in his ministry, he comes to his hometown of Nazareth and goes to the synagogue on the Sabbath day. He is handed the scroll of the prophet Isaiah, unrolls it to the passage in chapter 61, reads the portion referenced above (including the line about the "year of the Lord's favor"), and

5. For an enlightening discussion of this question, see Gregory C. Chirichigno, *Debt-Slavery in Israel and the Ancient Near East*, JSOTSup 141 (Sheffield: JSOT Press, 1993), 145–85.

then sits down and declares, "Today this scripture is fulfilled in your hearing" (vv. 18–19, 21). He announces that his ministry and work, that for which he has been anointed, is to bring about the restoration, the year of Jubilee. We should also note that Jesus's following speech takes a decided turn toward the gentiles (vv. 23–27). If there was any question as to whether the slave-release provision of Jubilee applied to foreign slaves in its original Old Testament context, there is no question with regard to Jesus's Jubilee declaration in Luke 4. The gentiles too will be among the oppressed who are set free.[6]

What is especially interesting about Jesus's proclamation is the connection that it has with the Day of Atonement. This account of Jesus reading from Isaiah 61 is preceded immediately by two other incidents in Luke 3–4, the baptism of Jesus and his encounter with Satan in the wilderness. I argued in the commentary above (on chapter 16, Live the Story, pp. 215–17) that Jesus's baptism and wilderness experience correspond to the two goats offered on the Day of Atonement, one of which was slain as a sin offering and the other of which was led into the wilderness. Jesus's baptism, in which he submits to a ritual of repentance from sin, though he had no sins to repent of and that anticipates his crucifixion, corresponds to the slaughter of the one goat for the sin offering. Jesus being led/driven into the wilderness for an encounter with Satan corresponds to the goat driven into the wilderness for demonic Azazel. In these two actions Jesus symbolically fulfills the Day of Atonement.

So when Jesus reads from Isaiah 61 that day in the synagogue at Nazareth, it is significant that this is one of the texts that were read on the Day of Atonement in ancient Judaism. This is the case because, as we have already seen, the proclamation of the Jubilee was to be made on the Day of Atonement (Lev 25:9). When Jesus says, "Today this scripture is fulfilled in your hearing," he does so having already symbolically performed the Day of Atonement in his baptism and temptation experiences.

We should also note that in Luke's citation of what Jesus read from Isaiah 61, there is a conflation that occurs. The phrase in Luke 4:18, "to set the oppressed free," is not from Isaiah 61, but Isaiah 58:6. The larger passage in Isaiah in which this verse occurs, Isaiah 57:15–58:14, was also a passage associated with the Day of Atonement.[7]

So, to both reiterate and sum up, in conjunction with the immediately prior baptism and temptation narratives, it is significant that Luke portrays

6. For two attempts to address the issue of slavery in light of the larger canon, see Swartley, *Slavery, Sabbath, War, and Women*; Webb, *Slaves, Women & Homosexuals.*

7. François Bovon, *Luke 1: A Commentary on the Gospel of Luke 1:1—9:50*, Hermeneia (Minneapolis: Augsburg Fortress, 2002), 152–53.

Jesus as reading from two related passages in Isaiah that were associated with both the Day of Atonement and the Year of Jubilee. When Jesus reads from the scroll of Isaiah and claims that the passage is fulfilled in him, he does so having recently performed actions corresponding to the actions involving the two goats on the Day of Atonement. The congregation in the synagogue that day perhaps did not know of these incidents or catch these connections. But Luke wants his readers to do so. The Jubilee will happen because Jesus has already symbolically fulfilled the Day of Atonement, and he will do so in reality when he offers himself as a sacrifice for sin at the end of Luke's Gospel.

We should also note that the Greek word *aphesis*, which the NIV rightly translates as "freedom" and "free" in Luke 4:18, is translated as "forgiveness" and refers to the forgiveness of sins in all of its other occurrences in the New Testament (of which half are in the Lucan literature [Luke-Acts]). It is quite possible that we should indeed read undertones of forgiveness in this statement. The captives (prisoners) would be understood as captives of sin, and the *aphesis* would indicate both release from captivity and forgiveness of sins.[8] This is again another clue that the "freedom" of the Year of Jubilee will only be accomplished by atonement and the forgiveness of sins.

It is nevertheless important to note, as Joel Green appropriately warns, that we should not understand Jubilee to be a controlling rubric for Jesus's earthly ministry. Rather, Jubilee provides the "backdrop" against which to see Jesus's mission. "There is no need to posit Jesus's demand here for the immediate implementation of jubilary legislation."[9] Indeed, it could not have been Jesus's goal to bring in the Jubilee during the time of his earthly ministry, since this Jubilee was only to be established by his death on the cross. The Year of Jubilee is dependent on the Day of Atonement. In this respect, then, when Jesus performs miracles (such as the healing of the blind), pronounces an *aphesis* (a forgiveness of sins), or when he makes pronouncements like those found in the Sermon on the Mount (which are consonant with the Year of Jubilee), these should be seen as anticipatory of the great eschatological Jubilee that will be fully implemented only at Jesus's second coming. This provides the proper perspective on Jesus's answer to John the Baptist when, from Herod's prison, he sends messengers to Jesus to ask him if he really is the Messiah. Jesus's answer is couched in Jubilee-like motifs (e.g., "the good news is preached to the poor;" Luke 7:18–23). Yet, John remains in Herod's prison (the captives are not freed),

8. See, for example, I. Howard Marshall, *The Gospel of Luke: A Commentary on the Greek Text*, NIGTC (Grand Rapids: Eerdmans, 1978), 184; Craig A. Evans, *Luke*, Understanding the Bible Commentary Series (Grand Rapids: Baker, 1990), 73–74.

9. Joel B. Green, *The Gospel of Luke*, NICNT (Grand Rapids: Eerdmans, 1997), 212 n. 33.

and he will eventually be beheaded. Likewise, the "restoration" of all things referred to in Acts 1:6 and 3:21, which many commentators rightly connect with the Jubilee, is nevertheless one that will not happen until Jesus's return.

In the meantime, the church has the responsibility of showing the watching world what Jubilee looks like. Indeed, at her best moments the early church did just that. Acts tells of how the believers in Jerusalem sold their property, shared their possessions, and gave to anyone who was in need (Acts 2:42–45; 4:32–37). In particular, Acts 4:33–34 notes that "God's grace was so powerfully at work in them all that there were no needy persons among them." This appears to be an intentional echo of the related seventh-year debt legislation in Deuteronomy 15:4: "there need be no poor people among you." And yet it is also important to note how we learn from Acts that the selling of property was not mandatory but voluntary (Acts 5:3–4). The commonality of possessions that seems to have characterized the early Jerusalem church seems after a while to have receded; indeed, such an arrangement has its own inherent problems (Acts 6:1). In any case, there are repeated calls throughout the New Testament for generosity and sharing with those who are less fortunate, particularly in light of the grace manifested by Jesus Christ himself (e.g., Luke 12:33; 14:13; 2 Cor 8:1–9; 9:6–15; James 1:27; 2:1–7, 14–17). Today's church should be proactive in finding just, impartial, and creative ways to play out the Jubilee.

A more complex and controversial issue has to do with what the church has to say to the state. Some denominations and Christian organizations have been quite vocal in telling governments not only that they must have programs for those who are poor and less fortunate but also how they should go about it and what specific policies they should put in place. On the one hand, there is a measure of justification for this, since the argument can be made that the legislation in Leviticus 25 is exactly that: government sponsored and mandated to ensure that none should fall into dire poverty. On the other hand, the line from Old Testament Israel runs to the church, not to the secular governments of the world. It seems to me that the church must be very careful about advocating not only for the "what" of care for the poor but also for the "how." Some religious groups have advocated for something very close to communism, and this would actually violate the principles in Leviticus 25. As Robert North cleverly puts it, "Where communism decrees 'None shall have property,' Leviticus decrees 'None shall lose property.'"[10] And Christopher Wright states:

10. Robert North, *Sociology of the Biblical Jubilee*, Analecta biblica 4 (Rome: Pontifical Biblical Institute Press, 1954), 175.

> The jubilee thus stands as a critique not only of massive private accumulation of land and related wealth, but also of large-scale forms of collectivism or nationalization, which destroy any meaningful sense of personal or family ownership.[11]

First, the church must examine itself to see if its own policies, perspectives, and methods are consistent with the vision of Leviticus 25 and the biblical Jubilee, as refracted through the lens of Jesus and the New Testament. Then she will be the beacon, the city on the hill, demonstrating for the rest of the world how to justly and compassionately care for those who have become impoverished. With regard to this responsibility, there is no dispute. It is the church's mandate.

11. Wright, "Leviticus," 155.

Leviticus 26:1–46

LISTEN to the Story

[26:1]“‘Do not make idols or set up an image or a sacred stone for yourselves, and do not place a carved stone in your land to bow down before it. I am the LORD your God.

[2]“‘Observe my Sabbaths and have reverence for my sanctuary. I am the LORD.

[3]“‘If you follow my decrees and are careful to obey my commands, [4]I will send you rain in its season, and the ground will yield its crops and the trees their fruit. [5]Your threshing will continue until grape harvest and the grape harvest will continue until planting, and you will eat all the food you want and live in safety in your land.

[6]“‘I will grant peace in the land, and you will lie down and no one will make you afraid. I will remove wild beasts from the land, and the sword will not pass through your country. [7]You will pursue your enemies, and they will fall by the sword before you. [8]Five of you will chase a hundred, and a hundred of you will chase ten thousand, and your enemies will fall by the sword before you.

[9]“‘I will look on you with favor and make you fruitful and increase your numbers, and I will keep my covenant with you. [10]You will still be eating last year’s harvest when you will have to move it out to make room for the new. [11]I will put my dwelling place among you, and I will not abhor you. [12]I will walk among you and be your God, and you will be my people. [13]I am the LORD your God, who brought you out of Egypt so that you would no longer be slaves to the Egyptians; I broke the bars of your yoke and enabled you to walk with heads held high.

[14]“‘But if you will not listen to me and carry out all these commands, [15]and if you reject my decrees and abhor my laws and fail to carry out all my commands and so violate my covenant, [16]then I will do this to you: I will bring on you sudden terror, wasting diseases and fever that

will destroy your sight and sap your strength. You will plant seed in vain,
because your enemies will eat it. [17]I will set my face against you so that you
will be defeated by your enemies; those who hate you will rule over you,
and you will flee even when no one is pursuing you.

[18]"'If after all this you will not listen to me, I will punish you for your
sins seven times over. [19]I will break down your stubborn pride and make
the sky above you like iron and the ground beneath you like bronze. [20]Your
strength will be spent in vain, because your soil will not yield its crops, nor
will the trees of your land yield their fruit.

[21]"'If you remain hostile toward me and refuse to listen to me, I will
multiply your afflictions seven times over, as your sins deserve. [22]I will
send wild animals against you, and they will rob you of your children,
destroy your cattle and make you so few in number that your roads will
be deserted.

[23]"'If in spite of these things you do not accept my correction but
continue to be hostile toward me, [24]I myself will be hostile toward you and
will afflict you for your sins seven times over. [25]And I will bring the sword
on you to avenge the breaking of the covenant. When you withdraw into
your cities, I will send a plague among you, and you will be given into
enemy hands. [26]When I cut off your supply of bread, ten women will be
able to bake your bread in one oven, and they will dole out the bread by
weight. You will eat, but you will not be satisfied.

[27]"'If in spite of this you still do not listen to me but continue to be
hostile toward me, [28]then in my anger I will be hostile toward you, and
I myself will punish you for your sins seven times over. [29]You will eat the
flesh of your sons and the flesh of your daughters. [30]I will destroy your
high places, cut down your incense altars and pile your dead bodies on the
lifeless forms of your idols, and I will abhor you. [31]I will turn your cities
into ruins and lay waste your sanctuaries, and I will take no delight in the
pleasing aroma of your offerings. [32]I myself will lay waste the land, so that
your enemies who live there will be appalled. [33]I will scatter you among
the nations and will draw out my sword and pursue you. Your land will be
laid waste, and your cities will lie in ruins. [34]Then the land will enjoy its
sabbath years all the time that it lies desolate and you are in the country
of your enemies; then the land will rest and enjoy its sabbaths. [35]All the
time that it lies desolate, the land will have the rest it did not have during
the sabbaths you lived in it.

36“‘As for those of you who are left, I will make their hearts so fearful in the lands of their enemies that the sound of a windblown leaf will put them to flight. They will run as though fleeing from the sword, and they will fall, even though no one is pursuing them. 37They will stumble over one another as though fleeing from the sword, even though no one is pursuing them. So you will not be able to stand before your enemies. 38You will perish among the nations; the land of your enemies will devour you. 39Those of you who are left will waste away in the lands of their enemies because of their sins; also because of their ancestors’ sins they will waste away.

40“‘But if they will confess their sins and the sins of their ancestors—their unfaithfulness and their hostility toward me, 41which made me hostile toward them so that I sent them into the land of their enemies—then when their uncircumcised hearts are humbled and they pay for their sin, 42I will remember my covenant with Jacob and my covenant with Isaac and my covenant with Abraham, and I will remember the land. 43For the land will be deserted by them and will enjoy its sabbaths while it lies desolate without them. They will pay for their sins because they rejected my laws and abhorred my decrees. 44Yet in spite of this, when they are in the land of their enemies, I will not reject them or abhor them so as to destroy them completely, breaking my covenant with them. I am the Lord their God. 45But for their sake I will remember the covenant with their ancestors whom I brought out of Egypt in the sight of the nations to be their God. I am the Lord.’”

46These are the decrees, the laws and the regulations that the Lord established at Mount Sinai between himself and the Israelites through Moses.

Listening to the Text in the Story: Biblical Texts: Genesis 8–9; 15; 17; Exodus 19–31

The idea of covenant comes to the fore in this chapter in a way it has not previously in the book of Leviticus. The biblical passages listed above provide the narratival background for the role of covenant, dealing chronologically with the Noahic, Abrahamic, and Mosaic covenants.

In my study of covenant in the Old Testament, I have come to the conclusion that there are seven basic elements in the covenants that God makes with human beings.

Unilateral. God alone determines the terms of the covenant. There are no negotiations. The only proper human response is to reply, "We will do everything the Lord has said" (Exod 19:8). Over fifty times in the Old Testament God refers to the covenant as "my covenant." Of the eight occurrences of the word "covenant" in the present chapter, six of them are phrased "my covenant."

Promise. One or both parties to the covenant make promises to the other party. The essence of the Mosaic covenant is Yahweh's promise that he reiterates in verse 12, "I will walk among you and be your God, and you will be my people."

Bond/Relationship. The Lord of the universe owes no one anything and is not obligated to anyone. But, in covenant, he now puts himself under obligation. He binds himself to the covenant partner and obligates himself to keep his solemn promises. Furthermore, he brings the covenant partner into a familial relationship with himself; he adopts the covenant partner into his family.[1]

Stipulations. As opposed to the idea that there are both conditional and unconditional covenants, it is more faithful to the biblical data to understand that all covenants are conditional, either for entrance to the covenant, for maintenance of the covenant, or both. The stipulations of the Mosaic covenant are the various commands, laws, and decrees, many of which can be found in Exodus 19–31, that are reiterated in this chapter.

Blessings and Curses. All covenants have, either explicitly or implicitly, blessings and curses. The blessings are basically the promises. The curses are the punishments that will be brought on the covenant partner should they fail to keep their covenantal commitments. The present chapter contains both blessings and curses.

Signs. The covenants have one or more covenantal signs (or ceremonies). Furthermore, the covenantal sign resembles the curse of the covenant in a kind of "cross my heart, hope to die" symbolism. For example, for the Abrahamic covenant in Genesis 15, the sign was the "smoking firepot with a blazing torch" (v. 17) passing between the cut-up pieces of the sacrificial animals. In this sign, God (symbolically in the smoking firepot and blazing torch) calls upon himself the curse of the covenant should he fail to keep his covenant promises to Abraham.[2] There is no

1. See especially Scott W. Hahn, *Kinship by Covenant: A Canonical Approach to the Fulfillment of God's Saving Promises* (New Haven: Yale University Press, 2009).

2. On this sign and how it represents the curse of the covenant, see Tremper Longman III, *Genesis*, SGBC (Grand Rapids: Zondervan Academic, 2016), 203–4.

reference to a covenantal sign in Leviticus 26, but it is important to note that the covenant mentioned in this chapter was put into effect by the covenantal ceremony recorded in Exodus 24, which also involved sacrificial blood.

Mediators. The covenants are given to a larger group of people through one mediatorial figure. In the Old Testament these mediatorial figures are Adam, Noah, Abraham, Moses, and David. Moses is the mediator for the covenant referred to in this chapter and is in fact the one delivering to the people the words of the Lord.

It is vital to understand this chapter in the context of the previous covenantal narratives.[3]

The blessings and curses sections of this chapter (vv. 3–45) also bear similarities to both treaty literature and law codes of other civilizations in the ancient Near East. From the second half of the second millennium BC, the Hittite suzerainty treaties, between the rulers (suzerains) of the Hittite empire and the smaller countries or city-states (vassals) that the Hittites conquered and brought under their control, have a structure which seems to be mirrored in the Pentateuch, but especially in the book of Deuteronomy. This is not the case with Leviticus as a whole, but this chapter does seem to correspond to some degree with the blessings and curses sections of these treaties, in which the gods are called upon to reward the vassals if they keep the treaty or punish them if they break it.[4]

EXPLAIN the Story

This chapter easily divides into three sections. Verses 1–2 contain statements about idolatry, Sabbath, and sanctuary. Verse 46 provides a concluding summary statement. The bulk of the chapter, verses 3–45, lists the blessings for covenantal obedience (vv. 3–13) and the curses for covenantal disobedience (vv. 14–45). The curses further divide into seven sections. The first five sections (vv. 14–17, 18–20, 21–22, 23–26, 27–35) present a rising crescendo of disobedience and corresponding punishment, with each section representing a further stage in the people's lack of repentance. The sixth section (vv. 36–39)

3. For an older but still very good introduction to the Old Testament covenants, see O. Palmer Robertson, *The Christ of the Covenants* (Phillipsburg, NJ: P&R, 1980).

4. For a good introduction to the ancient Near East treaty literature, see John H. Walton, *Ancient Israelite Literature in Its Cultural Context* (Grand Rapids: Zondervan Academic, 1989), 95–109.

deals with "those who are left" and presents a bleak picture of desolation. But the seventh section (vv. 40–45) presents a hope of repentance and restoration.

Idolatry, Sabbath, and Sanctuary (vv. 1–2)

There is no introductory "The LORD said to Moses" to begin this chapter. Therefore many commentators see this chapter as forming one unit with the previous chapter, with the primary concern being the necessity of Israel's obedience for their continuing existence in the land; disobedience results in exile to the lands of their enemies and captors. These transitional verses emphasize the necessity of obedience in right worship. Israel must not worship other gods; she must not attempt to worship Yahweh by means of images of Yahweh; she must respect the LORD's Sabbaths, including the Sabbaths of the land itself; and she must not defile the LORD's sanctuary. There are different suggestions as to what the "carved stone" (v. 1) refers to, but it is certainly regarded as some kind of idolatrous object, a representation of either another deity or even of Yahweh himself. Both are prohibited by the first two commandments of the Decalogue.

Blessings (vv. 3–13)

If the Israelites obey the LORD's commandments, they will enjoy the blessings of the land. The LORD will walk among them. This is both the essence of the LORD's promises in the Mosaic covenant as well as an indication of the recovery of the blessings of Eden, where the LORD apparently walked in the garden with its first inhabitants (Gen 3:8). These verses also recall the blessings promised to Abraham in Genesis 12:1–3. Somewhat hauntingly, the LORD says that he will "look on you with favor" (Lev 26:9). In the next verses, however, his looking at them will take on a different character. Also hauntingly, verse 13 refers to how they will walk without a yoke on their necks and with heads held high. This refers to their redeemed state from Egyptian bondage. This situation will be reversed in the next section.

Curses: Level One (vv. 14–17)

The eleven verses of blessings are now followed by twenty-six verses detailing the curses, almost as if the "blessing section can be seen as a mere preparation for the curse section in terms of its language and content."[5] The reason is violation of "my [the LORD's] covenant" (v. 15). Interestingly, the Hebrew word for covenant (*berit*) occurs eight times in this chapter, joining the other two

5. Kiuchi, *Leviticus*, 487.

occurrences in the book for a total of ten. This is perhaps an intentional allusion to the Ten Commandments, which form the foundation of the covenant. Also, ominously, "I will look on you with favor" in verse 9 is now changed in verse 17 to "I will set my face against you." This means that the use of the passive voice in verse 17, "you will be defeated by your enemies," is not merely a prediction but points toward God as the "divine causer."[6]

Curses: Level Two (vv. 18–20)

The failure of the Israelites to repent after the first round of punishments for their disobedience leads to a second round. Again, a symbolically and ritually significant number is employed. As Gorman remarks,

> The association of "sevenfold" punishment with sins suggests that the punishment itself is now viewed as a ritual process, of sorts, in which Yahweh attempts to move the people from the status of sin to that of repentance and obedience.[7]

A ritual reversal takes place: the number seven, which has played such a huge part in the various rituals described in the book, now becomes a number that represents Yahweh's ritual punishment of his people.

Curses: Level Three (vv. 21–22)

The only explicit punishment visited on the people in these verses is that of wild animals and the destruction they would cause among both herds/flocks and children. Second Kings 17:25–26 is one recorded instance of this threat become reality, in the wake of the Assyrian exile of the Northern Kingdom.

Curses: Level Four (vv. 23–26)

These verses speak of plague, capture by Israel's enemies, and famine in the land. The word translated as "hostile" is *qeri*. It only occurs seven times in the Hebrew Bible, and all seven are in this chapter (vv. 21, 23, 24, 27, 28, 40 ["hostility"], 41). Some other possible renderings are "contrary to" and "opposed to"; it is possible that these somewhat softer translations better capture the sense of the word. Nevertheless, we must admit that God's actions toward Israel in this chapter are in fact hostile and violent. Thus, for Israel to stubbornly rebel against God's covenant is to be construed as an act of hostility.

---

6. Milgrom, *Leviticus 23–27*, 2307.
7. Gorman, *Divine Presence*, 145.

It is especially important to note that the punishments God visits on Israel are referred to in verse 25 as God acting "to avenge the breaking of the covenant;" more literally, this can be translated as "avenging the vengeance of the covenant"—that is, "executing covenantal vengeance." Hartley appropriately remarks: "Breaking the covenant does not mean that they get out from under the covenant, but rather that they must be punished by the curses enumerated in that covenant."[8] Yahweh does not break the covenant by visiting punishment on the Israelites; rather, he is actually keeping the covenant by enforcing its punitive provisions.

Furthermore, it is important to note that these punishments do not happen automatically; they are not the "natural" result of Israelite disobedience. They "were not self-operating" but occurred "only when Yahweh activated them, and he would direct their course."[9] Calvin says this eloquently:

> He calls the Assyrian His axe, and the rod of His anger which He wields in His hand, (Is. 10:15, and 5;) and Nebuchadnezzar His hired soldier. He says that He will call the Egyptians with a hiss, and will arouse the Chaldeans by the sound of His trumpet. (Is. 7:20, 18, and elsewhere.) But since this point is sufficiently well known, there will be no occasion of further proofs. The sum is, that all wars are stirred by His command, and that the soldiers are armed at His will, and are strong in His strength. Hence it follows that He has innumerable forces by whose hand He may execute His vengeance whensoever He pleases.[10]

Curses: Level Five (vv. 27–35)

In this fifth level the first threat is that, most probably during famine and/or siege, the people will be reduced to cannibalism. A severe fulfillment of this curse is recorded in 2 Kings 6:24–30, a famine Samaria endured when besieged by Aram (see also Lam 2:20; 4:10).

The word translated "idols" in verse 30 is from the Hebrew word *gillulim*; this is a word of uncertain meaning but one that very possibly refers to excrement. "Lifeless forms" in verse 30 is more literally rendered "dead bodies" or corpses," so that the verse reads, "pile your dead bodies on the dead bodies of your idols"—a remarkable instance of the punishment fitting the crime. The Israelites worshiped dead idols, so their dead bodies will be joined to the dead bodies of their idols.

---

8. Hartley, *Leviticus*, 464.
9. Ibid., 472.
10. Calvin, *Last Four Books of Moses*, 3:235.

Again, the passage emphasizes the active involvement of Yahweh in the punishment of his people. Not only does he send his people into exile among the nations; he pulls out his sword and pursues them there.

The reference to the land finally resting and enjoying the Sabbaths it did not have during the time the Israelites lived there demonstrates that chapters 25–26 comprise a unit dealing with the land and Sabbath.

"Those who are left" (vv. 36–39)

A bleak picture is given here of the exiles' existence in the lands where they will be scattered, wasting away in the lands of their enemies. The verb translated "waste away" (from the Hebrew root *maqaq*) is the same one used in Ezekiel 24:23 to refer to how the exiles in Babylon will "waste away" when they receive reports from Jerusalem of the destruction of the Temple, as well as the death of the sons and daughters they were forced to leave behind when they were taken into exile. The woes of the exiles multiply in the lands of their captors.

The Hope of Repentance and Restoration (vv. 40–45)

After all that has been said in this chapter about the execution of the LORD's punishments on his people, this section holds out the hope of repentance and restoration. Some commentators see here evidence that what the LORD does or says he will do to his people should not be understood as retributive but only as restorative. The purpose of the expanding levels of punishment was that of restoring Israel, not executing retributive justice against them. However, these purposes should not be set in opposition to each other. The punishments should be seen as both retributive and restorative. When God does restore the fortunes of his people, it is a remnant that is restored, not the entire nation nor the many, many people who died during the execution of these punishments. Even when the exile comes to an end in Babylon, those who return to Judah will largely be those of a new generation—not those taken into exile but those born in exile. Yet the LORD keeps his covenant promises to the ancestors, and he redeems and restores a remnant to dwell in the land again.

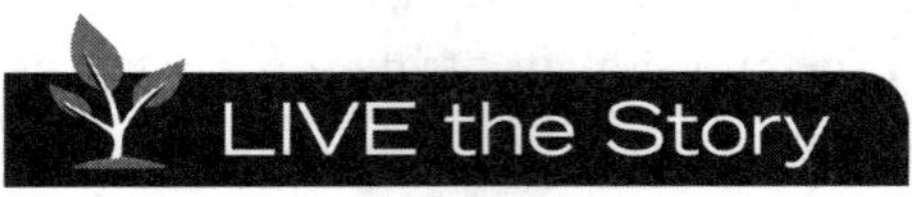

There are a number of ways in which Leviticus 26 connects to the New Testament. In what follows I draw attention to these connections under the rubric of covenant.

Jesus Came to a Nation of Covenant Breakers

Jesus came to dwell ("tabernacle"; see comments on chapter 1 above, Live the Story, pp. 43–44) among his people and to "walk" among them (Lev 26:12). He came to bring his people the blessings of the covenant. Even his first recorded sermon, the Sermon on the Mount in Matthew 5–7, begins with a series of beatitudes corresponding to the blessings section of Leviticus 26. Additionally, his life portrays and exemplifies the blessings of the covenant. When he feeds the crowds, multiplying the loaves and fishes, he fulfills in his own ministry the blessings that Leviticus 26:3–5, 10 pronounce on the crops and on the land. When he lies down in a boat during a raging storm and sleeps, he portrays the blessing of the covenant in which "you will lie down, and no one will make you afraid" (Lev 26:6).[11]

But having come to his own, his own would not receive him (John 1:10–11). So, instead of bringing the blessings of the covenant, Jesus also brings the punishments of the covenant and, in his role as prophet, becomes a "covenant lawsuit prosecutor," a role the Old Testament prophets played as they pronounced the enforcements of the punitive provisions of the covenant. Even in the Sermon on the Mount, various statements have more to do with curses than blessings.[12] This is even more pronounced in Luke 6:20–26, with four blessings followed by four woes. The closing of the Sermon on the Mount in Matthew 7:24–29 (par. Luke 6:46–49) also highlights the blessings/curses dynamic.[13]

Bernard Batto has convincingly argued that in Matthew 10:34 (par. Luke 12:51), when Jesus says that he has not come to bring peace but a sword, this intentionally both reflects and contrasts with Leviticus 26:6, "I will grant peace in the land."[14] In addition to the arguments Batto provides, it should be noted that in the adjacent verse 7, it is promised that the "sword will not pass through your country." Then in the curses section the LORD himself will bring the covenantal avenging sword against the people. So Jesus's words here should be seen as withdrawing peace and instead bringing the sword on a nation of covenant breakers.

In Luke 21:20–24 Jesus announces that the days of "punishment" (v. 22, better translated "vengeance") will come against Jerusalem "in fulfillment of all that has been written." This echoes Leviticus 26:25 (as well as other passages) and the vengeance of the covenant. Earlier in Luke's Gospel Jesus had said,

---

11. Blomberg, "Matthew," 33.

12. Hartley, *Leviticus*, 473–74.

13. Pao and Schnabel, "Luke," 298.

14. Bernard F. Batto, "The Covenant of Peace: A Neglected Ancient Near Eastern Motif," *CBQ* 49.2 (1987): 201–7.

> Therefore this generation will be held responsible for the blood of all the prophets that has been shed since the beginning of the world, from the blood of Abel to the blood of Zechariah, who was killed between the altar and the sanctuary. Yes, I tell you, this generation will be held responsible for it all. (Luke 11:50–51)

So Jesus has in mind not only that vengeance will come against the nation of covenant breakers, but also that vengeance for the sins of their ancestors in murdering the prophets will come upon them. This reflects Leviticus 26:39–40, in which the curse on the covenant breakers is that, in exile, they will also be paying for the accumulated sins of the previous generations.

In addition to this material in the Gospels, we can also note that Stephen, in his defense against the charges brought against him by the Sanhedrin, refers to his accusers as having "uncircumcised" hearts and ears (Acts 7:51). This echoes Leviticus 26:41, the first passage in the Pentateuch to refer to "uncircumcised" hearts. Stephen, in response to the charges against him, declares his accusers to be covenant breakers.

Finally, Paul declares that the covenants have very much to do with the people of Israel (Rom 9:4), yet he also recognizes that the covenant curses have come upon Israel for rejecting the revelation of God's Messiah. So Paul, in accordance with Leviticus 26:14–39, regards the hardening that has come upon the Israelites to be a fulfillment of the curse of the covenant (Rom 9–11). But he also reckons that this hardening has only happened in part, and that God, the God who has faithfully executed the vengeance of the covenant, is the same God who will also faithfully fulfill the promises in Leviticus 26:40–45; indeed, a remnant will be saved, precisely because God keeps his covenant promise (Rom 3:3–4; 11:1–6, 11–36).

Christians Can Also Be Covenant Breakers

Hartley correctly says, "Paul recognized that the new covenant made by Jesus comes with blessings and curses."[15] I mentioned earlier in this chapter that the ancient covenants had curses attached to them, and that the symbols and ratifying ceremonies symbolized this curse (see pp. 347–48 above). When we come to the New Testament, we find that there are two symbols, two ceremonial signs of the new covenant: baptism and the Lord's Supper. Both of these covenantal ceremonies are, in fact, death signs. Baptism is considered a dying with Christ in Romans 6; in two different passages it is analogized to

15. Hartley, *Leviticus*, 474.

the flood (1 Pet 3:20) and to the crossing of the Red Sea (1 Cor 10:2). Both analogies are death signs. On the one hand, they refer to salvation—but they also refer to the death of those who were not on the ark but died in the flood and those who did not cross the Red Sea on dry ground but drowned in those waters. Furthermore, in 1 Peter 3:21 baptism is spoken of as a pledge made from a good conscience. This puts baptism under the category of a covenantal vow, a promise made to God. The person who is baptized is pledging to turn their back on all that is unholy and to become a loyal follower of Jesus Christ. Should they fail to follow through on this commitment, then, "cross my heart, hope to die," their baptism serves as a death sign symbolizing the curse of the covenant.

In the same way, the Lord's Supper serves as a renewal of the original baptismal covenantal vow. Paul, in a haunting passage in 1 Corinthians 11:17–34, talks about those who approach the Lord's Supper in an "unworthy manner" (v. 27) and thus "eat and drink judgment on themselves" (v. 29). He goes on to say that this is the very reason "why many among you are weak and sick, and a number of you have fallen asleep" (v. 30). In other words, God has executed the curse of the covenant.

In addition to this, the author of Hebrews refers to those who have turned their back on the faith and have "trampled the Son of God underfoot" and have "treated as an unholy thing the blood of the covenant that sanctified them" (Heb 10:29). He then goes on to say that such persons will be subject to the covenantal vengeance and judgment of God, and they have every reason to dread falling "into the hands of the living God" (v. 31).

So those who are baptized and those who partake of the Lord's Supper should consider that they are taking part in a covenantal ceremony in which they are pledging themselves to follow the Lord. They are calling upon themselves the curse of the covenant should they turn their backs on the faith or sin in a particularly egregious manner and thus fail to meet their covenantal obligations.

In this regard, we should take note of passages that call upon believers to live holy lives. Second Corinthians 6:16–18, for example, calls believers to holiness in light of the incongruity that would exist between persons living in an unholy manner yet still claiming the covenantal blessings that God walks among them, that he is their God, and that they are his people (Lev 26:12). Paul considers this situation absolutely unthinkable.[16]

---

16. For a good discussion of this passage against the backdrop of Lev 26, see Peter Balla, "2 Corinthians," in *Commentary on the New Testament Use of the Old Testament*, ed. G. K. Beale and D. A. Carson (Grand Rapids: Baker Academic, 2007), 770–72.

Jesus Came to Take upon Himself the Curse of the Covenant

As mentioned before, when God in a theophany passed between the halves of the animals that Abraham had cut up and laid opposite each other, he "cut a covenant" (a more literal translation of Gen 15:18) with Abraham, calling upon himself the curse of the covenant should he fail to keep the promises he made to Abraham (see pp. 347–48 above). By this ceremony God established the Abrahamic covenant. Likewise, when Jesus, the night before his death, distributes the wine to his apostles and declares, "This cup is the new covenant in my blood" (Luke 22:20; 1 Cor 11:25), he calls upon himself the curse of the covenant; in this ceremony, as well as in his sacrificial death on the cross the next day, he establishes the new covenant. But in this case, the curse of the covenant that he calls upon himself is the curse that should have fallen on the apostles—and on us. Matthew, in his quotation of Jesus's words that night, makes it more specific, "This is my blood of the covenant, which is poured out for many for the forgiveness of sins" (Matt 26:28). Jesus established the new covenant by dying a death that would provide forgiveness for those who enter into covenant with him, taking upon himself the curse that rightly was upon them. The apostle Paul says, "Christ redeemed us from the curse of the law by becoming a curse for us" (Gal 3:13). We could ask Paul, "Where is this curse of the law found?" In addition to the answer he provides in that passage, citing Deuteronomy 21:23, he could just as easily have answered, "In Leviticus 26."

Ephraim Radner has intriguingly suggested that "we must see in the bulk of Lev. 26 the outline of the passion of Christ."[17] Indeed, using Irenaeus's theology of recapitulation, we can say that Christ recapitulates the experiences of Israel; he replicates in his own person the curses of Leviticus 26 that fell upon the Old Testament Israelites, and now fall upon him. Here are a few of the ways in which we can draw a line from Leviticus 26 to the passion of Christ.

Jesus experiences the "sudden terror" of verse Leviticus 26:16, as the "hour—when darkness reigns" surrounds him (Luke 22:53) and when he asks that he might not have to drink the terrible cup of the wrath of God, his sweat falling like drops of blood to the ground (Luke 22:42–44).

Jesus's strength was sapped (Lev 26:16), such that God sent an angel to strengthen him in his dark hour (Luke 22:43).

Jesus was surrendered to his enemies (Lev 26:17) who hated him and in that terrible hour ruled over him (Luke 22:52–53).

17. Radner, *Leviticus*, 275. See also his ensuing discussion on pp. 275–77. He suggests that Lev 26 should be a Holy Week reading.

The sky above him became iron (Lev 26:19), such that his prayers seemed to be directed to one who had forsaken him (Matt 27:46).

Jesus knew what it was to experience the threat from wild beasts (Lev 26:22), when during his temptation in the wilderness the wild beasts (Mark 1:13; symbolic of the raging animals of Ps 22:12–13, 16, 20) reminded him of the path of suffering that he was to follow.

Jesus was the object of the avenging sword of the covenant (Lev 26:25) that God said he would bring against his covenant-breaking people. On the night of his betrayal, Jesus quotes from Zechariah 13:7 in Matthew 26:31, "I will strike the shepherd, and the sheep of the flock will be scattered." And in Zechariah 13:7, the verse just prior to the one which Jesus quotes, the LORD says,

> Awake, sword, against my shepherd,
> against the man who is close to me!

In his passion and death Jesus experienced the avenging sword of the covenant, the sword that God said he would wield against covenant breakers but now wields against his own Son, who bears the curse of the covenant.

And the exile that was threatened against Israel (Lev 26:33–34, 38), Jesus himself experiences. First, he undergoes this exile as the Spirit drives (Mark 1:12, NRSV) him into the wilderness (compare the "pursues" of Lev 26:33). Then in his crucifixion he experiences the exile again, suffering "outside the camp" (Heb 13:12–13).

Jesus not only establishes the new covenant in his blood, but he also in his sacrificial death takes on himself the sin and the curse of his covenant people that he might purify them, make them his own special people, and bring upon them the blessings of the covenant.

> And I heard a loud voice from the throne saying, "Look! God's dwelling place is now among the people, and he will dwell with them. They will be his people, and God himself will be with them and be their God." (Rev 21:3)

> I did not see a temple in the city, because the Lord God Almighty and the Lamb are its temple. (Rev 21:22)

> No longer will there be any curse. (Rev 22:3)

LISTEN to the Story

27:1The LORD said to Moses, 2"Speak to the Israelites and say to them:
'If anyone makes a special vow to dedicate a person to the LORD by giving
the equivalent value, 3set the value of a male between the ages of twenty
and sixty at fifty shekels of silver, according to the sanctuary shekel; 4for
a female, set her value at thirty shekels; 5for a person between the ages of
five and twenty, set the value of a male at twenty shekels and of a female
at ten shekels; 6for a person between one month and five years, set the
value of a male at five shekels of silver and that of a female at three shekels
of silver; 7for a person sixty years old or more, set the value of a male at
fifteen shekels and of a female at ten shekels. 8If anyone making the vow
is too poor to pay the specified amount, the person being dedicated is to
be presented to the priest, who will set the value according to what the
one making the vow can afford.

9" 'If what they vowed is an animal that is acceptable as an offering to
the LORD, such an animal given to the LORD becomes holy. 10They must
not exchange it or substitute a good one for a bad one, or a bad one for
a good one; if they should substitute one animal for another, both it and
the substitute become holy. 11If what they vowed is a ceremonially unclean
animal—one that is not acceptable as an offering to the LORD—the animal
must be presented to the priest, 12who will judge its quality as good or bad.
Whatever value the priest then sets, that is what it will be. 13If the owner
wishes to redeem the animal, a fifth must be added to its value.

14" 'If anyone dedicates their house as something holy to the LORD, the
priest will judge its quality as good or bad. Whatever value the priest then
sets, so it will remain. 15If the one who dedicates their house wishes to redeem
it, they must add a fifth to its value, and the house will again become theirs.

16" 'If anyone dedicates to the LORD part of their family land, its value
is to be set according to the amount of seed required for it—fifty shekels

of silver to a homer of barley seed. [17]If they dedicate a field during the Year
of Jubilee, the value that has been set remains. [18]But if they dedicate a field
after the Jubilee, the priest will determine the value according to the number
of years that remain until the next Year of Jubilee, and its set value will be
reduced. [19]If the one who dedicates the field wishes to redeem it, they must
add a fifth to its value, and the field will again become theirs. [20]If, however,
they do not redeem the field, or if they have sold it to someone else, it can
never be redeemed. [21]When the field is released in the Jubilee, it will become
holy, like a field devoted to the LORD; it will become priestly property.

[22]"'If anyone dedicates to the LORD a field they have bought, which is
not part of their family land, [23]the priest will determine its value up to the
Year of Jubilee, and the owner must pay its value on that day as something
holy to the LORD. [24]In the Year of Jubilee the field will revert to the person
from whom it was bought, the one whose land it was. [25]Every value is to
be set according to the sanctuary shekel, twenty gerahs to the shekel.

[26]"'No one, however, may dedicate the firstborn of an animal, since
the firstborn already belongs to the LORD; whether an ox or a sheep, it is
the LORD's. [27]If it is one of the unclean animals, it may be bought back at
its set value, adding a fifth of the value to it. If it is not redeemed, it is to
be sold at its set value.

[28]"'But nothing that a person owns and devotes to the LORD—whether
a human being or an animal or family land—may be sold or redeemed;
everything so devoted is most holy to the LORD.

[29]"'No person devoted to destruction may be ransomed; they are to
be put to death.

[30]"'A tithe of everything from the land, whether grain from the soil or
fruit from the trees, belongs to the LORD; it is holy to the LORD. [31]Whoever
would redeem any of their tithe must add a fifth of the value to it. [32]Every
tithe of the herd and flock—every tenth animal that passes under the
shepherd's rod—will be holy to the LORD. [33]No one may pick out the good
from the bad or make any substitution. If anyone does make a substitution,
both the animal and its substitute become holy and cannot be redeemed.'"

[34]These are the commands the LORD gave Moses at Mount Sinai for
the Israelites.

Listening to the Text in the Story: Biblical Texts: Leviticus 1–26; Ancient Near Eastern Texts: Hittite Votive Records

This last chapter has sometimes been regarded as an anti-climactic conclusion to the book, dealing with apparently more mundane matters than the previous chapters. However, there are several ways in which the material in this chapter provides a fitting conclusion to what has gone before. First, Wenham notes that this chapter has quite a bit to say about vows that may be made to God. In this way, it provides a fitting contrast to the previous chapter, the bulk of which consists of punishments which God would bring against Israel for having violated their covenantal vows of obedience.[1] It is times of great distress, such as those that would have come about because of the covenantal curses of the previous chapter, that often occasion the making of vows.[2] A variation on this is to contrast God's faithfulness to his covenantal obligations in chapter 26 versus the potential of unfaithfulness for the Israelites in chapter 27.[3]

Second, chapters 25–27 can be seen as a kind of chiastic unit, with chapters 25 and 27 emphasizing Israel's covenantal responsibilities and acts of redemption, and chapter 26 dealing with God's covenantal responses of blessings and curses as well as his ultimate commitment to the redemption of his people.[4] Both of the outer chapters contain multiple references to the Jubilee.[5]

Third, chapter 27 can be seen as forming an inclusio (or bookends) with the first three chapters Leviticus. Both bookends, chapters 1–3 and chapter 27, have to do, for the most part, with offerings that are more voluntary in nature.[6] This correspondence would be especially evident with the fellowship offering described in chapter, one form of which is an offering to make or fulfill a vow. Thus, both chapters, 3 and 27, are dealing with vows.

Fourth, in addition to the preceding suggestions, which are of a more literary nature, there are two practical possibilities. The editor(s) may have felt that chapter 26, with its emphasis on punishments, was too negative to serve as a conclusion for the book and chose the material in chapter 27 as a more positive conclusion. Additionally, the chapter may have been chosen to provide additional information regarding the funding of the tabernacle operations and personnel.[7]

Vows to a deity were a prominent feature of various ancient Near Eastern religions. Vows to present a sacrifice or special offering to a deity could be made either on account of a particular deliverance from a distressing situation or a

1. Wenham, *Leviticus*, 336.
2. Ibid., 336.
3. Kiuchi, *Leviticus*, 494.
4. Balentine, *Leviticus*.
5. Gane, *Leviticus, Numbers*, 464.
6. Balentine, *Leviticus*, 212–13.
7. Kleinig, *Leviticus*, 588.

particular blessing already received, or conditionally upon the deity's answered prayer to the one making the vow. The prayers were usually for long life, healing from sickness, deliverance from enemies, or any rescue from a dire situation. The vows in ancient Israel seem to have usually involved food offerings and animal sacrifices. In the larger ancient Near East, the vows could be sacrifices, monetary gifts, statues of various sizes, or items of gold, silver, or other precious metals. A few examples from the Hittite Votive texts will illustrate. In this text, a Hittite queen makes a vow to the goddess Hebat on behalf of the king:

> If you, O goddess, my lady, will preserve the life of His Majesty, i.e., you will not allow him to come to harm, I will make for Ḫebat a gold statuette, and I will make for her a gold rosette, and they shall call it "Ḫebat's rosette." I will also make a gold toggle pin for your breast, and they shall call it "the goddess's toggle pin."[8]

In this text, the queen makes a vow for the king's healing from illness:

> If the prince recovers from this illness, I will [. . . . . .] and I will give to the deity on behalf of the prince, the king of Išuwa, a sword, a dagger (?), and one silver ZI-ornament of unspecified weight.[9]

And then in another text the king prays for the protection of a city:

> If the city of Ankuwa survives, i.e., it isn't totally burned, I will make for the Stormgod of Zippalanda one silver (model of a) city of unspecified weight, and I will give one ox and 8 sheep.[10]

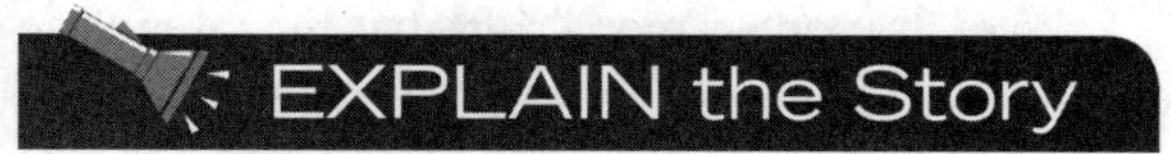

The chapter can be broken down into the following nine sections

Instructions about Vows of Persons (vv. 1–8)

Israelites could make vows of their own persons or other persons (presumably family members) to the LORD. This would probably be for service at the tabernacle, and most likely for limited, specified periods of time—though

8. "Votive Records," trans. Harry A. Hoffner, Jr. (*COS* 3:36.66).
9. Ibid., 67.
10. Ibid.

lifetime or very long periods of service were also possible (e.g., the boy Samuel in 1 Sam 1–2). In lieu of actually offering the person, the instructions provide for monetary payments to be made instead. It has been argued that in a number (perhaps even the majority) of the cases, the person enters into the vow of himself or another person, fully intending from the outset to make a substitutionary monetary payment.[11] That may be the case, but it seems more likely that the fairly high monetary payments expected as substitutions may have been set high for the very purpose of discouraging rashness in the making of these vows.[12]

The higher substitute payments for males over that of females has nothing to do with any idea that the male is intrinsically or inherently more valuable than the females. Rather, it has to do with the labor or productivity that would be expected from the person dedicated. Sklar helpfully suggests that rather than the NIV's "value," "assessment" would be the more appropriate translation in his instance.[13] Wenham notes that the prices set in this section are comparable to those that would have been paid for slaves in the slave market, and this may have been intended to reinforce the idea that these dedicated persons were largely thought of as Yahweh's slaves.[14]

Instructions about Vows of Animals (vv. 9–13)

Verses 9–10 have to do with clean animals that a person could present at the tabernacle in fulfillment of a vow. Most commentators seem to assume that the person actually offers the animal as a votive sacrifice, a form of the individual fellowship offering. But it is also possible that the vower could present the animal not as their own sacrifice but as an animal that could be offered as a community sacrifice, such as the daily morning and evening sacrifices.

Unclean animals could also be used to fulfill a vow. Of course, such animals could not be used as sacrifices, but one can envision that the tabernacle personnel would have need of animals that could be used for bearing burdens, plowing, riding, and so forth.

In this and subsequent sections in the chapter, provisions are given for redeeming or buying back one's vowed or dedicated offering—in case the person realized they might have made their vow or dedication rashly and unwisely.

With this passage, the chapter's concern with vows comes to a conclusion. One could misconstrue the making of vows as simply a crude bargaining-

11. So Gerstenberger, *Leviticus*, 439–40.
12. Ross, *Holiness to the Lord*, 492; Kaiser, "Leviticus," 1188.
13. Sklar, *Leviticus*, 328.
14. Wenham, *Leviticus*, 338.

with-God process. But Hartley more accurately and eloquently characterizes what is involved:

> Paying a vow is a joyous occasion. In fulfilling the conditions of the vow, the worshiper has a profound sense of living up to one's words. One psalmist exclaims joyfully and confidently, "You, O God, have heard my vows; you have given me the heritage of those who fear your name" [citing Ps 61:5]. In fact, the paying of vows is frequently made parallel to praising God [citing Pss 22:25; 61:8; 63:1] or making a praise offering [citing Ps 50:14].[15]

Instructions about Dedication of Houses (vv. 14–15)

Israelites could dedicate their houses to the Lord. These houses would most likely have been within walled cities and therefore not subject to the provisions regarding the return of property in the Jubilee Year.

Instructions about Dedication of Family Lands (vv. 16–21)

This passage is not entirely clear, and various scenarios have been put forward by commentators. What seems to be clear is that Israelites could dedicate their ancestral property to the Lord. This evidently meant that the proceeds from what the land produced would go to the sanctuary. At some point before the Jubilee, the person could redeem their field; indeed, they are expected to do so. But if they do not redeem it, the property passes over and becomes priestly property, holy to the Lord, belonging permanently to the sanctuary.[16]

Instructions about Dedication of Purchased Lands (vv. 22–25)

Again the passage is not entirely clear in all of its particulars, but it seems to also be possible for the purchaser (or leaser) of someone's else's ancestral property to dedicate some value from the property to the sanctuary and priesthood. In the Jubilee, the land returns to the original owner.

Instructions about Firstborn Animals (vv. 26–27)

The main concern here is that firstborn animals already belong to the Lord; therefore, one cannot actually dedicate them to him. Certainly, the same principle would also apply to the instructions in verses 9–13. One cannot vow to the Lord what already belongs to him.

---

15. Hartley, *Leviticus*, 487.
16. Sklar, *Leviticus*, 329–30.

Instructions about Devoted Things and Persons (v. 28–29)

The term "devoted," though it also occurs in verse 21 as a point of comparison, now appears in these verses as a point of instruction. The word "devoted" is the Hebrew word *herem*, which refers to something that is completely given over to the LORD's purposes. Famously, the word is used in several Old Testament texts to refer to the complete destruction of the Canaanites during the military campaigns of Joshua in particular cities. The word does not in itself mean "devoted to destruction," as has often mistakenly been understood. The destruction element has to be specified by the context. Rather, the word simply refers to the fact that a person or thing is given over to the LORD completely for his purposes. In verse 28, a person "devoted" to the LORD probably becomes a permanent worker in the service of the tabernacle. Verse 29 probably anticipates the practice of persons being devoted to destruction in a warfare or capital crime context. The main point is that previous statements about the possibility of redeeming or buying back what one has vowed or dedicated do not at all apply when it comes to the *herem*.

Instructions about Tithes (vv. 30–33)

Interestingly, the last set of instructions in the chapter, in contrast to the previous ones, has to do with the tithe as a mandatory contribution, and therefore essentially a tax.

> Giving a tithe to the king, the gods or the priests was a well-known practice in the Ancient Near East. . . . Since the Lord was not only Israel's God but also their divine King (cf. 1 Sam. 8:7), it was especially appropriate for them to acknowledge and honour him in this way.[17]

So the Israelites must pay to the LORD tithes of their produce and livestock. Those who wish to redeem their actual offerings of produce and livestock must pay a monetary substitute for them, as well as an additional 20 percent. The last two verses indicate a selection process to decide which animals will be tithed. Unlike what has sometimes been suggested, the different passages in the Pentateuch that deal with the tithe are not describing multiple tithes but rather one single tithe.[18]

Concluding Notice (v. 34)

With the statement in verse 34, the book of Leviticus comes to an end. The NIV, in my opinion, appropriately preserves the ambiguity of the Hebrew

17. Ibid., 332–33.
18. Richard E. Averbeck, "*ma'aser*," *NIDOTTE* 2:1041.

preposition (*be*) attached to the phrase "Mount Sinai." While some argue that the phrase means "on" Mount Sinai," "at" is definitely within the range of possible translations for the preposition. As opposed to the argument that suggests that the four places where this phrase occurs in the book of Leviticus (7:38; 25:1; 26:46; 27:34) mean that the revelation was given on top of the mountain, I believe the intention of 1:1 to show that the words of this book were spoken "from the tent of meeting" still holds. Regardless, 1:1 and 27:34 serve as bookends to declare that the content of the book was revealed to Moses, and from Moses to Aaron, his sons, and all the Israelites. Balentine remarks:

> From a theological perspective, the beginning and ending of this book invite readers, both ancient and modern, to receive God's commandments from Sinai as a *gift*. . . .
>
> In the end, Leviticus dares to hope and believe that both God's commands and Israel's opportunity for faithful response to them are a gift, not a burden. Such a gift becomes a summons to exuberant celebration, the ancient and abiding echo of which has been preserved in the words of the psalmist:
>
> I find my delight in your commandments,
> because I love them.
> I revere your commandments, which I love,
> and I will meditate on your statues. . . .
> Oh, how I love your law!
> (Ps. 119:47–48, 97a)[19]

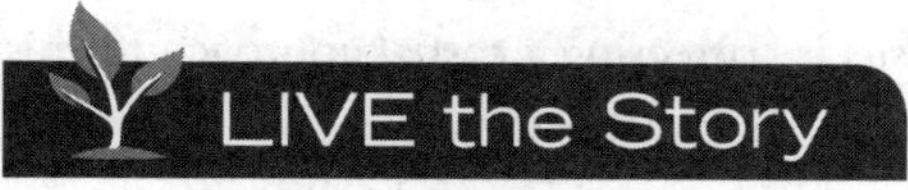

On the Making of Vows

Some have argued, in light of Matthew 5:33–37, that Christ has done away with the practice of making vows.

> Again, you have heard that it was said to the people long ago, "Do not break your oath, but fulfill to the Lord the vows you have made." But I tell you, do not swear an oath at all: either by heaven, for it is God's throne; or by the earth, for it is his footstool; or by Jerusalem, for it is the city of the Great King. And do not swear by your head, for you cannot make

19. Balentine, *Leviticus*, 213.

even one hair white or black. All you need to say is simply "Yes" or "No"; anything beyond this comes from the evil one.

The literature on the topic of Jesus and the law is voluminous, especially in light of Jesus's earlier statement in the chapter that he had not come to abolish the law but to fulfill it (Matt 5:17–20). But I think it is important to note that, in this passage, Jesus refers first to vows to the Lord but then branches off to talk about oaths in which one invokes God's name to indicate the veracity of one's statements. These are actually two different concepts, so there is a bit of conflation of concerns in what Jesus says, and he never actually suggests that vows should not be made. Most likely, like all the other items in Matthew 5, Jesus is not reflecting on the original commands in Scripture but on how that Scripture had been hermeneutically refracted through the rabbinic casuistry of the time. This is indicated by the fact that Jesus never, in any of these passages, says "It is written, but I say to you. . . ." Rather, it is always, "you have heard that it was said" (e.g., v. 33). In fact, whenever in any of the Gospel accounts Jesus uses the phrase "it is written," his purpose is always to uphold the teaching of the passage that he cites. His concern in this chapter is not with what is written in the Old Testament but with how the texts have been misinterpreted and misapplied by the use of casuistry in an attempt to avoid the "jots and tittles" (see, e.g., Matt 15:1–20; Mark 7:1–23).

Indeed, Jesus himself takes an oath (Matt 26:63–64), and Paul does as well (2 Cor 1:18; Gal 1:20). Additionally, Paul still makes vows (Acts 18:18). This probably indicates the hyperbolic nature of Jesus's statements regarding the topics he addresses in this chapter. For at least some of these, and I would include the vow/oath teaching in this category, Jesus is correcting a casual approach to this issue, not banning the practice absolutely. As Hartley says, "All in all it may be affirmed that the NT adopts the OT teaching on making and fulfilling vows."[20]

The making of a vow can be a meaningful act of worship, and the fulfillment of that vow, as indicated above in the Explain the Story section (pp. 362–63), is a joyous occasion. Indeed, in the messianic psalm par excellence, Psalm 22, Jesus is not only the one who laments in the first part of the psalm, but he is also the one who praises God in the last part of the psalm. Thus Hebrews 2:12 puts the words of Psalm 22:22 on the lips of Jesus:

I will declare your name to my brothers and sisters;
in the assembly I will sing your praises.

20. Hartley, *Leviticus*, 488; see also Kleinig, *Leviticus*, 595.

But then note that, in verse 25 of the psalm, the lamenter, now turned praiser, declares:

> From you comes the theme of my praise in the great assembly;
> before those who fear you I will fulfill my vows.

It would not at all be a stretch to see the author of Hebrews understanding Jesus to be the one who fulfills his vows to God in the midst of the gathered assembly of worshipers. I would argue, from the New Testament evidence, that vows of praise can still be a very significant part of a Christian's worship of God, not mandated by any means but part of the Christian's freedom of worship.

I know of individuals who, in particularly dire and distressing situations, prayed and vowed to God that if he would answer their prayers and provide deliverance, they would perform particular acts of devotion to the Lord. The Lord did indeed answer their prayers, and they joyfully kept their vows as acts of worship, adoration, and thankfulness to God.

Jesus, the One Devoted to Destruction?

It may seem strange and even jarring to put the question this way. But, in a very real way, we should see Jesus as the one who fulfills the motif of a person who has been declared to be *herem*, devoted to destruction. George Knight writes as follows:

> The substitute which is sacrificed must be "devoted" to the Lord, for only then is the substitute "most holy to the Lord" (v. 28). The sacrifice must be totally and utterly destroyed (v. 29). The word here is the Hebrew *cherem*. This term describes what Joshua did to the city of Jericho when he sent it up in smoke to God, completely and utterly. So "the devoted thing given to the Lord" (vv. 28–29) cannot ransom itself, though it is now the *asham* or guilt offering. So it must be another who now becomes the ransom for the sinner, one who is willing to make the absolute and ultimate commitment for the price of man; and that can happen only if he be willing to be a *cherem*, that is, a total sacrifice. As Paul insists, it is only God himself, uttering his Word, which is both blessing and curse at the same time, who can do this thing: and it is just this that God actually does, in Christ (2 Cor. 5:19).[21]

---

21. Knight, *Leviticus*, 172; see also Radner, *Leviticus*, 283–84.

The term *herem* is perhaps most associated with what Israel was commanded to do to Canaanite inhabitants of the land when they carried out their military campaigns in the conquest. However, what has not been emphasized is that individual Israelites, and even the entire nation, could be regarded as *herem*. When, in Joshua 7, Achan stole the devoted things of the Lord for himself, he actually made the entire Israelite people become a *herem*.

> That is why the Israelites cannot stand against their enemies; they turn their backs and run because they have been made liable to destruction. I will not be with you anymore unless you destroy whatever among you is devoted to destruction. (v. 12)

"Liable to destruction" here is literally "have become a *herem*."

> When Achan disobeys and takes of these items, Israel's army is defeated by the people of Ai and God says that Israel has now become a devoted thing itself until the devoted thing (Achan in his sin) is destroyed from its midst (7:12). Thus, the heathen city Jericho was devoted because it stood in the way of God's work through Israel in making conquest of Canaan. Israel became devoted because of sin that entered and made the nation unfit for use in God's work. Achan in his sin became devoted because he was the reason for Israel's hindrance as the people of God.[22]

Achan becomes the one who is "devoted to destruction," the one whom Leviticus 27:29 declares as unransomable and who must be put to death, so that the entire Israelite nation is not put to death. It only takes a slight bit of imagination to jump ahead twelve hundred years and listen to a high priest declare that "it is better for you that one man die for the people than that the whole nation perish" (John 11:50). Of course, there is a huge difference in the two situations. Achan was truly guilty of taking the devoted things and bringing the entire nation into the danger of annihilation. Jesus was truly innocent, but he is made *herem*, devoted to destruction, so that the nation, and not only that nation but all "the scattered children of God" (John 11:52), would not perish if they would own him as King and Redeemer. Indeed, Jesus so devoted himself (Heb 10:5–14). It is no wonder then that Paul can talk about the sacrificial death of Christ in the starkest terms:

22. Jackie A. Naudé, "*Herem*," *NIDOTTE* 2:276.

> God made him who had no sin to be sin for us. (2 Cor 5:21)

> Christ redeemed us from the curse . . . by becoming a curse for us. (Gal 3:13)

> He [God] condemned sin in the flesh [i.e., the flesh of Jesus Christ]. (Rom 8:3)

Christ was the one devoted to destruction for us that we might not be condemned but enjoy the pleasures of God for evermore.

Conclusion

As we come to the end of this commentary, we conclude by recalling that the book of Leviticus points forward to Christ in numerous ways. Sometimes this seems to be in fairly straight lines. At other times the route seems more circuitous, in a variety of intersecting, overlapping, crossing, winding, and shifting arcs, circles, and spirals. Christ is the high priest who officiates at the offering of the sacrifice. Yet he is also the sacrifice to be offered, in all its varieties: burnt, grain, fellowship, sin, and guilt. He is the atonement cover on which the priest is to sprinkle the blood of the sacrificed animals. Yet in that moment he is also the priest who does the sprinkling, and he is the sacrifice whose blood is applied to the cover. He is the priest who officiates in the tabernacle, yet he is also the tabernacle itself, the one in whom the fulness of the Godhead dwells bodily. He is the one who presents offerings at the tabernacle, yet he is also the sacrifice who takes the offerer's place. He is the one who enters into the covenant with Israel, yet he is also the one who takes upon himself the curse of the covenant to pay the penalty for Israel's covenantal violations. He is the slain goat of the sin offering, yet he is also the goat driven away into the wilderness. He is the one who makes a vow of praise to God, yet he is also that which is vowed. He is the lamb that is unblemished, yet he is also the lamb that absorbs the blemishes, sins, and impurities of those who offer. He is the one who dedicates himself fully to God, yet he is also the one who is devoted and delivered over to destruction. Jesus recapitulates in his own person and in his own body the history of Israel, fulfilling in his own life, death, resurrection, and exaltation what Israel was meant to be. And in doing so he constitutes his followers into a holy people, the holy people of God—indeed, the Israel of God.

Scripture Index

Leviticus

Numbers

Deuteronomy

Joshua

Judges

Ruth

1 Samuel

2 Samuel

2 Kings

2 Chronicles

Ezra

Nehemiah

Job

Psalms

Amos

Micah

Zephaniah

Zechariah

Malachi

Matthew

Mark

Luke

John

Acts

Romans

Philippians

Colossians

1 Thessalonians

1 Timothy

2 Timothy

Titus

Hebrews

Subject Index

Author Index